The German Army at Cambrai

To my mother,

Margaret Sheldon,

- a constant source of encouragement,
with my love.

By the same author:

The German Army on the Somme 1914- 1916
The German Army at Passchendaele
The German Army on Vimy Ridge 1914 - 1917
The Germans at Beaumont Hamel
The Germans at Thiepval

With Nigel Cave:

The Battle for Vimy Ridge 1917
Le Cateau

The German Army at Cambrai

Jack Sheldon

Pen & Sword
MILITARY

First published in Great Britain in 2009
and republished in this format in 2020 by
Pen & Sword Military
An imprint of
Pen & Sword Books Ltd
47 Church Street
Barnsley
South Yorkshire
S70 2AS

Copyright © Jack Sheldon 2009, 2020

ISBN 978 1 52676 672 4

A CIP catalogue record for this book is
available from the British Library

Printed and bound in England
By CPI Group (UK) Ltd, Croydon, CR0 4YY

Pen & Sword Books Ltd incorporates the Imprints of Pen & Sword Aviation, Pen & Sword
Family History, Pen & Sword Maritime, Pen & Sword Military, Pen & Sword Discovery,
Pen & Sword Politics, Pen & Sword Atlas, Pen & Sword Archaeology, Wharncliffe Local
History, Wharncliffe True Crime, Wharncliffe Transport, Pen & Sword Select, Pen & Sword
Military Classics, Leo Cooper, The Praetorian Press, Claymore Press, Remember When,
Seaforth Publishing and Frontline Publishing.

For a complete list of Pen & Sword titles, please contact
PEN & SWORD BOOKS LIMITED
47 Church Street, Barnsley, South Yorkshire, S70 2AS, England
E-mail: enquiries@pen-and-sword.co.uk
Website: www.pen-and-sword.co.uk

Contents

Foreword

Jack Sheldon is a former regular officer whose career included graduation from the German Staff course at Hamburg and serving as military attaché in Berlin. Now, in retirement, he is putting his language skills to good account by providing detailed, documentary descriptions of the German side of some of the most famous battles of the Western Front. Since the German side is often ignored or only superficially treated in British campaign studies, the author has already made an important contribution to historiography by his previous publications : *The German Army on the Somme 1914-1916* (2005), *The German Army at Passchendaele* (2007) and *The German Army on Vimy Ridge* 1914 – 1917 (2008)

This, the fourth volume of the series, will be especially welcome to the numerous British readers already familiar with the Battle of Cambrai, justly famous for the first employment of tanks on a large-scale. Sheldon's revelation of what was happening on 'the other side of the hill', or in this case of Bourlon Ridge, follows a similar pattern to his other books; namely a succinct description of the strategic scene with linking, explanatory and summing-up passages as the setting for extensive quotations from German sources. These are drawn from a wide range of archives, memoirs and unit histories and over all ranks from privates to generals.

The opening chapters vividly document the tremendous surprise achieved on the first day of the British offensive, 20th November 1917 and its devastating effect on the defenders at all levels. The German divisional commander, von Watter, who bore the brunt of the attack, kept his nerve but wrongly expected that the division (107th) in immediate reserve would quickly come to the rescue.

Bourlon Wood soon became the vital feature for the defenders and was only just held onto on 21st November. The commander of the German Second Army, von der Marwitz, described the fighting in the dense wood as 'pure hell'. It had been an 'evil experience' for the British defenders, particularly because the Germans had drenched the entire area with mustard gas. Sheldon quotes an unusual German order stating that the danger of contamination from gas-infected clothing was so great that British prisoners captured in Bourlon Wood must immediately take off their uniforms – or be shot.

Even during the chaotic conditions at the opening of the battle, the German high command began planning a counter-attack but, in the event, it took ten days to launch. The British defenders were then in turn completely surprised because they thought the battle was over. The Germans recovered most of the ground lost on 20th November by penetrating the exposed British right flank, but were held up south of Bourlon Wood and failed to achieve the breakthrough which had briefly seemed possible. Both sides accepted that the outcome was a draw.

The German high command promptly circulated a report on the lessons to be learnt: the organisation and equipment of the army fell short of the demands of mobile warfare. Deficiencies would have been even more sharply exposed had the counter-attack lasted longer and over a wider front. The mobility of all formations was a vital issue but improvements would be limited by the shortage of horses.

This interesting study concludes that, in most respects, including casualties and gains and losses in territory, the battle ended with honours even. But the shock effect of the mass tank attack with the novel use of predicted artillery fire had a lasting consequence which worked against the Germans for the rest of the war. Precious resources had to be diverted to anti-tank defences and to ensuring that a surprise attack, like that of 20th November, could never be repeated. In short, as Crown Prince Rupprecht warned: 'there can be no more mention of quiet fronts'. The resulting diversion of scarce resources was, in Sheldon's words, 'possibly the greatest legacy the tanks of Cambrai gave to the Allied war effort'.

Brian Bond
Emeritus Professor of Military History
King's College, London.

Introduction

By mid November 1917 fighting had died away in Flanders as the Third Battle of Ypres drew to a close. There had always been an assumption on the German side that the Allies would continue to press their attacks there until worsening winter weather brought operations to a halt. It was then believed that no other major operations would be carried out in the west that year. Yet, only a few days later, at Cambrai, making use of massed armour, the British army launched the most ambitious tank attack that the world had ever seen. It was so completely unexpected, surprise was so total and such rapid progress was made on the first day of operations that church bells throughout the United Kingdom were rung in celebration.

For a fleeting moment it appeared that the large scale deployment of tanks, supported by concentrated, predicted artillery fire, designed to neutralise the German batteries and lay down a lifting barrage just ahead of the advancing tanks and infantry, had provided the means to break through the massively deep barbed wire defences of the Hindenburg Line, suppress the German machine guns, pin down their defending infantry and so clear the way for their infantry to advance. There was also hope that cavalry moving up behind the assaulting troops would be in a position to pour through any gaps in the defences and wreak havoc in the German rear areas. In practice, however, things were not so simple. Once surprise was lost, once the defence began to react in a coordinated way, the ten day battle for Bourlon Ridge and the approaches to Cambrai degenerated into an all-too-familiar attritional slog, which exhausted the British forces committed to the operation and left the German defenders in possession of the key terrain.

The choice by the British of the rolling chalk land of Cambrai as a battlefield was probably the least worst option available to it at the time. The ground lent itself to disguising the preparations and the terrain had not been cut up by previous battles, so it was relatively dry and firm for the tanks. The German defenders, relying on the passive defences of the Hindenburg Line and under the assumption that the usual preparatory bombardment would provide sufficient time to reinforce the area if it came under threat, meant that there were many deficiencies in the defensive posture in this sector. In short, it was an adequate, but far from an ideal, choice. Water obstacles, in particular the St Quentin Canal, which acted as a moat defending Cambrai from the west and south, strictly limited the freedom of action of these early tanks.

The Battle of Cambrai has always been controversial. Launched with high hopes which were sustained by good initial progress, the British could not resist the temptation to go on attacking but, because the St Quentin Canal represented a formidable obstacle which, without the specialised armour available to later generations of tank men, was effectively impassable once the bridges were down, their decision to press on meant that they had no choice but to attempt to turn Cambrai from the north by capturing the Bourlon Ridge. The importance of this feature was equally clear to the German commanders, who, profiting from excellent rail links into the Cambrai area from elsewhere and the frequently proven ability of the German army to improvise, held on grimly along the ridge and rapidly assembled a large counter-attack force. Launched ten days after the battle began the German counter-attack also enjoyed remarkable success to begin with, but it, too, stalled quickly in the face of obstinate British defence. A few days later the British army withdrew from the untenable salient left by the battle and the fighting came to an end with honours fairly even.

The tactical surprise achieved on each occasion was due to intelligence failures by both sides. The initial British attack and the subsequent German counter-attack were so completely unexpected, so far from the expected pattern of enemy action, that intelligence staffs failed to pick up on the slight clues available, which might have provided at least some slight warning. It goes against human nature, especially that of senior officers, to be willing to accept responsibility for being caught out so, on the German side, although their morale benefited from their achievements later in the battle, unjust attempts were made at the time and post war to make the weakened 54th Infantry Division the scapegoat for the initial reverse whilst, on the British side, the unsatisfactory post-battle investigation also placed the blame unfairly on the lower echelons of the British Third Army so, in yet another way, the outcome of the battle was much the same for both.

The tactics each employed in the attack were, however, quite different. The British pioneered the use of modern all arms tactics at Cambrai. For the first time the mass use of tanks was coordinated with predicted artillery fire and close air support to create a starting situation which, at the time, was unique in the military history of the world. The Germans, for their part, made extensive use of what would later be called 'storm troop' tactics, though, in fact, hardly any trained storm units were present and the new tactics of isolating strong points and villages with fire and bypassing them, so that they would either wither on the vine, or be susceptible to mopping up operations from follow up forces, had to be explained to the troops carrying out the attack, who had no time to prepare properly for their ambitious missions and who therefore committed a series of errors, suffering disproportionately high casualties amongst the junior leadership at company level and below.

When the Germans came to assess the first part of the battle, which they referred to as *Die Tankschlacht bei Cambrai* [the Cambrai tank battle], they drew two main conclusions. Reviewing their performance on the battlefield and taking into consideration the very real shock effect these weapons caused at times, nevertheless they remained sceptical about the value of the tank, pointing out, with some justification, that at Cambrai, at least initially, everything had been in their favour. The attack came as a complete surprise, whilst a combination of poor light, battlefield obscuration and foggy weather meant that tanks could not be observed at normal battle ranges by the artillery in the anti-tank role. Had this been possible, it is highly probable that the serious attrition suffered by the tanks on the approaches to Flesquières, in particular, would have begun sooner and the results would have been even worse for the British. They also went round after the battle and counted the numbers of tanks knocked out, ditched or broken down. On the basis of this survey they decided, especially in view of the existing pressure on their armaments industry, that there was no possibility of justifying the procurement of large numbers of tanks in their current state of development. General der Kavallerie Georg von der Marwitz, Commander Second Army, held very strong views on the subject, declaring it would be impossible to defend adding expensive tanks to the inventory when it could be expected that over a third of them would become casualties every time they were committed to battle.

The Allies, with their vastly superior resources, could afford to take a far more relaxed view about the inherent profligacy associated with the use of the tanks of that period, as indeed they could about the loss of relatively large numbers of artillery pieces. It was far harder for the Germans to absorb their losses in *materiel*. In any case, Cambrai was virtually the swansong of the Mark IV tank. 1918 would see the arrival in service of improved types in even larger numbers. However, even though they were not committed to the tank in the way that the Allies were, its arrival on the battlefield was a factor which the German army could ignore no longer. There had always been both quiet and active sectors along the Western Front. The quiet ones were valuable, especially during periods of sustained fighting elsewhere, because formations could be sent to these places to rest, absorb reinforcements and train. Furthermore these sectors could be allocated lower grade formations, fewer guns and smaller stocks of ammunition.

This had been precisely the role of the Cambrai front during the heavy fighting in Flanders throughout the summer and autumn of 1917, but the policy depended on the fact that previous major attacks had all been preceded by lengthy bombardments designed to soften up the defences and destroy their associated barbed wire obstacles. The time taken to achieve these objectives had always provided the notice the defence needed to rush reinforcements of all types to the threatened front. The move to predicted artillery fire and the large scale use of tanks meant that surprise had been restored to the Western Front and the consequences for the Germans were profound. It forced them to assume that on any front where tank movement was possible, they had to be ready to face an armoured threat. This placed an almost intolerable burden on their rapidly diminishing resources in 1918.

The logical extension of this train of thought, bearing in mind that he who attempts to defend everything defends nothing, was the fact that simply staying on the defensive in the west as they had during lengthy periods of the war and certainly throughout 1917, was no longer a viable option. For this reason, whilst accepting the need to concentrate effort on countering the continuing tank threat, by far the greatest effort was made to evaluate the lessons learned during *Die Angriffsschlacht bei Cambrai* [the Cambrai counter-offensive]. They decided, for example, that systematic preparation was an essential pre-requisite for offensive operations. Unless adequate training had been provided, unless there was time for reconnaissance and rehearsal, they could not expect to enjoy real success in the attack.

There were many other lessons learned, some important, others less so, but one real problem was battlefield logistics. The reinforcement of the Cambrai sector had demonstrated that, where the infrastructure was in place, theatre logistics was not a concern but, forward of the railheads, there were major difficulties. The inability of horse-drawn logistics to sustain the advancing armies had played a large part in the failure of the Schlieffen Plan in 1914 yet, more than three years on, lacking sufficient motorised transport, the German army was to embark on its offensives in 1918 still reliant on horse drawn vehicles. Had there been a sufficient number of these and had the horses been equal to the task all might have been well but, if the manpower situation in the German army was critical by this stage of the war, there was a complete crisis in terms of the quality and quantity of horses available to it. There had been huge, irreplaceable losses during the past three years and, which was worse, one effect of the Allied blockade was that not only was the population of Germany going hungry, so were the horses. There was a chronic shortage of fodder, which meant that losses were high when horses were worked hard during operations and also that teams had to be increased in size to compensate for their weakness. Much thought had to be devoted about how to make use of this scarce, dwindling resource.

The warning signs were there during the Cambrai counter-offensive, but the relatively small depth of the operation and its short duration prevented the problem from being brought into sharp focus. Tactically, all involved in the counter-offensive had learned a great deal, but the experience had also thrown up a number of dilemmas. For example, the 08/15 machine gun had transformed the firepower available to the infantry in defence, but it had proved to be a difficult weapon to employ in the attack. Weighing in at eighteen kilograms, it was heavy for a light machine gun. It was a water-cooled, belt fed, crew-served weapon, which was complicated to operate and far less handy in the advance than, say, the Lewis gun. Nevertheless it was all they had and much time had to be devoted during the winter of 1917 to tests and trials regarding how best to deploy and transport it in the attack.

All this analysis and evaluation, however, was still in the future when the storm broke around the forward defenders on 20 November. Severely pressed, driven back, they yielded ground but did not actually break. Reinforcements brought up and thrown in to the battle played their part and helped the German army score a notable defensive success during the battle for Bourlon Ridge. Their counter-attack, though falling short of all it set out to achieve, nevertheless brought the German army its greatest success over the British army to date. Measured against their unfavourable starting position, the eventual outcome of the Battle of Cambrai was a feather in its cap and, after a depressing year of attritional defensive fighting, it provided a boost to its morale and was a source of considerable pride to the men who had fought there.

Jack Sheldon
Vercors, France
October 2008

jandl50@hotmail.com

Author's Note

Sources used for this book include items from the archives in Freiburg, Stuttgart and Munich, though on this occasion the fact that so few Bavarian formations were involved at Cambrai reduces the utility of that normally very helpful provider of information. Nothing can fully substitute for the losses suffered when the Royal Air Force bombed the Prussian archives in Potsdam on 14 April 1945, but careful exploitation of surviving material in other places means that the cupboard is far from bare as far as primary sources in Germany are concerned. Once more the preparation of this account has drawn heavily on regimental histories and other books produced in Germany during the 1920s and 1930s. It is evident that there was an attempt, post war, to gloss over misunderstandings between 54th Infantry Division and 107th Infantry Division when these books came to be written but, with the aid of surviving primary documentation, it has proved possible to reconstruct the events of 19 – 20 November 1917 with a good degree of confidence in its accuracy.

Generally the material in the regimental histories can be relied on as an accurate portrayal of the events which occurred on the battlefield and, as far as Cambrai is concerned, almost every fact obtainable from British sources is confirmed in the German record, though, naturally there is often a different slant on how matters unrolled. In the final analysis, the German histories are similar to the British ones. Their overall worth depended on the ability of the author concerned and the amount of time and effort put into them. As a result, most are of generally high quality, some are mediocre and others, often barely more than expanded chronologies, are of little use to the researcher. Nevertheless, as a body of work, they represent an irreplaceable asset and it is fortunate that they exist in such large numbers.

The Germans never differentiated between English, Scottish, Irish or Welsh soldiers and units, referring to them all as Engländer.   This usage was frequently extended to contingents from the Dominions as well. Engländer has been translated throughout as 'British' for troops from the United Kingdom and usually adjusted where other nationalities were involved.

German time, which was one hour ahead of British time, is used throughout the book.

Acknowledgements

I am most grateful to Professor Brian Bond for providing the Foreword to this account of the Battle of Cambrai from the German perspective. Professor Bond's commitment, during a lifetime of study, to the placement of the First World War in its proper historical perspective, has done much to teach us not to accept oft-repeated myth or glib superficiality in our examination of this great conflict and, instead, to focus unemotionally on the facts. I am also grateful to Dr Bryn Hammond, who kindly provided me with an advance copy of his book *Cambrai 1917: The Myth of the First Great Tank Battle*. His insights were most helpful to my understanding of German accounts of certain aspects of the battle. Dr Alex Fasse in Germany has been a great help and support to me over the years, but I should like to pay special tribute to his generosity in allowing me access to a great deal of primary source material relating to the Battle of Cambrai, which he painstakingly collected during the production of his outstanding doctoral thesis *Im Zeichen des 'Tankdrachen'*. I also wish to express my particular indebtedness to him for his work clarifying the muddle which existed within Group Caudry at the beginning of the battle and the subsequent attempts to downplay the role of 54th Infantry Division and to enhance that of 107th Infantry Division on 20 November 1917.

I should also like to thank the numerous members of the Great War Forum, who provided me with source material, information or identifications of tank casualties and were able to explain obscure references to particular signs, symbols and flags displayed by British tanks during the battle. Those who helped included Tom Mc Cluskey, Bob Grundy, Gerald Moore, René Senteur (who also kindly permitted me to publish his photograph of F5 Fervant), Andi Lucas, Paul Hederer, Conor Dodd, Charles Messenger, Jeremy Banning, Jonathan Saunders, Stephen Broomfield, Mark Hone and several others who operate behind pseudonyms, but contribute to an extremely lively and informative internet community which, collectively, is the repository of an immense amount of information about the Great War. My thanks, as always, go to my editor Nigel Cave, the friendly team at Pen and Sword Books and, most especially, to my wife Laurie, who drew the maps and sustained me throughout the lengthy gestation period of this book through her loving support.

CHAPTER ONE

The Flanders Sanatorium

1916 was an exceptionally difficult year for the German army. The Battle of Verdun, which had been raging since spring had, by the autumn of that year, changed completely from an offensive to a defensive operation, which was costing it appalling losses in men and *materiel*. Meanwhile the Battle of the Somme continued as well, imposing an incessant drain on resources. On 27 August Romania declared war on Germany and, although that nation was defeated in an extraordinarily swift victory (by 6 December Bucharest was in German hands), this new theatre of operations also required troops, some of whom had to be withdrawn from the Western Front. In consequence, the German manpower situation at the turn of the year 1916-1917 was critical, because the main effort lay unmistakeably on the Western Front, which was precisely where its forces were most stretched.

The decision to establish a new defensive line in rear of the main battle front had in fact been taken shortly after Hindenburg and Ludendorff had assumed responsibility for overall command in the West the previous September. It was one of the main outcomes of the conference held at Cambrai on 5 September. Ludendorff directed that reconnaissance was to begin immediately to select defensible positions along the lines Arras – Laon and Verdun – Metz. Two weeks later this directive was expanded. The first position, to be known as the *Siegfriedstellung* [Hindenburg Line], was to be constructed along the line Arras – St Quentin – La Fère – Condé (to the north of Soissons). When built this would obviate the need to hold a very large salient. A second position, the *Michelstellung*, was intended to achieve the same purpose and to run between Verdun and Pont à Mousson. Initially the purpose of this work was two fold. The first reason was to ensure that any Allied breakthrough could not be operationally expanded or exploited in any significant way; the second, and the reason that ultimately dictated the occupation of the *Siegfriedstellung*, was that it would permit the German forces to withdraw in the face of a serious Allied offensive, provided only that the latter was recognised in a timely manner. Immense resources of manpower and *materiel* were devoted to its construction which, while it continued, absorbed almost the entire cement, sand and aggregate production of occupied France and Belgium, together with that of western Germany.

Because these positions were laid out well to the rear of the battlefronts, work on them could be carried out virtually under peacetime conditions. They were intended to reflect the latest defensive tactics and to exploit the inherent strength of reinforced concrete fortifications placed on ground of the defenders' choosing. By far the most important was the *Siegfriedstellung*. Such was the urgency that work began on it as early as the end of September 1916. As planned it was to be no less than 143 kilometres long and to comprise several defensive positions in considerable depth. In order to ensure that as little time as possible was lost, the line was divided into sectors, each the responsibility of a planning staff comprising General Staff officers, gunners and engineers. Once planning and marking out was complete in each sector, a staff responsible for overseeing its construction was established. The demands were endless and it was of key importance, for example, to ensure that supplies of building materials arrived in a timely manner in the required locations.

Hundreds of barge and train movements were needed which, given the priority for transport that the Battle of the Somme required, proved to be far from straightforward to arrange and manage. The works absorbed the total effort of a labour force approximately 65,000 strong. All these engineers, labour units and civil contractors had to be accommodated and administered as well, adding greatly to the difficulties. It was estimated that the entire line would take about five months to construct but, before it could be begun in earnest, a complete infrastructure had to be established to service it. This included the construction of hundreds of kilometres of broad and narrow gauge railways, together with sidings, unloading ramps, halts and stations. So complex and extensive was this work that, in addition to the construction gangs, manning it absorbed no fewer than twenty two railway companies.

In parallel, frenzied work started to build engineer, ammunition and supply depots and dumps, not to mention workshops, hospitals and all manner of canteens and other facilities. There was no choice in the matter. The construction of such a major defensive line simply could not be improvised. By mid-autumn, plans covering the mechanics of the move to these new positions were also well established and, so extensive were the works, it was impossible to conceal what was going on from the ordinary soldiers. All manner of rumours abounded – none of which was helpful in terms of motivating the men at the front to give their all in the face of persistent Allied offensive operations. Finally, on 26 November, in order to underline the official position that there was at that time not the slightest need or intention to withdraw (even if the work had been complete) an order went out down the chain of command.

"By order of Supreme Army Headquarters, rearward positions of great extent are being constructed at various places along the Western Front. These measures were based on a wide range of considerations and warnings have been given regularly against premature withdrawal. Just as we build fortresses in peacetime, so we are now developing depth positions. In the same way as we freed ourselves from our fortresses, so too are we keeping our distance from these depth positions. These positions provide greater security for our operations and demonstrate that the commanders of the army, aware of their responsibilities, have to take all possibilities into consideration. Only he who stands fast and has thought through everything in advance can expect to prevail."[1]

Be that as it may, the very fact of the existence of such a major defensive position meant that it was more or less inevitable that it would be used at some point. The question was, when – and in what circumstances? This decision was far from easy. Ludendorff wrestled with it for weeks during the winter of 1916 – 1917. Its necessity was debated constantly and heatedly at the highest level, because it was not considered to be the only possibility. Much time was devoted, for example, to an examination of whether forces could be accumulated for a German offensive in the early New Year. It was calculated, during a meeting at Stenay on 19 December, called to discuss the French successes at Verdun of 15 December, that, by March 1917, a total of seventeen divisions could be earmarked, provided that a further four could be withdrawn from Russia; but, equally, it was clear that they could achieve nothing decisive in the west.[2]

Other staff checks continued and papers evaluating the different options were written. Ludendorff, under immense personal pressure, changed his position several times. On 15 January, during a meeting at Headquarters Army Group Crown Prince Rupprecht, he declared himself convinced that no offensive would be possible[3] but, following the issue of a directive by Supreme Army Headquarters on 29 January: 'On politico-military grounds, a voluntary withdrawal to the *Siegfriedstellung* cannot take place...'[4] by 31 January, Ludendorff, knowing that the commanders of both First and Second Armies were opposed to a withdrawal from the positions on the Somme, was back seeking the views of General der Infanterie von Kuhl. What would the effect of *Alberich* [i.e. the move back to the *Siegfriedstellung*] have on the troops? Kuhl's view was that, initially, it would be unfavourable, but that they would soon understand the necessity.[5] By now Ludendorff was becoming more convinced than ever about the need to withdraw, but still the decision was delayed. This was to have consequences for the preparation of the *Siegfriedstellung* and, arguably, ultimately, the Battle of Cambrai.

The problem was that the uncertainty meant that right into January and February 1917 resources were being devoted to strengthening the defences of the Somme, in case either the withdrawal did not take place, or a partial solution, the so-called *Wotan-Siegfried-Riegel* option (i.e. withdrawal to the line Arras – Sailly), was adopted. The choices did not end there, however. As late as 6 February, First Army (presumably drawing on the Supreme Army

Directive of 29 January) placed a demand on Army Group Crown Prince Rupprecht for a further three divisions and 15,000 labourers for six weeks in order to move to new positions and improve their defences.[6] This demand was turned down flat, but it illustrates the differences of opinion within the German chain of command at a critical time and the way shrinking from a decision, which was effectively inevitable, compromised the outcome. In the end and after numerous additional staff papers had been produced which investigated, *inter alia*, if the withdrawal could be combined with a minor offensive or whether the move should be made in one gigantic operation, or be phased and nuanced, so as to slow the Allied follow up as far as possible, the only viable decision was taken.

Clear sighted thinkers had felt all along that there was no alternative. During a visit to General von Kuhl as early as 20 January, Generalleutnant von Fuchs had made it clear that there was no realistic alternative to withdrawal. Kuhl noted that he had stated,

> "Enemy superiority is so great that we are not in a position either to fix their forces in position or to prevent them from launching an offensive elsewhere. We just do not have the troops... We cannot prevail in a second Battle of the Somme with our men; they cannot achieve that any more. Therefore we must direct all our efforts into building up *Siegfried* and devote no effort to our current positions - especially not on the Somme. The positions produced will be worth nothing and we shall simply exhaust the men. We can save a lot of divisions, train them and deploy them elsewhere against the enemy with good prospects of success... if not we shall lose the campaign. A big decision must be made, not a half-hearted one. We must not shrink from withdrawal into the *Siegfriedstellung!*" [7]

Of course, those who opposed the move had several valid points on their side. To relinquish voluntarily ground which had been bought at a huge price in blood earlier was hard for both soldiers on the ground and the civil population of Germany to understand and accept. To yield to the Allies far more ground than they had ever won in over two hard years of fighting could only boost their morale and, in association with the haughtily rejected *Friedensangebot* [Offer of Peace][8] of December 1916, would simply lead to an assumption of German weakness. Yet, unpalatable though it undoubtedly was, that was the very point. The German armies were facing a crisis and the question of manpower was the clinching argument; the stark, serious, overriding fact which could not be ignored. Even after the move of some divisions from the Eastern Front, with only 154 German divisions along the Western Front pitted against about 190 Allied ones, which were frequently numerically superior, the unfavourable force ratio meant that the expected major Allied spring offensive was a source of major concern and could be ignored no longer.

Despite all views to the contrary, in order to save manpower and especially, in view of the coming offensive, to generate urgently needed reserves, there was only one realistic solution: to shorten the line. The *Wotan-Siegfried-Riegel* plan, it was calculated, would only reduce the front by thirteen kilometres and save six divisions, whereas a bold move straight back to the *Siegfriedstellung* meant a shortening of forty to forty five kilometres and manpower savings of thirteen divisions.[9] So it was that 'the big decision', desiderated by Fuchs and others, was taken. The line would be withdrawn an average of fifteen kilometres into the *Siegfriedstellung* between Soissons and Arras.[10] This highly controversial operation, the mechanics of which almost caused the resignation of Crown Prince Rupprecht, who was adamantly opposed to the excessive scorched earth policy employed, was code named the *Alberich Bewegung* [Alberich Movement].[11]

Finally, after continued heart-searching, in a move which took the Allies completely by surprise, the order was given on 16 March 1917 to occupy the new positions. The German assessment of Allied intentions meant that the decision could be delayed no longer. The withdrawal plans, so painstakingly worked out and implemented, worked more or less perfectly. The Allies followed up hard on the heels of the retreating troops, but were forced to postpone their offensive intentions until they had reorganised their forces and closed right up in front of the new defensive lines. There was only one problem. In mid-March 1917, the *Siegfriedstellung* was not complete and in many places, including forward of Cambrai, it turned out not to have been optimally sited. There is little doubt that it would ultimately have been an extraordinarily powerful defensive position, but time had not been on the side of the German army. In a telling proof of the dire situation that army found itself in as a result of the Allies' major offensives of 1916, it was forced to move earlier than it wished and certain major planned projects, such as the total felling of Havrincourt Wood, simply could not be carried out in time. A heavy price would be paid later for this deficiency in particular.

Incomplete the line may have been, but an assault on Cambrai played no part in Allied offensive plans for the time being, so all through the spring the front settled down to an uneasy stalemate, broken only by minor operations designed to improve certain perceived deficiencies in the forward layout and to correct an oversight by incorporating La Vacquerie into the main forward position. Throughout the spring and summer a constant succession of formations assumed responsibility for the Cambrai front. Almost all had come from serious fighting elsewhere, were very worn down, overstretched and not well placed to make major improvements to the positions. The tours of duty here, however, did have the great advantage of being quiet. 'Live and let live' prevailed and the morale of the troops benefited from the break it offered. The regimental history of Grenadier Regiment 123 commented that, with the exception of a small area near Banteux, there was hardly any enemy artillery fire for hours at a time, which enabled the trench garrison to lie at their leisure outside their dugouts and enjoy the early summer sunshine in peace.[12] Things were never so easy in their Outpost Line and there was a great deal of low level mortaring and patrol activity to contend with but, overall, it was a great deal more relaxing than the battles around Arras and to the north in Flanders later in the year.

In its turn, following a hard tour of duty in Flanders, which had included the Battle of Langemarck in August 1917, 54th Infantry Division was withdrawn from the battle and sent south in early September to rest and reconstitute. On arrival it assumed responsibility for the *Siegfriedstellung* from Havrincourt to La Vacquerie and the first of the forces which would be involved in the Battle of Cambrai were in position. Here they found that great belts of barbed wire and other obstacles protected positions well supplied with deep dugouts and the area really was quiet. Not for nothing had it become known to the German army as the *Flandernsanatorium* [The Flanders Convalescent Home]. However the situation was not quite as comforting as it might have been. The length of the divisional sector was nine kilometres as the crow flew; ten as the trenches were dug. With each of the three regiments finding one battalion forward, one in support and one in reserve, battalion sectors more than three kilometres wide meant that garrisoning the trenches and improving them was extremely demanding and strenuous.

Another serious disadvantage was the lie of the land in this area and the way the positions had been laid out. Despite the fact that the *Siegfriedstellung* had been designed and constructed completely out of contact with the enemy, in this particular sector, the main defensive line ran along the forward slope of the crest line so that it was difficult to watch the enemy trenches and from nowhere was it possible to observe the enemy rear areas or approach routes. In contrast, the British, with observation posts established on the dominating heights west of Havrincourt, had views stretching as far as Cambrai. The consequence was that the division had to place great priority on despatching regular reconnaissance patrols forward at night to gather essential information. This was an additional burden on the hard-pressed forward troops. These deficiencies in the sector forward of Cambrai caused some disquiet amongst the arriving troops and led to a great deal of exhausting labour for the newly arrived trench garrison.

Leutnant A Saucke Officer Commanding 6th Company Infantry Regiment 84 [13]

"From the very beginning I was disappointed with the much praised Hindenburg Position. I had imagined it to be a shining example of a modern field fortification equipped with all the fruits of the latest technology of war but, at first glance, all I could see was a non-uniform, temporary and incomplete [construction]. There was nothing for it but to set to and to build it up if we were to be in a position to hold the further advance of the enemy successfully. [As a result], we did not derive much benefit from this 'quiet' position. I believe that seldom did we perform so much physical labour as we did before Cambrai."

Arriving in the closing days of August, the formations of 54th Infantry Division deployed to relieve 18th Infantry Division. Initially units of Infantry Regiment 84 defended Sector *R1* (Flesquières – Havrincourt), with Reserve Infantry Regiment 27 to its south.

*Oberleutnant Karl Nissen Adjutant 3*rd *Battalion Infantry Regiment 84* [14]

"Hardly was the mud of Flanders washed off and beaten out of our uniforms, than orders arrived at the regiment directing us to deploy to a quiet sector of the *Siegfriedstellung* southwest of Cambrai. Already, by 26 August, leading elements of the regiment (3rd Battalion) had marched via Cambrai and Noyelles to points in rear of the new sector. The 2nd and 1st Battalions followed during the next few days. By 29 August all units of the regiment had arrived in their new positions and 3rd Battalion had already deployed its companies in Sector *R 1 South*, whilst those of 2nd Battalion were located in *R1 North*. The 1st Battalion spent ten days resting and training at Noyelles.

"The regimental sector, *R1*, which had been allocated to the regiment, was delineated roughly as follows: on the western side, northwest edge of Havrincourt – northwest edge Flesquières – immediately southeast of Cantaing – one kilometre north of Noyelles; on the eastern side, 300 metres east of Fémy Wood – cutting through the road Ribécourt – Havrincourt 500 metres to the west of Ribécourt – 500 metres east of the *Großer Stern* [Great Star][15] on the Flesquières – Ribécourt road – Premy Chapelle – southeast edge of Noyelles. It was a good two kilometres in width and was divided into two sub-sectors – *R1 North* and *R1 South* – the boundary running along the eastern side of the pond in Havrincourt Park, then just to the east of *T Copse* and as far as the eastern edge of Flesquières.

"Each of these battalion sectors was further sub-divided into two company sectors. The deployment of the battalions was so arranged that two companies acted as outpost companies and two others were in support. All the machine guns and grenade launchers were distributed across the full width of the battalion sectors. The final battalion of the regiment remained in Noyelles in reserve, resting and carrying out training. Rationing of the forward battalions was carried out from Havrincourt for that in *R1 North*; whilst that in *R1 South* was supplied from field kitchens dug into *Stollenweg* [Dugout Way]. Trench stores and ammunition were supplied from the engineer park at the exit of Flesquières in the direction of Ribécourt.

"For the most part, the forward positions *K1* and *K2* ran through the park belonging to Havrincourt Chateau. From *K1*, numerous advanced saps ran forward well into No Man's Land. The forward ends of these saps were manned by sentries or sections, commanded by unteroffiziers. A short distance behind the *K2* line of the First Position were the remains of Havrincourt Chateau, which had been blown up. The *Zwischenstellung* [Intermediate Position] ran a mere one hundred metres south of the village of Flesquières, whilst the rear lines had only been marked out on the ground."

For its part, Reserve Infantry Regiment 27 deployed forward to positions south of Ribécourt; the war diary of its 3rd Battalion providing a description of the sector from west to east at trench level: [16]

"The line is divided by two re-entrants: Beaucamp and Bilhen. The position itself is divided into the Outpost Line, Battle Lines *K1* – *K3* and the *Zwischenstellung* [Intermediate Position]. The outpost zone features both advanced saps and *Widerstandsnester ('Widas')*[17] [fortified strong points]. The enemy lines were located on average 600 – 700 metres from the outpost trenches, though on the left flank at Bosquet Copse[18] and on the right flank the distances were 400 and 350 metres respectively. This meant that the enemy frontline positions were higher than ours, affording them good views over the forward area and the two re-entrants.

"The fortified strong points were scattered throughout the area between the Outpost Line and *K1*. The Outpost Line itself was only manned during the night, but the *Widas* were also manned during the day, some of them commanded by unteroffiziers. The distance from the Outpost Line to *K1* averaged 500 – 800 metres and the *K2* line was approximately 200 metres behind *K1*. Both these trenches were plentifully supplied with good dugouts. The *K3* Line was out of sight of the enemy. During the past weeks the sector had been extremely quiet, though the enemy conducted small scale raids against our Outpost Line from time to time. There was also little enemy artillery fire, though during periods of good weather enemy aircraft were very active."

The overall geography and the way in which the defensive positions had been planned, demanded a fresh look at deployment within the regiments and battalions and adjustments to normal trench routine.

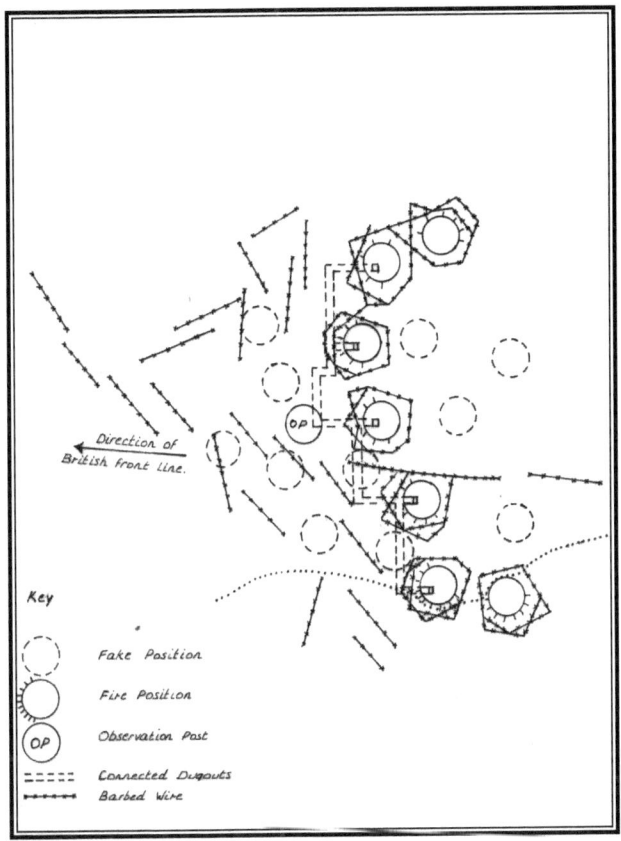

A Typical Wida

Leutnant A Saucke Officer Commanding 6th Company Infantry Regiment 84 [19]

"The new feature of the position was, above all, the explicit exploitation of the outpost zone which, in our area, varied between 300 – 500 metres in width. In conformity with that fact, the deployment and organisation of the companies deviated from the normal [procedure], each company formed four fighting platoons and one pioneer section, the latter being under the command of the Battalion Trench Officer. Whenever the company was in the front line, two platoons manned the *K1* Line, whilst the other two, divided into sections, deployed forward into the outpost zone. These forward piquets were approached by means of one single shallow trench, whilst all other movement, between piquets and section commanders' posts or between individual double sentry posts had to take place above ground and with no cover. It was not until later that this was improved...

"Reliefs within the outpost company took place on a twenty four hour rotation at about midnight. The operation had to be conducted with the utmost care, because we were extremely vulnerable to possible enemy harassing fire. The wire obstacle furthest forward was extremely weak, but that before *K1* was very strong indeed. Double sentry positions were established every thirty to fifty metres in short sections of trench about shoulder high. The length of sentry duty varied according to the weather and the amount of light. Relief within the posts themselves was not possible due to the lack of manpower. As a result, sentry duty made the most extraordinary mental and physical demands on the men. In view of the poor rations and the wet, cold, autumn weather, such a special performance could only be maintained over a long period by troops as well disciplined as ours.

"On more than a few occasions thick fog meant that the sentries were forced to maintain their positions without any sort of relief until 11.00 am or even midday. In other words they had to stay in their muddy holes for up to ten to eleven hours without a break. Once the visibility improved then, on order of their platoon commanders, they could pull back to their section positions, which were generally located about 150 to 200 metres in front of the barbed wire and were mostly protected from the elements only by a rough piece of corrugated iron. There the Unteroffizier and his eight men had to spend the day jammed in like herrings in a barrel, freezing cold and hungry, because warm food could not be brought forward in daylight.

"As soon as it began to go dark it was a matter of preparing to move forward to the wet muddy holes once more until, with midnight, came the longed-for hour of relief. But, having made it back to the *K1* Line, our brave musketeers still had no chance to rest. One would have to go to the kitchen to fetch the warm food and the remainder of the daily rations; another would have to take over the relaying of signals calling for defensive fire. Someone else would go in search of the mail, while yet another went to collect firewood. It would be almost dawn before their worn out bodies could lie down on the rough bunks, made of wood or metal and certainly not padded with feather or down, there to attempt to stretch out for a few hours of sleep. Of course the day brought another round of fatigues which had to be carried out until at about 11.00 pm the word would come down, 'Everybody out! Stand by to relieve forwards!'

"That, in broad outline, is how our men spent their days when they were deployed facing the enemy. Despite the fact that Cambrai was a quiet front, our men did not live a sleepy existence. However, it is a fact that this sort of soldierly activity must be regarded as a suitable way of preparing and toughening up of mind and body for the hard conditions associated with a major battlefront."

Settling down in their new sector and familiarising themselves with the micro-geography of their trenches, the units of 54th Infantry Division then began in the time-honoured manner to improve the defences of the outpost zone and the main positions, together with their billets to the rear. A divisional training area was set up near *Neufwald* [Bois des Neuf, one kilometre north of Marcoing], where battalions, allegedly at rest, spent many hard days training and exercising as they gradually, but all too slowly, absorbed returning wounded and a trickle of replacements into their ranks.

Oberleutnant Karl Nissen Adjutant 3rd Battalion Infantry Regiment 84 [20]

"The mission of the regiment was principally to develop further the sector which had been taken over and to hold it against enemy attacks. As a result, over time, enormous barbed wire obstacles were constructed in front of all lines and positions. Specially designated squads were formed to build and maintain [these obstacles] and their main task was to wire up Havrincourt Park to the highest standard. Development of the trenches and dugouts, the machine gun and grenade launcher posts was placed in the hands of the companies. The demands which these tasks made on our men, worn down and exhausted by the heavy fighting in Flanders, were enormous. However, with magnificent devotion to duty, they held on to achieve an immense amount.

"The effect of the weather, together with enemy artillery and mortars, often destroyed more in one night than had been achieved the previous day. Again and again the damage was repaired and new work accomplished – all in addition to the main tasks of the companies, which were to man the outposts and carry out patrols. Sentry duty was still the main task; the object being to establish by careful observation what was happening in the enemy positions, where the enemy sentry positions were, etc. It was also essential to capture prisoners by means of small scale raids, which were prepared by means of numerous preliminary reconnaissance patrols, so as to establish the make up and grouping of enemy forces, as well as to determine patterns of relief and planned operations.

"Over the weeks this developed into No Man's Land becoming a very active place as we first of all learned every detail of the terrain. Later patrols often forced their way into the enemy trenches. One example occurred during the night 8/9 October, when a patrol from 3rd Battalion, commanded by Vizefeldwebel Panse, achieved this and repeated the feat on 2 November. Unfortunately, during the crossing of the second enemy wire obstacle, Panse and some of his outstanding comrades were wounded by enemy hand grenades and that particular operation failed. Fahnenjunker Meentzen, an outstanding young soldier who had only spent a few days at the front, fell badly wounded into the hands of the enemy."

During the early days of the deployment, some of the raids and patrols were quite modest in scope. Nevertheless, their successful completion was good for morale and prevented staleness or too defensive a mindset from becoming widespread. Already, by 2 September, junior ranks of 7th Company achieved a minor success on the *Kalkberg* [Chalk Mountain], an area of high ground in No Man's Land about one kilometre southwest of Havrincourt, which had recently been captured by the British and pressed into service as an observation point.

Reserve Leutnant Schmid Officer Commanding 7th Company Infantry Regiment 84 [21]

"When the artillery fire lifted at 9.55 pm and the machine guns opened up, the men in the forward sentry positions started to work their way forward. Unteroffizier Post 2 of Field Sentry Position 1 shook out, moved to the right hand corner of the *Kalkberg* and established a covering position on its upper edge. It appeared that the enemy had already pulled back from here. The remainder of the group then moved along, about half way up the slope, as far as the left hand corner. When it had approached to within about ten metres, the enemy threw hand grenades from a fortified position on the left hand corner. This post seemed to comprise about three men. We then began to throw grenades at the position, following which one man pulled back, taking the machine gun with him.

"The other two continued to offer resistance, but our men pushed forward energetically, repeatedly throwing hand grenades. At that the remaining enemy pulled back, defending themselves with rifles and hand grenades. We immediately occupied the fortified post and part of the trench which ran to the rear from it. Despite repeated hand grenade attacks by the enemy the post was defended. The entire section now occupied the hill and searched it. The enemy had begun to dig a trench on the far side of the slope, but it was not quite complete; planks for lining dugouts were found in it. Captured materiel recovered included, one carbine, several mortar bombs, two boxes which contained some hand grenades, several drums of machine gun ammunition, flares, a coat and a water bottle.

"Whilst [the men of] Field Sentry Position 1 were advancing onto the *Kalkberg*, Field Sentry Position 2 was also moving towards it along the streambed. Enemy sentry positions along the *Kalkbergstraße*, had already been withdrawn, probably because of the artillery fire. Our old sentry positions were reoccupied and contact was made with Field Sentry Position 1. The enemy had also dug in along *Kalkbergstraße* and prepared the crossroads for defence by erecting a barricade and a barbed wire obstacle. Digging tools, rapid obstacles, baulks and planks of timber still lay around the place and we immediately made use of the material we had found against the enemy. A communication trench had already been dug almost up to the crossroads, so we blocked it and wired it off.

"A repetition of the British operation can only be prevented if our outpost line is heavily wired. It will also be necessary to harass the British positions behind the *Kalkberg* constantly with artillery and mortar fire. The enemy is able by day, unseen and undisturbed by us, to work and also to occupy our forward posts. During the driving off of the enemy sentries, Gefreiter Gier, ably supported by Musketiers Knoop and Reizig, distinguished himself; whilst from Field Sentry Position 2 there were outstanding contributions from Unteroffiziers Lisch and Riggelsen."

Also departing Flanders, but not moving into position around La Vacquerie and Banteux – Bantouzelle until towards the end of September 1917, were regiments of 9th Reserve Division, which were to play a large role during the battle. Severely depleted by losses suffered around Zandvoorde, battle casualty replacements began to arrive shortly after the relief of 10th Bavarian Infantry Division was complete. The majority of the new arrivals had no front line experience and time had to be devoted to training them in such basic skills as the use of hand grenades and fighting from positions amongst craters, which had been the daily routine of much of the infantry for more than a year at this point. In this area and south towards Honnecourt, the German defences to the west of the canal were restricted to outposts, intended only to secure the crossings and bridgeheads at places such as Honnecourt itself. To the east of the canal was the so-called *Scheldestellung* [Escaut/St Quentin Canal Position]. This comprised a series of strongpoints with, to the rear, the two main lines of the *Siegfriedstellung*, which were linked by communication trenches.

Initially, because of the width of the divisional sector, all three regiments took over one part of the frontage. Reserve Infantry Regiment 6 deployed on the right between La Vacquerie and Banteux, Reserve Infantry Regiment 19 was in the centre to the west of Banteux and Infantry Regiment 395 covered the left flank between Bantouzelle and Honnecourt. Because 9th Reserve Division had been terribly weakened by its losses in the Flanders battles, 183rd Infantry Division, which itself was not very strong, sent one battalion of Infantry Regiment 440 to help and 36th Division released a battalion of Infantry Regiment 141. Generally speaking the positions were in reasonably good order and the troops were pleased after the muddy shell holes of Zandvoorde to find that they were to occupy well constructed deep dugouts, equipped frequently with battery-operated electric lights. No Man's Land varied between 800 and 1,300 metres in width and, although there were minor exchanges of artillery fire, on some days not a single shell was exchanged.

9th Reserve Division was in fact one of the original divisions to occupy the *Siegfriedstellung*, but they had left this very same sector in April 1917 and they noticed a number of significant developments on their arrival. It had been realised early that La Vacquerie had to be incorporated into the defences so, as a result of many minor actions and a great deal of difficult digging, the previous outpost line was transformed into the *Vacqueriestellung*, becoming the main line of defence from La Vacquerie down to Banteux and relegating the original *Siegfriedstellung* to a support line in this sector. To the rear of the fortified area was the *Zwischenstellung* [Intermediate Position]. This was heavily wired, but in many places the line of the trenches was only spitlocked and the planned concrete constructions were frequently only indicated on the ground, there having been neither manpower nor materials to complete their construction.

The formations quickly settled down to a pattern of fourteen days in the forward trenches, followed by seven days 'rest' and training to the rear. Reinforcements began to trickle in and, despite the considerable width of No Man's Land, a full programme of patrolling began. Some experienced officers and NCOs needed no urging and the personal cost could be high.

Reserve Hauptmann Hollender 3rd Battalion Reserve Infantry Regiment 19 [22]

"[Unteroffizier von] Rosadowski was an exceptionally determined man and daring patrol commander. He volunteered to go on every single patrol. He had already begun to render much valuable service to the battalion and his company back in Flanders in 1914 and now he was doing so again near Cambrai. Repeatedly he ranged far out in front of our own lines and, on several occasions, brought back prisoners. During one reconnaissance patrol ordered by the regiment he was killed as he was crawling up to the enemy lines in order to examine their precise layout."

His loss was a bitter blow to his comrades. They were not prepared to leave his body lying out unburied, so an officer and several volunteers returned in darkness and recovered his body from a position hard up against the British lines – a not inconsiderable feat in itself. Naturally patrolling was not confined to the 3rd Battalion. At the beginning of November, 2nd Battalion Reserve Infantry Regiment 19 mounted a successful prisoner snatch. Its commander later wrote one of the most honest and evocative accounts of a prisoner snatch ever to appear in print.

Reserve Leutnant Vocke 5th Company Reserve Infantry Regiment 19 [23]

"During the evening of 31 October 1917, I was ordered to go to the battalion command post. Rittmeister von Massow explained to me that we had to discover if the British, in connection with the Italian offensive, had withdrawn any troops. Prisoners had to be captured. From each company I received an Unteroffizier and four men, one of whom was Unteroffizier Köhler of 7th Company. During the night 31 October/1 November I carried out a reconnaissance in No Man's Land and the following night the patrol was carried out. Ten paces short of the British wire, I had my men lie down and crawled forward alone to look for an entry point. I was challenged by a British sentry post. I tried to reply in English as best I could, but the necessary words failed me and I started to curse in German, which caused me to be on the receiving end of a number of 'blue beans' [bullets].

"A considerable fight with hand grenades then broke out either side of the barbed wire. We won the exchange; the enemy fell silent. To have attempted to fight our way in would not have brought us any prisoners, but we should undoubtedly have taken casualties. Although it was rather annoying, we had to withdraw. The following night I set off again with Unteroffizier Köhler and fourteen men. Everything was perfectly still, so the slightest noise could be heard. It was a moonlit night and a bit foggy, with visibility about fifteen metres. Slowly we crawled forward on all fours, a well-trodden path leading towards the British. After some hours, though the positions were only eighty to 350 metres apart, we managed to find a gap in the enemy wire. We crawled through intending to grab the British sentry who we could hear coughing.

"We came across a second wire obstacle, but we were able to crawl through it. I had the Unteroffizier and the men lie down between the obstacles, with orders to follow me on my signal, or if I shouted, but not to throw grenades or shoot without express instructions. Each of us carried a pistol and three grenades, but nothing else, so as to avoid being betrayed by rattles. As I was crawling through the second obstacle, the British sentry suddenly began shooting. I reached for my hand grenades. I had lost one somewhere whilst crawling. I could not activate the second; the mechanism was blocked with mud, so I threw my final one. As agreed, a particular gefreiter threw grenades simultaneously which exploded to the right of mine and cut off the sentry post. I leapt up and in one movement ran to the trench. I then fired my pistol at the sentry post. After the first round, it jammed; mud had blocked the ejection opening. Oh well! I jumped down into the trench.

"I found myself standing between two traverses. I was just asking myself, 'What now?' when somebody came running along the traverse to the left. With the moon behind him, I could not recognise who it was. Taking a quick decision, I threw my heavy Dreyse pistol in his face, which knocked him down. I could see the shadow of his pistol on his face. Its long barrel could have been that of a German pistol, so I shouted at the man, asking him who he was. Answer: 'Unteroffizier Köhler!' He had recognised me in the moonlight, even though I could not see him. What luck that my pistol had jammed; he got away with a large bump on his head. 'Where are the others?' 'Behind me.' 'Right let us continue.'

"Completely unarmed, I ran off towards the other direction. Just as we reached the next traverse, twenty five metres away, a British soldier was just coming round the corner. This time I had no trouble distinguishing his helmet. We were wearing caps. He pointed his large revolver at me. I threw myself at him, punching him in the face, grabbing his hands and shouting, 'Hands up!' He did not get a shot off. Violently he was thrown against the wall of the trench and his revolver ripped off him. Together with Unteroffizier Köhler who was following up, he was grabbed. Pushed up out of the trench, he was seized by some of the others.

"Lying near the traverse was the first British sentry who had been hit by fragments from my first grenade. We left him lying there and sprang up out of the trench. Urged on by shoves and thumps, we made the violently struggling prisoner return with us. In the hurry and the darkness we all tripped over in the British wire, the Tommy underneath all of us, so his uniform jacket and trousers were full of triangular tears. Soon we were through the wire and I gave orders that the British were to be kept at bay behind it by means of grenades and shots. We fired and bawled so loudly that, back in our own lines, people thought that a full scale battle was underway. Thanks to my luminous compass I could choose the exact route and, within a few minutes, we were back in our own trenches and being greeted heartily by our comrades.

"My men celebrated. I handed round cigarettes then, together with a gefreiter, I headed for the battalion command post and introduced the commander to this 'Trench Corporal'. It had been his task in the event of the arrival of another German patrol to raise the alarm so that they could be captured. Thank heavens, it was the other way round!"

Not all patrol actions met with the same success. A few days earlier an operation mounted by 1st Battalion Reserve Infantry Regiment 27 very nearly led to self-inflicted casualties. During the evening of 24 October, Reserve Leutnant Poppendieck of 4th Company led forward a fighting patrol drawn from picked men of the entire 1st Battalion. It was to be his last operation. One of its members described what happened.

Musketier Bode 1st Company Reserve Infantry Regiment 27 [24]

"Shortly after we left our trenches we spotted a British patrol. Leutnant Poppendieck immediately decided to try to capture it. We split up left and right so as to surround it, whilst Leutnant Poppendieck and a few others [prepared] to charge it. The right hand group was commanded by a Gefreiter, whose Christian name was Ignatz. I believe he was from 2nd Company but, because I later lost my diary in the confusion at Havrincourt, I have forgotten his name. Ignatz had set off in what he thought was the direction given by Leutnant Poppendieck, when suddenly four figures loomed up in front of us. Bawling, 'Burn Tommies!' Ignatz hurled his grenade, which was fully primed, at them. Our commander must have become disorientated in the dark, because his group hit the ground and threw grenades back at us, fortunately without injuring anyone. It could have turned into a great disaster, but for the fact one of us shouted out and the error was realised. Unfortunately our Leutnant Poppendieck (who had only recently returned to us, having recovered from a wound suffered in the *Hillerwald*) had been killed by the grenade thrown in the darkness. Who was to blame? In my view, given the situation, nobody could be held responsible"[25]

Given the hair trigger reactions required of those who operated at night forward in No Man's Land it is, perhaps, surprising that more such incidents did not occur. Four days later, on 28 October, in front of the sub sector of 12th Company Reserve Infantry Regiment 27 there was an occurrence which could have had serious consequences for British operational security. Unteroffizier Knoop came across the corpse of a British soldier, who had been killed a couple of days earlier when men of 12th Company opened fire on a British patrol. The body was found lying by the road Ribécourt – Trescault. It and all its personal equipment were recovered because the Germans were constantly trying at this time to verify the identities of their opponents and this was a very welcome find. Medical examination suggested that the body had been dead about two days. Initially the Germans were puzzled because it bore no badges or identification marks but, when the contents of the man's wallet were examined, he was found to be carrying the insignia of a British tank unit.

Information concerning the find was transmitted instantly to higher headquarters, where it was assessed that the man must have been part of a tank crew, who was conducting a reconnaissance for a possible tank attack along the so-called *Bilhenmulde* [Fonds de Beaucamp on the modern map]. No other collateral or confirmatory evidence was found subsequently and, furthermore, with the Third Battle of Ypres still raging to the north, the intelligence staffs decided that the incident and its potential implications fell outside their expected pattern of Allied operations, so they discounted the entire affair. This was unfortunate, but not untypical of the work of intelligence officers, who tend to be extremely good at explaining why something has happened, but not at predicting what is going to occur.

After the brief flurry of interest caused by the discovery of the tank man, life continued much as before in the Flanders Sanatorium. Patrol activity by both sides continued to be conducted at a brisk tempo, with neither side gaining any particular ascendancy – both had their successes and their failures. There was not much else which could be done. The fighting in Flanders was absorbing almost the entire effort of the Army Group and beyond. There was not even sufficient artillery ammunition to permit the launching of ambitious raids. Every shell had to be directed north to Flanders. The adjutant of 108 Brigade later described how the gunners pleaded with him on one occasion to get them off the charge of squandering precious shells:

> "Absolutely everything which could be stripped out of the Cambrai front was taken for Flanders. There was such a shortage of ammunition that the gunners came to me one day, wringing their hands and pleading for my help. Apparently an extremely painful investigation was underway to determine why a few shells had apparently been frittered away on some British infantry on the *Kalkberg*. Finally we calmed down higher headquarters by explaining that movement on the *Kalkberg* could easily appear to be like [the opening of] an attack, so it was clear to everyone that the artillery simply had to open fire."

It has always been a tenet of German military thinking to take risks elsewhere, so as to reinforce the *Schwerpunkt* [Point of Main Effort]. It is, perhaps, indicative of the immense pressure being exerted on the German army in Flanders at the time that risks, which in any other circumstances might have been regarded as verging on foolhardiness, had to be accepted. Putting their trust in the strength of the passive defences of the *Siegfriedstellung* and comfortable in their assessment that any major attack would have to be preceded by a significant bombardment, which would provide ample warning and permit the redeployment of defending forces and resources, as November opened it appeared to all on the Cambrai front that autumn would turn into winter and still nothing would occur to alter the accustomed pattern of events. It would be harsh and unjust to accuse the commanders and staffs of complacency. Nothing in the history of warfare to date could have prepared them for the surprise they were about to receive, but it would equally be wrong to assume that all aspects of command and control in the German army were as they should be.

An impression has developed over the years that, during the First World War, the German army was a well-oiled machine, comprising superb soldiers well led and commanded and with the *Großer Generalstab* [Great General Staff] providing the glue which held the entire structure in place. In fact, on many occasions the staff was a hotbed of back-biting, scheming and political manoeuvring. Whilst it is true that many staff officers holding key appointments were quite brilliant and extremely hard working, inevitably the enormous wartime expansion of the army had led to dilution of quality in places – it could hardly be otherwise. One of the functions of the General Staff had always been to ensure that military professionals stood alongside key commanders, who might have owed their positions more to their belonging to royalty or the aristocracy rather than any particular military merit. This was intended to ensure that sound decisions were made on the battlefield in the context of unity of command.

One by-product of this was that two distinct chains of command developed because, in addition to the normal one, it was and always had been the duty of General Staff officers at all levels to keep their staff superiors fully briefed on evolving situations and to react, not only to their commanders, but to instructions emanating from their superiors on the staff. Naturally commanders had the formal power of decision and command but, frequently, they would be steered towards a particular course of action by their chiefs of staff and, if they made a decision contrary to the advice of the staff, it was also a requirement for the chief of staff to make an official entry in the war diary detailing his alternative decision and providing the necessary justification. Bearing in mind that there were very few General Staff officers in the German army (a situation which persists to this day), relatively junior officers often had a disproportionate influence over the planning and conduct of operations. The Chief of Staff of the German Second Army, for example, was Major Stapff. His equivalent in the British Third Army was Major General Louis Vaughan.

This was not the only issue associated with the Great General Staff. It was a short step from using staff channels for purposes of coordination and to improve efficiency to manoeuvring actively behind the backs of commanders. Whispering campaigns conducted over the telephone network or during staff talks were, of course, extremely difficult to prove, although many commanders, including Generalleutnant von Moser, Commander Group Arras, were convinced that they were occurring. Lest it be thought that these fears were simply the products of the over-active imaginations of commanders, the diary of General der Infanterie Hermann von Kuhl, Chief of Staff Army Group Crown Prince Rupprecht, contains a very interesting example of the phenomenon relating to General der Infanterie Sixt von Armin, Commander Fourth Army, which occurred in June 1917, just prior to the opening of the Third Battle of Ypres.

It is also relevant in respect of the Battle of Cambrai because the officer that Oberst von Loßberg replaced as Chief of Staff Fourth Army in the wake of the Messines disaster was Major Stapff. Stapff's undoing was a lack of decisive thinking in the wake of the first day of fighting. Despite urging by von Kuhl and an opportunity to formulate a clear plan of action, Stapff, noted as a clever, hard-working staff officer under normal circumstances, was still unsure and unclear over the telephone to von Kuhl on 10 June 1917. Fourth Army was in crisis, so Stapff had to go, but the issue did not end there. Kuhl decided that General Sixt von Armin was not equal to the challenge either, describing him in his diary on 12 June as, 'rather weak, insufficiently decisive: old, too; not sharp enough.'[26] Kuhl felt that the best solution was to swap the commanders and chiefs of staff of Fourth and Sixth Armies.

Loßberg, having been consulted, agreed but, in the event, it was decided (in Ludendorff's absence) between Hindenburg and the Kaiser that only the chiefs of staff would move. On 14 June, von Kuhl discussed this again with Loßberg, who had by now taken over at Fourth Army and who told him that Sixt von Armin ought to go. At that, von Kuhl discussed the matter with Ludendorff, who confirmed that, even at this late stage, if Loßberg really could not work with Sixt von Armin, moves would be set in train to remove him, regardless of the reservations of the Kaiser. In fact *Oberst* von Loßberg decided that he would be able to work with or, rather, through, *General der Infanterie* Sixt von Armin and so the fate of one of the most senior field commanders in the German army was decided by his Chief of Staff several ranks junior to him – a truly amazing situation and unthinkable in any other army.

The Commander XIV Reserve Corps, also known as Group Arras, had much to say on this subject in his personal diary. Because Generalleutnant von Moser was the commander responsible for the Battle for Bourlon Ridge, he is an important witness, but it is essential to remember that he did not rate Commander Second Army, General der Kavallerie Georg von der Marwitz, professionally and he also disliked him personally. These negative feelings were mutual, which impacted on relationships within the chain of command and the efficiency with which the battle was conducted.

Generalleutnant von der Moser Commander Group Arras: Diary Entry 5 – 11 November 1917 [27]

"We have been transferred to Second Army deployed immediately to the south of us [and commanded by] von der Marwitz. We were grateful for the parting words of the Commander Sixth Army, who said that Group Arras had, since March 1917, been an unshakeable corner stone of Sixth Army. We were all reluctant to leave Sixth Army. As far as the new one was concerned, from the very beginning I had the feeling that, as I have often mentioned, the misuse of the telephone system was in full swing here. It appeared to me that one of my general staff officers was more than keen to participate in this. The officer had occupied exactly the same position almost since the beginning of the war. As a result his attitude to all around him and, indeed, to the fighting troops was insufferably high handed. He had become accustomed to thinking that he was quite infallible, I discussed this matter in serious terms with my Chief [of Staff] and directed that this general staff officer was to be posted without delay to a frontline unit; this to occur after the Chief returned from leave, so that he could follow the matter up and make sure it happened. Quite rightly the endless retention of totally fit and able unwounded general staff officers in the higher level staffs is the source of much ill feeling in the army.

"17th Reserve Division has now left us...and was replaced by the 11th Infantry Division. It is almost constantly foggy; the few aircraft available to us were very hampered in their ability to conduct surveillance over the enemy lines. The enemy is remaining quiet... According to all impressions, observations and intelligence, our front, as well as that of our left hand neighbours, Group Caudry, which is responsible for the town of Cambrai, is regarded as totally quiescent."

As Generalleutnant von Moser had noted, from 12 November onwards the weather was primarily foggy, rendering both ground and air reconnaissance virtually impossible. Enemy artillery was almost completely inactive and the sound ranging troops had nothing to report. In consequence the divisional commander ordered a series of patrols and raids. Each night raiding parties pushed their way into the British trenches, sometimes with artillery support and sometimes without. On most occasions, however, the enemy did not contest the raids, which triggered suspicion. Previously the British troops opposite 54th Division had always fought back vigorously, but now the opposite was the case; it could only have been the result of following orders. Suspicions had already been increased when Reserve Infantry Regiment 27 discovered from items found on the body of a dead soldier that he was a member of a tank battalion. Opposite La Vacquerie, for example, it was noticed, during the short periods when the visibility improved, that flags of various colours and bundles of twigs had been placed, presumably to indicate directions and boundaries.

Leutnant J Langfeldt 2nd Battalion Infantry Regiment 84 [28]

"There had been a noticeable increase in aerial activity but, unfortunately, this was ascribed to the choice of the enemy of this quiet sector as an exercise area for trainee pilots. Nobody of course actually knew where the aircraft had come from, but this explanation was passed on without further consideration to Division. To our left the 90th came across the body of a British soldier forward of their lines. Examination of the uniform led to the conclusion that the man belonged to a tank unit, but this was explained away as possibly dating from when the British had closed up on the new position and people felt reassured.[29] The companies holding the forward positions frequently reported hearing the whistles of locomotives and the rumbling of trains, but this was [assumed to be] the British preparing for winter. So the situation remained calm and free of concern up the chain of command. The 90th regiment was withdrawn completely and elements were deployed near St Quentin and so we were flanked, left and right, by Landwehr regiments. In other quiet positions we had had anti-tank batteries; here they were removed. The teams of horses for the guns of the field regiment were miles away from the gun lines and the batteries had very little ammunition in stock

"The forward battalions maintained a routine typical of quiet fronts. Two companies in the forward trenches maintained a thin outpost line, whilst the two companies to the rear were told off for digging duties. There was a certain amount of patrol activity on both sides and this was not completely without casualties, but nothing of great importance was obtained. I should also mention that after our tour of duty in Flanders we received, for the first time, replacements who were not of particularly high quality. One night a sentry disappeared, allegedly as a result of a British patrol, but there was talk of desertion. It was the first bad sign of what was to occur later."

In fact 54th Division had been reporting its disquiet. Unfortunately the events cited were not interpreted in the same way by higher headquarters. Frequently they were simply disbelieved. Confirmation, at least as far as 54th Division was concerned, came as a result of a raid. In the early hours of 18 November, 2nd Battalion Infantry Regiment 84 launched a raid forward of its positions and south of Havrincourt. Designed to capture prisoners, it succeeded in alerting the defenders of 54th Infantry Division that an attack was being prepared against the divisional sector. It was led by Reserve Leutnant Hegermann, who had only recently returned from a training course organised by Jäger Storm Battalion 3, which was later to spearhead the attack of 28th Infantry Division on 30 November. As always, the operation was prepared with meticulous care, the dress rehearsal being attended by the divisional commander himself.

Fähnrich H Carstens 2nd Battalion Infantry Regiment 84 [30]

"For a long term a number of us had been keen to teach a lesson to the Tommies who, during recent days, had begun to behave with an excess of arrogance. As a result, it was a simple matter to raise a sufficient number of volunteers from all four companies to permit the launch of a minor raid against the enemy trenches. Following extremely detailed preparation and once our artillery had had time to range in, the business was scheduled to take place during the early hours of 18 November. For the operation we had sought a section of enemy trench which was sticking out forward and which we knew was occupied by several outposts.[31] The aim was to launch forward in four assault groups; one from each company and eight men strong. Each was to be accompanied by three engineers, equipped with a Bangalore torpedo for dealing with the enemy obstacle.

"From left to right the groups were from 6th, 8th 7th and 5th Companies respectively. The assault group furthest to the left was to roll up the trench to the right and the three others to the left. In overall command was Leutnant Hegermann, who was co-located with the 8th Company assault group. Every man had his own particular place [and knew exactly what to do] so the best possible result was to be expected. The main thing was to be up and at 'em, like Blücher, and under no circumstances to falter – which, for all of us, went without saying. At 4.00 am 18 November each of the groups left the outpost line at their appointed places. The artillery fire was due to begin at 6.30 am. So there was ample time to occupy the starting positions and to push the Bangalore torpedoes under the enemy obstacle. Once I had reached my starting point with my assault group, the next task was to insert the charge. I crept forward as silently as possible with my three engineers, with a pistol in one hand and a grenade ready to throw in the other.

"Carefully, we approached the first enemy obstacle. It was only a lightweight piece of rapid wiring which, taking the greatest care, we cut through then crept on. We soon arrived at the second obstacle which was significantly thicker. It was now 6.00 am, so we had to hurry because our artillery fire was due to come down at 6.30 am. We quickly laid the charge then returned to the place where our comrades were waiting for us. We had hardly arrived than the first of our artillery shells roared towards the objective, followed by more. The shells were well placed and we were able to make our way forward to the first enemy obstacle while the fire was still coming down. Punctually three minutes later our fire lifted onto the enemy support lines. That was the signal for us to start. We rushed forward as one for the enemy trench. Our Bangalore torpedo had been set off when our first shell landed and had been very effective.

"To the front our route was more or less clear. With a few leaps we were down in the trench, exactly where a British double sentry position was located but, instead of firing, the two Tommies attempted to escape to the left. However they had made a mistake, because the assault group from 8th Company had also reached the trench and had them in a trap. The other assault groups had also grabbed a few Tommies by the collar then, at a signal from our commander, it was time to head back. Our battalion commander, Hauptmann Soltau, was waiting at the Outpost Line to congratulate us on our success. The operation had been worthwhile; we brought back six prisoners with us, including an officer deputy [*sic*] and a very lanky corporal. Apart from a few slightly wounded, we suffered only one painful casualty: our dear Leutnant Störzel[32] was so seriously wounded that he soon closed his eyes for ever. But even though the loss of our Leutnant hurt, we were delighted to have shown the Tommies that German soldiers would not take provocation lying down, that the old aggressive spirit, which our enemies had already learnt to fear, still dwelt within them."[33]

Despite all the care that had been taken with the preparation and planning of the raid, it would have turned out badly had the commander, Reserve Leutnant Hegermann, not noticed that, in the confusion, orientation had been lost. One section of wood in the dark looked much like another and some of the groups, having seized prisoners, were seen heading the wrong way and deeper into the enemy lines. Checking his compass quickly, Hegermann raced after them, turned them round and, with the exception of Leutnant Störzel, hit in the forehead by a shrapnel ball, led his men and their prisoners successfully back. Following interrogation of the six men captured, it was increasingly clear that an attack was in the offing, but it was difficult to be specific about the nature of the threat. The commander of 108 Brigade, Oberst Weck, however, lost no time in publishing a congratulatory order:

"I wish to express my fullest appreciation to Leutnant Hegermann and all participants in today's operation which, following the break in to the enemy position, led to the capture of six British [soldiers]. This applies not only to the daring act itself, but also to Hauptmann Soltau for mounting this most carefully devised and prepared operation. May those comrades who sealed their courage with their blood all make speedy recoveries."[34]

In the wake of the raid and as a result of the information obtained from the prisoners, 54th Infantry Division increased its state of readiness. All available small arms ammunition and hand grenades were moved forward. There was a serious lack of S.m.K. ammunition.[35] Deliveries were not forthcoming but, acting on its own initiative, the division managed to lay its hands on several thousand rounds, which were quickly distributed. 18 November also saw a visit by General der Kavallerie von der Marwitz to Headquarters Group Arras. Everything about the visit irritated and annoyed Generalleutnant von Moser, who sat down that evening and let off steam in a lengthy diary entry.

Generalleutnant von der Moser Commander Group Arras: Diary Entry 18 November 1917 [36]

"Today an Irish deserter announced, admittedly as has often happened previously, that there would soon be an enemy attack near Fontaine. 240th Infantry Division took all the usual precautionary measures, as did the rest of the Group, at least to the extent it could, given the lack of reserves. A report was despatched upwards.

"The Army Commander visited the Group for the third time, together with his Chief of Staff [Major Stapff]. This third visit brought home to me with final and complete, but totally dispiriting, clarity what a dreadful, fated, professional relationship I had landed in. The Army Chief of Staff placed unachievable demands on us, by sketching out on the map the location of a new infantry defensive position on the high ground near Fontaine which was overlooked on all sides by the enemy and dominated by their fire. Despite our calm raising of convincing objections, which were based on months of experience, he stuck obstinately to his view and impossible demand. The result will once more be a written order with entirely predictable negative consequences.

"The impossibility of carrying out the order will lead to passive resistance amongst the troops. There will be fresh pressure from above, which will produce a half – hearted attempt at a position. This will appear as a thin line on the map of the defences, but will, in reality, barely exist. The discovery of this dismal fact by officers sent from Army Headquarters will lead to sharper, harder pressure from above and [the troops] will be forced to work. The end result will be that the men will be extremely angry, a lot of unnecessary exertion and casualties will have been caused and there will still not be a defensible position.

"The effect the demeanour and tone of the Army Commander has on me and the words I am setting down on paper with a heavy heart, reflect not only my own recent experiences but, at the same time, numerous discussions I have had with colleagues. Two running sores are affecting our command body: one is the climate of mistrust that has built up in many instances between the army commanders and the corps commanders; the exceptions simply prove the rule. This mistrust manifests itself in the fact that the corps commanders are given only the absolute minimum information possible about the overall context in which the large scale operations are conducted. This means that they are not in a position to form their own judgements; which in turn means that they are in no position to express divergent opinions or even suggestions.

"As far as positional warfare is concerned, it manifests itself in patronizing treatment when directives go into the smallest detail and this is made worse because these bureaucratic ideas are put out by staff officers, to whom the army commanders have delegated full powers. Again and again the result is mentally deadening and, amongst some generals, complete surrender to a blind obedience, which is really questionable in a senior commander. This is precisely what is desired, even though it means that the essential intellectual cooperative effort of all levels of the army remains untapped. As a result, visits by army commanders to their corps commanders seem ever more frequently to involve supervision, checking and oppression; almost never is there any question of open, frank discussion in an atmosphere of trust.

"Corps commanders are regarded by higher and the highest headquarters as nothing more than ciphers charged with the uncritical, or, rather, awestruck fulfilment of the infallible directives which are handed down from on high. Anyone who counters the views or directives from above is a *Frondeur*[37]; anyone who raises subjects such as difficulties, overloading the troops, excessive casualties, evacuation of indefensible positions or similar matters, is unpopular and suspected of personal weakness. Independent decisions are prohibited; basically they are treated as unviable, unless they fit exactly into the army scheme of operations – or, rather, that of the army chief of staff.

"Unfortunately some corps commanders adopt the same procedure as far as their relationship with the divisional commanders is concerned. This damages both their authority and personal satisfaction. All this affects more and more the truthfulness of upward reporting because anybody who reports grievances or setbacks brings not only himself, but also his troops, into disrepute as far as the ruling system is concerned. Everything must be and must run exactly how it is required from above – it is impossible to shake off this feeling.

"The second running sore is the way the ever increasing grip that the General Staff exerts on affairs; that is to say the parallel control the General Staff officers are conducting by misuse of the telephone system behind the backs of the commanders. This way of working is even more questionable, because the sheer length of the war means that the officer corps of the General Staff is so youthful and diluted that its branches, right up to chiefs of staff, are frequently very lacking in experience of life or the ability to make accurate assessments of their own capabilities, duties and rights. Despite this, the most important tactical matters dealt with from army chief of staff down to the operations officer of a division are often thrashed out totally over the telephone, or so arranged that, when the commander gets to hear about them subsequently, he can hardly do other than agree to what has been decided.

"Naturally, all independently-minded commanders battle against these dangerous abuses – some of them even stick close by the telephone day and night. However, because... it is impossible to monitor the totality of telephone traffic, it is a struggle with no prospect of success. The climate of mistrust, the patronizing system and the way the General Staff operates, unavoidably damages the authority of the corps and divisional commanders and, at the same time, denies them the necessary and important inner pleasure which comes from the exercise of high command. Complaints about this are general because not only does it encourage the impression, in fact it is often directly expressed that, as far as the success or failure of tactical operations are concerned, not only is this not exclusively the responsibility of the commander; rather it is due in equal, if not greater measure, to the General Staff officer.

"Only if this thought process is followed is it possible to understand why it is, following failed operations, that frequently the chief of staff of an army or corps is relieved, but not the army or corps commander. This procedure would have been impossible under the old Kaiser or the great Moltke. These two men dealt only with the commanders, who had been trusted, given all imaginable authority, but who also carried full responsibility. Quite correctly the General Staff officers ranked simply as their assistants. I regard it as disastrous that we have become ever less faithful to this proven principle, which served us well in the wars of 1866 and 1870/71, as well as in peacetime and at the start of this war. The corps commander is no longer seen as an intellectual prop of the higher command; rather, more as a simple mechanical clamp. A house held together by however many such clamps is bound to collapse in a storm if it lacks strong supports. Never do the above mentioned running sores show themselves in a worse light than during times between battles. When a battle is being fought, the corps commander will allow nobody to usurp his responsibility for his front. Writing this down has lifted my spirits inwardly a little, but it does not change the situation."

Was Moser being over-sensitive or even paranoid? Had the constant strain of front line command ever since the outbreak of war begun to wear him down? He had been an outstanding divisional commander of the first class 27th Infantry Division, which had borne the brunt of the August fighting for Guillemont during the Battle of the Somme the previous year, but he had exercised command frequently from his sick bed, which must have taken a toll. Had he been over-promoted? A good divisional commander does not necessarily take the transition to command of a corps in his stride. Nevertheless a considerable part of his argument is confirmed by Kuhl's description of the manoeuvrings against Commander Fourth Army noted above and he may well have been correct in the rest of his judgements.

The significant point, however, is what this demonstrates about the tensions, doubts and difficulties which beset the German chain of command in the Cambrai area on the eve of what was to be one of the most serious crises of the entire war on the Western Front. The exercise of command and control in battle has always been a difficult matter; never more than during the First World War, when communications problems meant that vital decisions frequently had to be made on the basis of fragmentary, dated or even misleading information. When to these problems was added an atmosphere of mistrust, there were bound to be adverse consequences: in this case, as will be seen, time-wasting, nugatory staff work and the relative failure of the ultimate German counter-offensive.

As if that were not difficult enough to cope with, Reserve Infantry Regiment 27 had been withdrawn earlier, complete, to provide a reserve for Group Caudry. It was relieved by one of the regiments from 20th Landwehr Division, but this was not a like-for-like replacement and did nothing for operational readiness. The same could be said for the provision of artillery. This wide sector could only call on three light field howitzer batteries and six field gun batteries – a total of thirty four weapons. The situation was even worse for heavier guns. Medium artillery was provided by one battery each of captured Russian, French and Belgian guns, some of which had a range of only 5,000 metres. The only other support was provided by an obsolescent battery of coastal howitzers and one single battery of 150mm heavy field howitzers.

To make matters worse, there was insufficient ammunition for these weapons. The nine batteries of Field Artillery Regiment 108 only had stocks of between 1,000 and 1,500 rounds per battery stored in the gun lines. In reserve were a mere 4,600 shells, which could not be made available to the batteries in position on 20 November; firstly because the batteries of the reinforcing Field Artillery Regiment 213 arrived in the area on 19 November without any ammunition (allegedly due to restrictions on the transport of ammunition and troops on the same trains, even in an emergency) and, secondly, because in the event of an assault in the Havrincourt area, batteries of 20th Landwehr Division to the north, which would be firing in support of 54th Infantry Division, were also to be supplied from the same ammunition depot. All attempts by the division to draw attention to the potential dangers were rebuffed on the grounds that the positions were effectively impregnable and that the usual preliminary artillery bombardment prior to an attack would allow sufficient time for the necessary reinforcements of men and munitions to be moved forward.

As has been mentioned, the commander of 54th Infantry Division had had the greatest difficulty in getting his superior headquarters to accept his assessment that his sector faced the threat of imminent assault. The official view remained that the positions were so strong that they could not be stormed without a lengthy preparatory bombardment and that, even when tanks had been involved in attacks previously, they too had been linked with comprehensive bombardments and, when they were launched, had generally not been particularly successful. Somewhat frustrated that his initial attempts and those of his staff by telephone and in writing to obtain reinforcements and increased supplies of ammunition had only elicited a conditional, somewhat half-hearted, response from Group Caudry, Generalleutant Oskar Freiherr von Watter went in person to discuss the matter with the Group Commander, General der Infanterie Theodor Freiherr von Watter, who happened to be his cousin.

After a lengthy conversation, Generalleutnant von Watter came away convinced that he had made his case, that the additional support would be forthcoming and, in particular, that the 107th Infantry Division, which was in the process of arriving by train from the Eastern front, would be deployed at the time and place of his choosing. In the meantime his staff continued to request the return of Reserve Infantry Regiment 27, including its 3rd Battalion, which was deployed down near St Quentin, to 54th Infantry Division. These telephoned requests also extended to the provision of at least two battalions of heavy artillery, both field guns and howitzers, more lighter field guns and large stocks of ammunition, both artillery and S.m.K. armour piercing small arms ammunition.

Apparently the response from Group Caudry was that this would, 'as far as possible be done'.[38] When these statements were taken together with the assurances which commander 54th Infantry Division had received from the Group Commander, the former felt certain that the arriving formations of 107th Infantry Division would be his to deploy once they had arrived. This impression was further confirmed when, at about 7.00 pm 19 November, the Operations Officer of 107th Infantry Division, Hauptmann Glokke, arrived in the operations room of 54th Infantry Division and reported the arrival of the first infantry elements of his division. This was the news for which the division had been waiting.

Generalleutnant Oskar Freiherr von Watter Commander 54th Infantry Division [39]

> "My operations officer and I greeted most warmly this fresh General Staff officer, whom I had known in Posen. Help in time of crisis! He was briefed fully on the situation, the divisional assessment and its deployment. He himself briefed us about 107th Infantry Division, its organisation and its time and method of arrival. According to this, the final infantry contingents would arrive during the evening of 19 November. The remainder were already there and the artillery commander would be reporting in shortly. After this, I took it for granted that I could expect to be able to employ the division. In fact I took the first steps towards this, giving instructions that this same night one regiment was to be moved to each of Cantaing, Marcoing and Cambrai. My orders stated, 'From 6.00 am 20 November the whole of 54th Infantry Division is to be on high alert. The infantry regiments of 107th Infantry Division are to be in position by 6.00 am and ready to move: Regiment Cantaing towards Flesquières; Regiment Marcoing towards Ribécout-la Vacquerie, Regiment Cambrai towards Rumilly. With the exception of one battalion, the artillery will be deployed tonight.'"

Glokke noted these orders, then the 54th Infantry Division Operations Officer dealt with the coordinating instructions. At the end of these discussions, the commander of 107th Infantry Division, Generalleutnant Havenstein, arrived. Watter expressed his regrets to Havenstein that the situation meant that he would not be able to deploy the division as a single entity. Havenstein declined a repetition of the complete briefing in view of the fact he had received the main threads and that his Operations Officer was fully informed. At that, Havenstein returned to his own headquarters in the Cambrai suburbs and, a short time later, Watter released Glokke, so that the necessary orders could be given to the regiments of 107th Infantry Division and he was instructed to return to headquarters 54th Infantry Division at 6.00 am the following day. Watter later remarked, 'From the very beginning both I and my Operations Officer were convinced that we had been given the right to make use of the 107th Infantry Division'.[40]

At some stage of the evening the Group Commander arrived at Headquarters 54th Division. Watter explained his plans to move Reserve Infantry Regiment 27 forward to Marcoing and, although some of the detail was not entirely clear when Watter came to recall the incident in later years, he certainly discussed how he wished to use 107th Infantry Division. 'He declared himself to be in agreement', wrote Watter after the war, 'and did not mention that I should not be able to make use of the division.'[41] In retrospect it is, of course, clear that there was a misunderstanding about this, but there is no reason to doubt Watter's version of events. He was universally known as a man of the utmost integrity and, as will be seen, his actions the following day were entirely consistent with those of someone who firmly believed that he had been granted the power to deploy the formations of 107th Infantry Division as he saw fit. The resulting confusion and subsequent recrimination provides yet another proof of the stresses and strains within the German chain of command.

As requested, Reserve Infantry Regiment 27, which had been acting as Group Caudry reserve, was subordinated to 54th Infantry Division once more, but was not immediately sent back into its old positions. It was felt that the move would have been too disruptive. Instead, Generalleutnant von Watter sent orders directing the regimental staff to move forward to Marcoing, to go into bivouac there and to be on standby to conduct a counter-stroke to Havrincourt, via Flesquières. 108 Infantry Brigade was informed about this and 3rd Battalion Reserve Infantry Regiment 27 was instructed, as soon as it arrived in Cambrai, to find billets and to be deployed at the southern exit of Cambrai by 6.00 am, ready to move in the direction of Marcoing. Accordingly, its 1st and 2nd Battalions were moved forward during 19 November to counter-penetration positions near Marcoing, where they would be well placed to move to the apparently threatened Havrincourt sector. Its 3rd Battalion, which had been deployed down near St Quentin, was withdrawn; returning during the night 19/20 November and being moved forward from Cambrai to Marcoing during the early morning of 20 November.

On 19 November there was, in fact, some slight reinforcement from 107th Infantry Division. The commander, the battalion staffs and the battery commanders of its direct support artillery, Field Artillery Regiment 213, were directed to move forward to Headquarters 54th Infantry Division for briefing and orders. One of those present, Leutnant Breusing, later wrote, 'Quite unforgettable for me was the way Generalleutnant von Watter pointed out the sector where we were to carry out our relief during the coming days and said to us, literally, 'Gentlemen, you are being deployed to a very quiet sector. The British have no plans here. It could be that they will attempt from time to time to capture a sap; that is something they have done in the past, but I regard even that as unlikely'.[42] Generalleutnant von Watter, on the other hand, confined himself post-war to the remarks, 'Towards 6.00 pm the commander of Field Artillery Regiment 213, Oberstleutnant Borchert, arrived, together with his staff. Having greeted this former chief of the horse artillery battery of Field Artillery Regiment 11, whom I knew from the time when I was a battalion commander in Kassel, I orientated him quickly over the main points of the situation. He then reported to me that the regiment, less one battery, which had been involved in a railway accident, was following close on his heels. [He added] that the regiment lacked any sort of ammunition and that the gun crews were not trained on the new sensitive fuzes. We had a quick discussion concerning how we could help, then I turned him over to the divisional artillery commander, trusting absolutely that everything would be sorted out.'

The battery commanders then rode out to carry out a reconnaissance of their appointed positions but, even before that task was complete and in the wake of the general increase in alert ordered by 54th Infantry Division, orders arrived for an immediate move forward of their batteries. The order applied to the 2nd and 3rd Battalions of the regiment, which were to be deployed along the general line: Ribécourt – Flesquières – Graincourt. In extremely difficult circumstances the guns set off in total darkness for the front. One of the main priorities was to secure stocks of ammunition for the three guns of each battery (the fourth gun, together with all ammunition on hand, had had to be left behind when the regiment was transferred from the Eastern Front). The situation regarding ammunition came as a considerable shock, as Reserve Oberleutnant Tröger of the 2nd Battalion later noted: 'When we went to collect ammunition in Neuville, it transpired that there were serious deficiencies in the way the depot was stocked. The only ammunition suitable for our guns was a supply of delayed action shells, which were unusable at long range. However, for close engagement of infantry or direct fire at tanks, they were very suitable.'[43]

The situation proved to be even worse for the howitzers of the 3rd Battalion. No ammunition of this type was available in Cambrai, or for the ammunition column which was sent to Marcoing to seek supplies. It was not until 4.00 am 20 November that some howitzer ammunition was got forward to the battery positions and, even then, the quantities were derisory: 240 rounds for each of 7th and 8th Batteries and only slightly more for the 9th – 380 rounds. Even a three gun battery could fire off these amounts extremely quickly. These reinforcements, which hardly amounted to more than a gesture, were deployed as follows: 4th Battery was 1,100 metres southwest of Graincourt, just to the north of 1st Battery Landwehr Foot Artillery Battalion 37. They found only one prepared gun pit; the other two guns were completely exposed and there was no time to dig pits. There was, in addition, one deep dugout, with a single entrance.

5th Battery was deployed three hundred metres south of Graincourt, with gun positions dug into the bank of the sunken road leading south towards Flesquières. This position had three dugouts but, once again, each had only one entrance, a practice abandoned elsewhere long before as too dangerous. 6th Battery was placed 400 metres north of Flesquières, where it later carried out a number of important fire missions, despite the fact that it occupied a long-established position which was well known to the British artillery and which, therefore, came in for a great deal of counter-battery fire. Fortunately it was of exemplary construction and featured one major dugout, with no fewer than six entrances.

All the batteries of the 3rd Battalion were clustered quite tightly around

Flesquières. The 7th Battery was near the ruins of the sugar refinery just to the east of the village, the 8th about one and half kilometres to the east and the 9th about 1,200 metres north east of the village, in the direction of Orival Wood. In the short time available to them there was little the battery commanders could do in the way of orientation or fire planning. They each had maps with the rough areas of the defensive fire zones marked on them but, in the darkness and the fog, all they could do was to prepare the guns for action, distribute the meagre supplies of ammunition and stand by for whatever might happen – their concern increased by the fact that, in contrast to the normal situation on the Eastern Front, their battery positions were not encircled with wire. Unsure about the locations of their neighbours, or where the nearest friendly infantry was located, they waited anxiously for the dawn.

On the basis of statements made by the prisoners captured by Vizefeldwebel Runkel of Reserve Infantry Regiment 90 during the early morning of 19 November, all elements of 54th Division were warned that they were to expect an attack by tanks though, naturally, the full extent of the risk was still unknown. Reports were passed by the forward units telling of the roar of heavy enemy traffic behind their lines. Either through ignorance, or simply because they had refused to provide the information, the Germans did not know for sure which day the attack would occur, so Generalleutnant von Watter assumed that it would be 20 November and that the whole of his frontage would be affected. He was reasonably confident that his men would be able to hold. By the standards of the day, his positions were beyond reproach and even though a Landwehr regiment had been inserted into his sector, which was not ideal, he could at least count on the fact that he had Reserve Infantry Regiment 27 available to him in the *Eingreif* [counter-stroke/counter-attack] role when the attack opened.

Despite the small reinforcements, as has been noted, the defending artillery was weak. Ammunition of the correct type and in sufficient quantity was lacking; whilst repeated demands during the past few weeks for heavy artillery had fallen on deaf ears. Nevertheless, von Watter contented himself with the thought that, in addition to Reserve Infantry Regiment 27 in rear of the centre of his sector, by morning the three regiments of 107th Infantry Division would be deployed forward, thus ensuring that, should his front be broken, immediate counter-measures would be taken to throw the attackers back and restore the original front line. He also believed, in response to earlier orders, that the bridges and crossing points along the St Quentin Canal had all been prepared for demolition by the divisional engineers, thus providing him a last line of defence if necessary. It seems that there was very little thought that any such demolitions would have to be carried out, because the trenches of the *Siegfriedstellung* had been designed to be wider than the three metres that was known to be too much for the British Mark IV tank to cross.

Group Caudry, although it accepted that the prisoner statements suggested the proximity of a major attack, reasoned that there had been no artillery bombardment and that, even if such a bombardment was dispensed with, nevertheless, on the actual day of the attack, any British assault would be preceded by several hours of gunfire, which would provide time for the regiments of 107th Infantry Division to deploy in support of 54th Infantry Division. As a result, its chief of staff, Major Müller-Loebnitz, probably with the connivance of Group Caudry, issued completely different orders to 107th Infantry Division than those given by Generalleutnant von Watter earlier that day.[44] The only possible additional excuse might be the fact that because all prisoners previously taken by formations of 54th Infantry Division were from the same division and that even though those captured on 19 November stated that they would be relieved by the 51st (Highland) Division for the offensive, it was still not unreasonable to assume that the attack was not actually imminent.

If the German chain of command was completely wrong in its assumptions about preliminary gunfire and the strength of its passive defences, its view concerning the maximum width of trench which could be crossed was also awry. The British had given much thought to a means of crossing the trenches of the *Siegfriedstellung*, which were three and a half meters wide. The solution was the use of fascines, hastily manufactured with great effort prior to the battle. These could be released as required from within the tank and dropped into a trench or other gap, thus enabling the advance to continue. This unexpected development was one of the biggest contributors to the shock effect generated after the advance began. Time and again front line defenders believed that if they fell back behind the next line of trenches, they would be immune from further forward movement by the tanks: their subsequent disabuse was exceedingly damaging to morale and willingness to stand and fight.

If the situation as far as the chain of command was far from perfect, what of the strength and assessed capability of the forces stationed in the Cambrai area? In this respect it is important to note that, despite receiving replacements and reinforcements, the regiments deployed forward who were about to defend against the British assault were still understrength in mid-November. Reserve Infantry Regiment 27 was better served than most, however. It received reinforcements on thirty one occasions between 22 August and 17 November 1917 so, by the eve of the battle, its strength had almost doubled to a near-normal total of fifty six officers and 2,335 other ranks, equipped with thirty six heavy machine guns, thirty eight light machine guns, twenty four grenade launchers and twelve light mortars.[45] For its part, Reserve Infantry Regiment 19 received 540 reinforcements during October and November, bringing its battalions up to an average strength of twenty officers and 730 other ranks.[46]

Overall, however, the picture was far less favourable. Against a late 1917 target strength of 800 men per infantry unit, the battalions of 20th Landwehr Division, for example, averaged 684. Not only that, but many were of low quality or limited employability. Of the overall total of 5,082, 637 were classed as *garnison-verwendungsfähig* [rear area duties only] and these men had no business forward in the line of battle. The battalions of 54th Infantry Division averaged 694, those of 9th Reserve Division 678 and 183rd Infantry Division 674.[47] To have to begin operations fifteen to twenty percent understrength (and very possibly more in the rifle companies) was far from ideal.

The bayonet strength of the units is, however, only one measure of potential battle effectiveness, so the evaluation of Headquarters Second Army sent to Army Group Crown Prince Rupprecht on 17 November is particularly interesting.[48] Overall it painted a dispiriting picture – and not only as far as the formations most closely associated with Cambrai were concerned. It was estimated, for example, that 54th and 183rd Infantry Divisions required at least two more weeks of so-called rest and training to reach full battleworthiness. 9th Reserve Division was reckoned to be 'suitable for employment only on quiet fronts' and 20th Landwehr Division could only be used to garrison static sectors of the front. In fact, such were the losses that this division had suffered in Flanders, that it was intended to move it to the Eastern Front as soon as 107th Infantry Division had had time to arrive, shake out and relieve it. As far as the 107th Infantry Division was concerned at that point it was still being transported from the Eastern Front, and Second Army could not even venture an assessment of its value as an operational formation in the west.

Group Caudry went slightly further, however. By this time the loyalty of men from Alsace-Lorraine was being called into question and the Group noted that there were 350 men from that region in the ranks. Coupled with the fact that it still had no light 08/15 machine guns in its inventory and that its artillery batteries had only been permitted to bring three guns each from the east, it was felt that this cast doubt over its overall utility in the short term.[49] The situation was much the same for Group Arras and even further afield in the Group Quentin area. According to Army Group Crown Prince Rupprecht on 17 November, not one of the Arras divisions (111th, 240th and 20th) or those of Group Quentin (79th Reserve, 36th and 238th) was rated as fully battleworthy. Following the mauling that they had received during the earlier battles in Flanders, this was hardly surprising, but it was far from satisfactory. The general impression at Army Group level and above was that there were critical shortages of manpower and equipment in the Cambrai area, but that the priority still had to be given to the primary focus of the autumn battles (i.e. Flanders) and that risks would have to continue to be run elsewhere.

There were indicators that the fighting around Ypres had run its course by mid-November, but this was not matched by any assessment that the Allies might shift the point of the attack. In the higher level staffs, work had already begun on planning for operations in 1918 and the prospect of having to face another major defensive challenge during the closing weeks of the year was more or less ruled out. In an overall appreciation of the situation, issued on 17 November, Army Group Crown Prince Rupprecht stated: 'For the time being it is improbable that major attacks will occur anywhere. Minor operations in the Second and Sixth Army sectors are still possible...It is possible to envisage that the British, if they abandon their offensive in Flanders, may move to secondary operations in other areas.'[50]

There is ample evidence that, in the final days and hours leading up to the offensive, 54th Infantry Division became increasingly concerned that such an operation was likely. For example, on 16 November it requested, in the event of an attack on Havrincourt, that Landwehr Infantry Regiment 384 of 20th Landwehr Division be placed under its command.[51] Similarly it requested and was granted the return of Reserve Infantry Regiment 27 to its ranks. As has been mentioned, from the evening of 19 November, all elements of 54th Division were placed on the highest state of alert. All artillery ammunition was prepared for firing. The projecting pins for the sensitive impact fuzes were all inserted, ammunition stacks, such as they were, were moved closer to the gun lines and all gunners resting back in the horse lines were ordered forward to reinforce. All available artillery observation points were manned, communications were tested and increased where necessary. It is, however, interesting to note that, whereas Generalleutnant von Watter was convinced that there was about to be an attack on his divisional sector, it was still not a view shared by many either at superior headquarters or amongst the forward sub-units.

Leutnant J Langfeldt 2nd Battalion Infantry Regiment 84 [52]

"The result of the [Hegermann] patrol was that the previous generally carefree atmosphere came to an abrupt end. Certain information was now known about future enemy intentions. They were planning a major attack and were hoping to push forward as far as the *Oertinger Riegel* [Oerting Stop Line] on the first day. Nevertheless it was in the rear that the excitement and increase in activity began. Those of us holding positions forward did not believe it at all - which is surprising. In the battalion we had often discussed the point that a surprise attack offered far greater chance of success than one which had been prepared by days of drum fire. Why was it now that we did not believe the enemy capable of it? Well probably because we felt fully equal to any such thrust. We received orders to issue each man with rations for five days and to distribute ammunition. I was fully occupied with this work throughout the afternoon of 19 November.

"The company commanders were summoned to a conference, but none of them treated the threat seriously either. Towards evening the number of orders increased. I had to pass on most of them myself, because Leutnant Elson and several other officers had gone to Noyelles for the burial of young Störzel. There was constant traffic in and out of battalion headquarters. Runners came and went from the regiment and the companies. Contact was established with the neighbouring Landwehr battalion. Questions, together with reports, arrived from the Machine Gun Company and from the mortars. During the late evening several machine guns, which had been put at our disposal, arrived from Reserve Infantry Regiment 27 and had to be allocated positions. The 3rd Battalion reported that it had occupied the *Oertinger Riegel* and we did everything possible to obtain S.m.K. ammunition, but there was none to be had."

On the eve of the battle, therefore, the outlook on the German side of No Man's Land was about as bad as it could be. Almost the only man who thought that there was going to be an attack was Generalleutnant von Watter of 54th Infantry Division and even he had no idea of the scale of what the British had planned. There was bad blood between the General Staff and the commanders and a climate of mistrust and suspicion prevailed throughout the chain of command. The troops were understrength, overstretched and, in many cases, not fit to be holding forward trenches. The artillery was inadequate and the reserve stocks of ammunition derisory. Given the success of British operational security, surprise was going to be complete. Had the British commanders realised just how unprepared the German defence was for what was about to hit them, they would have been justified in expecting the assault to be a walkover. That it most certainly was not. Unknown to the British there was one unforeseen, indeed unforeseeable, factor in favour of the defence in the critical part of the battlefield which helps to explain why.

In order to understand why the anti-tank defence conducted by units of 54th Infantry Division was so effective, it is necessary to go back in time a few months to when artillery units of 27th Infantry Division were involved in early engagements against British Mark I tanks during the Battle of the Somme. Towards the end of the battle, Oberstleutnant von Watter, commander Field Artillery Regiment 49, who was none other than the younger brother of Generalleutnant von Watter, commander 54th Infantry Division, was promoted Oberst and took over as commander 27 Artillery Brigade. In this capacity he was responsible for drawing together the lessons learned by those of his batteries which had engaged tanks. Generalleutnant von Watter, whose background was in horse artillery, summoned his brother towards the end of 1916 and quizzed him in detail about the new threat and the type of counter-actions which had proved to be effective.

Armed with this information, as soon as 54th Division was withdrawn from the Verdun battlefield in November 1916, von Watter called together all the officers of his direct support formation, Field Artillery Regiment 108, for a conference, during which he stressed that it was an absolute certainty that the appearance of the tank meant that the artillery was going to be forced out of the purely static role which positional warfare had imposed on it. He then went on to insist that, with immediate effect, every battery was to train to engage moving targets over open sights and that individual guns were to be practised in galloping forward to take up aggressive forward firing positions in broad daylight: in the midst of battle, if necessary. The necessary training and amendment to tactical procedures having been carried out, the first use of the new methods occurred early in 1917 during the Aisne-Champagne battles when, in April 1917, the gunners of Field Artillery Regiment 108 knocked out French tanks with direct fire at Berry-au-Bac and Guignecourt.

Building on this, at the Battle of Langemarck on 16 August 1917, batteries of Field Artillery Regiment 108 galloped forward and successfully engaged British tanks at ranges of up to 2,000 metres. This was not a matter of luck. From November 1916 onwards, whenever the 54th Division was not engaged, an instructional battery, usually under command of Leutnant Erwin Zindler, was established and was responsible for conducting a series of four week courses, with the following training aims: daily practice in direct fire missions using live ammunition, with emphasis on switching at high speed from indirect to direct fire and swapping sighting arrangements; driving exercises, including rapid call forward of teams and deployment at the gallop over challenging terrain; use of light signalling and semaphore equipment in addition to telephones, to improve communications between different elements of the batteries. The course was conducted on at least eight separate occasions prior to the Battle of Cambrai.

In order to promote improved understanding of the new methods, all the infantrymen of the division were directed to observe demonstrations and to participate in the exercises, as were all officers of the division, regardless of their arm or service. In addition, numerous high ranking officers of neighbouring or superior headquarters were also invited to attend. Part of the infantry training involved them occupying a specially constructed trench system, whilst co-located artillery observers brought down various types of fire all around them. Defensive fire, destructive fire and rolling barrages were all practised, but the main emphasis was on anti-tank work. One of the most sophisticated of the exercises involved the use of elaborate target arrays, simulating the approach of tanks. The targets moved on rails set at various angles and were towed by teams of horses pulling cables hundreds of metres long. Information was passed back by the observers and, at a given moment, whilst the remainder of the guns continued with their indirect fire missions, individual guns, or sections would be ordered to gallop forward, take up fire positions and engage the advancing 'tanks.'

As training progressed, the exercises were all against the clock. Everything was noted: *viz.* length of time from passage of information to harnessing up and moving; to the first shot; to the effective destruction of the target. At ranges up to 1,000 metres, a hit was expected within three rounds; at less than 500 metres first round hits were the norm. With constant drilling, all the gunners of Field Artillery Regiment 108 became extremely effective at this type of work and that was not all. In parallel, both engineers and infantrymen of the division were instructed and rehearsed in engaging tanks at short range. By means of models and diagrams, they learned all the vulnerable parts of the tanks and how to exploit them. Tactics practised included learning to hide in dugouts then emerging to tackle tanks as they descended into or, in particular, when they attempted to climb out of, trenches - a moment when they were very vulnerable to the placement of charges on their fuel tanks or running gear. Machine gunners continually practised shooting at targets with the same dimensions as the viewing slits of these early models. It is probably no exaggeration to say that of all the divisions in the German army, none was better prepared to resist a tank attack than 54th Infantry Division at Havrincourt and Flesquières on 20 November 1917.

What a stroke of luck for the defence.

Notes

1. Kuhl: *Der Weltkrieg 1914-1918 Band II* pp 57-58
2. Soo: *Persöhnliches Kriegstagebuch des Generals der Infanterie a.D. von Kuhl BA.-MA.*
    RH 61/50652 pp 37-38
3. *ibid.* p 39
4. Directive *OHL Ia. Nr. 2079* See: *Persöhnliches Kriegstagebuch des Generals der Infanterie a.D. von Kuhl BA.-MA. RH 61/50652* p 43
5. *ibid.* p 44
6. *ibid.* p 47
7. Original emphasis. See: *Persöhnliches Kriegstagebuch des Generals der Infanterie a.D. von Kuhl BA.-MA. RH 61/50652* p 41
8. The *Friedensangebot* was an initiative by Bethmann-Hollweg to bring the war to a negotiated end. It was treated with complete contempt by German senior military leaders, who believed that it would be taken by the Allies as a sign of weakness and, in any case, its terms were so ludicrously unacceptable that it was instantly dismissed by the Allied leadership.
9. Kuhl: *op. cit.* p 61
10. Of course, the withdrawal was far greater in the centre of the salient, amounting to about fifty kilometres at its widest point.

11. Alberich is a central character of Wagner's Ring Cycle. He is an ugly deformed dwarf, who in *Rheingold* seeks world domination through the theft of gold from the Rhine maidens. Ultimately he is betrayed by his instinctive boasting and exhibitionism and, thwarted, places a curse on the ring and, by extension, all those who oppose him. But his fate is as nothing compared with that of those corrupted in turn by the cursed ring and what it stands for – especially Wotan, chief of all the gods, who gradually becomes ever more entangled in lies and deceit and constrained in his freedom of action. In the end Wotan is as big a loser as Alberich, when the ring and its powers are finally returned whence they came. If you enjoy parallels, the course of the Great War is full of them from this point. This operation was not so much an *Alberich Bewegung* as the start of *Götterdämmerung* (which, interesting to relate, was the codename chosen later by Group Caudry to describe its part in the German counter-attack of 30 November 1917) during which even Siegfried, that embodiment of youthful heroic vigour – a Germanic superman – proves not be the source of redemption; that hope turns out to be illusory and Siegfried, too, succumbs to his fate.

12. Bechtle: History Grenadier Regiment 123 p 104
13. *Erinnerungsblätter der ehemaligen Mansteiner 4. Folge Nr 8* pp 69-70
14. *Erinnerungsblätter der ehemaligen Mansteiner 4. Folge Nr 6* p 45
15. The road/track junction by modern Hill 110 and 400 metres southwest of the centre of Flesquières, was named by the German defenders after the major road junction in Berlin where the Victory Pillar, commemorating the Franco-Prussian war, still stands.
16. Dahlmann: History Reserve Infantry Regiment 27 pp 345-346
17. *Widas* (pronounced vee-daz) were relatively small strong points, constructed using reinforced concrete and designed primarily to provide cover for advanced machine gun crews.
18. This copse, which no longer exists, was located on high ground about one kilometre east northeast of Trescault.
19. *Erinnerungsblätter der ehemaligen Mansteiner 4. Folge Nr 8* p 70
20. *Erinnerungsblätter der ehemaligen Mansteiner 4. Folge Nr 6* p 46
21. *Erinnerungsblätter der ehemaligen Mansteiner 4. Folge Nr 7* p 54
22. Schwenke: History Reserve Infantry Regiment 19 p 277
23. *ibid.* pp 277-279
24. Dahlmann: *op. cit.* p 348
25. The body of Reserve Leutnant Gustav Poppendieck was recovered. He is buried in the German cemetery at Cambrai Block 2 Grave 17.
26. This entire episode is covered on pp 69-74 of the personal diary of General der Infanterie Hermann von Kuhl. See: *Persöhnliches Kriegstagebuch des Generals der Infanterie a.D. von Kuhl BA.-MA. RH 61/50652*

27. Moser: *Feldzugsaufzeichnungen* pp 306-307
28. *Erinnerungsblätter der ehemaligen Mansteiner 4. Folge Nr 8* p 65
29. Langenfeld's memory of events is wrong. This is a reference to the discovery by Reserve Infantry Regiment 27 of a body near Trescault on 28 October.
30. *Erinnerungsblätter der ehemaligen Mansteiner 4. Folge Nr 7* pp 56-57
31. The location of the raid was a point on the Route Royale in Havrincourt Wood, approximately three hundred metres east of the pond located seven hundred metres south of Havrincourt Chateau and two hundred metres southwest of Grand Ravine CWGC cemetery.
32. Leutnant Georg Störzel, who was originally interred at Noyelles, is buried in the huge German cemetery at Neuville St Vaast/Maison Blanche Block 1 Grave 516.
33. *Erinnerungsblätter der ehemaligen Mansteiner 4. Folge Nr 8* pp 64-65
34. Weck had obviously overlooked the fate of Störzel. *Erinnerungsblätter der ehemaligen Mansteiner 4. Folge Nr 7* p 58
35. S.m.K.= *Spitz-Munition mit Kern* [armour piercing ammunition]
36. Moser: *op.cit.* pp307-309
37. This is impossible to translate. The word is French, deriving originally from the time of *La Fronde*, a short civil war in France between 1648 and 1653, during the Franco-Spanish war which began in 1635. It is a complicated story, which actually involved two separate *Frondes* (a word originally meaning 'slingshot', used by some of those involved to break the windows of those they opposed). These were the *Fronde Parliamentaire* and the *Fronde des Nobles*. It was the latter which caused the greatest disruption within France. The impulse was not revolutionary; rather it was intended to mark out the limits of the prerogatives of the crown which, in the wake of the Thirty Years War, was attempting to impose a harsh regime of taxation nationally and so override feudal rights and liberties held by towns and corporations and working in favour of local interests. During the second half of the period the *Frondeurs* formed armed bands under noble leadership. There were insurrections, battles, intrigues and ceasefires until, eventually, the country wearied of the anarchy and the royalists eventually defeated and disarmed the *Frondeurs*. The crown was then regarded generally as a force for stability and the main outcome of this hiatus was the emergence of absolutism under Louis XIV. In this instance it appears from Moser's choice of words that the term was used by the German chain of command in a pejorative sense to describe any subordinate who rocked the boat or attempted to question anything emanating from a superior headquarters.
38. *General Oskar Freiherr von Watter* p 73
39. *ibid.* p 74
40. *ibid.* p 75

41. *ibid.* p 75
42. History Field Artillery Regiment 213 p 158. There is some reason to doubt the veracity of this statement. At the very least it seems strange that the message allegedly given to the officers of Field Artillery Regiment 213 should have been so at variance with the assessment reported up the chain of command in the light of events of the past forty eight hours by Headquarters 54th Infantry Division. In addition, when a new General Staff officer, Hauptmann Gädeke, arrived at his headquarters on 18 November, von Watter allegedly greeted him by saying, 'Make no mistake about it. Within the next few days we shall have to fend off a major attack.' See *General Oskar Freiherr von Watter* p 72. There was undoubtedly bad blood between 54th and 107th Divisions post war. The regimental histories of the latter may be searched in vain for any suggestion that the division, collectively, bore any responsibility for the reverses of the first day of fighting. Instead (and aided by remarks by Ludendorff in his Memoirs – *Meine Kriegserinnerungen* p 396) the accepted version of events was that 54th Division was simply rolled over and 107th Infantry Division rode to the rescue in the nick of time, thus averting total disaster. To preserve that illusion, no suggestion that the regiments of 107th Division could have deployed sooner or more appropriately and, therefore, have prevented any crossing of the St Quentin Canal on 20 November by the British, could be allowed in the public domain.
43. History Field Artillery Regiment 213 p 158
44. Later, according to General der Infanterie Ernst Kabisch (*General Oskar Freiherr von Watter* p 78), Müller-Loebnitz stated that, without the authority of the Army Group, never mind Second Army, the 107th Division could not be deployed. Be that as it may, it is hard to escape the conclusion that greater transparency and an increased willingness by commanders and staff to discuss the situation might have led to better mutual understanding and 107th Division might have been far better placed to respond to the demands of the following day. Even if that had not happened, it is difficult to explain why it was not made clear to von Watter that his understanding of the command relationships was, in fact, incorrect. Kabisch goes on to speculate, 'There can hardly be any other explanation than that whichever [staff officer] conducted the conversation with the General Staff Officer of 107th Infantry Division concerning the tasks of the division must have said, 'General von Watter is too anxious. It is unnecessary for you to move forward tonight. For the time being you are the Army Group reserve. Move into billets there and there.' If Kabisch was right, not only was this another example of the General Staff working behind the backs of the commanders and

blundering, it also suggests that those involved were too arrogant even to keep Watter informed about their decisions.

45. Dahlmann: *op. cit.* p 347

46. Schwenke: *op. cit.* p 281

47. Hauptstaatsarchiv Stuttgart M 33/2 Bü 894 p 196 *Stärkemeldung Gruppe Caudry Abt. IIb. Nr. 20920 13.11.1917*

48. Kriegsarchiv München HGr Rupprecht Bd 125 p 35 *AOK 2 Kampfwertmeldung vom 17.11.1917*

49. Hauptstaatsarchiv Stuttgart M 33/2 Bü 256 p 142 *Gruppe Caudry Ia Nr.300 op. 11.11.1917*

50. Solger: *Akten und Tagebuchauszüge (Heft/Akt 240) Schreiben der HGr Rupprecht an die OHL vom 29.10.1917 und Telegramm Ludendorffs (Ia Nr. 5337 geh. Op.) an die HGr Rupprecht vom 14.11.1917 BA-MA RH 61/51714*

51. See Hauptstaatsarchiv Stuttgart M 33/2 Bünd 143 p 1 54. *Infantry Division Ia Nr. 2884 16.11.1917*

52. *Erinnerungsblätter der ehemaligen Mansteiner 4. Folge Nr 8 p 66*

CHAPTER TWO

20 November 1917:
The First Clash

Ordered to be extremely watchful, the defending sentries and observers all along the 54th Division sector strained to detect any sign of enemy activity as midnight came and went. Out to their front all appeared to be calm, though there were reports from time to time that red flares were being fired. It was believed that the British were doing this to induce the artillery to bring down defensive fire and so waste ammunition. About 2.00 am a report was flashed down to the ground holding units that, according to the prisoner who had been captured the previous morning, the enemy had positioned an unknown number of tanks forward. In those regiments where the distribution had not yet occurred, this was the signal to issue what little S.m.K. armour piercing ammunition was available. In many cases there was insufficient even to equip every machine gun, but all stocks on hand were given out and the fact reported back up the chain of command. All remained quiet then, suddenly, at about 5.00 am, forward sub-units of Infantry Regiment 84 sent up flares calling for artillery defensive fire. What had happened was that the troops stationed around Havrincourt, who had in any case been on especially high alert for any sign of an attack, spotted some British infantry cutting gaps in their wire, sent up flares calling for defensive fire and opened up with their own mortars and small arms fire.

There was a response by the artillery in accordance with the 54th Division plan and all German artillery within range brought down fire at an intense rate in defence of Havrincourt. Fairly quickly demands for fire stopped and, within half an hour, all was quiet once more. Unfortunately by then this apparently false alarm had seriously depleted the already inadequate stocks of ammunition dumped forward at the gun lines and, as a result, when the real attack began later, the guns were soon in difficulties. For the time being, however, it appeared that the increased alert state had been maintained for nothing. Dawn broke. The night sky began to lighten and, as on so many autumn mornings in the Cambrai area, everywhere was blanketed in dense, damp fog. 7.00 am came and morning reports concerning the previous night's events were passed up to superior headquarters. 7.15 arrived and the sky was noticeably lighter, despite all the fog.

Five minutes later and with shocking suddenness, at 7.20 am the fire of 1,000 guns crashed down with hysterical violence all along the German front as the entire British artillery opened up as one. In all directions the positions were lit up by a seemingly endless series of explosions as shells of all calibres poured down on the shocked defenders, bringing to a sudden end the relative tranquillity of the 'Flanders Sanatorium'. The front line positions were especially targeted, but heavy harassing fire began to come down simultaneously on the *Zwischenstellung* [Intermediate Position = Hindenburg Support Line], Flesquières and the other villages in the forward zone and all the approach routes from the rear. There was just time for fleeting instructions and orders to be passed from command posts, then virtually all the telephones went dead, their cables cut. Despite all subsequent heroics by the signallers, only a few deeply buried cables remained intact and, from the start, the defensive battle was fought in an almost complete communications blackout, made worse by the appalling visibility. Yet again the only means of passing information was to rely on runners.

As soon as the bombardment began, the noise of the engines of the British tanks, which had been quietly ticking over for the previous ten minutes, rose to a roar as they began to move forward. Above them squadrons of the Royal Flying Corps flew past and started to engage any targets they could see. The Battle of Cambrai, upon which so many British hopes were pinned, was underway. Probing forward, the tanks soon encountered the massively dense belts of German wire. The question as to whether it would impede the progress of the armour was soon answered. It did not prevent forward movement and, more important, it did not tear apart and foul the running gear. The passive defence offered by the barbed wire proved to be illusory as the tanks flattened it with complete ease. It was the first serious shock of the day for the defence and there were to be many more before the day was over. The men in the companies defending Outpost Line and the *K1* line of the *Siegfried Stellung* (SI) [Hindenburg Main Line] just to the south of Havrincourt were amongst the first to be confronted with the reality of facing a mass armoured attack.

Sergeant Schwarz 3rd Company Infantry Regiment 84 [1]

"The night 19 – 20 November passed as quietly as it had been during the past few days. Around 6.00 am 20 November I was relieved in Number 2 Picket then I headed back to the *K1* line where we intended to go down into our dugout for a few hours of refreshing sleep. We never reached the dugout; all of a sudden the British brought down appalling drum fire on our position, forcing us to take cover in the nearest dugout. When, at about 7.20 am,[2] the fire was lifted to the rear, we immediately occupied our positions. The sight that greeted us was completely unexpected. About twenty to thirty tanks were bearing down on us and they were only about fifty to sixty metres away.

"Following up behind, in section groups, came the British infantry. Initially we fired at the tanks but we soon realised that this fire was in vain, so we directed our fire mainly against the assaulting infantry. This caused the enemy heavy casualties. Unfortunately our ammunition soon ran out and, on orders of the company commander, we pulled back to the village of Flesquières, where we attached ourselves to the *Halberstädter* [Reserve Infantry Regiment 27]. To the front of the position we could clearly see twenty British tanks, which had been completely destroyed by artillery fire."

Leutnant A. Mestwarb 7th Company Infantry Regiment 84 [3]

"7th Company occupied positions in *R1* (South), maintaining contact with Landwehr Infantry Regiment 387 to the left. 8th Company was to our right. I was located in Outpost I on the left flank, where I had established a junction point with the 387th. As far as I remember, Outpost II was off to my right, under the command of Vizefeldwebel Wunderlich. Outpost I was linked to the *K1* Line by means of a long communication trench, a shorter trench joined us to the neighbouring Outpost II and our link to the left was by means of a short stretch of defensive trench... During the night 19/20 November the British artillery was relatively quiet and the hours before dawn were strikingly still: the calm before the storm. I was on duty throughout almost the entire night, despatching patrols forward to ensure that we were not surprised but nothing untoward was reported. Just as dawn was breaking I felt that it was time for an early morning snack and headed back from the outpost to the dugout. I had barely made the necessary preparations than the storm broke.

"Just after 7.00 am British drum fire came down all along the front. I leapt up, grabbed the flare pistol and, stuffing my pockets with red and green cartridges, I rushed up. I soon saw that the fire was coming down to our rear along the *K* lines, which were currently swathed in smoke and fire. Instinctively the sentries out forward pulled back into the outpost line and the trench was occupied. We continued to observe keenly whilst this was happening. The sentry standing next to me suddenly made an extraordinary remark. His actual words were, 'Herr Leutnant, something four-cornered is coming!' I looked and immediately recognised that it was a tank; the fascine perched on its roof did indeed give it a square appearance. Well we thought that we could deal with one or two tanks. We had no idea that there were masses of them and we opened fire immediately – unfortunately without making the slightest impression on this monster.

"It carried on towards us, firing, then veered off to the left so as to make room for those following it, who were emerging one by one from the corner of the wood to our front. What a superb target this wood corner would have made for our artillery! But there was no sign of any such intervention; not a shot landed. From the minute the tanks first appeared I shot off flares. I eventually fired off every flare I possessed but nothing happened. The telephone had been put out of action immediately, so runners were despatched to battalion headquarters. We heard nothing from them either; we were completely cut off. Meanwhile the tanks made rapid progress, crossing the trench to our left and right and firing constantly. Some of them paused, maintaining heavy fire against the trench, whilst others pressed on beyond the *K2* [Line].

"What was to be done? The fact that we were utterly defenceless in the face of these monsters and our artillery was silent was very depressing. Worse still, numerous aircraft flew low over the trenches bringing down heavy fire. This was no longer a battle; this was a massacre. Leutnant Mory completely lost his head once the first tanks were reported, but something had to be done. I sent a runner, ordering the other Outpost to withdraw then, taking with me every man who was still capable, I pulled back to *K1*. The communications trench was raked by fire. It was only possible to use it if we ducked down, but we nevertheless hurled ourselves into the hail of fire. There was terrible confusion and not many men made it. *K1* had already been evacuated, so we pushed straight on to *K2*. Here Leutnant Mory and his party, who had linked up with Leutnant Saucke and some men of 6th Company, were already pulling back.

"I myself was completely exhausted and had to get my breath back, so I stayed behind in *K2* with a few men who were in a similar condition. Once we had recovered somewhat and were able to move once more, we realised that our route to the rear had been cut by yet more tanks and that we had no chance of escape. Together with a few men, I occupied a section of trench and attempted to bring down fire on the tanks, but it was totally pointless. Our fate was sealed. A short time later the British came at us with hand grenades. I was seriously wounded by two fragments and, knocked out of the fight, I was captured. That was the end of 7th Company, with which I had, with only short breaks, fought in so many hard battles – Champagne, Russia, Verdun and Flanders. What a dismal thought!"

Leutnant B Hegermann 8th Company Infantry Regiment 84[4]

"I was awakened by the shout, 'Defensive fire is being called for to our right!' Our artillery responded promptly, but the fire died away quickly and a few minutes later all was calm once more, until one hour later when enemy drum fire came down with a sudden crash...we were not under direct fire, so it was a simple matter to alert the sentries and deploy the garrison very swiftly. Looming out of the darkness we saw British infantry. There was a swift fire order and they were greeted with rifle and machine gun fire. The effect on the British was dreadful. They went down like cornstalks or raced for the rear...But, what was that? 'Herr Leutnant what is that half-left in front of us?' It seemed as though a blackboard was moving about and approaching us. Half right, we saw exactly the same thing. 'A tank! Tanks! Fire! Fire S.m.K. ammunition!' The tanks drew closer, heading straight for us. Eventually they halted, a mere fifteen metres from us. 'Attack them with hand grenades!'

"They moved right up to our trench. The first of them crossed over and then halted. It was still really dark. We came under fire from the tank and had to take cover. 'Keep throwing grenades at that monster!' – but they had no effect on it. It dawned on us that we were powerless against this tank. It, on the other hand, had sized up the situation and was making life hell for us in the trench...In response to a firm order, 'Man the firestep!' new life was breathed into the defence...[Here] in *K1* small arms fire was brought down on the British infantry which was advancing 150 – 250 metres behind the tanks then, once the tanks were close enough to be engaged with close quarter weapons, bitterly hard fighting broke out everywhere.

"For several minutes we held up some tanks immediately to our front, all the time under heavy fire from their machine guns. Eventually it was no longer possible to hold out on the firestep because some tanks had got in behind us and were driving along the trench firing, as also were very low flying aircraft. Pressing in tight against the walls of the trench, making use of every bit of cover, we continued to try to deal with the tanks with our hand grenades. I myself threw a continuous stream of grenades from the front and the sides, attempting to get one through one of the apertures in the side, but our only success was to prevent them from advancing for a time..."

Virtually all the initial attempts to counter the approximately one hundred tanks which were attacking the Infantry Regiment 84 sector failed. Reserve Leutnant Hallum launched a solo attack using hand grenades, but was shot dead during the attempt. The forward companies poured small arms fire at the infantry accompanying the tanks and against the tanks themselves, but their efforts were largely in vain. Outnumbered, overrun and overpowered they fell where they stood or were swiftly captured and sent back to the

British rear in large numbers. The advance continued in the direction of Flesquières.

Leutnant A Saucke 6th Company Infantry Regiment 84 [5]

"Around 7.00 am ...all hell broke loose as the concentrated fire of hundreds of guns crashed down as one. I raced across to the foot of the stairs leading out of the dugout and, looking upwards, I could see the trench lit up in the gloom by a sea of flame caused by the ceaseless detonations of exploding shells. There could be no more doubt. This was an attack! Despite this our morale was high; we felt ourselves the superior of the British by far. Within minutes the enemy lifted their fire to the rear. This was the moment we had been waiting for and a few seconds later we were manning our posts in the trench. Whistles blew: Stand to! Stand to! There was a light machine gun in the neighbouring dugout. Before an order could be given, the weapon was in position above cover, ready to fire. But there were no targets to engage; the entire area to the front was cloaked by fog. Behind us a yellowish-grey wall of smoke rose into the sky, caused by the incessant exploding shells.

"I was rather surprised about how little damage the enemy shelling had caused. The trench was almost untouched; there had been barely two or three direct hits. I later heard that the British had only moved their batteries into position the previous night and, in order to protect the essential surprise, upon which the success of the operation depended, had used predicted fire from the map. What was the situation in the forward company positions? I was just about to despatch a runner to find out, when a wounded man from 7th Company approached us from the right and gasped a few, heavily charged words, 'The British have got tanks!' A cold shiver ran down my spine; the effect of this information on the morale of my men was plain to see. They, who had just been pouring scorn on the British, saying that they would all be tearing their trousers on our barbed wire, suddenly looked disconcerted.

"At that precise moment Reserve Leutnant Mory, second in command of 7th Company, appeared. He was slightly wounded, totally out of breath and with his morale in tatters. We were very struck by this, for we knew him to be a fearless man, who had made his name within the regiment as a daring patrol commander. In order not to unsettle my men unnecessarily, I took Mory to one side and learned from him that his company had simply been overrun and wiped out by the tanks. So the British could be expected to appear before *K1* at any moment. I immediately despatched runners to the platoons to alert them to the danger and reported what I knew of the fate of the outpost companies to the battalion. There was still no sign of the enemy.

"All of a sudden there was a muffled shout from a neighbouring sentry post. Everyone rushed to the parapet and then we saw, looming out of the swirling fog, a dreadful colossus heading straight for us. Every single one of us could almost hear his heart beating in his chest! However, we were seized only momentarily by leaden indecision. With weapons tucked into our cheeks we fired shot after shot at the enemy. Unfortunately this affected them not in the slightest. Slowly, but unstoppably, they drew closer. Firing also began left and right of us. As I pulled myself up to look over the parapet, I could see a whole chain of these steel monsters advancing towards our trenches. The tank to our front was barely one hundred metres away by now. The light machine gun had fired off its last belt of ammunition without visible effect. What was to be done?

"I clung onto the hope that that the *K1* [trench] would be wide enough to present the tanks with an impassable obstacle and gave orders to pull back to *K2*. Evacuation of the first trench took place swiftly but in good order. The behaviour of the men was faultless. Removing armfuls of grenades from boxes dug into the walls of the trenches, assisting in the transport of the machine guns, not even forgetting the empty machine gun [ammunition] belts [they withdrew]. It was high time. The tank had now got damned close to us. Most unfortunately the communication trench back to *K2* had no kinks in it. It was as straight as a die. We were roughly at the mid point when the tank arrived at *K1* and was able to bring its machine guns to bear on us. I was second last. The man bringing up the rear was hit, as were two further forward, but I was untouched. It really was a life or death race.

"When I arrived at the safety of the *K2* trench I was so worked up, my knees were trembling. 5th Company, commanded by Reserve Leutnant Beuck, had already occupied part of *K2*. The platoons and sections were quickly reorganised and deployed. Weapons at the ready, each man stood by grimly awaiting what was bound to happen. The hopes that we had pinned on *K1* soon proved to have been ill-founded. For a time it appeared that the advance of the tanks had stalled; we could see them moving up and down, apparently aimlessly. Had we had a gun available the situation would have been saved, but our artillery was silent, only enemy shells roared overhead. We were on our own resources; cut off from the reserves by a wall of smoke and fire, whilst our fate unfolded in front of us.

"To our right in the narrow valley south of Havrincourt Park the tanks appeared to have broken through; certainly we noted a squadron of tanks already to our rear and advancing on Flesquières, whilst our opponents had still not crossed *K1*. I watched one tank, which displayed a white flag as a special recognition mark and had some sort of attachment on its front.[6] It approached the trench at right angles then, when it reached the lip of the trench, the attachment suddenly fell vertically. I assumed that the tank had been hit or at least been damaged and could scarcely believe my eyes when it continued onwards and its outline gradually became more clearly defined. There could be no doubt, it had crossed the trench and was pressing on towards us. What I had seen must have been a large wooden object or a great bundle of sticks which it had released at the appropriate moment in order to cross the trench.

"The following moments were difficult. We felt betrayed and sold out. Once more the most violent firing broke out as every barrel was brought to bear against these monstrous opponents. If only its infantry had put in an appearance! We could have dealt with men of flesh and blood like ourselves, but we were defenceless against these armoured machines. Nevertheless, a breakthrough in our area was remarkably delayed. The going was unsuitable for tanks. We were located in a former copse and the numerous tree stumps seemed to hinder the tanks considerably. It is also possible that we were located where there was a gap in the enemy attacking waves. Whatever the facts, the battle ground to a halt here for a considerable period of time.

"I made use of the opportunity to obtain instructions from battalion personally. On the way to the battalion command post, I could see tanks well to our rear, manoeuvring against Flesquières. I came across Hauptmann Soltau [commanding officer 2nd Battalion] in front of the entrance to his dugout. He had been slightly wounded in the back and his uniform jacket was hanging loosely from his shoulder. Leutnant Beuck arrived at exactly the same time. Hauptmann Soltau was very agitated. He could not understand why we had simply evacuated the first trench and now appeared equally powerless to defend the second one. He ordered us to hold *K2* at all costs. He had just been in contact with the regiment. A counter-attack, designed to restore the situation, was expected shortly. I asked if the artillery would be advancing alongside and tried to stress the hopelessness of an unsupported infantry attack all the time that the enemy was operating with tanks.

"Hauptmann Soltau interrupted me impatiently several times. He seemed not to want to comprehend the situation and constantly repeated his order that the newly adopted positions were to be held at all costs, so Beuck and I returned forward, with the clear knowledge that for us the day was lost. The battle picture had not altered essentially, but the remaining fighting elements of the battalion were closing in instinctively towards the sunken road, from which, remarkable to relate, the tanks were keeping their distance. The final phase of our resistance began. The British infantry appeared, following the routes of the tanks. As they flattened the barbed wire, the British tanks unrolled white tape, making the resulting lanes obvious to the assault troops, who gradually began to observe, then move forward with extreme caution. The battle flared up once more. Wherever a live target offered itself, shots cracked out. However, it was not an even fight. We were completely surrounded and to our left, in the sector of Infantry Regiment 387 around Ribécourt, the enemy had achieved especially deep penetrations.

Leutnant J Langfeldt 2nd Battalion Infantry Regiment 84 [7]

"During the night the British were supposed on one occasion to have brought down a concentration of heavy fire on our positions. This drew our artillery into replying with defensive fire and so depleting their already meagre stocks of ammunition. I heard none of it; I was sleeping the sleep of the dead. In the morning I was rudely awakened by drum fire, which came down suddenly. I instantly looked at my watch; it was, unless my memory fails me, 7.15 am. I hurried over to the entrance of the dugout. The trench leading to it was under heavy high explosive and shrapnel fire and, above all, with the smoke shells which took your breath away. As soon as the fire eased slightly, I rushed forwards along the *Stollenweg* [Dugout Way]. In the dugout were company cooks and one platoon of 6th Company. I pressed them to emerge and to occupy a section of trench which forked off a little way forward of *Stollenweg*. Leutnant Hallum was very helpful to me and led the men into the section of trench where this keen, faithful officer was the first to be mortally wounded.

"Meanwhile the first reports had arrived from the front. Leutnant Mory arrived breathless and panicky. Almost his entire company had been captured; the British had countless tanks. I can remember to this day how the scales suddenly fell from my eyes when I heard the word tanks. It was all clear now or, rather, it was unclear, exactly what it meant to be opposed by tanks. We had a short council of war to decide what to do. The Hauptmann ordered us to occupy the short stretch of trench. Because it only had very short traverses, tanks driving over it would not be able to sweep it with machine gun fire. The aim was to let the tanks calmly pass us by then, leaving them for the artillery to deal with, we would attempt to close with the British infantry. If that was successful, the effect of the tanks would be neutralised. The first step was to clear the supply dump of all available hand grenades and other ammunition and to distribute it to the infantrymen. Above all, however, we had to make contact with the regiment and inform them that we needed S.m.K. ammunition. We then saw that masses of tanks were already climbing the slopes behind us towards Havrincourt, whilst on the other side they had already passed Ribécourt. It was essential to direct the artillery, which was still engaging the former defensive fire tasks, onto these targets.

"However, the first of the artillery fire cut off the link to the regiment. A runner was despatched but, because of the presence behind us of a wall of flame and smoke in the valley bottom, he did not get through. I raced over to the light signalling station…[where] the men did their damnedest to get in contact with the regiment. I soon saw that it was impossible; a thick curtain of smoke, which even the sun's rays could not penetrate, hung there, cutting off our view of Flesquières completely. Then I spotted the tactics that the British were using. British infantry appeared at the far end of the trench, but when they saw that we were occupying it, they pulled back immediately. They obviously had orders not to get into a fight with us, but to leave it all to the tanks. I then raced back to the Hauptmann to inform him that it would be hopeless to try to link up with the regiment."

One telephone line which did survive initially was that between regimental headquarters Infantry Regiment 84 and *KTK North* [battalion command post, north] in *R1* near Flesquières. The 1st Battalion commander, Reserve Hauptmann Wille, was able, therefore, to pass on a situation report at about 8.00 am - and a dismal tale it told. He informed the regiment that Reserve Leutnant Hegermann of 8th Company had joined him, that enemy thrusts had overrun the *K1* and *K2* lines in *R1 South* and that they had reached the *K1* line in *R1 North*.

Reserve Hauptmann Wille 1st Battalion Infantry Regiment 84 [8]

"At 7.00 am on 20 November a heavy artillery shell landing near to the battalion command post signalled that the battle had begun. It was followed by five minutes of intense drum fire, to which our artillery replied vigorously. Then the enemy fire ceased. There was a brief pause, then the British drum fire resumed with extraordinary force. In no time all the telephone links, with the exception of that from the regiment, were severed. Outside everything was wreathed in smoke and dust. British machine gun bullets whistled overhead and impacted in the rose garden. The ear-splitting racket of battle surpassed anything experienced in Flanders.

"The regiment demanded report after report. There was no news from Soltau and the regiment had no information either. Finally, after an hour, an unteroffizier from Dunkelgod's company staggered in, almost exhausted, reporting, 'Leutnant Dunkelgod can hold out no longer. To his right twenty British tanks have pushed on over the *K1* line.' Outside the picture was the same, but the hellish racket seemed to be moving forward. I put a question to the regiment, asking them, in due of the threat to the right flank following the tank breakthrough, whether the battalion should conduct a fighting withdrawal. 'No, the front line is to be held' [was the response].

"At that I requested the regiment most urgently to despatch Fürsen's [commanding officer 3rd Battalion] reserves forward in a counter-stroke, in order to restore the situation. Major Hofmeister, deputy regimental commander, released one of Fürsen's companies for this purpose and ordered it to advance at once. The telephone line to Fürsen had been shot away. Runner after runner was despatched to him, but it was all in vain..."

The commander of *KTK South*, Hauptmann Soltau, was already engaged in desperate hand to hand fighting against troops of 2nd and 6th Battalions West Yorkshire Regiment of the British 62nd Division by this time, though he did manage to pass a couple of brief reports back by runner. Casualties were mounting. In addition to all the men taken prisoner, key members of the regiment began to fall out of the fight. Eventually, after six tanks had been knocked out, a male tank, commanded by Lieutenant William McElroy, managed to force a way into the village. With its support Soltau and his men were driven back to buildings on the edge of Havrincourt, but the end was approaching. During a concerted attack along the line of *Kabelgraben* [Cable trench], Hauptmann Soltau was killed, together with his staff, whilst Reserve Hauptmann Christiansen, who had only just assumed command of 8th Company, was shot through the head and moved into a dugout, where he died some time later when a grenade was thrown into it. Members of 6th Company, who had been forced back out of their original positions, were present to witness the unfolding of these traumatic events.

Leutnant A Saucke 6th Company Infantry Regiment 84 [9]

"There were enemy tanks everywhere, followed by two waves of British assault troops at 200 and 300 metres distance. Nowhere did our artillery appear to be having any sort of effect. Finally the enemy realised that we had been forced into one final pocket of resistance. Tanks approached from all sides, the guns in their small turrets bringing down unbroken fire. We suffered considerable casualties and our gallant band shrank constantly as we repeatedly yielded sections of trench. Finally, faced with a hopeless situation, we gathered in the sunken road. Tanks appeared at the western edge of the ravine, which enabled them to bring their guns to bear all along it. The game was up...

"We pulled back past the two dug-in field kitchens, where fires still burned beneath the cooking pots, to the battalion command post...to see what our commander would now order. In contrast to earlier, Hauptmann Soltau was very calm. He had a strange look in his eyes – just as though he knew that Death was lying in wait for him. Leutnants Elson, Ritzmann, Beuck and Hinkeldeyn were with him, together with the battalion runners and a few vizefeldwebels, unteroffiziers and men. That was all that was left of the 2nd Battalion. Few words were spoken. What could we have said? It was not yet every man for himself. A feeling of togetherness still prevailed and we waited for our leader to give the word.

"The moment arrived. A sentry observing up on the parapet shouted down that several tanks were approaching the eastern end of the ravine. This meant that our direct withdrawal route was now cut. There remained only one slight chance of avoiding being enveloped. Directly opposite the battalion dugout the so-called *Kabelgraben* led off. It was two metres deep, very narrow and a cable ran away along its base to the rear. The tanks would not be able to touch us in this narrow trench. We should be able, in a manner of speaking, to run between their legs. If the trench was not occupied by the British infantry, we should be able to escape, but it called for the utmost haste. British helmets could be seen in the trenches leading from the sunken road. Shots were exchanged and I saw a lanky Scotsman fall to the ground. The others pulled back into cover like lightning.

"At that, Hauptmann Soltau gave us the signal and, one by one, we raced across the ravine and into *Kabelgraben*. An unteroffizier was in the lead, then came Hauptmann Soltau with Leutnant Elson behind him. I was next, followed by my batman, Dinse, my runner, Gefreiter Turlach, Leutnants Ritzmann and Hinkeldeyn and the remaining NCOs and men. I later discovered that Reserve Leutnant Beuck stayed in the ravine, where he was captured together with several vizefeldwebels of his company. A few minutes later, tragedy struck amongst us in *Kabelgraben*. Hardly had we covered one hundred metres when we bumped into British soldiers coming the other way. There was no means of escape left. Hauptmann Soltau jumped up out of the trench, as did the leading Unteroffizier. A few machine guns opened up and seconds later the Unteroffizier, bleeding from an arm wound jumped back in, blurting out, 'Hauptmann Soltau is dead!'...

"I looked carefully over the edge of the trench. There were two tanks not fifty metres away half left. Over by the sunken road a dozen of our men were being disarmed. Automatically I raised my rifle and fired two or three shots, hitting one of the kilted soldiers...It must have been about midday when we were captured. As we were led to the rear we saw what masses the British had concentrated for the attack. In our old *K2* and *K1* lines, packed together, were cavalry, artillery and engineers. Ammunition columns were lined up in the open. During the late afternoon, on our way to the wire cages where we would spend our first night of captivity, our accompanying guards told us that the British had occupied Cambrai. Worn down mentally and physically we could not bring ourselves to doubt their word and, heads hanging low, we trudged towards a dismal, inglorious future."

Previously, at 6.50 am, as part of the reaction to the firing of the defensive fire missions forward of Havrincourt, Major Krebs, commander of Reserve Infantry Regiment 27, had already received the order from 108 Brigade to advance to Flesquières: '6.30 am. Direction of La Justice; gas alert. Heavy enemy artillery fire. We are firing a defensive fire mission at Havrincourt. Regimental staff is to move immediately to command post Infantry Regiment 84. 2nd Battalion is to move immediately to the *Zwischenstellung*. The remaining two companies, currently at Fontaine Notre Dame, are also to be moved there, making use of trucks located there for the purpose. 3rd Battalion is to be held back in Cambrai, ready to move.'[10] Back in Marcoing, where heavy fire was also coming down on the assembly area of Reserve Infantry Regiment 27, Major Stubenrauch despatched the companies in the order 7th, 6th, 5th and 8th to Flesquières via Premy. His Machine Gun Company moved on vehicles. It was a difficult move forward, as this description by a member of 6th Company shows:

Unteroffizier Senftleben 6th Company Reserve Infantry Regiment 27 [11]

"What a dreadful move! In front, behind, to the side and overhead the shells crashed down. Sulphur fumes and powder smoke filled the air and, together with the fog, made it impossible to see into the distance. Our company commander rushed here and there, cracking jokes at the soldiers bent over because of the roaring shells and saying, 'Lads, that is not going to help you!' The behaviour of the regimental staff, accompanied by some hussars and grooms, also earned them complete admiration. Completely ignoring the exploding shells, they galloped along the bank alongside the road. That sort of thing certainly makes an impression and encourages others to do likewise!

"Finally the area under fire was traversed and, after a short pause to get our breath back, we pushed on across the open hillside to the protection of the trenches. Here we could have a proper breather, then we moved further forward on the slippery duckboards. We looked at each other in astonishment. Surely that could not be the *K1* line? Were the British already in the front line trenches? Just a minute, Tommies! You are not going to get further forward! These were our thoughts and the words which we exchanged. Some of our comrades were standing in ones and twos in front of the dugouts; their faces smiling at the help [which had arrived]. Our company commander, Leutnant Krings, was out in front, leading us, just as we knew he would!"

On the basis of the reports that did filter through, a local counter-stroke was hurriedly arranged. In view of the anticipated attack against Havrincourt, Reserve Hauptmann Fürsen, commanding officer of 3rd Battalion Infantry Regiment 84, had already discussed possible counter action with his company commanders the previous evening and, by 8.10 am, just as the Army Group Commander, Crown Prince Rupprecht, was informing OHL of the seriousness of the situation, his battalion, less 12th Company, had launched forward. Leading elements of Reserve Infantry Regiment 27, the only uncommitted regiment of 54th Infantry Division and extremely quick off the mark, was rapidly on the scene with its 1st and 2nd Companies, followed closely by the entire 2nd Battalion, commanded by Major Stubenrauch. This attack soon clashed with British tanks whilst it was still north of the *Oetinger Riegel*[12] and it quickly stalled. Falling back on Flesquières, these troops occupied the first line of the *Zwischenstellung* to the west of the *Großer Stern*, whilst the second line to the east of Flesquières was garrisoned by the regimental staff, 3rd and 4th Companies and 1st Machine Gun Company of Reserve Infantry Regiment 27.

Although he still had no clear picture of the overall situation, Generalleutnant von Watter, commander 54th Infantry Division, was sufficiently concerned about events to his front that, having already committed Reserve Infantry Regiment 27, he now telephoned through to 107th Infantry Division and ordered the implementation of the plans which he had discussed the previous evening with its chief of staff: 'Regiment Cantaing is to move to Flesquières and link up with Reserve Infantry Regiment 27 or support it in its attack on Havrincourt. Regiment Marcoing is to advance to reinforce Reserve Infantry Regiment 90.'[13] Had these regiments been where von Watter expected them to be, i.e. the two places mentioned above plus Masnières; and had they been able to advance as he directed, it is highly probable that the British would have been prevented from crossing the canal later in the day. As it was, for some extraordinary reason, nobody mentioned to von Watter at the time, nor contacted him subsequently, to inform him that neither of these formations were located in the places he expected them to be, or were even subordinated to him.

In the meantime, at about 8.40 am, Major Stubenrauch arrived at Flesquières together with the leading elements of his battalion and linked up with Major Hofmeister. Although he was captured later, he was able to provide a description of events in a report he sent from captivity:

Major Stubenrauch 2nd Battalion Reserve Infantry Regiment 27 [14]

"Major Hofmeister told me that the British had forced their way into Havrincourt and that Hauptmann Wille, commanding officer of 1st Battalion Infantry Regiment 84, which was located in *R1 North*, had sent an urgent request for support. Contact had been lost with Hauptmann Soltau, commanding officer of 2nd Battalion Infantry Regiment 84 in *R1 South*. Things did not seem to be going well in that area and he had received no information whatsoever about it. (In fact a report was despatched a little later by Soltau saying that he, together with some courageous comrades, was engaged in a battle with tanks at his command post – 'We shall hold out until the last man!' – Soltau fell during this heroic fight.) I could not orientate myself adequately. The smoke of battle, together with the fog, cut out long range visibility at the time. Major Hofmeister regarded immediate support for Havrincourt as essential. In accordance with a divisional order that, in the event of an advance by Infantry Regiment 84, Reserve Infantry Regiment 27 was automatically to occupy the *Ötinger Riegel*, I decided to move forward to it and to hold it."

7th Company was deployed in the *Havrincourtgraben* [Havrincourt Trench] and 6th Company in *Grenzweg* [Boundary Way], whilst 5th and 8th Companies moved into reserve, occupying the *Zwischenstellung* to the south of Flesquières. Major Stubenrauch moved forward to a place of observation, whilst Major Hofmeister despatched Leutnant Brockes back to direct 1st and 2nd Companies Reserve Infantry Regiment 27 to launch a counter-stroke towards the *KTK* in *R1 North*. Brockes searched all over the *Zwischenstellung* for the two companies, but only came across a few members of Infantry Regiment 84, a security detachment of Pionier Company 108 and some stragglers from Infantry Regiment 387. At 9.00 am, Brockes located 1st Company taking shelter in the catacombs and the 2nd Company in the process of carrying out a previous order to occupy the *Zwischenstellung*.

Meanwhile enemy shells were raining down on and around Flesquières; the curtain of fire and poor visibility making the move forward of the German infantry extremely difficult. Nevertheless progress was made and, at around 8.45 am, Major Krebs and his adjutant arrived at the Infantry Regiment 84 command post. Quite independently, Reserve Hauptmann Fürsen, commanding officer 3rd Battalion Infantry Regiment 84, also gave orders to his companies, less the 12th, which remained in the *Zwischenstellung*, to launch a counter-stroke forward. As a result of all this activity, shortly after 9.00 am, the following troops were deployed in the *R1* sector ready to fight their way forward:

> From the Flesquères area - 2nd Battalion Reserve Infantry Regiment 27 complete, 1st and 2nd Companies Reserve Infantry Regiment 27.
> From the *Ötinger Riegel*, those elements of 3rd Battalion Infantry Regiment 84 located there.

In fact the situation was rather more complicated and less favourable than this apparent availability of troops would suggest. In any other circumstances and based on recent experience on Flanders, a counter-attack in more than battalion strength on a narrow front might reasonably have been expected to make good progress, but here the presence of tanks, the speed of the British movement and the depth of some of the penetrations already achieved meant that as soon as 3rd Battalion Infantry Regiment 84 attempted to move, it became unexpectedly entangled in a close-quarter battle with both British tanks and infantry. Further north, 8th Company and 2nd Machine Gun Company Reserve Infantry Regiment 27 were still moving forward. By the time they arrived, the deteriorating situation meant that these sub-units had to be directed to advance, avoiding Flesquières. There were also enormous problems with artillery support. The shortage of ammunition, poor visibility and conflicting demands on the guns meant, even where communications had not failed, that essential fire support was not forthcoming.

Forward of Flesquières, members of 7th Company Reserve Infantry Regiment 27 were hurrying forward along the *Havrincourtgraben* [Havrincourt Trench] in an attempt to link up with the command post of 1st Battalion Infantry Regiment 84. On the way they repeatedly encountered wounded members of that battalion who were making their way back to the aid posts, but none of them could provide a coherent account of events forward. The sector towards which they were moving was unknown territory for them and the fog was virtually impenetrable. In order to avoid bumping into the British off-balance, the company deployed left and right of the trench and began to advance across open ground.

Reserve Leutnant Hermann 7th Company Reserve Infantry Regiment 27 [15]

"To give the men their due, I must say that their behaviour was excellent, despite the heavy enemy fire. It was just as though they were on the exercise area in Cambrai, as they had been three days previously when the regimental commander visited the company for the last time. I felt uplifted by them and felt sure that we should be able to recapture the forward position. Of course we did not realise at the time that we were not only confronting men but also tanks. I called a short halt at the railway embankment [about 500 metres short of *Oetinger Riegel*] and here we were troubled by aircraft which swooped down very low. They were engaged by our light machine guns and riflemen. It was claimed that Gefreiter Hesse and Musketier Smuda shot one aircraft down. Leutnant Patzer[16] made the same claim. Both he and Gefreiter Hesse were killed a little later. I did not witness the event myself due to the fog and the fact that I was located on the right flank, which was in the air and, therefore, at greatest risk. Looking through the telescope, I could see movement in the *Oetinger Riegel* to our front, but could not make out what it was. I directed bayonets to be fixed in order to eject the British from the *Oetinger Riegel* if they had managed to occupy it already. The enemy fire increased further in intensity and then a dark mass emerged from the fog and then took on the form – of the first tank.

"When we reached the *Oetinger Riegel*, we came across a few men of Infantry Regiment 84. It was impossible to advance any further under cover because even more tanks had arrived. I also thought that I should lose contact with the other companies, because we were already a long way forward. I decided, therefore, to defend the *Oetinger Riegel* for the time being, hoping that the weather would clear more and, above all, that our artillery would join in the battle against the tanks. During our approach we had already noticed that some batteries were already out of ammunition, but every minute that we could hang on forward provided more opportunities for fresh stocks of ammunition to arrive. We did not succeed in keeping the tanks at bay with grenades and small arms fire. Minute by minute our situation became more critical. Tanks advanced across the trench on both flanks and now began to attack from the rear. British officers later commented to me that they had feared that we had already widened our trenches to such an extent that the tanks would have been unable to cross them, even with the aid of fascines.

"I could see that we should not be able to hold on for much longer and I sought an escape route. It was out of the question to think of getting away where there was no cover. The *Havrincourtgraben* was already blocked, but when we attempted to move along the *Oetinger Riegel* towards *Grenzgraben* [Boundary Trench] - which meant crawling most of the time in order to remain concealed from tanks which were patrolling up and down on both sides - we found that blocked too. Sitting on a great fascine, a tank was astride the trench.

We were unable to hold back the British infantry for very long with our fire. As our ammunition ran out and as increasing numbers of tanks dominated the *Oetinger Riegel* with fire from their machine guns and main armament, the enemy assault troops (51st Highland Territorial Division [*sic*]) were able to force their way into the trench. They had worked their way forward by sheltering behind the tanks. Further resistance was pointless. It could only have lasted a few minutes and we could do nothing against tanks with bayonets. Not many took any notice of us; instead they pushed on and attacked other troops to our rear: presumably 5th Company. Because of the casualties we had suffered and the way we were scattered along a lengthy section of trench, the remainder of the company was swiftly overwhelmed. I do not know exactly what the time was, because my watch was immediately ripped off its chain but, when I arrived in a headquarters building in Trescault, a clock on a desk read about 10.00 am [11.00 am German time] and it could have taken us about one hour to get there."

One of the junior NCOs of 7th Company also left a description of this abortive attempt to restore the situation to the front.

Gefreiter Bär 7th Company Reserve Infantry Regiment 27 [17]

"We stopped for a short breather at the railway embankment. It seemed as though the company commander was not sure if we should stay at the embankment and defend it or if we ought to push on, but the battalion order had been 'Forwards at all costs!' Reserve Leutnant Hermann, our courageous and much-loved company commander, came to a quick decision and ordered, 'Fix bayonets and advance by sections over the railway embankment'. This was because British machine gun fire was sweeping the railway tracks. At the cost of only light casualties we achieved this; then 7th company calmly advanced in extended line, as though we were on the drill square, heading for enemy on the crest line from where fire was being poured down. Now and then somebody fell, killed or wounded, but we pressed on through very heavy machine gun fire; the British yielding everywhere before our assault. By the time the railway embankment was approximately 500 – 600 metres to our rear the company was suddenly attacked from all sides by masses of British infantry and numerous tanks. The hellish situation was made worse by British aircraft flying at very low level. I saw two of them crash. 'Get in the shell holes and bring down rapid fire', came the shouted orders. An appalling, almost volcanic, eruption of fire poured down from all around. We fought back like men possessed. 'Fire at the infantry', I bawled above the din of battle. These [men] were following the tanks and they fell in great masses. Without artillery we were powerless against the tanks. They literally showered us with shells and our casualties were high. Leutnant Patzer died heroically as part of a machine gun crew which engaged the nearest tank. Ratajczak, a hairdresser from Berlin and a member of my section, leapt into my shell hole and shouted, 'Wilhelm, I shall not leave you!' The firefight continued; the ammunition began gradually to run out. General Haig [sic] threw ever more masses at us. This superiority was too much for the company which, almost totally surrounded, went into captivity. Yet Unteroffizier Uhlich, Gefreiter Fensterer and I managed to break out from this inferno. Clearing a way with grenades we raced off, running in zig zags so as not to offer good targets for the shots which pursued us. Finally we arrived at a section of trench, where we took up defensive positions. There was ammunition here. At the last moment the Berliner, Rataczak, was hit in the leg below the knee by a machine gun bullet from an aircraft. 'Wilhelm, save yourself, otherwise you will be captured', he shouted at me. He lay lying there by a small wood. Now there was no time to care for the wounded, as the three of us pushed on backwards. In the meantime the massed tanks had pushed on forwards and past us in the direction of Flesquières and Marcoing. The infantry, mostly Scottish, followed up gingerly. We fired and defended ourselves as best we could but, with great speed, the wing of the British who were attacking here swung round as far as the railway embankment. We had been caught once more. In vain we looked around for an escape route, we still hoped for a swift German counter-stroke, but none came: just masses and masses of British soldiers. We were surrounded again and this time the Tommies had a firm grip of us."

Also advancing towards the southwest exit of Flesquières, 1st Company Reserve Infantry Regiment 27 began taking casualties. Feldwebelleutnant Reinsch's platoon had two men killed and two wounded. A shell landed very close to Unteroffizier Tuschling, who was forced to halt and clean his machine gun. Then, when he attempted to follow up, he found that he had lost contact. All these checks meant that the company commander, Reserve Leutnant Stoltenberg, only had the two platoons of Reserve Leutnant Reuter and Vizefeldwebel Barner with him when he attempted to advance along the Flesquières – Havrincourt road. Despite this setback, his company, too, reached the *Oetinger Riegel*, when he bumped into a mass of advancing tanks.

Reserve Leutnant Stoltenberg 1st Company Reserve Infantry Regiment 27 [18]

"The enemy trapped us between two columns of tanks, engaged us with their guns and so enabled their infantry to overwhelm us. Throughout the entire battle I only counted three German artillery shells landing in my sector. There were few infantry targets to be seen and then they were only fleeting glimpses of individuals. The fire which we put down instinctively did not check the enemy at all and had no effect on the tanks – especially because my requests for S.m.K ammunition [had] received no attention. The battlefield was quiet as we were moved to the rear. Only when we were actually at Havrincourt did the occasional shell crash down or did we hear the tack! tack! of a machine gun."

Unteroffizier Drücke 1st Machine Gun Company Reserve Infantry Regiment 27 [63]

"At about 8.00 am twenty tanks advanced on a broad front out of the wood to the left [south] of Havrincourt (Fémy Wood). They were presenting their flanks to us and they opened fire. I immediately ordered my machine gun to be brought into action then suddenly I saw columns to the left of the wood [advancing] in a ravine which ran alongside it. At that I gave the order to open fire, observing that barely a man rose to his feet afterwards. From this I assumed that the British had suffered heavy casualties. From that position I fired off 2,500 rounds then, turning around I saw a tank behind me, barely ten paces from the trench! I ordered that the machine gun was to be removed from its mount and told [the crew] to follow me. We moved further left and I brought the gun back into action and fired my last 250 rounds at the columns. At that point the infantry moved further to the left, because the British were moving to the left along the trench. I remained with my machine gun with Infantry Regiment 84. A shell landed just in front of me, killing my gunner. The infantry stormed past me then I picked up my gun and, together with my two remaining crew members, rushed from shell hole to shell hole, because we were attacked with machine gun fire and bombs by aircraft. Eventually we passed through Flesquières..."

Gefreiter Döring 1st Machine Gun Company Reserve Infantry Regiment 27 [64]

"Shortly after 8.00 am we observed fifteen to twenty tanks to our left. We brought fire down on them and, as a result, the leading tank came to a halt. Because it was heavily wooded to our front, we had not noticed that the British infantry had worked its way forward. By the time we did, they were within ten metres of us. I ripped out the working parts and raced after my men. By the time we had run about 500 metres we met up with some men who informed us that we had been outflanked by the British and were cut off. Not wanting to be captured carrying machine gun working parts, I threw them away. We then tried to break through and succeeded."

Meanwhile the detached platoon of 1st Company pressed on down *Havrincourtgraben* and met advancing elements of 2nd Battalion Reserve Infantry Regiment 27. Continuing beyond them it moved towards the *Oetinger Riegel*. The platoon commander described the action in a letter to his wife, written at the end of November.

Feldwebelleutnant Reinsch 1st Company Reserve Infantry Regiment 27 [19]

"I myself was slightly wounded above the right eye by a shell splinter. The lenses of my spectacles turned red and blood ran down my cheeks. There was not time to spare to dress it; that was too valuable. A feldwebel of Infantry Regiment 84, whom I knew, orientated me about the situation. He added that the first line was already taken and that the second line, though only weakly held, could be defended. I decided to go to the aid of the hard-pressed Infantry Regiment 84. I had not gone much further forward when several people coming the other way reported that tanks were already 250 metres to my left at the *Oetinger Riegel*. I scrapped the idea of getting further forward; we climbed out of the trench, took up positions in shell holes and fired at the tanks and the infantrymen who were following them. Unfortunately we had no success against the tanks. We hung on until they were within twenty five paces, then we dropped back into the communication trench. Too late! The route to the rear was cut off and the same was true forwards. I broke off to one side towards a sunken road. Pursued by machine gun fire from the tanks, hurling myself from hole to hole, I reached a sunken road covered by an eight metre wide wire obstacle. A quick breather, then I gathered everyone together from Reserve Infantry Regiment 27, Infantry Regiment 84 and Pionier Battalion 108 and we headed back to join the defence of the village of Flesquières."

Men of 6th Company Reserve Infantry Regiment 27 had a similar experience. Their role was to advance along the line of *Grenzweg* in an attempt to link up with 2nd Battalion Infantry Regiment 84 but, before they even reached the *Oetinger Riegel*, they became bogged down in a battle with tanks and infantry, during which the company commander, Reserve Leutnant Krings, fell, killed by a shell which burst directly on the parapet of the trench next to him.

Unteroffizier Albrecht 6th Company Reserve Infantry Regiment 27 [20]

"Suddenly we spotted three tanks to our front and we engaged them with the ammunition we had with us. That proved to be in vain, whilst throwing grenades as they neared us did not help either. We tried to evade them off to one side, but our surprise was beyond description as these things closed in from right, left and, finally, from the rear. We then quietly and calmly divided our fire between them but we could achieve little. The number of tanks, the fire of their main armament and the accurate shooting of their machine guns had a devastating effect. Each of us stood his ground but, as we were increasingly outnumbered – the Scottish infantry had closed up on our positions under the protection of the tanks - we were forced to smash our equipment and surrender to the enemy. Furious and drunken,[21] the soldiers hurled themselves at us and, hitting, pushing and cursing us, they robbed us of all our valuables such as watches, chains and rings as 'souvenirs'."

Vizefeldwebel Lemme 6th Company Reserve Infantry Regiment 27 [22]

"I was ordered by my company commander to remain behind and to ensure that everyone followed Leutnant Krings forward. Although I was placed there as a block, I have to report that every man moved forward courageously, despite the heavy fire. The whole of 6th Company reached the trench [presumably *Grenzweg*] without casualties, then they advanced along it until they passed the Flesquières – Ribécourt road. This was where, just after the road, the company commander, Leutnant Krings, was killed. Ignoring this, despite the fact that we were so upset about it, the company continued. Suddenly another order arrived – everybody back. I immediately sent word forward to discover where the order had come from, but I did not receive a reply, because the company was split in two by a direct hit and the sudden arrival of a tank which brought the trench under fire. We then pulled back together with some of Infantry Regiment 84 behind the Flesquières – Ribécourt road and took up positions there; the tanks had already closed right up to us. However their advance stalled slightly in the face of small arms fire and their further advance was hindered."

Another of the 6th Company NCOs describes the confusion after the shell fell on the trench.

Unteroffizier Senftleben 6th Company Reserve Infantry Regiment 27 [23]

"We hurried on over collapsed sections of trench. To the right, next to the trench, stood a small barn or shed. Some sections of roof were still sitting on the few remaining uprights. All hell had broken loose here. At this point we left the trench and made for our objective across open country. Suddenly everything halted and shouts went up from the front, 'Back!' *Schleswigers* [men of Infantry Regiment 84] hurried past us, calling out, 'Turn round lads, the Tommies are in the trench!' They carried on past. We stayed where we were, despite the fact that shells were coming down behind us. There was a question from the rear, 'Who gave the order to pull back?' The question had come from Vizefeldwebel Lemme. That is what you call good Prussian German sense of duty!

"A leutnant of the *Schleswigers* eventually provided an explanation. 6th Company was, to a large extent, cut off; our beloved leader, Leutnant Krings, was dead, though we did not want to believe it! We headed back along the trench then rushed across the road. By the barn the trench had almost entirely collapsed and we pulled up short again. There on the ground, blown there by a shell, lay five of our comrades bleeding heavily. Over there lay a leg, a bloody brain was stuck to the wall of the trench, a head detached from its body fixed us with a stare. 'I cannot give you my hand, but may you have eternal life, my good comrade!'[24] We made our way slowly past. Nobody gave the falling shells a thought except [the fact] that they could cause the fallen no more pain."

All the while the abortive thrust towards Havrincourt was underway, shells continued to pour down on Flesquières. Pushing forward, Major Stubenrauch decided to hold 5th Company and elements of 8th Company back and so occupy part of the *Zwischenstellung*, which still offered a certain amount of cover and protection. They had barely moved into position than a tank loomed up out of the fog at 9.20 am. Despatching a message via Major Hofmeister, commander Infantry Regiment 84, calling for artillery support, Stubenrauch left the men of 8th Company to hold out against further tank thrusts and moved further forward, leading 5th Company towards Havrincourt. Once again the advancing troops bumped into British tanks and accompanying infantry and once again the men of Reserve Infantry Regiment 27 attempted to hold forward and so deny the British attackers room to manoeuvre before the tanks could be countered more effectively by the artillery. These efforts were barely more successful than earlier ones had been, but some members of 5th Company did succeed in knocking out one of the tanks. Reporting from captivity, a platoon commander explained what happened.

Reserve Leutnant Bleß 5th Company Reserve Infantry Regiment 27 [25]

"Our fire directed against the tanks enjoyed no success. They outflanked us on both sides and cut us off from the rear, obliging us to take cover in the trench [*Havrincourtgraben*] once more. The company continued to advance along the trench until it was found to be blocked by a tank. There was no turning back because the trench was blocked there too by another tank. A third tank drove along the trench, keeping it under constant fire. After I and a group of brave men had thrown all the grenades at the tanks, I decided to leap up out of the trench and move to a better defensive position. However the machine gun fire was so intense that of the men who followed me, all were wounded or killed..."

Later, one of Bleß's men recalled:

Wehrmann Hohmann 5th Company Reserve Infantry Regiment 27 [26]

"Each of us looked for a firing position up above, then we saw the British tanks about one hundred metres to our front. I counted five from my position. We poured fire at the tanks with rifles and machine guns, but it did not seem as though we were making any impression on them. Slowly they advanced towards us, firing on us from all sides. Right and left of me my comrades were going down. All of a sudden, just above our heads, came a roaring, cracking sound as the great bundle of wood or steel that the tank was carrying on its top slid to the ground and the tank appeared to slew onto its side. A loud cheer went up from us because we thought that the tank had received a direct hit but, a few moments later it continued on its way firing.

"There was another loud crash then another. This time the tank had received a direct hit. Within an instant it was enveloped in a large cloud of black smoke and the tank itself seemed to be ablaze. We suddenly saw the crew bale out and run away from the tank; naturally they did not get far under our fire. Suddenly the cry went up, 'Here come the Tommies!' Protected by their tanks, the British infantry had forced their way in to the trench and were now attempting to roll it up. Grenades were thrown at us; one of them landing right next to me on the parapet, but I quickly ducked down. My comrades to the left and right, who were not so quick, were both seriously wounded in the head. Later I bandaged several men up and led them back [to Flesquières]."

The battle picture elsewhere was also becoming critical, not least in Sector *R2*, defended by Infantry Regiment 387. Drum fire was coming down everywhere and the forward positions were under direct attack by the advancing tanks. Though the survivors from this regiment left no detailed account of their experiences, general remarks in their regimental history confirm what a chaotic, traumatic experience the tanks assault was for them.

"Spectral beings, which soon revealed themselves as the outline of tanks, loomed up out of the fog. Immediately our rifle and machine gun fire clattered against them. It was an extremely uncomfortable sensation to discover that our fire did not appear to have any effect at all on the tanks. The protective barbed wire was also a failure: the wires tore apart and clung together in heaps. The tanks crossed the trenches, pouring fire down into them with their main armament and machine guns. They then pushed on into the depth of the position, leaving follow-up waves to complete the destruction of the trench garrison. Before we had time even to appreciate the totally novel situation, the tanks were in amongst us. In the regimental sector they broke in, with only twenty five to fifty metres spacing between tanks. The attack developed from the south after our neighbouring regiment was overrun and driven back. The 9th Company on the left flank was commanded by Reserve Leutnant Stuthe, who was killed by a shot to the stomach. This company was the first to be hit. All the officers and NCOs of this company, together with the larger proportion of the soldiers, were killed or captured...

"The enemy advance continued, supported by strong enemy reinforcements who approached from the west. Enemy aircraft flew low over the positions constantly, bringing down machine gun fire against the trenches and surrounding area...Our own troops were entirely on their own. There were no reinforcements or ammunition resupply. The light and heavy machine guns of the regiment fired until they were knocked out or ran out of ammunition. The S.m.K. ammunition was used up quickly and the stock of hand grenades was soon exhausted. We were simply powerless against the tanks, especially because we had had no training or experience whatsoever in countering them.'[27] An assault pioneer from Reserve Infantry Regiment 27 later provided a clear impression of the confusion in this area at the time:

Unteroffizier Wacker Assault Pioneer Platoon Reserve Infantry Regiment 27 [28]

"Such thick clouds developed as a result of all the smoke bombs and incendiary shells that it was impossible to see from *K1* to *K2*. As a result I went down and ordered the assault pioneer platoon to move to immediate standby alert state. During this period of time the drum fire was lifted onto the *K2* line and further to the rear and throughout extremely heavy machine gun fire could be heard coming from the outpost and the *K1* lines. Gradually visibility improved until it was once more possible to see from the *K2* to the *K1* line. A man of the security group asked me what the object was forward of the *K1* line.

I went towards it and saw through the fog that it was a tank which had reached the *K1* line and that another was following close behind it."

Unteroffizier Wacker then rushed first to the battalion command post and then to regimental headquarters of Infantry Regiment 387 to report and to raise the alarm in Marcoing. Other members of the regiment carried out similar tasks, whilst Sergeant Schäfer, in the process of passing information on the latest situation to Infantry Regiment 84, raced over to a nearby artillery battery position to the south of Marcoing. There then began a frantic struggle to haul the guns out of their pits.

Sergeant Schäfer Reserve Infantry Regiment 27 [29]

"Because of the delay of about a quarter of an hour which this caused, a tank was able to close up on us from the southwest. The heavy fire [it brought down] scattered us. The gunners raced in all directions and we threw ourselves down in a knee-deep communication trench, intending to move to the Infantry Regiment 84 command post along it. In this we were not successful. We were suddenly surprised and surrounded by an eight man tank crew – English and Scotsmen – who threw themselves at us and took us prisoner."[30]

In anticipation of tank action to their rear, two guns of 3rd Battery Field Artillery Regiment 108 had already been hauled out of their pits and were ready to engage tanks advancing against Flesquières and the Zwischenstellung more generally. At about 9.15 am, in an attempt to overcome the communication problem, Hauptmann Fürsen moved his command post forward into the front line of the Zwischenstellung to the south of the Flesquières – Ribécourt road, from which point he continued to control the forward battle. This was typical of the independent actions taken by subordinate headquarters in an attempt to bring order amongst chaos, but it was extremely difficult. For lengthy periods, regimental headquarters had no news at all other than the brief written reports brought by runners. Infantry Regiment 84 was pressed repeatedly for information by 108 Brigade, but runners struggling to pass through curtains of artillery fire had great difficulties in getting through and their information was frequently overtaken by events as the battle developed.

Around 10.30 am Major Hofmeister was mortally wounded by a tank shell and attempts were made to move him back to Noyelles for treatment. However, by the time the party reached the village, the British 7th Dragoon Guards had already captured it and it was occupied by men of the Royal

Fusiliers. The stretcher party had already suffered casualties from machine gun fire during its journey and finally had to abandon the attempt 300 metres south west of the village, where the dying Hofmeister fell into British hands.[31]

Musketier Sörensen 12th Company Infantry Regiment 84 [32]

"On 19 November we were deployed to provide security in the first line of the *Zwischenstellung*. Suddenly, at 7.20am on 20 November, heavy British drumfire started coming down. A short time later we were ordered to occupy the railway embankment near the *Oetinger Riegel*. In the meantime several tanks had already passed through Havrincourt, followed at approximately one hundred metre intervals by columns of infantry. Because we were aware that there was no point in shooting at the tanks, we simply fired at the infantry. [We] spotted that a red flag was poked out of one of the tanks several times. Whenever this happened the following infantry moved forward a bound and the artillery brought down a great weight of fire. We in the regiment fired as fast as we could and observed that our fire had caused a great many casualties. Because the tanks were getting very close and one of them drove along the line of *Havrincourtgraben*, firing into it, I was given the task by the company commander of taking a report over to regimental headquarters. Major Hofmeister [acting regimental commander] sent me back with a message that if we could not hold along the railway line, to pull back to the sunken road which runs from Flesquières cemetery to Havrincourt.

"We also came under terribly heavy fire and the tanks had soon outflanked us to the left and right. I got through and immediately informed regimental headquarters. When I got there Major Hofmeister was lying badly wounded so, together with six comrades, I was ordered to carry Major Hofmeister to the Main Dressing Station in Noyelles. When we had covered two hundred metres out of the trench, three of my comrades were wounded by machine gun fire and we bandaged them up immediately. One of them died a short time later. Under heavy machine gun fire, four of us carried the major further. When we were about three hundred metres from the field fortifications at Noyelles, rapid fire was opened on us from the nearby woods[33] and the British infantry swarmed towards us. Because we could see that Major Hofmeister had not long to live and in order to avoid being taken prisoner, we had to leave the major lying where he was. We were fortunate enough to reach a small trench and so avoid falling into the hands of the enemy. We had another attempt to reach the major and bring him in, but we did not succeed."

When the attack was originally launched, covered by fog and artificial smoke, the defending artillery had been placed in an almost impossible position. The well practised, standard operating procedure of Field Artillery Regiment 108 of 54th Infantry Division to throw forward guns, once it was clear that tanks were involved on a large scale, faltered because complete uncertainty reigned.

Reserve Leutnant H Zindler 1st Battery Field Artillery Regiment 108 [34]

"The battle had been in progress since the early morning. Swirling fog made it impossible to see into the distance. Even at only a few hundred metres it was difficult to make things out. The battery, neighbouring positions, villages and approach routes were all under extremely heavy fire. It was impossible to obtain accurate information about the enemy; patrols which had been despatched had not yet returned. At about 10.00 am two slightly wounded *Mansteiners*,[35] making their way to the rear and showing all the signs of nervous shock, reported, 'The enemy is attacking on a broad front, making mass use of tanks, which are advancing in waves. The wire obstacle, the *K1* and *K2* lines have already been overrun.'

"The report sounded almost unbelievable. Mass use of tanks, with wave after wave of them; that would amount to something entirely new, compared with the previous weak deployment of these weapons of war. Nevertheless, from within the slender resources of the battery, two guns were hauled out of cover and set up in the open. Hauptmann von Köller, who had been posted to receive a general staff officer's artillery training a few days earlier, assisted energetically, as did one of the wounded *Mansteiners*. Both remained by the gun as the close-quarter anti-tank battle began and thus played a part in knocking out the seven of the monsters which the battery destroyed."

Initially, with only planned defensive fire missions to fall back on, all the guns, with the exception of two which had managed to move forward, opened at between 3,000 and 4,000 metres. Such was the shortage of ammunition, however, that fire was far from continuous. Furthermore, at the expected rate of advance of the tanks, it was assumed that they would be threatening the gun lines within an hour of the start of the assault and that ammunition would have to be preserved for that battle. As a result the first enemy assaults were countered mainly by mortar and small arms fire. It is indicative of the ferocity of the close-range battle and the first class performance of the forward infantry that the first of the tanks did not begin closing up on the gun lines on the Flesquières Ridge until towards midday, more than four hours after the offensive began. Here the artillery located to the northeast of the village, in particular 2nd and 3rd Batteries Field Artillery Regiment 108, played a very significant role in the defence once the visibility improved. Where there had been casualties amongst the gunners, improvised reinforcements were summoned, thus helping the guns to maintain a desperate rate of fire as long as the ammunition lasted.

Unteroffizier Petzold Mortar Company 1st Battalion Reserve Infantry Regiment 27 [36]

"Suddenly the crew of one of the guns bawled that they needed manpower. The mortar men, the so-called 'flea artillery', were quickly on the spot. The shell baskets began to fly. It was warm work and we soon removed our jackets. One of us was better trained than the rest. He knew how to load and to pull the lanyard. Curious, he asked the gun commander what we were shooting at. 'Nothing to do with you,' came the answer and the work went on. Suddenly we received a report that tanks were moving up onto the high ground. Order: 'Guns out of their pits!' Everyone set to with a will and, in no time flat, they were out in open positions. Some people thought that this meant that the guns were about to be withdrawn, but forward we knew better. In our forward positions we longed for the gun to perform and it did its work brilliantly. Soon every shot was impacting on those stinking boxes known as 'tanks'. Each time one of these objects went up in flames, the brave lads of the infantry cheered and exchanged ribald comments. 'It must be warm for the crew in there!' Yes, our guns shot really well."

Repeated direct hits took a considerable toll on the tanks. Some accounts state that 2nd and 3rd Batteries between them dealt with eight tanks, others mention six. Altogether Field Artillery Regiment 108 claimed the destruction of forty nine tanks and there is no doubt that in places the guns were served to the very last before being overrun. [37] Examination of the battlefield later suggested that much of the damage to the tanks in this sector was the work of one individual and later, in an extraordinary passage in his post-battle despatch, Field Marshal Haig stated,

"Many of the hits upon our tanks at Flesquières were obtained by a German artillery officer who, remaining alone at his battery, served a field gun single-handed until killed at his gun. The great bravery of this officer aroused the admiration of all ranks." [38]

Leaving aside the controversial reasons for the inclusion of these remarks, it is certainly the case that once they became known post war in Germany, considerable interest was aroused. The subject was not addressed in the regimental history of Field Artillery Regiment 108, because that appeared as early as 1919 and, initially, it was thought that, because an officer was specifically mentioned, it might have been Leutnant Müller, battery officer [= gun position officer] of 6th Battery. One of the reasons for this was probably that this battery, which claimed twelve tanks destroyed, enjoyed the greatest success that day. However, more detailed work in the late 1920s, including close questioning of survivors, narrowed the search down and it became clear that, in all probability, the man involved was Unteroffizier Theodor Krüger of 8th Battery. Krüger's gun was located on the boundary between Sectors *R1* and *R2*, about one kilometre east of the Flesquières sugar refinery. There witnesses reported that he did indeed continue to serve his gun completely alone as one by one his comrades became casualties and he was last seen standing firing his pistol as the British attacking troops closed in, until he, too, fell dead.[39]

It was extremely fortunate for the defence that, coincidental with the approach of the tanks, came the first significant improvement in the weather and general visibility as the fog cleared. Almost without the need for orders, such was the standard of training of Field Artillery Regiment 108, the guns moved rapidly into dominating open positions and began to engage the advancing tanks. It was later claimed that these guns knocked out fifty two tanks with direct fire[40] and, although the exact figure might be disputed, there can be little doubt that all the practice of the previous months paid off at the critical moment and that large numbers were destroyed or immobilised. The field howitzers of 6th Battery Field Artillery Regiment 108, for example, commanded by Landwehr Leutnant Kurz, accounted for no fewer than twelve tanks, despite the slower rate of fire of the howitzers as compared to the more generally available field guns. It was perhaps fortunate for the British assault that so much of it during the early stages took place in extremely poor visibility. Had the tanks come under aimed artillery fire earlier in the morning, the course of the day could have been quite different.[41]

There was also success for the guns elsewhere along the front. Even though it was not until 4.00 am on 20 November that sub units of Field Artillery Regiment 213 of 107th Infantry Division received some ammunition – in inadequate quantities and of a type unsuitable for anti-tank engagements – nevertheless their guns were in most cases well placed to intervene once the battlefield obscuration had cleared. 4th Battery, for example, located just to the north of 1st Battery Landwehr Foot Artillery Battalion 37, 1100 metres southwest of Graincourt, more than held their own until their guns were knocked out and they were seriously outflanked.

Leutnant Jakubasch 4th Battery Field Artillery Regiment 213 [42]

"In response to flares the battery fired defensive fire in the direction of Trescault at about 7.00 am. A British aircraft circled over our position and reported it, because we were suddenly engaged with heavy artillery fire. About 10.00 am one of our guns was knocked out by a direct hit and, simultaneously, the infantry began to flood to the rear through our position. There were large numbers of enemy aircraft about then, towards 11.00 am, tanks suddenly appeared to our front around Flesquières. In order to be able to engage them successfully we pulled the two serviceable guns out of their covered pits and moved them forward to where we could engage them with direct fire. With the manpower we had available it was not possible to push them up the steep slope to our front in order to obtain a perfect position.

"I ordered sights to be set at 700 metres and, with our third shot, we knocked out a tank. In short order we followed this with three more, then suddenly one of our guns failed mechanically. I then continued with my one remaining gun and dealt with four more tanks – the last of them at a range of eight hundred metres – so my total score was eight. In the meantime the British infantry had closed in to within four hundred metres and there was a tank already on our flank. As a result the battery position began to be engaged with tank main armament and machine gun fire, as well as small arms fire, from the south and southeast.

"The neighbouring 1st Battery Foot Artillery Battalion 37 (Heavy Field Howitzer 02) had long since evacuated their position...In order not to be captured I first removed the breech assembly from the last serviceable gun and, together with a few faithful comrades, withdrew. On our way we frequently had to take cover in shell holes because we were under more or less constant machine gun attack from low flying British aircraft. We were in a wretched state when we finally rejoined our limbers in Proville."

In the event, weight of numbers prevailed and, by between 3.00 pm and 4.00 pm, the majority of the German infantry gun lines had been overrun and lost. The explanation was quite simple. Quite apart from the strength of the assaulting troops, the German gunners had no more ammunition to fire. All day long the batteries had been sending urgent requests for replenishment, but the necessity to supply the five batteries of Field Artillery Regiment 213 and the guns of 20th Landwehr Division from the meagre stocks held forward ruled this out; the 4,600 shells were soon expended and, by evening on 20 November, only one field gun and one howitzer of Field Artillery Regiment 108 were still firing.[43] There was nothing for it in Flesquières but for the embattled troops of Reserve Infantry Regiment 27 under the valiant Major Krebs to hold on and trust to their own efforts in an attempt to retain possession of this vital sector.

Back in the *Zwischenstellung* Hauptmann Fürsen, who had been forced by enemy pressure to move his command post to the area of the battlefield cemetery and sugar refinery [known as *Süßer Emil* = Sweet Emil] about 500 metres northeast of Flesquières, set about rounding up all troops and stragglers who were making their way to the rear in order to bolster the defence of this critical sector. All of them, infantrymen, gunners and sappers were halted and placed in defensive positions, prior to being used as a reserve. Those who had arrived without personal weapons were directed to the artillery to help move shells to the guns. Setting a first class example of coolness and courage, Fürsen helped check what might have escalated into panic. Leaving Fähnrich Carstens, Fürsen, accompanied by his adjutant and his recently assembled sixty strong band of men, headed for regimental headquarters, now commanded by Major Krebs, Reserve Infantry Regiment 27, to receive orders. He was directed to attempt to link up with 2nd Battalion Reserve Infantry Regiment 27 and he set about the task immediately.

Advancing along the low ground between Ribécourt and Marcoing, the first of the tanks was approaching the latter at around 11.00 am. At that time Offizierstellvertreter Bergmann, Reserve Infantry Regiment 27, was in command. Hurriedly assembling whatever personnel he could find, Bergmann set about defending the village for as long as possible.

Musketier Walter Neumann Signal Detachment Reserve Infantry Regiment 27 [44]

"The fire had stopped. The gunners pulled back and explained that the Tommies had already reached the Market Place in Marcoing. In other words, they were about five minutes away from us. As we pulled on our equipment we could hear the crack of rifle bullets in the streets. Just as we were emerging from a house, a tank drove straight past us. Together with five other men, I rushed up behind the tank and dealt with the crew, all of whom burnt to death."

Unteroffizier Thiele 12th Company Reserve Infantry Regiment 27 [45]

"Suddenly the shout went up, 'Here come the Tommies with tanks'. A comrade and I rushed off to the western exit to the village, so as to put ourselves at the disposal of the local commander. As we moved along behind the last houses in the village a tank had already broken into the village. We were outnumbered by the twenty to twenty five British soldiers who were following the tank. My comrade wanted to pull back into the village, but I shouted, 'Come on man, turn and face them and let's see what happens!' We managed to get off two or three shots, then the enemy was upon us. I looked around for support, but in vain. Resistance was pointless. Gritting my teeth I stood in front of the sergeant who was in command of the party and who held his bayonet to my chest. We were then completely plundered: money, wallet, pocket knife, comb, epaulettes, Iron Cross ribbon. Everything was taken off me, even my handkerchief, which my 'conqueror' threw away. As I attempted to retrieve it I was prevented by the bayonet from doing so. The first grab was for my watch pocket, so I secretly pushed my wristwatch further up my arm and so was able to save it."[46]

Offizierstellvertreter Otto Alt 4th Company Reserve Infantry Regiment 27 [47]

"Our 4th Company was deployed on the left flank of the battalion. From here we had superb fields of fire. The Tommies were pouring fire on us. When their heavy shells burst they sent up fountains of earth as tall as houses. It was not long before we heard the clatter and rumble of tanks approaching us from the dip in the ground to our front. Some hove into view, spewing fire, climbing the slopes unstoppably towards our positions and breaking into them. Some of our valiant comrades, with Küster, Zimmers and Bader to the fore, launched themselves at these puffing, fire breathing monsters with hand grenades and, having caused explosions in their fuel and ammunition, succeeded in bringing some of them to a halt in front of and on our position, whilst their crews tried to abandon their blazing vehicles. One tank was forced to turn away after well-aimed fire was directed against its viewing slits and one tank crew – Scots in kilts – was successfully captured.[48]

"It was our gunners who were able to deal quickly and most effectively with these 'mobile forts'. At close quarters, with direct fire, our courageous artillery, which unfortunately only had a few guns, destroyed all tanks within range. An impressive number of these expensive pieces of fighting equipment was strewn around the extensive battlefield like so much scrap iron. These devices, designed to clear the way for the infantry and upon which the enemy set such store, failed here. For us the battle with the infantry which followed up immediately after the tanks came next and we prevented a breakthrough. This battle was fought hard everywhere and was very bloody. On the left flank of our neighbouring company and our right, a group of Tommies broke into the trench. With shouts of *Hurra*, they were ejected once more by the neighbouring company. Those who broke in on our right flank were dealt with through the use of grenades, mainly by Zimmers, Küster and Bader. Not one single Tommy forced his way into our left hand platoon.

"Well aimed heavy fire caused the enemy considerable casualties and their repeated attempts to conduct energetic assaults withered away immediately in front of our lines. Unfortunately our losses, during the battle with the tanks as well as the infantry, were also rather heavy. My friend and compatriot Bader received a serious head wound. Zimmers, too, that unshakeable dare devil, also had to leave the position after he was wounded, as did many other comrades from the company.

At about 11.45 am the situation to the west in the Flesquières sector was as follows: despite all efforts, position by position, the remaining forward parties of Reserve Infantry Regiment 27 and Infantry Regiment 84 had been fought to a standstill, overwhelmed and killed or captured. In *R1* the British had advanced to the second line of the *Zwischenstellung* at Flesquières village and were forward of the park, just to the north of *Großer Stern*. Hauptmann Fürsen's *ad hoc* reserve was in position in Flesquières park ready to conduct a local counter-stroke if necessary. Following a fire fight with units of the 51st (Highland) Division, this is precisely what happened around midday. Meanwhile the pace of the battle began to quicken for those defenders manning positions in the village or remaining in reserve in the catacombs near the church.

Leutnant Brockes 2nd Company Reserve Infantry Regiment 27 [49]

"Outside the *Pionierpark* [Engineer Park, located three hundred metres south of Flesquières church], I heard a roaring noise coming from both sides of the trench, which was probably caused by British tanks. An instant later I bumped into advancing British soldiers. Because I had no sort of weapon with me, I raced backwards as fast as I could go until I came across some hand grenades lying on the edge of the trench. I took them and moved forward a few metres and threw them at the British."

This situation had developed because of the location of the defending troops, the bulk of whom, operating forward of Flesquières, were either in *Havrincourtgraben* or *Grenzweg*, or clustered in the Intermediate Position southwest of the village or around the junction of *Grenzweg* and the *K1* line near *Großer Stern* southeast of it. This left sizeable gaps in the *Pionierpark* [Engineer Park] sector which the British troops were able to exploit, especially because of the very poor visibility that morning. As the dangerous situation became clear, troops from 1st Battalion Reserve Infantry Regiment 27 were rushed into position to parry the attack, 2nd Company going straight into action.

Musketier Seiffert 2nd Company Reserve Infantry Regiment 27 [50]

> "Up until then we had suffered very few casualties. We had no proper contact to our left or right. Suddenly we spotted Tommies forty to fifty metres to our front. We defended the *Pionierpark* and drew great satisfaction from it. We fired light machine guns, grenade launchers and threw hand grenades in profusion."

Deciding that the main danger lay on his right flank from British troops who had already broken into Flesquères, Leutnant Brockes took over the right hand platoon.

Leutnant Brockes 2nd Company Reserve Infantry Regiment 27 [51]

> "I moved initially to the hedge at the northwest end of the park and brought down fire on the British who had already forced their way in strength into the village along the line of the road from Havrincourt. At that the British pulled back into an area of dense scrub behind a hedge and returned rapid fire. We worked our way forward in bounds, but our losses from the heavy fire were so high that I felt it better to take cover in the shell holes some two hundred metres short of the village and to send out contact patrols to the right and rear."

Whilst Brockes was thus occupied, his company commander, Reserve Leutnant Höfer, was drawing on the local knowledge of Leutnants Ofenbrück and Bielenberg of Infantry Regiment 84 to organise a sharp local assault which regained the southern boundary wall of the eastern end of the park – but at the cost of his own mortal wounding.

Musketier Seiffert 2nd Company Reserve Infantry Regiment 27 [52]

> "It was not long before the Tommies took to their heels. Because we attacked with great aggression, they must have assumed that we were there in strength. I should also like to make mention of the fact that, in the course of what was effectively hand-to-hand fighting, our company commander, Leutnant Höfer and a Feldwebelleutnant [Hausmann: Infantry Regiment 84] were shot right before my eyes. We were all saddened by this, but it did not affect our will to fight. We then occupied positions that the Tommies had vacated. From there we had open fields of fire and we brought down a heavy weight of fire on the enemy with our light machine gun."

A slightly different and somewhat breathlessly written version of these events appeared later.

Leutnant Ofenbrück Orderly Officer 3rd Battalion Infantry Regiment 84 [53]

"Gather together anyone you can find and launch a counter-stroke against the *Havrincourt-Riegel!*' – Yes sir! (Major Hofmeister). A company of Reserve Infantry Regiment 27 emerged from the village where they were in danger of running straight into two tanks located at the crossroads. 'Halt! Tanks! Move right into the *Pionierpark!*' In no time I was there too. Two officers of the other company introduced themselves. 'No time to lose! Counterstroke in this direction! Deploy right! Further forward on the right! You, on the left, up and out of cover!'

"Herr Leutnant There they are.' 'Where? Open fire lads! Machine gun over here! Rapid fire!' 'It's jammed!' 'Then use hand grenades! Up and at 'em. Charge! Leutnant Brockes take the right flank, let's go! Leutnant Höfer push forward with your platoon!' Tac-tac-tac-tac! The tank at the crossroads engages the tops of the trees with its machine gun. 'OK lads, go! Forwards! Can't you see that it is shooting at the trees?!' 'Herr Leutnant a tank behind us is driving into the village.' 'Never mind; let it go. The artillery will deal with it as it emerges. Double march! *Hurra!*' 'Herr Leutnant the tank is still moving' '*Donnerwetter!* Let it go. Forwards, let's go!'

"Tac-tac-tac-tac! Boom! Crash! There is a stink of phosphorous. The tank in the village really is engaging us now. Calm is essential. 'Everyone take cover! The enemy must not get any closer. Machine gun forward; man the piles of sand. Leutnant Hausmann, remain with the machine gun.' Tac-tac-tac-tac! Leutnant Hausmann is shot in the stomach. 'Two volunteers forward!' Leutnant Höfer is also hit in the stomach. Leutnant Bielenberg, Take over command! This line is going to be held. I shall go and fetch reinforcements.' The British pulled back into Flesquières at a trot and their tank was soon dealt with."[54]

When it came time to recall the events of the history of Infantry Regiment 84, Ofenbrück had toned down his remarks somewhat, but his thrust remained the same.

Reserve Leutnant Ofenbrück 3rd Battalion Infantry Regiment 84 [55]

"When, at 10.00 am, two tanks approached the southern corner of Flesquières Park, I reported this orally to the regimental commander, Major Hofmeister. He then gave me the task of informing Hauptmann Fürsen that he was to conduct a counter-stroke with 10th and 12th Companies Infantry Regiment 84 in order to extract those elements of Reserve Infantry Regiment 27, under Major Stubenrauch, which were cut off in the *Havrincourt-Riegel.* 10th and 12th Companies, however, had already launched a counter-stroke at 9.00 am and I was not able to reach them. I then bumped into 2nd Company Reserve Infantry Regiment 27 at the entrance to the engineer park of Infantry Regiment 84, who risked running straight into the clutches of the tanks which had halted near Flesquières. I directed them into the engineer park.

"Towards 10.30 am, the enemy had closed in on the village from the line Flesquières cemetery – *K1* Line of the *Zwischenstellung* and had already set foot in the western section of the Park. I assumed command of 2nd Company Reserve Infantry Regiment 27 and had them occupy a defensive line. During the course of a counter-stroke, where I was well supported by Leutnants Brockes and Höfer of Reserve Infantry Regiment 27 and Landwehr Leutnant Bielenberg and Feldwebel-Leutnant Hausmann of Infantry Regiment 84, I worked my way forward. During the counter-stroke, we came under heavy fire from a tank which was moving through Flesquières and it was extremely difficult for me to hold the terrified men in check. In fact I only succeeded thanks to the support of the above mentioned officers, Landwehr Leutnant Bielenberg in particular, and approximately two sections of Infantry Regiment 84.

"At about 11.00 am I handed over command responsibility for this section of the line to Landwehr Leutnant Bielenberg, whilst I went and reported the success to Major Krebs (Reserve Infantry Regiment 27) and requested support. Unfortunately I did not receive any, but all remaining members of Infantry Regiment 84 were deployed in a fresh counter-stroke. Commanded by Hauptmann Fürsen, this achieved a shining success. The whole of Flesquières Park was cleared and we went firm in the second line of the Intermediate Position. We then sealed off *Kabelgraben* and occupied the southern edge of the Park as far as Red Point 8512, with the remaining elements of 2nd Company Reserve Infantry Regiment 27, who gradually trickled in. Because of lack of troops and the approach of two tanks from Flesquières cemetery, this line had to be withdrawn. There the remainder of 2nd Company Reserve Infantry Regiment 27 and Infantry Regiment 84 held until 5.00 am on 21 November. Had sufficient support been available for the counter-strokes, the *Zwischenstellung* could have been held easily."

This bold action enjoyed some success and the German defenders were once more in control of the village itself, the engineer park and the second line of the *Zwischenstellung* as far as *Havrincourtgraben*. Furthermore they had made a definite contribution to the battle. Delay had been imposed on the British advance, effort had to be deployed and therefore dispersed to deal with pockets of resistance in and around the approach to Flesquières. As a result some of the impetus was lost from the attack and time was provided for additional reinforcements to make it through to Flesquières, which was to become the primary focus of the fighting during the coming hours. Naturally there had been further losses. Hauptmann Fürsen was wounded eleven times by fragments when a grenade exploded, forcing him to hand over command to Oberleutnant Nissen, who was to suffer the same fate later in the day. During the final hours at Flesquières, the remnants of Infantry Regiment 84 were commanded by Reserve Leutnant Ofenbrück.

To the north of Infantry Regiment 84, the formations of 20th Landwehr Division simply buckled under the violence of the initial attack. As soon as Havrincourt, which was inclusive to Infantry Regiment 84, fell, the British thrust through the depth of the adjacent sector of Infantry Regiment 384 simply could not be held. The extreme weakness of this regiment after a severe mauling in Flanders earlier, the total absence of battle casualty replacements, the lack of mortars and grenade launchers, which had had to be left behind near Ypres, meant that the regiment was in no shape to defend a four kilometre frontage against any sort of attack, let alone one of this unprecedented nature. So depleted was it that no fewer than ten of its twelve companies had to be deployed in the front line.[56] All initial attempts to counter the advance of the tanks having failed utterly, the defenders quickly gave ground and attempted to conduct a fighting withdrawal through the various communication and battle trenches. Advancing tanks pressed on unstoppably and were soon manoeuvring around the *Zwischenstellung* to the west of Flesquières. One of the main difficulties was the lack of visibility. The small arms fire, hand grenades and mortar bombs used by the defenders completely failed to halt the advance and tanks appeared continually out to a flank, or in rear, of the few pockets of resistance. One sub-sector after another fell and in many cases the defenders, outflanked, were simply cut off and captured. A final desperate attempt was made by men of 5th and 6th Companies and some fragmented elements of 3rd Battalion, who had broken out to the rear, to hold out in the *Zwischenstellung* southwest of Graincourt, but no reinforcements appeared, ammunition ran out and there was no resupply. The scattered remnants appeared later at Cantaing, which had originally been the location of the rest billets of regimental headquarters. When the roll was called later that evening back at Proville, on the southwest outskirts of Cambrai, there was still a total lack of clarity about the losses. The best that could be recorded was that the regiment, already grossly understrength, had suffered casualties of three killed, thirty seven wounded and 1,135 missing.[57] Already weak before the battle opened, it had effectively been wiped off the order of battle.

As the tanks appeared just to the southwest of Graincourt, batteries of 1st Battalion Field Artillery Regiment 282 and 2nd Battalion Field Artillery Regiment 213 opened direct fire on them, whilst the heavier artillery - 6th

Battery Landwehr Foot Artillery Battalion 32, 3rd Battery Landwehr Foot Artillery Battalion 37 and 6th Battery Landwehr Foot Artillery Battalion 61 – equipped with a motley assortment of captured weapons, fired off the remainder of its very limited stock of ammunition against the approaching infantry. This fire was, however, not very effective. Counter-battery fire by the British artillery had already accounted for all three remaining guns of 6th Battery Field Artillery Regiment 213, whilst two field guns of 1st Battery Field Artillery Regiment 282 were buried and badly damaged. Its 2nd Battalion had some limited success against tanks operating to the north of Flesquières, but it was not possible to haul some of the guns out of their pits, so they could not be used and gradually the battery positions were overrun and the weapons had to be abandoned.

Around midday and into the afternoon, some guns of 1st and 2nd Batteries Field Artillery Regiment 282 were able to continue to fire from positions in and around Graincourt, but finally they and the remaining guns of 5th Battery Field Artillery Regiment 213, located about 500 metres southwest of the village, fell silent as the last of their ammunition was fired off towards 3.00 pm. Just to one side of the main assault, the British made attempts to expand their break in the direction of the Bapaume – Cambrai road. Infantry Regiment 386, the right forward formation of 20th Landwehr Division, which had initially been under heavy fire when the bombardment opened, noted with some disquiet that everything had been calm on its front since 8.30 am. To the left the noise of battle could be heard through the fog, but the situation was completely unclear. Towards midday the sector came under heavy artillery bombardment once more and patrols were sent out by the flank companies to find out what was going on.

Their reports, coupled with stories told by stragglers from the overrun Infantry Regiment 384, indicated that the deep British thrust was threatening to cut them off from the rear. In an attempt to counter any such development, the divisional artillery commander, Major Vollerthun, had ordered 4th and 5th Batteries Field Artillery Regiment 282 to move some of their guns into open positions near the sugar refinery northwest of Graincourt on the main Bapaume-Cambrai road. From there, as the visibility improved, they enjoyed success against both tanks and infantry but overall the threat of being outflanked meant that it proved to be impossible for the units of Infantry regiment 386 to hold south of the road and 2nd and 3rd Battalion (which came rushing forward from reserve) moved to take up positions in front line trench of the *Zwischenstellung*. The commanding officer of the 3rd Battalion, Reserve Hauptmann Erlinghagen, extended the line east along the road in the direction of Anneux and despatched patrols in an attempt to link up to the left. This was not successful and there appeared to be a wide gap in the defences and little to prevent the British from thrusting right up to Cambrai.

To the south of Infantry Regiment 84, where the front line was being held by Infantry Regiment 387, the situation quickly became critical. All communications failed as soon as the attack began and no runners were able to get back to report the situation to the regimental commander. As a result, an hour and a half after the assault began, he reported to Generalleutnant von Watter at Headquarters 54th Infantry Division that all was quiet in his sector. It was almost a case of famous last words when, just a few minutes later, he realised that his own command post was directly threatened by tanks. His regiment had been totally knocked out of the battle, its members, all bar a few, killed or captured.[58] Similarly, operating down on the southern flank of the 54th Infantry Division sector, the inexperienced troops of Infantry Regiment 376 were simply brushed aside by the attack. Its troops, already unnerved by the weight of bombardment and such extensive use of incendiary shells and mortar bombs that the entire front appeared to be in flames, gave ground rapidly or simply surrendered in the face of the tank assault.

Naturally it had not been anticipated that Infantry Regiment 376 would have to do anything more than man a quiet sector of the front. Only a few days previously it had been deployed on the Russian front; it was certainly not fitted in terms of manpower, training or equipment to repel an attack of the violence of this one. Its failure meant that the British were able to make a further deep thrust – this time between Infantry Regiment 84 and Reserve Infantry Regiment 90 which was defending La Vacquerie. There was considerable consternation in the command post of the latter as the news from the front became ever more serious, then finally dried up as one point of resistance after another was overwhelmed. At 8.00 am a report from the front, sent using the earth telegraph system, contained the information that the outpost line and forward trenches had already been overrun. The news that the great belts of wire, in which so much trust had been placed, had simply been flattened by the tanks as though they were beds of brambles came as a profound shock.

The plan in the event of an attack in this area had been for the right hand battalion of 9th Reserve Division to come under command of Reserve Infantry Regiment 90, the left forward formation of 54th Infantry Division. It was just possible to pass a warning order before the hail of shells of all calibres came down so violently around the command post that all external communications, with the exception of a deeply buried cable running back to Brigade headquarters, were severed: never to be re-established, despite the continuing heroic efforts of the signallers. Runners began arriving at regular intervals bearing the most urgent requests: for artillery support; for reinforcements; for ammunition resupply; but there was little that could be done, especially by the artillery, which began the battle under strength and was suffering the repeated loss of guns as they were caught under the bombardment which was creeping forward from one pre-registered target to another. Finally fewer runners arrived and the earth telegraph system fell quiet as its operator was overrun. The regimental adjutant later recalled:

Leutnant Bibeljé-Schwerin Adjutant Reserve Infantry Regiment 90 [59]

"The situation became more and more serious. The Brigade commander was given a short orientation briefing by telephone and support was requested very, very urgently, because the enemy, supported by tanks, was advancing unstoppably. I can remember very clearly the brigade adjutant informing me that the 90th was performing brilliantly in comparison with our neighbours the 376th, in whose sector the tanks had already crossed the *Zwischenstellung*. We could no longer bear to remain in the command post. The flow of reports from the front had dried up, we could not plan on receiving any support from the rear, so out we went where every man who could fire a weapon was required.

"As we emerged into the trench we could see clearly off to our right individual tanks crossing the hills northeast of Marcoing and heading towards the low ground in the direction of Noyelles. In our regimental sector we could see them advancing towards us in line and some of them were already uncomfortably close. Altogether that day our ten kilometre divisional sector was attacked by 350 – 400 tanks, which advanced deeply echeloned. The infantry held on well, tackling the dark monsters, which sprayed machine gun and small calibre shells from their interiors, with armour-piercing ammunition and bundles of hand grenades. Great fascines sat on top of the tanks, which could be released from within the tank if it had to negotiate a particularly wide trench. As a result, not even the relatively wide trenches of the *Siegfriedstellung* posed much of an obstacle and, even though they moved only slowly, these dreadful machines of war advanced surely and steadily.

"Now and then our artillery succeeded in scoring a direct hit. Even a 75mm shell could wreck a tank, or at least bring it to a halt and thus remove it from the battle. I personally counted a dozen burning tanks in front of our position, but what was this tiny number compared with the great mass which finally succeeded in capturing the second line of the First Position and was now bearing down on the *Zwischenstellung*? Some of our infantry, unable to hold off the enemy any longer, pulled back; others allowed the tanks to bypass them calmly, then brought down murderous fire on the British infantry which was following hard up behind the protective steel walls of the fire-spewing machines.

"But some tanks halted at the edge of the trenches and brought down enfilading fire on our trench garrison. This fire from a flank drove the now helpless infantry down into the dugouts, into which the tanks poured fire or which were set on fire by the enemy infantry, which was equipped with incendiary grenades for the purpose. So, gradually, the enemy arrived in front of the first line of the *Zwischenstellung*. Some of our men still held out in *Widerstandsnester (Widas)*, but they must have felt that the cause was hopeless. Three or more of the terrible black monsters drove up to these *Widas* and fired at them with their guns until resistance died away and eventually they fell silent.

"Towards 11.00 am the enemy artillery fire slackened temporarily. Apparently they were moving their artillery further forward. At the same time we saw fresh enemy tanks rolling forward bringing up ammunition and fuel. Out of others sprang six to eight infantrymen who had been carried forward under armoured protection.[60] This was the point when the regimental command post ought to have been withdrawn more to the rear. My proposal to this effect was rejected by the regimental commander, who quite rightly feared that a move to the rear by the staff would be taken by those fighting brilliantly to our left and right as a general signal for retreat. So, with the exception of the artillery commander who moved back after the last of our guns was knocked out by a direct hit, we stayed where we were as the danger became ever more acute.

"At the very moment that the enemy began once more to bring down extraordinarily heavy fire, we received word that Reserve Infantry Regiment 227 had been despatched forward to support us. The divisional commander himself [Generalleutnant von Watter] informed us by telephone that its units had set off from Cambrai at 9.00 am and he was quite amazed to hear that not even its leading elements had yet reached us. In actual fact only one of the battalions of the regiment had arrived at Masnières. The other two became held up, then embroiled, in heavy clashes with enemy advancing from Noyelles and Cantaing. The single battalion decided that the counterstroke ordered by us offered absolutely no chance of success. Instead it took up positions along the northern bank of the canal in the sector from east of Masnières to the area of Marcoing. Here and in the direction of Marcoing everyone capable of handling a weapon was thrown into the breach. The final divisional reserve, Storm Detachment Pries, was transported by lorry from Cambrai, divided between the regiments and helped their remnants to stem the violent assault.

"Perhaps it would have been more appropriate to evacuate the positions that we held around 11.00 am and to fall back on the line of the canal. We did not realise at that time that Pionier Kompanie [Engineer Company] 108 had not managed to blow the sturdy stone bridge that spanned the canal at Marcoing and so make a further advance by the tanks impossible. There was another strong bridge over the canal at Masnières, but this one was at least so weakened that the first tank which attempted to cross it and so enter Masnières collapsed it and sank in the river, together with an officer and several other ranks.[61] Meanwhile we remained where we were and continued to defend our positions, which had become the front line. Right and left of us British infantry pressed forward. Elements of the enemy column advancing through the *Herzogsschlucht* [Duke's Ravine] veered off to the left and cut us off. Five tanks, which we could not counter, began to pour fire into our section of trench, which was about one hundred metres long and was being defended on all four sides by about forty men and one light machine gun.

"The ammunition began to run low. All the grenades had been thrown and the light machine gun only had about twenty rounds left. In contrast to our comrades of Infantry Regiment 84 who, having been encircled in Flesquières for over a day, managed to make their way through enemy lines back to the German ones, we did not succeed. Just before 1.00 pm we conducted a further telephone conversation with division and spoke personally to the commander, *Excellenz* von Watter. We described the desperate position once more, he thanked us all again, then we had to smash the telephone switchboard and set the dugout on fire. All the maps were thrown on a straw palliasse and set on fire. Soon all the wooden items in the dugout were blazing. Up above the regimental commander had ordered bayonets to be fixed and bitter hand to hand fighting began. In this the British had two advantages. They had ammunition and they could either fire or stab downwards at us; whereas we, lacking a single bullet, could only defend ourselves by lunging upwards [with our bayonets].

"Whilst we were fighting for our lives with the courage of desperation, men such as Reserve Leutnant Demant and Feldwebelleutnant Nehmer sealed their loyalty to the Fatherland in blood through their deaths and, further to the rear, bitter fighting was taking place at the canal. Hauptmann von Both, the regimental machine gun officer, who was primarily responsible for organising the resistance in Masnières, Hauptmann von Milczewsk, commanding officer of 2nd Battalion Reserve Infantry Regiment 90 and Reserve Leutnant Quantmeyer distinguished themselves particularly in this action. The commanding officer of 1st Battalion, Hauptmann Grebel, was seriously wounded in the arm; the same shell killing his faithful adjutant, Harder...

"It is impossible to describe each of the thousands of incidents which showed that our brave men of 1917 fought with the old 1914 spirit, nor how young and old, active and reserve officers gave their best, their noblest, for the Fatherland. We were defeated by overwhelming numbers of the enemy and their superior technical war material. So confident was the enemy of success that they had readied several cavalry brigades to follow up defeated opponents and, if possible, to occupy Cambrai that same day.[62] The way that both riders and horses were wiped out was pitiful to behold."

The day had begun badly for 54th Infantry Division and, for its commander personally, things were about to get worse. He was operating with only inadequate, inaccurate information to guide him. The Landwehr regiments under his command had failed completely when put to the test and he had already deployed his main reserve, Reserve Infantry Regiment 27, in an attempt to bolster the critical Flesquières position. He had told his forward regiments in good faith that formations of 107th Infantry Division were hurrying forward to reinforce them and now he realised that somehow this critical part of his plan had unravelled. Despatching one of his staff officers to investigate, he must have felt as though he had betrayed the trust of all his subordinate commanders and their men, as he sat in his headquarters maintaining an air of calm, so as to set a good example to his staff, whilst outside all was chaos and uncertainty.

Notes

1. *Erinnerungsblätter der ehemaligen Mansteiner 4. Folge Nr 7* p 60
2. Inevitably the various witness reported that the opening bombardment began at different times ranging from 7.00-7.30 am. In fact the first shells were fired at 7.20 am and the armour moved simultaneously.
3. *Erinnerungsblätter der ehemaligen Mansteiner 4. Folge Nr 10* pp 84-85
4. *Erinnerungsblätter der ehemaligen Mansteiner 4. Folge Nr 8* p 86
5. *Erinnerungsblätter der ehemaligen Mansteiner 4. Folge Nr 8 & 9* pp 71-75
6. Tanks participating in the attack used various colours of flags or panels to indicate their function or to provide information to others on the battlefield. White panels were meant to be displayed on the roofs of knocked out or immobilised tanks and blue and white flags were used to indicate the centre tank of each section of three – certainly within 51st (Highland Division). It is not completely clear in this case what the function of the white flag was, or even if the witness was reporting accurately what he had seen.
7. *Erinnerungsblätter der ehemaligen Mansteiner 4. Folge Nr 8* pp 65-67

8. *Erinnerungsblätter der ehemaligen Mansteiner 4. Folge Nr 10* p 90
9. *Erinnerungsblätter der ehemaligen Mansteiner 4. Folge Nr 8 & 9* pp 71-75
10. Dahlmann: History Reserve Infantry Regiment 27 p 355
11. *ibid.* p 358
12. Oertinger is a German surname, so the probability is that this stop line was named after an officer associated in some way with its construction.
13. *General Oskar Freiherr von Watter* p 84
14. Dahlmann: *op. cit.* p 358
15. *ibid.* pp 362-364
16. Reserve Leutnant Gerhard Patzer died aged twenty two. He is buried in the *Kamaradengrab* of the German cemetery at Neuville St Vaast/Maison Blanche.
17. Dahlmann: *op.cit.* pp 364-365
18. *ibid.* p 365
19. Dahlmann: *op.cit* pp 355-356
20. *ibid.* p 356
21. *ibid.* pp 365-366
22. *ibid.* p 366
23. There are such constant references in the German literature to British attackers being drunk that it appears almost to have been a standard expression. There is little reliable evidence to show that there is any real truth in these statements.
24. Dahlmann: *op.cit.* p 366
25. *ibid.* p 367
26. Here Senftleben is quoting from the poem *Ich hatt' einen Kamaraden* by Ludwig Uhland, which is the traditional German soldier's farewell to a fallen comrade.
27. Dahlmann: *op. cit.* p 368
28. *ibid.* p 368
29. Arnold: History Landwehr Infantry Regiment 384 p 13
30. Dahlmann: *op. cit.* p 360
31. *ibid.* p 360
32. It is probable that the identification was made because some of the British soldiers were wearing kilts. If so, this suggests that some of the party were actually infantrymen from the 51st (Highland) Division
33. Major Fritz Hofmeister, who was forty years of age when he died, had just returned to duty, having recovered from a minor wound suffered in Russia. He had previously fought with Infantry Regiment 84 from the beginning of hostilities. His body was moved to the German cemetery at Cambrai after the war and he is buried in the *Kamaradengrab*.
34. *Erinnerungsblätter der ehemaligen Mansteiner 4. Folge Nr 8* p 62

35. This is a reference to *Neufwald* = Nine Wood, which dominated the approaches to Noyelles and was occupied by 16th Battalion Middlesex Regiment at the time
36. *Erinnerungsblätter der ehemaligen Mansteiner 4. Folge Nr 12* pp 109-110
37. The full title of Infantry Regiment 84 was *Infanterie Regiment von Manstein (Schleswiges) Nr. 84*: hence *Mansteiners* as a short hand description of its members.
38. Dahlmann: *op. cit.* p 386
39. The Field Artillery Regiment 108 claim breaks down as follows: 1st Battery (Kuskop) 7; 2nd and 3rd Batteries (Müller and Roß) 6; 4th Battery (Vieth) 3; 5th Battery (Reusch) 2; 6th Battery (Lorenzen) 12; 7th Battery (Heller) 5; 8th Battery (Behrmann) 6; 8th Battery (Müller) 8. They also claimed that some tanks were forced to turn away as a result of their fire, but this cannot be substantiated in any meaningful way. See Rockstroh: History Field Artillery Regiment 108 p 97
40. Quoted by Cooper *The Ironclads of Cambrai* p 106
41. There is an interesting postscript to this story. In June 1966 the Bundeswehr, strictly constrained in its ability to draw on the history of the German army prior to 1945, nevertheless felt that this story of simple battlefield heroism, praised by a former enemy, could be utilised to inspire future generations. Accordingly, the artillery barracks in Kusel (Hunsrück) was named after him. It was the first time an NCO had been honoured in this manner. Unteroffizier Krüger Barracks is, at the time of writing, home to *Artillerlelehrregiment 345*.
42. *General Oskar Freiherr von Watter* p 144
43. Writing later, JFC Fuller, quoted by Cooper in *The Ironclads of Cambrai* p 105, claimed that, 'The hold-up on Flesquières Ridge was entirely due to faulty tactics. It would have been in no way disastrous had the infantry been on the heels of the tanks, for then they could have settled with the German gunners in a few minutes.' Of course Fuller felt that he had to defend the tanks against the general charge that their vulnerability against an organised anti-tank defence called their value into question, but it is also a classic example of a British writer failing to give the enemy any credit for a well fought engagement. As has already been described, Field Artillery Regiment 108 was at that time probably the best trained formation in the German army as far as anti-tank operations were concerned. Had the visibility been better earlier, it is entirely possible that its guns would have been taking out British tanks long before either they or any accompanying infantry – regardless of their spacing – would have been in a position to do anything about it.
44. History Field Artillery Regiment 213 pp 160-161
45. Rockstroh: History Field Artillery Regiment 108 p 96

46. Dahlmann: *op. cit.* p 360
47. *ibid.* p 361
48. Thiele was not held prisoner for long. He and another man succeeded in escaping from a prison camp on 26 January 1918 and, after a series of adventures, managed to regain the German lines. For this feat he was awarded the Iron Cross First Class.
49. *Mitteilungen des Reserve-Infanterie-Regiments 27 Heft 24*
50. This seems improbable. It is far more likely that these were men of the 51st (Highland) Division.
51. Dahlmann: *op. cit.* p 370
52. *ibid.* p 372
53. *ibid.* p 372
54. *ibid.* p 372
55. *ibid.* p 373
56. This interpretation of events was strongly disputed by Reserve Infantry Regiment 27 after the war. In particular they objected to the suggestion that Ofenbrück had gripped the situation, had assumed command of a company of another regiment and taken its two officers under command. Be that as it may, it was clearly a critical moment and for a time the decisive action by the defenders had stabilised the situation, albeit temporarily.
57. *Erinnerungsblätter der ehemaligen Mansteiner 4. Folge Nr 8* p 61
58. Arnold: History Infantry Regiment 384 p 12
59. Strutz: *Die Tankschlacht bei Cambrai* p 50
60. *General Oskar Freiherr von Watter* p 84
61. Pries: History Reserve Infantry Regiment 90 pp 240-241
62. Whilst it is the case that old tanks were used to drag sledges carrying combat supplies forward, there are no properly attested accounts of troops being carried forward in tanks. It is possible that a few men managed to obtain a lift forward in this manner, but it is more probable that what was seen were groups of infantrymen who had moved forward using the armoured bulk of the tanks for protection from direct fire weapons.
63. This was tank F22 operating in support of 88 Brigade 29th Division. In fact the crew managed to escape through the hatches as the tank settled on the remains of the broken bridge.
64. This was far from the case. The dimensions of the break-in had caught both sides by surprise. In point of fact very little British cavalry was deployed forward on 20 November.

CHAPTER THREE

20 November 1917:
The Attack Continues

The mid-morning conversation involving Major Hermsdorf, commander Reserve Infantry Regiment 90, and Generalleutnant von Watter, commander 54th Infantry Division, was profoundly disturbing for the latter. As has been noted Watter, despite his previous night's assessment of the potential seriousness of the situation, had drawn some personal comfort as the attack opened from his belief that he had laid the groundwork for the initial deployment of reinforcements from 107th Infantry Division and that, should an attack occur on 20 November, he would be reasonably placed to counter it. His feelings when it dawned on him that the counter-stroke he had promised Reserve Infantry Regiment 90 was not underway and that the various forces he thought were at his disposal were not even ready for action, can barely be imagined.

Specifically, Watter had promised Hermsdorf that a regiment from 107th Infantry Division was already on its way to his location from assembly areas near Marcoing and that all he had to do was to hold on until he was reinforced. Not only that, he had also informed the command post of Infantry Regiment 84 in Flesquières at about 11.00 am that it was to launch an attack to recapture Havrincourt and that Reserve Infantry Regiment 52 of 107th Infantry Division was marching forward to come to its assistance and that of Infantry Regiment 387. Already concerned, however, that there had been no sign of reinforcements and no contact from Headquarters 107th Infantry Division, Generalleutnant von Watter had despatched his assistant divisional adjutant, Major von Finckh, to Cantaing at about 10.00 am, with orders to move via Marcoing, Masnières and Rumilly to link up directly with units of 107th Infantry Division and to ensure that his orders to them to get forward were being carried out. He was further to ensure that the defence of these localities and the canal bridges were all in hand.[1]

What von Watter could not know, however, was that his understanding of events was shared neither by Group Caudry nor 107th Infantry Division. Quite separately from the contact battle being fought by formations of 54th Infantry Division, once the extent of the crisis became clear, Reserve Infantry Regiments 52 and 227, together with 1st Battalion Field Artillery Regiment 213, had been brought to readiness at 9.00 am, but they were far from ready to move, being scattered around carrying out low level administration and training – in the case of Reserve Infantry Regiment 52 these were as far away as Carnières, Boussières and Bévillers to the east of Cambrai - and certainly not located forward as Watter had expected.

Finally, at 9.40 am, Group Caudry passed operation orders to 107th Infantry Division.[2] According to these orders, two battalions of Reserve Infantry Regiment 227 were to move under command of Reserve Infantry Regiment 90, crossing the canal at Masnières. A further battalion was to be despatched to 9th Reserve Division in Crèvecoeur. 1st Battalion Field Artillery Regiment 213 was subordinated to 54th Infantry Division and Reserve Infantry Regiment 52 was to occupy a blocking position along the line Fontaine – Proville in order to deny the approaches to Cambrai to the British from the southwest and west. 1st Battery Field Artillery Regiment 213, which had just been issued with new guns that morning, passed a quiet day moving into position at Fontaine Notre Dame but, as will be seen, the experience of the remainder of this unit that day was rather different.

Reserve Infantry Regiment 232 was directed to remain partly in Cambrai as army reserve and partly to take up screening positions along the line of the Canal de l'Escaut between Cantaing and Noyelles. At a time of such extreme crisis, this was a strange use of this formation but, according to the Group Caudry report referenced above, it came about as a consequence of a Second Army order dated 19 November. [3] In the event these orders were changed within little more than an hour, once messages came in from Infantry Regiment 387, desperately attempting to discover what had happened to the expected support from Reserve Infantry Regiment 52. The latter was then immediately placed under command of 54th Infantry Division and Reserve Infantry Regiment 232 was ordered to take up a semi-circular defensive line west and south west of Cambrai between Anneux and Rumilly.[4]

It is clear that Watter was still not fully clear about the overall situation during the late morning. Shortly after he had also reassured Reserve Infantry Regiment 27 at around 11.00 am that help was on the way, Leutnant Bertheau arrived from Infantry Regiment 84 to deliver a report concerning the situation at Flesquières. The 51st (Highland) Division, attacking with tank support, had established itself on the edge of the village. Firing over open sights, the artillery had engaged the tanks with considerable success and Hauptmann Soltau and his men of 2nd Battalion Infantry Regiment 84 were believed still to be fighting desperately in the front line against unequal odds.[5] Not that Bertheau was aware of it at that moment, but Hauptmann Soltau and all his party, including his adjutant, Leutnant Elson, and his machine gun officer, Leutnant Hinckeldeyn, were already dead, overwhelmed whilst trying to parry the advance. He was able, however, to pass on the news that Major Hofmeister, commander of Infantry Regiment 84, had been killed at his post in Flesquières and that Major Krebs, commander of Reserve Infantry Regiment 27, had assumed command.

After an anxious wait by the staff of Headquarters 54th Infantry Division,

Major von Finckh returned at midday to break the bad news that there was no sight of any of the formations of 107th Division in either Cantaing, Marcoing or Rumilly. It was a dreadful moment for Generalleutnant von Watter, faced as he was with all the signs of a major breakthrough and no reserve forces with which to counter it. Just as he was contemplating what to do next, into his headquarters walked Major Frühling, commander of Reserve Infantry Regiment 52. Watter later recalled greeting him by saying, 'Thank heavens! Has the enemy been ejected from Flesquières? How come you are here in person?' Frühling replied, 'I do not know anything about Flesquières. My regiment is on the march on the road leading from Le Cateau and I have come on ahead to be briefed.'[6] All that was left for Watter to do was to issue fresh orders and to make arrangements for the move forward of the reinforcing units to be accelerated by the use of trucks. For the time being matters were out of his hands. He could only keep his nerve and hope that those elements of 54th Division which were still fighting could hold out long enough to enable 107th Division to deploy and screen Cambrai.

To the south of the 54th Infantry Division sector, the men of 9th Reserve Division also experienced an extremely difficult day. It was a particular misfortune that, despite some slight warning that an attack might be in the offing, the already weak divisional artillery was further reduced just prior to the offensive. During the night 19/20 November the eight 90 mm field guns of 1st Battery Landwehr Foot Artillery Regiment 61 were pulled out of position. Their crews were sent to relieve the personnel of 874 Battery (150mm *'Ringkanonen'*[7]) who were withdrawn from the battle to be re-equipped with new weapons. In addition, one section of guns from 5th Battery Reserve Field Artillery Regiment 9 was switched to an isolated forward position by a tile works on the Le Pavé – Gouzeaucourt road.[8] Defending the sector from La Vacquerie southeast to Banteux, with its 1st Battalion right forward, 2nd Battalion left forward with 3rd Battalion in reserve, the units of Reserve Infantry Regiment 19 found themselves fighting for their lives almost from the moment the offensive opened. Initially the drum fire crashed down on the outposts and forward trenches then, a few moments later, this was lifted onto the second line and, after a further few minutes, there was a third lift. Advancing on a wide front against them came waves of tank, flattening the wire, pushing over trees and walls and catching the forward garrison once more completely by surprise. Later two of its officers, Reserve Leutnant Grieger, adjutant 1st Battalion, and Reserve Leutnant Kühnau, commanding 4th Company, which was located in depth positions behind 2nd Company in and around La Vacquerie, reported:[9]

"Day dawned. There was an unearthly silence all along the front. Would 20 November pass like all the previous quiet days? 7.00 am! The front line suddenly burst into flames as the drum fire came down with a crash. Nerves were stretched to breaking point. Where is the enemy? – Over there, looming through the fog, came huge black shapes – tanks – with, behind them, columns of infantry. Our battalion was deployed on the right flank of the enemy attack. The main thrust was directed against 2nd Company [defending La Vacquerie], commanded by Reserve Oberleutnant Meyer. A desperate battle developed. Small arms ammunition, hand grenades, even the S.m.K. ammunition was ineffective against the tanks. The artillery support in our sector failed completely.

"Fighting with inadequate weapons, with many of his men dead, wounded or captured, surrounded by tanks, Oberleutnant Meyer and his faithful companions had to give up their positions bit by bit. In constant contact with the enemy he arrived at the 4th Company sector, which had set up a blocking position with its machine gun nests and assault troops. Courageously, the crews of the light machine guns carried out their duty to the last but, once more, we had to accept that the enemy was fighting with weapons to which we had no counter. Unstoppable, the tanks pushed forwards, supported constantly by aircraft. Step by step, the remnants of the companies pulled back towards their left flank, exploiting every possibility to hold the enemy back.

"The tanks rolled up trench after trench, whilst we fought back with S.m.K. ammunition and hand grenades from such close range that we could observe their crews through the viewing slits as they aimed their guns at us from a mere thirty metres. From the *S1 Stellung* we withdrew across the Gouzeaucourt – Le Pavé road and so bumped into elements of 3rd Company under Leutnant Krüger. The foremost man in this desperate battle was Oberleutnant Meyer. Standing on the parapet and inspiring his men, he fired at the enemy, but soon fell mortally wounded, sealing his courageous behaviour with his death."

Leutnant Kühnau added, 'My little group of faithful comrades comprised almost the same men who had fought with me for the *Westfalenwald* [Westphalian Wood] during the Third Battle of Ypres. Close by me were my dear, faithful, platoon commanders, Offizierstellertreter Mittmann and Vizefeldwebel Lammers, together with Unteroffizier Reuther, who had received the Iron Cross First Class during the Battle of Arras in spring 1917 for daringly delivering an important report. Gefreiter Orth also distinguished himself greatly. Tirelessly he sought to bring his machine gun into action at every opportunity. I watched him as he engaged a tank at a range of thirty to forty metres. Step by step we were forced back along the *S2 Stellung* and there, where the field kitchens were established, the final stages of the battle were fought out. Surrounded by tanks which had crossed our trenches, there was nowhere else we could withdraw. We had to lay down our weapons. The battle was over about 11.00 am; we were prisoners.' It was a similar tale of disaster just to the south of the Gouzeaucourt – Le Pavé road.

Unteroffizier Sandt 1st Company Reserve Infantry Regiment 19 [10]

"I belonged to the Battalion 'Permanent Patrol Group'. Every second night, four men and an Unteroffizier of 1st and 2nd Companies under the command of an officer went on a reconnaissance patrol. On alternative nights this duty was done by 3rd and 4th Companies. There were no other duties for the participants and so it was that I used the opportunity to check out our own position, as a result of which I avoided being given 'lodgings' by the British. During the night 19 – 20 November the usual patrol went out under the command of Leutnant Damzog. The sound of digging could be heard clearly by the British wire and we assumed that damage, caused by a heavy mortar the previous afternoon, was being repaired. In reality work was being done to a sunken lane, which led from Gonnelieu to the Cambrai – Péronne road, in order to make it passable for tanks. At 4.00 am we returned 'home', none the wiser.

"At 7.00 am I was awakened in the dugout I shared with the commander of 1st Company [Reserve Leutnant Hofmann] by the sound of drum fire. Almost immediately one of the entrances to the dugout was collapsed. About 7.00 am the approach of tanks was observed. The effect on the morale of the young replacements, who had arrived after the *Flandernschlacht* [Third Battle of Ypres], was very considerable. Unteroffizier Ullmann, the commander of the grenade launcher, attempted to hit a tank. One round did hit, but it had no effect. The tanks closed up until they were uncomfortably close. We pulled back, moving partly across country and coming under heavy fire from the tanks. We fired frequently at the dense lines of infantrymen who were following up. Some of these men appeared to be drunk.[11] I watched as some individuals seemed to be dancing for joy, throwing their helmets into the air and catching them again.[12]

"In *S2* we met up with Leutnant Wintruff [a 1st Company platoon commander] and some men. Once more we fired at the tanks without damaging them and then pulled back along the valley leading towards Banteux as far as *Aichweg*. From the machine gun post there, Leutnant Wintruff engaged two of the approaching tanks with machine gun fire. When they continued, despite this, to advance, Leutnant Wintruff removed the working parts from the machine gun and we withdrew along *Aichweg*. A tank pulled up at an angle to *Aichweg* and the British forced their way into a section of the trench.

At the *KTK* we met up with Hauptmann Hollender [commander 11th Company]. Under his leadership, a few moments later we ejected the British from the *Aichweg*, though it was still sealed off at one end by the tank. Meanwhile Leutnant Wintruff had brought a machine gun into action. From *Aichweg* we brought down heavy fire on the British infantrymen who were advancing in dense lines from *S2*. At the short range of 150 – 200 metres we were very successful. We counted twenty seven tanks in our field of view. Of these four or five had been knocked out. We also saw prisoners from the 1st Battalion being led away in section columns by the British."

As has been noted, the situation was not helped by the weakness of the artillery on this nine kilometre frontage. It was precisely from this sector that the Landwehr artillery had been withdrawn. A high proportion of the remaining guns of Reserve Field Artillery Regiment 9 was undergoing repair, so that the Sub Group, commanded by Reserve Hauptmann Toeplitz, could only call on one pair of field guns from 5th Battery and two light field howitzers of 9th Battery, one of which was wrecked a short time later by a barrel explosion. The four obsolete guns of 874 Battery with their makeshift crews added little to the weight of fire. It was a deeply frustrating and embarrassing day for the gunners, who could do little more than man their command post in Lateau Wood and monitor a deteriorating situation. Around 10.00 am they were informed that about forty tanks, accompanied by waves of infantry, had overrun La Vacquerie and the *S* Line running north from Banteux and were already closing in on the *Zwischenstellung*.

Only a short time later the situation was much worse. The British 12th Division, supported by tanks of C and F Battalions, had thrust forward to a line running from the sugar refinery in Banteux via the quarry at Le Pavé to Quennet Farm. The Masnières – Le Pavé road had been crossed and the guns of 874 battery, located 300 metres northeast of Lateau Wood, had been captured by men of 37 Brigade. The two guns of the independent section had long since fallen into enemy hands.[13] The platoon commander kept firing right up until the moment when a tank arrived on the gun position.[14] The crew of one was captured, together with its crew, but the remainder managed to evade capture and make their way back to the main position of 5th Battery.

It had been a torrid day for the 1st Battalion. Having been attacked frontally and from a flank, it had had to yield its entire defensive position. The 2nd Battalion, to its south had a slightly easier time of it; its 6th Company, deployed forward left, even managing to maintain almost all its original sector. It is of course true that this was the southern limit of the British assault. Nevertheless, having fought hard at the end of the day, 6th Company, together with the remnants of 5th Company, still managed to provide a hard shoulder against further British thrusts and held a firm depth position in contact with Landwehr Infantry Regiment 395 to the south.

Offizierstellvertreter Redlich Mortar Company 209 [15]

"About 9.00 am we were attacked with machine guns by two British aircraft, which flew over the trenches at about sixty feet. We opened fire on the first of them at a range of twenty five to thirty metres. Immediately after the first volley it swerved off in a tight turn, flew on about thirty to forty metres in the direction of the enemy then crashed vertically into the ground. One man emerged from the cockpit and attempted to run off. We opened fire on him, he ran a few more paces, then fell to the ground. The second aircraft disappeared and troubled us no more."

Writing home after the battle, one of the junior NCOs of 6th Company, who was later commissioned, provided a vivid account of the events of the day.

Unteroffizier Moes 6th Company Reserve Infantry Regiment 19 [16]

"Drum fire came crashing down suddenly at 7.30 am on 20 November. Everything was enveloped in smoke and dust. The fire continued for forty five minutes, then the cry was heard, 'Here they come!' I raced with some of my men to our appointed place in the trench and there we saw infantry in several waves, being led by many tanks. We were fortunate; we were not in the direct line of the assault and were able, therefore, to fire into the British flank. This had no effect on the tanks, of course, and they brought down fire on us with their machine guns and heavy armament. It has a bad effect on the nerves when one of these monsters rolls slowly, but unstoppably, towards someone. This happened to us, too. Crawling slowly, getting closer and closer, spewing death and destruction, one came towards us; whilst above it circled low flying aircraft firing their machine guns. We shot one of them down and, joy of joys, suddenly our tank received a direct hit from an artillery shell and caught fire. We whooped with happiness and breathed a sigh of relief! The screams of the crew who were burned alive were truly dreadful. One emerged engulfed in flames and ran around with his hands up, crying with pain, until he finally collapsed.

"We then set about attacking in the flank the British soldiers who had forced their way into our forward trench and pushed them back. We managed to make good progress but then the British brought up a machine gun and we could not get to within grenade throwing range. I crawled forward a bit and looked round a corner to see what the British were up to. I suddenly saw two steel helmets pop up. I was about to shoot until I realised that they were German and recognised my platoon commander, Vizefeldwebel Lehmann. We waved and hurled ourselves happily at each other. Once more we had contact with the rest of our company – thanks to the brave, daring, Lehmann. Together with a few others, he had rolled up the neighbouring trench; moving partly along the parapet and partly along the base of the trench and constantly throwing grenades at the British. He was completely black from all the powder smoke. I still have a vivid picture, too, of Vizefeldwebel Tennies. His platoon stood firm in the trench, bayonets fixed, whilst he was in position up on the parapet. Despite heavy British small arms fire and exploding grenades, he fired from a standing position at the Tommies."

Improvising tactics and attempting to slow the advance of the tanks, men in the forward positions resorted to every type of expedient – some of which were more successful than others.

Feldwebelleutnant Biermann 6th Company Reserve Infantry Regiment 19 [17]

"The tanks could not be halted with small arms fire. I grabbed a grenade launcher and some ammunition. Fifty metres from a tank I set up the launcher and opened fire. Luck was with us. We could hear internal explosions coming from the tank as the ammunition caught fire. It was then a simple matter to adjust the aim of the launcher so that the rounds fell behind the tank and the crew was soon dealt with."

Altogether five tanks were knocked out on the 6th Company front; some by the defending infantrymen and others by a single gun of Reserve Field Artillery Regiment 9. This vigorous action caused the surviving tanks to veer off to the north, where the fighting continued to be intense. In the adjacent sub-sector the situation for the forward troops was very similar. Rarely can such an apparently one-sided battle have played out on such a narrow front.

Reserve Leutnant Dieckmann 7th Company Reserve Infantry Regiment 19 [18]

"Our sector [east of Gonnelieu] had been under fire for half an hour when a man came running up, shouting, 'We are being attacked by tanks!' At that we noticed that tanks were tearing apart and flattening the wire obstacle as though it were composed of spiders' webs. Some of our men were enraged when they realised that our S.m.K. ammunition and hand grenades were clattering uselessly against the armour. Making use of the huge fascines they had brought with them, the tanks blocked off the trench in the centre of the company sector and then dismounted some of the crews who took over the trench, established a barricade behind the fascine and swept the ground with fire from a machine gun which was established there, thus rendering a counter-attack impossible.[19]

"It was impossible to hold the first trench of the *Vacquerie Stellung*[20] with the eight men who were still left. I gave orders, therefore, that, taking the machine gun with us, we were to pull back to the main company trenches in the *Banteux Stellung*. Because artillery fire made the communication trench impassable, we had to move across country. As we approached the position we lost one man to our own fire. In the dreadful, swirling smoke, he was mistaken for a British soldier and a machine gun opened up on him. In the trench I met up with [Vize]Feldwebel Lehmann, who had set up a machine gun and was bringing down flanking fire on the British who were storming forward through gaps in the barbed wire. He stood amidst piles of empty cartridge cases and was already on his second set of working parts in the gun. As soon as the tank crews realised how destructive the fire of this machine gun was, the weapon itself came under heavy fire.

"However the tank was knocked out with S.m.K. ammunition: a situation which permitted us to attempt to continue the battle. Two machine guns, operated by Vizefeldwebel Tennies and me personally, were set up in a sap where we had excellent fields of fire at the masses of British troops who were pushing through the gaps. However we were soon spotted and brought under tank fire. One tank drove us out of the sap, back into the trench and drove towards this section of trench. Through use of an explosive charge made up of twelve stick grenades bundled together, which was thrown forward of the trench against the approaching monster, the left hand track was torn apart. It could advance no further, being able only to turn in circles. It brought down heavy fire against us and we responded with more made up charges. Just as it was going dark the petrol in the tank exploded and the crew baled out wreathed in flames. We shot them down swiftly. After that we searched the interior and rewarded ourselves by taking everything edible."

Situated just to the south, Infantry Regiment 395 was included in the artillery bombardment, but the greater part of its frontage did not come under direct attack. The most affected was its 1st Battalion, which was located right forward and adjacent to Reserve Infantry Regiment 19. To its left the 1st Battalion was subject to heavy fire and a gas attack which stretched south, interdicting movement and creating concern that the sector might subsequently be threatened. As sheets of massed machine gun fire neutralised all the known crossing points along this part of the St Quentin Canal, low flying Allied aircraft, diving low to machine gun the forward positions and strong points, forced most members of the regiment to spend the day under cover. Nevertheless, the 3rd Battalion, which had been in reserve, was warned to move forward as early as 8.45 am and to take up positions around Montecouvez Farm. From there, from about 1.30 pm, 3rd Battalion Infantry Regiment 395 launched a series of company-sized counter attacks, which were directed against targets from *Kochertal* to La Vacquerie, but progress was limited due in large part to enfilade fire from tanks directed against the companies as they attempted to get forward into Sectors *S1* and *S2*.[21]

Later in the day a strong British thrust to the north of the Reserve Infantry Regiment 19 sector overran German battery positions to the west of the Masnières – Le Pavé road and pushed on, unchecked, towards Masnières. One element swung to the east just to the north of Quennet Farm, bypassed Lateau Wood and appeared unexpectedly very close to Regimental Headquarters of Reserve Infantry Regiment 19. This same thrust caused considerable consternation at the command post of 3rd Battalion Reserve Field Artillery Regiment 9. As the assault closed in the entire staff, officers and men, took up firing positions and began to bring down heavy aimed rifle fire against the British infantry. This was sufficient to check the advance momentarily and the defenders made use of the pause to break clear towards the rear – a task further complicated by the presence of a British machine gun team on the northern edge of the wood.

Pfarrer [Padre] Pflanz Reserve Infantry Regiment 19 [22]

"The Tommies are coming!', bawled the sentry and, indeed the Tommies really were there and only fifty metres away. Fire was opened using the few weapons available in the command post. The enemy went to ground, but their numerical superiority was too great. Feldwebel Stickel was killed and several men were wounded. The regimental staff pulled back towards Vaucelles. Leutnant Damzog, Liaison Officer of 1st Battalion Reserve Infantry Regiment 19, was killed in heroic circumstances at the canal bridge. He had already crossed the bridge when he saw the British approach. At the head of a few men, he charged them, firing from a standing position, until he fell, mortally wounded."

Nevertheless the commander, his adjutant and certain other members of the staff arrived at Bonne Enfance Farm, where they set up in the command post of the heavy artillery and began trying to organise the recovery of the guns of 9th Battery. Initial attempts to save the guns, led by the battalion adjutant, Reserve Leutnant Kramer, foundered in the face of heavy British fire but, later that same day, the commander of 9th Battery himself, Leutnant Gustav

Müller, having reconnoitred a suitable route, succeeded in rescuing the remaining two guns, whose ammunition was recovered from the battery position the following night by a team led by Reserve Leutnant Tscheppen. As the day wore on, it became clear that the threat to the southern shoulder of the attack was not developing further. The opportunity to reinforce the artillery in this sector was seized, therefore. 4th Battery Reserve Field Artillery Regiment 9 took up positions just west of Bonne Enfance Farm and a further two batteries were withdrawn from the sector to the south and moved to counter the pressure on the left flank of 9th Reserve Division. At the same time, the light howitzers of 9th Battery Reserve Field Artillery Regiment 9, which had been undergoing repair, were finished at top speed and moved forward into firing positions.

These frantic efforts on the part of the artillery to improve the seemingly hopeless force ratio mirrored equally desperate attempts to force march infantry reinforcements forward all along the front under attack. Meanwhile British pressure continued to be exerted, including serious thrusts in the direction of Les Rues des Vignes.

Reserve Leutnant Höft Gas Warfare Officer Reserve Infantry Regiment 19 [23]

"When extremely heavy artillery fire began to crash down at 7.00 am I was at Les Rues des Vignes. That place and the nearby Crèvecoeur were engaged heavily, as were the bridges and the lock crossing points over the canal. The fire, which was controlled by aerial observers,[24] came down very accurately, so we suffered casualties amongst the runners, who had to make use of the bridges. The response of our artillery was weak to begin with, then died away completely towards midday. In answer to my shouted questions, the wounded coming from the front replied, 'The Tommies have overrun the *Siegfriedstellung* and are bearing down on the village!' I immediately sounded the alarm, so as to gather together all the personnel in the village and to hold it against the enemy which was pressing forward.

"At the assembly point, I came across Feldwebel Brandt, 10th Company, who, maintaining an iron calm despite the heavy fire which was coming down all around the place, was distributing weapons and ammunition to the men. Together with Brandt I organised the clerks, tradesmen and the men in the sickbay and led them to the southwest exit to the village. At 11.00 am I reported to the Regiment that I had established a line of defence with about sixty riflemen 200 metres forward of Les Rues des Vignes. The company feldwebels formed the heart of this defence. We were already coming under small arms fire as we moved into position. Whenever the wind dispersed the thick clouds of smoke we could make out individual British soldiers at a range of about 1,500 metres and bring fire down on them.

"After I had handed over the defensive line to the slightly wounded Hauptmann Bartsch, who had returned from the front line, I set off to carry out a reconnaissance to the right because we had heard the sound of shots from the right flank. Because of the dense fog, which was made even more impenetrable by the effect of enemy fire, initially I could not establish how far the enemy had pushed forward into the neighbouring sector. As I got back to my defensive line, I discovered that my men had just set off on a counter-attack, led by Leutnant Thurmann, who had returned from the regimental command post. I linked up with them. Enemy defensive fire was brought down on us from Lateau Wood in an effort to halt our forward movement.

"We could see that the eastern edge of the wood was occupied by the British and then a tank appeared at the northeast corner of the wood and engaged us with its main armament and machine guns, slightly wounding some of the men. There seemed to be no prospect of continuing the advance, so we returned to our starting point. During further reconnaissance at about 2.00 pm I was able to make out the enemy pushing out north and northeast. Enemy artillery was moving nose to tail along the Masnières – Le Pavé road and next to the road I spotted columns of marching British infantry. Squadrons of tanks moved into the hollows to the right of the road. Because we had fired off much of our ammunition and the range was great, we could do nothing to hinder the enemy advance.[25] In order to avoid being outflanked to the right, we adjusted our defences northwest to a line from the churchyard of Les Rues des Vignes to the canal, via Revelon Chateau. Two machine guns remained at the western edge of the village as protection against an attack launched from Lateau Wood."

Four kilometres away to the northwest, the battle for the key terrain around Flesquières continued unabated, as described by members of Reserve Infantry Regiment 27.

Feldwebelleutnant Reinsch 1st Company Reserve Infantry Regiment 27 [26]

"We were successful and the attack stalled. The tanks were dealt with by the artillery. During the afternoon the British attempted to bypass Flesquières with the tanks, but the attempt failed. When I heard that Graincourt had been captured, I pulled back onto a height about 150 metres north of Flesquières. Here I was in command of a company of men drawn from Reserve Infantry Regiment 27, Infantry Regiment 84, Pionier Battalion 108 and gunners from both the field and foot artillery. To our right everything had been pulled back.

Although we were hanging in the air, we did not fully appreciate the seriousness of our position. I had at all costs to cover the divisional right flank. From 2.50 to 3.50 pm, then again at 4.00 pm, cavalry appeared on the threatened flank. They got what was coming to them and it was a pleasure to bring our excellent rifle fire to bear against the cavalry."

Reinsch's account was confirmed by members of 7th Company Reserve Infantry Regiment 27.

Ersatzreservist Schäfer 7th Company Reserve Infantry Regiment 27 [27]

"We had to pull back behind Flesquières and occupy an artillery position. Led by Fledwebelleutnant Reinsch, we pulled the guns out of their firing positions. They had earlier knocked out with a direct hit a tank which emerged from the left (eastern) exit to Flesquières. At 2.00 pm an enemy cavalry patrol appeared but we beat it off and the same thing happened when another appeared. After that it was quiet."

Quiet was of course a relative term. As the fighting swept on towards the canal and Flesquières was deeply outflanked on either side, it was inevitable that the British troops would attempt to knock Major Krebs' small garrison back off this crucial and dominating piece of terrain.

Landwehr Leutnant Bielenberg Supply Officer Infantry Regiment 84 [28]

"A significant length of the Second Line of the *Zwischenstellung* was rolled up, but there matters stalled. Our courageous leader, Reserve Hauptmann Fürsen, was wounded and Landwehr Leutnant Becker died a hero's death. A German aircraft closed in, trying to establish where our front line ran. We laid out white towels, newspapers etc on the edge of the trench, but the pilot did not appear to spot these signs. I had my sheets brought out of my dugout and spread them out. The pilot gave the signal 'Understood' and flew away. My signaller informed me that the Tommies had already ransacked my dugout and had stolen numerous items.

"In the nearby *Pionierpark* [Engineer Park] ammunition and hand grenades were distributed once more. Several men whose wounds were being dressed were lying at the entrance to the ammunition dugouts. It had to be assumed that the enemy would soon renew their attack on our position, so particular measures to counter this were taken. All available men occupied designated defensive positions. Towards 3.00 pm the British attacked once more, supported by tanks. Most of the gunfire from the tanks hit the top of the trees, so we were showered with a great many splinters of wood.[29] The Tommies, who appeared on the edge of the park, were driven off easily with the help of the 27th.

Reserve Leutnant H Zindler 1st Battery Field Artillery Regiment 108 [30]

"When, having fired off the last of the shells, the position had to be evacuated, the remainder of the battery moved to Cantaing, up to which the enemy had already moved very closely on three sides and was already bringing fire down on it from the rear from *Neufwald* [Bois des Neuf = Nine Wood – located southwest of Noyelles]. There was then an advance with tanks on a wide front from here towards Cantaing: with good reason. The road Flesquières – Cantaing – La Folie was the only one in the divisional sector which was not subject to decisive attack. On it there were confused scenes, which made the senses reel. All arms and services were jumbled together, together with many wounded, supply wagons, convoys and civilians. Orders were being given and there was bustle and scurrying in all directions.

"Nobody spotted the danger of the threat building up from *Neufwald*. If the enemy succeeded in reaching the road to the north of Cantaing then Flesquières and, with it, Major Krebs and his men of the 27th, would be completely encircled. The attack frontage, therefore, was Noyelles – La Folie – Fontaine and [had this been achieved] the way would have been open by the evening of 20 November for an advance on Cambrai. Hauptmann von Köller and I, together with my little band of gunners, occupied positions in gardens and prepared to defend the built up area. For weapons all we had were carbines. We were reinforced by a small group of infantrymen, mostly men of the 84th. This included a machine gun. Nevertheless, the situation was desperate. What could we do against tanks with these arms, especially when the enemy were already bringing down artillery fire on the village?

"Then we had a stroke of luck. Two truck-mounted anti aircraft guns which were driving through the village were stopped, one of them by Hauptmann von Köller. They moved to take up positions at the exit to the village leading to La Folie. Now things became hot for the Tommies. It was a pleasure to see the [advance of the] tanks thrown into confusion as though they were part of a hare hunt. The infantry fled back into *Neufwald*, which was raked systematically [with fire] from front to rear and back again until it smoked. The lucky discovery of four wagons belonging to the light ammunition column of Field Artillery Regiment 108 which contained 360 shells permitted full exploitation of the rapid fire capability of the anti aircraft guns.

"Suddenly, in the midst of the raging fire, a man with his coat flapping open came rushing down the road from La Folie – my men maintained that he was from the 84th – shouting through the roar of the guns and gesticulating with his hand towards La Folie: British cavalry! Hearing this and without a word of command, gunners and *Mansteiners*, carbines, rifles and machine guns in their arms hared through the gardens, over hedges and fences, through the houses, over the road, through the houses once more, running wildly. What had caused it? A great mass of British dragoons[31], who had approached at full gallop, and were now milling about barely fifty metres from us. Opening fire from a standing position on them there were falls, rearing horses, shouts and others making off. It was all over in seconds.

"Between Noyelles and La Folie, the Schelde Canal [St Quentin Canal] ran through folds in the ground and was hidden from view by trees and bushes. Making use of the cover thus provided, the cavalry moved out of the murderous fire of the anti-aircraft guns, probably with orders, by means of an attack on Cantaing, to create a breathing space for the attack and to facilitate the encirclement. In the event this was thwarted by the actions of this man of the 84th – I accept the view of my men in this respect – and in my opinion this enabled Major Krebs and his men to continue holding on. I have never been able to discover the name of this man who, at the very last moment, got though with this report of such crucial importance."

It will be recalled that when the offensive opened, the only uncommitted troops in the Cambrai area were the regiments of 107th Infantry Division, which only one week previously had been deployed on the Eastern Front. The journey west lasted several days and was to have been followed by a rest week to permit time for clothing and equipment to be maintained and replaced and to provide an opportunity for rest and retraining, prior to the relief of 54th Division and the beginning of a planned gentle introduction to operations on the Western Front. As it was, only leading elements had had as much as a two day break in the Cambrai area before being flung piecemeal into a desperate situation. In addition, the journey itself had not been without incident. A train carrying officers and men of 2nd Battalion Reserve Infantry Regiment 52 was involved in a serious accident near Hirson on 18 November.

Oberleutnant Richter Adjutant Reserve Infantry Regiment 52 [32]

"We were all sitting happily together during the journey on 18 November 1917. I was seated in the first coach behind the locomotive. Suddenly there was a terrible crash. I was thrown forward, hitting my head on the wall opposite. There was then a second impact and I flew into the opposite corner. There then followed several seconds of bangs, crashes and screeching noises. To begin with all was dark then flames broke out. There was a small triangular hole in the wood and metal just to my right and somehow I managed to wriggle through it. Then, right up until the last minute, I helped with the rescue operations. Together with Leutnant Köpfel I managed to pull my clerk clear of the burning coach, but this was only because when the roof began to collapse his foot, which had been trapped, was freed. Between us we threw him upwards and clear and managed to escape ourselves. The hours which followed were dreadful and appalling. Our train had collided head on with an artillery transport travelling in the opposite direction. Our engine driver had overrun a stop signal at full speed. Some of the passengers heard the sound of emergency whistling, then came the collision. The third carriage, carrying baggage, was thrown forward over the second and the entire weight of the train crushed the first two coaches, which were carrying the officers."

In view of the intense overuse of the railway network, it is amazing that there were not more such incidents. The outcome of this was serious enough. Five officers were killed and their bodies burnt. Three officers and six men were seriously injured and there were numerous minor injuries and cases of shock. Despite the ensuing difficulties, the seriousness of the situation prevented any special consideration being given to these troops, who quickly found themselves flung into battle without time for orientation, proper briefing or systematic preparation. Compounding these difficulties there was total muddle within the chain of command concerning the subordination of the formations of 107th Division when they finally became available. In the circumstances it is little wonder confusion and misunderstanding within Group Caudry that day led to mistakes being made and the reinforcements being deployed late and less than optimally.

The exasperation felt by Generalleutnant von Watter, commander 54th Division, when he realised that, following his telephone conversation with Reserve Infantry Regiment 90 at 9.00 am, contrary to his firm belief and previously issued orders, none of the formations of 107th Division were moving forward to reinforce his embattled regiment, has already been discussed.[33] This self-inflicted contribution by the German chain of command to the fog of war that morning could have had catastrophic consequences for the defence but, once the problem was highlighted, steps were put in place to rectify the situation as soon as possible. Major Stapff, Chief of Staff Second Army, had broken the news of the tank assault to OHL at 8.00 am. Ludendorff, whose subsequent interventions during the battle were the source of much frustration and irritation to his subordinates, recognised the danger immediately and took steps to counter it.

First Quartermaster General Erich Ludendorff [34]

"When, shortly after 8.00 am, I spoke to Chief of Staff of Second Army, he briefed me that there were already enemy penetrations along our front. I immediately ordered the movement by rail to the Cambrai area of a number of divisions of varying degrees of readiness, which were located to the rear of Army Group German Crown Prince. I also directed Army Group Crown Prince Rupprecht to move formations in their area, located to the north of Cambrai. General von Kuhl [Chief of Staff Army Group Crown Prince Rupprecht] had already departed by car for Fourth Army before word was received from Second Army about the battle. As a result the initial moves of the divisions of this Army Group were delayed...I did not receive a clear impression of the extent of the penetration until around midday. When I did, I was filled with a feeling of great concern. However, everything that could be done had already been done. All I could do was to leave the course of the battle to fate."

All this friction meant that inevitably time was lost; whilst the pace of events led to a frustrating day of order and counter-order for those responsible for the conduct of the contact battle. By midday, when Reserve Infantry Regiment 52 had suspended its training session and marched back to its quarters before setting off for Cambrai, its original orders had changed. 'The order of 9.20 am is amended. Regimental staff and one battalion are to proceed to Cantaing, one battalion to Fontaine Notre Dame and one battalion to Proville. All vehicles are to be moved to the southwest outskirts of Cambrai '[35]

Riding on ahead of the main body, the regimental staff linked up with Rittmeister Schäffer from the staff of 107th Division, who informed them, 'The situation forward is bad; the British have broken through.' Having been told that Reserve Infantry Regiment 52 was to be subordinated to 54th Division and was to conduct a two battalion counter-attack in the direction of Flesquières, the commander drove direct to Headquarters 54th Division in Cambrai, but the situation there was unclear; he could not be briefed in any detail, but the counter-attack towards Flesquières was confirmed. At 2.05 pm, commander Reserve Infantry Regiment 52, Major Frühling, issued the following order to his battalion commanders:

"1. The enemy have occupied our positions between Flesquières and Ribécourt. Numerous tanks have crossed this line.
2. The regiment is to move to retake Flesquières and the *Zwischenstellung* [Intermediate Position] Flesquières – Ribécourt.
3. 1st Battalion is to attack, with its right flank directed at Flesquières; 3rd Battalion with its left flank directed at the *Zwischenstellung* near Ribécourt. 1st Battalion is responsible

for manning the junction point [between the units].

4. 2nd Battalion is to remain initially at my disposal in Cantaing.

5. A telephone line linking me with 108 Brigade on the road Marcoing – Graincourt is to be laid immediately." [36]

Every means possible was employed to hasten the movement of the regiment and one company was loaded onto trucks.

Gefreiter Skorna 2nd Company Reserve Infantry Regiment 52 [37]

"With mixed feelings we saw the hustle and bustle of Cambrai wash over us. Electric trams crowded with civilians and soldiers standing tightly pressed together drove past us. They had no idea the British soldiers had already advanced to positions near to Cambrai. Calmly and unconcerned, men of the widest variety of arms and services wandered about, bringing home sharply to us the contrast between front line soldiers and those serving in the rear areas...It was of far greater interest to us to note a British gun which, every now and then, brought down shells which exploded with loud crashes one kilometre away to our left. As a result we were all certain that forward not everything was going to plan.

"Whenever you move from life behind the lines to the front you inevitably think of death. Not, however, with any particular anxiety; rather with a certain resignation. At times I often thought it wrong that there were also men behind the lines. They all ought to have been exposed to enemy fire like my comrades and me. It was a thought born of feelings of self-preservation and it only came to me during the approach to the front line. When in the line...my thoughts were restricted to what was being played out either side of me.

"The town lay behind us. The route led forward through flat wooded country. To our right meadows opened out and behind them a deciduous wood on high ground. A shot down airman, apparently very seriously wounded, was being carried across these meadows towards Cambrai in a stretcher improvised from a ground sheet and two poles. He lifted his head a little and it was moving when he said in a loud voice, 'Keep closing on the British! Shout *Hurra* confidently and they will run away like hares!' Now and again old Landwehr men were seen making their way back, heading rapidly for Cambrai. Then we came across another shot down officer, arm in a sling, supported between two gunners and hopping along on his one good leg.

"We then passed an entire unit of older Landwehr soldiers who were defending the *Chausseegraben* [Highway Trench] in the wood. It was a battalion of Infantry Regiment 384. A constant stream of teams of artillery horses was coming the other way. Some of them were from

Field Artillery Regiment 213, our own divisional artillery...who explained that the British had attacked the *Siegfriedstellung* with heavy artillery and tank support during the early morning and that they had broken in to a depth of four to six kilometres. A number of guns had had to be destroyed; others were abandoned, their crews mown down by machine gun fire from tanks looming up out of the mist. It gradually became clear what we would find at the front. The gunners complained loudly about the lack of ammunition, which had proved to be very painful.

"We next came to a canal, which we crossed, and a little after that we saw the first of the houses running along the road to the village of Cantaing. There were still civilians in the village and they stared at us curiously...We passed the church and marched on. At long last – it might have been about 4.00 pm – we emerged from the village. About one hundred metres in rear of it was a counter-penetration position, which comprised a few shallow trenches protected by a barbed wire obstacle and several deep dugouts [the *SII Stellung*]. However, before we could actually occupy the position - we were still on the way there – there was an incident. To our front and probing the terrain about 800 metres away, was an enemy cavalry patrol, about ten men strong. The company commander, Leutnant Mann ordered the company to halt and to prepare to fire a volley.

"Immediately everyone made ready and took up fire positions but, before the company commander could give the order, one over-excited individual fired a shot. The British were startled and came to an abrupt halt. Previously they had not noticed us, but now they had. The company commander had no choice but to order fire to be opened. There was the crash of a volley, one cavalry man fell and the others turned around."

According to the history of Reserve Infantry Regiment 227, although they were aware on 19 November that one battalion of Field Artillery Regiment 213 had moved forward into position the previous evening in order to reinforce the limited artillery of 20th Landwehr Division, they themselves early on 20 November were still under no form of alert and they were somewhat peevish that, 'Nobody had even seen fit to provide us with a few topographical maps so that we could orientate ourselves to the new front in a manner to which we were accustomed'.[38] Ignoring the sounds of gunfire during the early morning, which could be heard clearly in their billets, the battalions continued with low level training and the testing of gas masks. It was assumed to begin with that the gunfire was friendly. There were, however, some who felt that things were a bit noisy for a supposed quiet front and concern grew further when, following a break in the clouds, aircraft were seen overhead and bombs began to fall. Those who had taken the aircraft to be enemy were proved correct and there followed a tense period of waiting until suddenly, at about 9.00 am, reports arrived from 54th Division via Group Caudry that the British, supported by tanks, had broken through the defences at several points.

Making use of whatever weapons and ammunition were to hand, the formations of 107th Division were to be thrown forward to intervene in the battle. Despite the lack of maps, Reserve Infantry Regiment 227, stationed in Cambrai, was actually best placed to respond to the new orders. It was a big demand to expect these units to advance into unknown territory with no knowledge of the situation, the enemy or even the terrain and there make a meaningful contribution to the defence. Nevertheless, even though the situation was far from ideal, training and administration was rapidly terminated. The battalions paraded ready to move and orders arrived stating that the regimental staff and two battalions were to be subordinated to 54th Infantry Division and were to advance via Rumilly and Masnières to be at the disposal of Major Hermsdorff, commander Reserve Infantry Regiment 90. This had always been the intention of Generalleutnant Freiherr von Watter of 54th Division.[39] Now, hours later than intended, the planned reinforcement was taking place. The 3rd Battalion was despatched simultaneously to Crèvecoeur, to the south of Cambrai; there to come under command of 9th Reserve Division. Setting off at fifteen minute intervals, beginning with the 2nd Battalion at 11.30 am, the units of Reserve Infantry Regiment 227 left to join the battle.

Major Buchholz Commander Reserve Infantry Regiment 227 [40]

"I trotted along the road. The weather was still foggy and damp and the visibility was poor. Rumilly was under heavy artillery fire, a large proportion of which was shrapnel, so I dismounted and followed the line of a shallow trench, only one foot deep, to the west of the road which led down to Masnières. I passed through two obstacle belts which had numerous wide gaps. I had no idea that this was the so-called '*S II' Stellung*, the second *Siegfriedstellung*. I dropped down to the village and, having searched around, came across the regimental staff of Reserve Infantry Regiment 90 in the cellars of the factory buildings of a spinning mill. This was, in fact, only a rear headquarters. The sole officer manning it was the machine gun officer, who had just returned from home leave. The commander was forward in the command post. The telephone line to him had just been cut, probably because he had been captured by the British.

"The situation appeared grave. The British had attacked with a great many tanks that morning, apparently overrunning the entire position. I could obtain no more detailed information here, despite the reports and alarming information which had arrived. The British, supported by tanks and moving in great groups, were closing in on the houses of the villages of Masnières and Marcoing. Small groups of soldiers, the remnants of the 90th, were pulling back past us. We left the cellar and took up positions of observation. There we saw the British, complete with tanks, just forward of the village. I asked if the canal bank would make a suitable defensive position and, upon receiving a positive answer, I decided to head back to the regiment and to deploy it in that position. If we were to be able to occupy it and then hold it, we should have achieved everything that was still possible in this situation.

"However, we need hand grenades for the forthcoming battle. 'Where were any to be found?' 'In the engineer park at the station north of Rumilly.' So I sent Leutnant Mandt on ahead to meet the battalions and to direct them to equip themselves there rapidly with hand grenades. I found myself standing in the *SII Stellung* on the high ground just north of Rumilly. I saw the long rows of British soldiers and, behind them, tightly packed houses on the ground which fell away on the far side to the Canal de l'Escaut [St Quentin Canal]. I could also see large numbers of tanks pressing forward. Marcoing was already in enemy hands. Were the canal bridges blown?

"Had we been alerted only one hour earlier and not once our duties had begun! In that case we should have held the line of the canal firmly and have been able to cause grim casualties to those over there! As we soon noted, the bridges had not been blown and, at the engineer park, because the personnel had already disappeared, only after lengthy searches of the dugouts, which cost valuable time, could hand grenades be located. I was burning up with impatience. Every minute was costly. The battalions had arrived towards 1.00 pm and now it was almost 2.00 pm. The two battalion commanders came forward and I gave out my orders. I wanted to seize the line of the canal, but it was essential to move quickly because our situation was becoming less favourable by the minute.

"At Marcoing the British had already crossed the canal. From there and from the far side of Masnières heavy rifle and machine gun fire was being directed at us as, at long last, our forward elements, including the 2nd Machine Gun Company, passed my position in the *SII Stellung*. I watched as Unteroffizier Bienert and his machine gun went by. During the time I was a battalion commander in Infantry Regiment 157 he had been my well-tried and trusty battle orderly and I had brought him with me to Reserve Infantry Regiment 227. During the final days in the east, in order not to hold up his promotion, I had transferred him to the 2nd Machine Gun Company and there he became an Unteroffizier. It would had been a waste to have him follow me around the positions carrying my gas mask and binoculars, but now I wished that I had had my tried and tested runner once more!

"I shouted out to him and he gave me a cheery reply, He was concerned only to do his best. A short time later he was carried to the rear, wounded in the stomach and he died at the aid post. Honour his memory!" [41]

At about 2.00 pm the commander gave out his orders that the enemy forces which had pushed across the canal were to be thrown back over it and that the line of the canal was to be held. 1st Battalion, attacking astride the road leading to Masnières, was reasonably successful in driving enemy forces back with heavy losses, but 2nd Battalion, advancing towards a long line of poplars marking Masnières itself, had a much more difficult time of it. Involved in stiff fighting from the moment the first of its three waves of attackers breasted a rise located roughly parallel to a track running from Rumilly-Noyelles, it came under extremely heavy machine gun fire. Two of the commanders of the leading companies later left descriptions of events here.

Oberleutnant Deutschmann 6th Company Reserve Infantry Regiment 227 [42]

"Ignoring [the machine gun fire] we crossed the *SII Stellung*, which was merely spitlocked[43] and wired. The fire seemed to be coming mainly from the right flank, partly from Masnières itself and partly from raised positions on the canal bank on the enemy's side. Isolated sections of Reserve Infantry Regiment 27 were still holding out on the northern side of the village and were absorbed by us as we passed. As we pushed on further we realised that the enemy was only in strength on the southern bank of the canal; whereas on the north bank and in the village they were established only weakly. After a short battle these detachments were driven off or captured. We occupied the southern edge of the village and brought down effective small arms fire against the enemy infantry which was attempting to cross the canal. We could see quite clearly that we had caused them serious casualties. How far the enemy had outflanked us to the right I could not judge, but apparently there was a threat from that direction."

Deutschmann was correct in his judgement. The 6th Company had, albeit at the cost of heavy casualties, pushed forward to the canal but, to their right, 7th Company had bumped into serious opposition. Making use of the crossings at Marcoing, strong British forces were established along the line of the *W[otan] III Stellung* and they moved against the right flank of Reserve Infantry Regiment 227.

Leutnant Ambos 7th Company Reserve Infantry Regiment 227 [44]

> "I was in charge of the right flank, but at this point I only had about twenty men available. The advancing lines of British infantry were well equipped with light machine guns and they made excellent use of them. In addition we came under enfilade fire from tanks. As a result it was not long before I was shot and wounded. Together with my runner, Gefreiter Stange, I made my way to the rear and was wounded once more in the leg on the way."

This thin line was swiftly overrun, with a number of men and heavy machine guns falling into British hands.

Leutnant Quehl 2nd Machine Gun Company Reserve Infantry Regiment 227 [45]

> "The first machine gun platoon launched itself daringly into the attack alongside the infantry. Visibility was bad due to the wet, rainy weather. Leutnant Fleischer was wounded. The four machine guns had pushed on so vigorously that all of a sudden only they were fighting and, lacking cover to the sides, they were swiftly outflanked by the British. The British attacked frontally in tightly packed columns and led by a commander mounted on a horse. This can only be explained if it is assumed that the British believed that they had broken through and that they simply wished to begin the advance to Cambrai. Our machine guns reaped a huge harvest. They too suffered casualties, but they kept up the fight to the last minute. Gefreiter Kammerer's gun fought excellently. After his gunner was wounded, he took over the gun himself and fired at the British, who were bearing down closely on him right up until he was surrounded and captured."

The situation was decidedly critical for the defence. 5th and 8th Companies Reserve Infantry Regiment 227 out on the right (northern) flank, attempted to shore up the line. Despite absorbing those making their way back and extending the position to reinforce the threatened flank, they were sorely pressed, but their machine guns were starting to have an effect on the British troops who were pushing up behind the withdrawing German forces and attempts were made frantically to stabilise the overall situation from positions in the *S II Stellung*. The regimental commander despatched his final reserve, 3rd Company, forward; a move which certainly improved matters for the defence, but meant that, for the time being, there was no means of reacting to a further crisis.

Leutnant Beck 1st Machine Gun Company Reserve Infantry Regiment 227 [46]

"As we moved forward, I noticed to my great alarm that, out to our right, men of our 2nd Battalion were rushing to the rear. They had pushed on too quickly and found themselves in a weak position vis-à-vis the lines of British infantry, which also had the support of a tank. I placed my reserve machine gun on the railway embankment to the right of the road and opened effective fire with four guns on the line of advancing British infantry. Within seconds they scattered and began to dig in. As soon as they attempted to advance, we pinned them down once more. For the time being the battle was a stalemate but, due to the threat to the right flank, over time our position was untenable."

Leutnant Hörold 5th Company Reserve Infantry Regiment 227 [47]

"Those troops who had pulled back took up positions level with my platoon. Some of us clustered around the dugouts, some of which were ready, whilst others were unfinished, others sheltered in isolated sections of trench. It began to rain! Soon we heard a grinding, roaring sound which was getting closer and a stink of petrol fumes was carried on the westerly wind. We knew what were on their way! – Tanks! Very shortly three of them appeared to our front, one of them in the wide gap by Flot Farm. Watching them crawling forward like great prehistoric monsters and crossing all obstacles with ease, sent unpleasant shivers up our spines. But they could not be permitted to get through!"

Leutnant Quehl 5th Company Reserve Infantry Regiment 227 [48]

"Leutnant Dresel quickly brought his machine guns into action. I had previously ordered that there was to be no firing until I blew a signal on my whistle and that the firing was to be concentrated on point targets. When the nearest tank was three hundred metres away, I gave the order to open fire. I rejoiced to watch the impact of the bullets on the tank sending showers of sparks in all directions. After a few seconds flames leapt up from the tank. This was followed by an explosion and the tank did not move again. This success was down to the fact that I had not carried out the order, issued when we left the east, to leave all ammunition behind. Instead I had taken with us a goodly quantity of S.m.K. ammunition, both belted and in boxes.

"Our joy over the destroyed tank was great, because it had been a highly unpleasant feeling to watch the beast draw near without any means of alerting our artillery, which was extremely weak anyway... Once the first was dealt with, the second, having sent a load of iron in our direction, disappeared in the direction of Marcoing behind a fold in the ground. Meanwhile Leutnant Posenski, working with amazing speed, had brought two grenade launchers into action against the third tank at Flot Farm. Unfortunately this was with high angle fire, the low angle mounts having been left behind. This tank also disappeared behind the farm buildings and did not reappear.

"As it went dark, a patrol moved forward to the crippled tank. They found it abandoned, but discovered all sorts of excellent booty within it: sparkling wine, cognac, chocolate and fruit cake; almost all luxury items which we had not seen for a very long time. That only increased our happiness further."

As has been noted, 1st Battalion Reserve Infantry Regiment 227 had been launched in an attack towards the canal. It reached its objective successfully but at more or less the same time as the British infantry surged forward in dense masses, supported by tanks, towards the three bridges. Hurried demolition attempts had not been at all successful, so 4th Company was hard pressed to defend the crossings, despite vigorous support from heavy machine guns, which took a considerable toll amongst the attackers. British tanks turned away from the wooden bridge, which was clearly not strong enough to bear their weight, whilst the defenders simply watched as tank F 22 attempted to cross the partly destroyed railway bridge and only succeeded in collapsing it. In the gathering darkness, its crew escaped. Nevertheless, as time passed, the situation forward became increasingly critical. 2nd Battalion Reserve Infantry Regiment 227 was greatly troubled by its vulnerable right flank, but the open left flank of 1st Battalion, which was hanging in the air, was equally problematic.

Hauptmann Otterstein 1st Battalion Reserve Infantry Regiment 227 [49]

"Unfortunately I had no contact on this (left) flank, because Reserve Infantry Regiment 90 [54th Infantry Division] had only been able to station about two platoons in that sector. During the day I was able to make use of a platoon from 6th Company, which had stumbled into our position during the fighting, to echelon my left flank to the rear and so protect it. As it went dark, visibility was further diminished by the rain and so this tactic was no longer viable and there was a risk that the British would cross the canal under cover of darkness and hit my battalion from the rear. I simply had to pull my left flank back to the *S II Stellung*, where I was able very roughly to link up with Reserve Infantry Regiment 90. If Regiment Bredelow[50], which did not reach us until 11.00 pm, had already been in position, we should have been able to hold Masnières and the line of the canal east and west of that place without difficulty. Because no other reserves had got forward, as soon as it went dark, the entire regimental line had to be pulled back to the *SII Stellung*. All that was left behind by the steel canal bridge was a courageous platoon of 4th Company, under Vizefeldwebel Bierwirth, with orders to deny the enemy its use, Despite the constant risk of being surrounded and captured by the British – he was one kilometre forward of the battalion's night position – he bravely stood his ground all night at a cost of one man killed and two wounded."

Elsewhere in this sector the final dramatic events of the day were being played out. The outcome could have been decisive for the defence of Cambrai, but the intervention of fortuitously arriving reserves staved off the crisis, demonstrating once again that the outcome of battles is frequently on a razor's edge. The regimental commander of Reserve Infantry Regiment 227, Major Buchholz, was established with his staff by the Cambrai – Masnières road. All were watching a tank which approached to within one hundred metres of 2nd Battalion, all guns blazing, prior to disappearing behind a rise in the ground, when the commander of 2nd Battery Field Artillery Regiment 213 [Leutnant Giebeler] rushed up with alarming news: 'British cavalry have broken through to our left, overrun my battery and is surging forward behind us and behind Rumilly. Enemy infantry is following up! Help me, I must recover my battery!'

Buchholz, having already committed his final reserve, could only despatch the men of the first mortar platoon to guard the left flank and anxiously await developments. Suddenly, coming from the direction of Cambrai, could be heard the rattle of heavy small arms fire. It appeared as though the regiment was surrounded. If true, the way to Cambrai would have been wide open. It was an exceedingly nervous moment and Buchholz ordered that the regiment was to remain in position and hold out to the last. In fact the situation had been saved. Just as the cavalry had forced its way around, reinforcements had arrived in the shape of the Recruit Depot of 54th Infantry Division and a reinforcement draft for 49th Reserve Division and they were able to shoot the cavalry advance to a standstill. One member of the draft later left this brief account of their intervention:

Gefreiter Albert Müller Ersatztransport 49th Reserve Division [51]

"On 17th November, about 1,000 men in Blankenburg were assembled as reinforcements for the Western Front. After a journey lasting several days we were off loaded in open country and formed up into companies. After a tough forced march, we were met by a German artillery officer: 'The British cavalry has broken through and is operating in rear of a German division which is heavily engaged in battle. They will be here any moment!' We had to deploy and moved forward a bit in extended line, then we took up position in a sunken road and received the advancing British cavalry with murderous small arms fire. The attack withered away, we took many prisoners. Dead horses, men and fine leather equipment lay around in tangled heaps. We also seized numerous riderless horses.[52] Our casualties were slight. We stayed where we were for three days, then moved to Reserve Infantry Regiment 225."

Despite such improvisations, the hours that had been lost due to the earlier command errors meant that events had generally overtaken the planned counter-measures. Even as they advanced, the marching sub-units could observe tanks manoeuvring. Finally arriving in Cantaing at 3.30 pm, Major Frühling, commanding officer Reserve Infantry Regiment 52, came across a scene of complete tactical breakdown. There were no battleworthy troops at all in Cantaing. A group of artillery officers informed him that, following an assault led by over one hundred tanks, their guns had been lost, the two forward Landwehr regiments had been completely wiped out, almost all of Flesquières had fallen and Noyelles was occupied. Meeting the commander of Landwehr Infantry Regiment 384, he was informed that the latter intended to fall back on Cambrai with approximately one hundred stragglers and to attempt to muster what remained of his regiment. All contact with the outside world had been broken and the situation to the front was completely unknown.

Major Frühling moved forward to carry out his own reconnaissance and swiftly determined that the forward line of enemy troops stretched from Flesquières to Noyelles, whlst enemy infantry and tanks could be seen moving around on the high ground only 1,000 metres south of Cantaing. The establishment of enemy artillery positions up there could only signify that an attack against Cantaing was being actively prepared. This changed situation called for swift and decisive action, so Frühling quickly issued a new order:

"1st Battalion is to occupy and defend the high ground immediately to the south and east of Cantaing. It is to despatch patrols in an attempt to make contact with the German troops said to be holding out on the northern edge of Flesquières and to reconnoitre the terrain towards Graincourt and Anneux. 3rd Battalion is to advance to the canal lock about one kilometre east of Cantaing. 2nd Battalion and the regimental staff will establish themselves on stand-by in the northern section of La Folie copse (about two kilometres northeast of Cantaing)."[53]

More or less at the same time 2nd Battalion Reserve Infantry Regiment 232 arrived in Cantaing under orders to defend the place in association with 1st Battalion Reserve Infantry Regiment 232, which was advancing to the east of the canal. As was so often the case in an emergency the German defenders were beginning to stabilise the situation and reinforce a threatened sector, though naturally the delay in beginning the forward deployment increased the difficulties encountered. 1st Battalion Reserve Infantry Regiment 232, for example, was seriously hindered by the constant stream of wounded, stragglers and administrative vehicles heading back pell-mell for the relative safety of Cambrai.[54] Meanwhile, 2nd Battalion Reserve Infantry Regiment 232 was ordered by Major Frühling to take up positions with its right flank linked up with 1st Battalion Reserve Infantry Regiment 232 and its left flank on the canal where 3rd Battalion Reserve Infantry Regiment 52 would go over to defence. The presence of enemy cavalry near Noyelles meant that the need to place flank protection out to the left through the use of a reserve company was stressed, because it would take some time yet for 3rd Battalion Reserve Infantry Regiment 52 to get forward into position.

Leutnant Herbert Ulrich Orderly Officer Reserve Infantry Regiment 52 [55]

"I rode at the head of the column with the commanding officer of 3rd Battalion, Hauptmann Bohtz. Just as we had crossed the bridge by the lock west of La Molière, we came under machine gun fire from the left. I met our signals officer, Leutnant Ahrens, who told me that the regimental commander was coming down the road towards us. I trotted on, so as to report the arrival of the battalions. The machine gun fire grew heavier. Because there was no more cover to the left I jumped down from my horse which, having become nervous as a result of all the fire, raced off, seemingly right into the arms of the British. I continued on foot, met up with Major Frühling and Leutnant Hansen and reported. They were on foot but had their horses with them. I also met Leutnant Dietz, adjutant of 3rd Battalion.

"At that very moment several squadrons of British cavalry burst out of the wooded area south of the Cantaing – Proville road to launch an attack on a broad front past the eastern entrance to Cantaing in the direction of Fontaine. We scattered. The commander, together with Leutnants Hansen and Dietz, headed off northwards on the horses. I, without a mount, set off along a dry trench running northwest towards Cantaing. In no time I found myself surrounded by six horsemen who threatened me with their sabres. Their leader fired at me from a range of five metres with his pistol, but without hitting me. However, because they came under small arms fire from Cantaing, they left me and charged on towards Fontaine. As the fire increased and they also came under fire from La Folie Wood (probably from our 3rd Battalion) they turned about. In the meantime I had carried on running towards Cantaing where I knew our men were located. As they galloped back two British soldiers took a swing at me with their sabres as they passed by. Arriving in Cantaing I met up with some of the men of the regimental staff who were located in the first house and also, to my great joy, I was reunited with my horse, which was unharmed."

Ulrich was luckier than members of regimental headquarters who were ridden over by the remnants of several squadrons of cavalry which had been turned back by the combined fire of the reserve company of 1st Battalion Reserve Infantry Regiment 52 and 2nd Battalion Reserve Infantry Regiment 232 in Cantaing. Major Frühling lost an arm, Gefreiter Krebs was also seriously wounded and the adjutant, Leutnant Hansen,was killed. The men of Reserve Infantry Regiment 232 had had much the same experience. First 6th and then 7th Companies came under heavy fire from the *Neufwald* as they moved to take up the positions to which they had been directed. Eventually they were able to take cover, engaging both the enemy positions in *Neufwald* itself and, a little later, the British cavalry with machine gun fire of their own, which ultimately drove the survivors back into Noyelles. The signallers, charged with establishing communications, were also caught up in this action.

Leutnant Ahrens Signals Officer Reserve Infantry Regiment 52 [56]

"Having come under heavy fire once more, the second group under Unteroffizer Schmidt made a bold sweep to the north and ran into British cavalry. The machine gun fire which was coming from the southeast was the work of dismounted British cavalry. At the lock I came across elements of Infantry Regiment 384 and a mortar detachment which had occupied the lock and mounted a machine gun. Leaving behind a sentry at the lock, who was to brief Schmidt's group which was following up, I went towards the lock building, where I came across a group of vehicles belonging to a machine gun detachment fleeing panic-stricken. I myself tangled with a horse pulling one of the vehicles.

"Just as I reached the building, Hauptmann Bohtz and Leutnant Ulrich came riding up looking for the location of Major Frühling. They rode off to meet him, but bumped into the attacking cavalry and Hauptmann Bohtz was captured. The machine guns at the lock opened fire and a little while later Hauptmann Wesemann arrived with 3rd Battalion, occupied the canal line and pushed an officer's patrol forward into La Folie Wood. The British cavalry patrol was badly shot up and the remainder disappeared just as it was going dark."

As has been noted, 2nd Battery Field Artillery Regiment 213 was also affected by the cavalry action. It had experienced a difficult day so far and had only recently taken up position roughly three kilometres to the south of Proville.

Leutnant Giebeler 2nd Battery Field Artillery Regiment 213 [57]

"We halted on a hill top to the west of Rumilly, only to be confronted by an indescribable view. We could clearly see a huge number of tank squadrons moving towards us and, following up, unmistakable lines of infantry. We set up our observation post along the line of the road Rumilly – Crèvecoeur, with the battery position behind a crest line to the east of Rumilly. The battery commander undertook a long series of engagements to the southwest which were directed against infantry targets...while the signallers did their best to maintain the telephone line which was frequently cut.

"All of a sudden bullets whistled over the observation point coming from the direction of the guns. One of the signallers managed to hear, 'We have just been attacked by enemy cavalry', before the link was lost. I immediately alerted the infantry close by. After many requests, the commander let me have a patrol of men and we set off in the darkness which had fallen in the meantime. However, such was the weight of the fire coming from the direction of the battery that we could not reach it. I went back to the infantry commander once more and categorically demanded the services of a company in order to recapture my battery. When he refused I went alone, accompanied by a one year volunteer, whose name I forget, following the cable to the gun position. This time I was not shot at and, once I arrived there, I found that everything was once more in 'first class order'.

"It transpired... that events had unrolled in this way: firing had been suspended due to the fog and some of the personnel had gone over to the limbers, about one hundred metres to the east of the road. A column from another unit whose own battery had already been lost, had just brought up some ammunition when, suddenly, on the left flank, an enemy squadron was coming at full gallop over a hill about 500 – 600 metres south of the battery. Because of the heavy ground it was only possible to swing around the left hand gun then it was a matter of 'Over open sights, rapid fire!' A few rounds were fired, the enemy had crashed into the battery then there was chaotic cutting, slashing and firing. The Canadian cavalry had the upper hand over the handful of our men. Lt Vogel, Unteroffizier Pöppelmann and a few others were led off by the Canadians, but they managed to escape when Leutnant Frohnhäuser, who was manning the observation post, spotted the group and got the infantry to open fire.[58]

"When the enemy forced their way into the battery position, Leutnant Bruns threw himself over the trail of a gun and played dead. As bullets were flying round the battery, he peered from under an arm, noticed that the cavalry was following the other unit's column, which was hurrying away, then watched as they went on to attack a group of recruits who had appeared and who were manning a sunken road.[59] Taking a quick decision, he ran over to this group with a few others. Härtel stayed in the battery position, together with three other comrades. Assuming that the battery was now between our own and the enemy lines, they removed the breech blocks and buried them. Then they attempted in vain in the darkness to make their way back to the limbers and ended up spending the night in a village right by Cambrai.

"In the meantime Leutnant Vogel, on the orders of the artillery commander to whom he had reported the loss of the battery, attempted with the aid of some infantry to recapture the battery, but he bumped into some dug in infantry, probably Canadian cavalrymen who had lost their horses, and could get no further. However, once it was fully dark, Bruns crept up, accompanied by a few gunners and infantrymen, and found that it was unoccupied. It was shortly after that that Leutnant Giebeler must have arrived. Gradually all the other stragglers assembled there then moved back to spend the night in the Curassier Barracks.

"The following morning Härtel and his comrades found the position empty. On their way back to Cambrai they came across seven Canadians and twenty unwounded, but completely equipped, horses, all of which they seized gratefully and led away."

In the meantime the urgency of the situation, which was becoming clearer as time passed, meant that increasing efforts were made to move forward as many of the marching troops of Reserve Infantry Regiment 52 as possible by truck. There were numerous deficiencies in the way the troops were deployed; briefing, adequate supplies and ammunition were lacking, but gradually, through the chaos, attempts of varying degrees of success were being made to fill the gaping gaps in the defence.

Oberleutnant Richter Adjutant 2nd Battalion Reserve Infantry Regiment 52 [60]

"The men had their rifles and 120 rounds of ammunition. Other than that there was nothing: no hand grenades, no flare pistols and no iron rations! This is how we were thrown into battle. Oberleutnant Fischer, who commanded the battalion, and I drove, together with twenty men, at a crazy speed through Cambrai in the direction of

Fontaine. Here I attempted to orientate myself. The streets were eerily empty. Finally I came across a house displaying a red flag with a small white 'F' on it [*Fernsprechstelle* = telephone point]. In we went. 'Connect me with 107th Division!' 'I do not have contact with 107th Division,' answered the duty shift leader. 'Then put me through to any of the command posts of the infantry to our front!' There is no infantry to our front!' '*Donnerwetter*! There must be *some* troops to your front!' 'No, Herr Leutnant', he replied, pointing out of the window. 'There is nothing forward of that and the first tanks have already arrived on the hill over there.'

"Does that mean that the British will be entering this room in a matter of minutes?' 'Yes.' That was enough for us. Out we went into the village, selected a line to defend and the twenty of us took up our positions. The battalion would be here any minute. At long last a messenger from the regiment arrived by bicycle. We were to return to Cambrai. We finally linked up with the battalion again that evening; it had joined together with the advance of 3rd Battalion.

To the south of Noyelles, there was still a large hole in the defences, which the British were engaging with machine gun fire. 1st Battalion Reserve Infantry Regiment 52 had pushed well forward, the regimental staff was scattered, 2nd Battalion, with its staff in Fontaine, was leaderless and the 3rd Battalion was deployed in La Folie Wood with its commander and adjutant out of action. As darkness fell, Hauptmann Wesemann assumed command of 3rd Battalion and despatched Leutnant Schneider at the head of a contact patrol to move to 1st Battalion and brief its commander, Major Steinkopff, about the situation. Handing over command to Oberleutnant Coßmann, Steinkopff assumed command of the regiment and moved to link up with 2nd and 3rd Battalions at the lock over the canal by the Cantaing – Proville road.

At long last an order arrived from Brigade, cancelling the thrust against Flesquières and ordering a redeployment. Reserve Infantry Regiment 232 was to assume positions to the west of the canal lock towards the southern edge of Cantaing. Reserve Infantry Regiment 52 was to move to cover from the southern and western edges of Cantaing along the line of the *SII Stellung* to the Cambrai – Bapaume road and Reserve Infantry Regiment 227, to the south of Reserve Infantry Regiment 232, was to form a front facing Noyelles. In the pitch black darkness and further hindered by pouring rain, the regiments of 107th Division moved into position and pushed forward patrols and listening posts. On paper a rough defensive line had been established, but the men lacked digging tools and, above all, ammunition, to face a probable continuation of the offensive the following morning.

Grenades and similar weapons had been left behind when the division moved westwards and there were no replacements and no S.m.K.

ammunition to be had in Cambrai. With tanks reported in the *Neunwald* and down towards Noyelles, the situation was extremely precarious. Finally, between 4.30 and 5.00 pm, 1st Battalion Reserve Infantry Regiment 232 arrived at the canal near Noyelles, where they linked up with scattered remnants of Reserve Infantry Regiment 27 of 54th Infantry Division; Hauptmann Schrader of that regiment, being the most senior officer present, took overall command of the situation.

Back in Flesquières, even early in the afternoon, Major Krebs was still under the impression that attempts were being made for reinforcements to be got through to him. A long-delayed message by light signal from 54th Infantry Division was finally flashed through at 1.20 pm, stating that a regiment intended to reinforce him was advancing on Cantaing. In view of the overall situation, Krebs was in a quandary. He felt that Flesquières could be defended for longer if the defensive garrison could be increased but, if it really was the intention to reinforce him, where was the advance party which should have been seeking briefing and orientation? Furthermore, how could this aim be reconciled with the fact that, according to other sources of information from stretcherbearers, ammunition carriers and others, the enemy had already driven forward to Marcoing and even Noyelles? It was equally clear that a serious thrust in the direction of Graincourt had made considerable progress.

In and around the village, the 51st (Highland) Division demonstrated that it still had unfinished business to attend to. The losses amongst its tank support had been extremely serious but, equally, it was unacceptable that the small German garrison could be allowed to continue to hold out and so continue to influence adversely the planned advance on Bourlon Wood. Time was being lost, together with momentum. The advance of the British 62nd Division on its left had already been paused to allow it to conform, so it was vital that this final point of resistance be reduced as soon as possible. Local fighting flared up along the perimeter throughout the afternoon then, towards evening, a further combined assault was attempted. Most of the weight of this attack fell on 2nd Company Reserve Infantry Regiment 27, a number of whose members subsequently reported on their experiences.

Landwehr Leutnant Paepke 2nd Company Reserve Infantry Regiment 27 [61]

"Just as it was going dark, two tanks appeared on our right flank, pouring fire against our lines, whilst a third tank pushed on along the road from Flesquières to Ribécourt...In order to avoid the risk of being cut off from the remainder of the line, we pushed our line right out to this road, which thereafter formed our right flank".

Although it was not possible to close up on the first pair of tanks, the third was engaged with some success.

Unteroffizier Kitschka 2nd Company Reserve Infantry Regiment 227 [62]

"The enemy had sent three tanks probing forward. One of them advanced as far as our line and turned away back to the enemy lines. A short time later another tank, this time accompanied by a strong assault troop, pushed towards us. The [infantry] was engaged by the company with flanking fire from light machine guns which virtually wiped them out; only a few managing to escape. The tank itself was attacked by several hand grenades thrown from a house. It was not possible to knock it out totally, but it was brought to a standstill and did not risk pressing on further."

It was obvious that, once the sun set at about 5.00 pm, the battlefield would be somewhat calmer and movement would become easier, but what use did his superiors intend to make of the changed situation? Krebs had to resolve the matter so, at about 4.30 pm, he despatched Leutnant Brockes and one of his runners on bicycles to move to Cantaing and obtain precise information and orders. Despite having to run the gauntlet of shell and machine gun fire, the two of them got through to that place safely. On arrival he found nobody to whom he could report. An old woman he met in the village headquarters building informed him that everyone had departed hurriedly. Heading for Cambrai, he met up with Hauptmann von Koeller (formerly of Infantry Regiment 84, but transferred to Field Artillery Regiment 108) and Reserve Leutnant Zindler, 1st Battery Field Artillery Regiment 108. The two of them were organising the engagement of cavalry and tanks in the La Folie area with truck-mounted anti-aircraft guns.

Whilst Brockes' odyssey continued, every effort was made by the small garrison at Flesquières to prepare for a long, difficult, night.

Landwehr Leutnant Bielenberg Supply Officer Infantry Regiment 84 [63]

"Gradually night fell. We could hardly reckon on support. From the sound of firing in the distance, we could tell that the enemy had thrust in depth to the left and right of us. It was absolutely essential to establish a continuous defensive line linking with the Second Line of the *Zwischenstellung* where the regimental staff was located. In the park of the chateau to the east of the road, *Kabelgraben* was readied for defence and a few machine gun positions were prepared. I reported into regimental headquarters and was directed by Major Krebs to ensure immediately that sufficient ammunition, hand grenades, flare pistols and cartridges were brought inside the defensive perimeter.

"I succeeded in obtaining the services of twelve volunteers, some of them members of the staff of Infantry Regiment 84. It had already gone quite dark. After we had crossed the park we reached the road. Ducking down in cover, we watched as a tank passed directly to our front, then we dashed across the road into the *Pionierpark*. There, working by torchlight, we took as much as we could carry from the depot and hurried back. All available officers assumed responsibility for a sector of the defensive lines. My men and I were deployed in the park to the east of the road. For the most part the hours passed quietly. Now and again small arms fire broke out on either side. Now and then flares were fired by us and others all the way to regimental headquarters in order to deceive the enemy that our strength was greater than it actually was."

Meanwhile, pressing on as rapidly as possible, Brockes and his accompanying soldier headed for Fontaine Notre Dame and tried, successfully, to avoid clashing with British cavalry. Once there he was faced with a frustrating half hour at the town headquarters as he attempted, in vain, to reach 54th Infantry Division by telephone. Tired of dealing with crossed lines and general confusion, he decided to press on to Cambrai and report in person. By now it was dark as he made his way along roads crammed with transport, stragglers, supply vehicles and horsemen.

Leutnant Brockes 2nd Company Reserve Infantry Regiment 27 [64]

"As soon as I had reported in to the chief of staff, Hauptmann Gädeke, I was led through to *Excellenz* von Watter in the main map room. I was covered in filth from head to foot and was completely encrusted with a thick layer of clay to above my hips. My face and hands were black. Despite my appearance, I was immediately offered a chair. An old Oberst, Otto Prinz zu Schaumberg-Lippe who, in consideration of his years, was employed as orderly officer of 54th Infantry Division, personally brought me a tray of sandwiches and a glass of wine, which I was urged to consume as I provided *Excellenz* von Watter and his chief of staff with a detailed summary of the situation. I was filled with pride and satisfaction when I saw the high appreciation of our superiors for the way we had fought for Flesquières – despite the fact that ultimate success was very much open to question.

"They were under the impression that Major Krebs and his entire detachment had already been captured around midday, that I must have been given my task before then and that I must have just managed to get clear of Flesquières before it was completely encircled. I insisted that I had been present in Flesquières until after 4.00 pm and that I was convinced that Major Krebs would still be holding out. My account was punctuated by *Excellenz* von Watter saying, 'That was heroic; that would be truly heroic.' I finally succeeded in getting the Division seriously to entertain the idea that Major Krebs would still be defending Flesquières. However, although nobody expressed any doubts and simply gave me words of praise and recognition, I could not be absolutely sure that *Excellenz* von Watter and the general staff officers who were present were totally convinced.

"On the basis of their long years of war experience, officers such as they were rightly sceptical of this type of oral report brought by individual, unknown officers returning from the front line.[65] Nevertheless I was not publicly doubted and *Excellenz* von Watter set about examining ways of helping Major Krebs if he really were still at Flesquières. Unfortunately there was nothing to be done; 54th Infantry Division had no forces left at its disposal. Hauptmann Gädeke provided me with a careful and very detailed situation report, including the fact that Cantaing 'ought now' to be occupied by elements of 107th Infantry Division."

The defences at Flesquières were probed and tested constantly during the early hours of darkness. The perimeter was pulled in tighter, so as not to leave vulnerable points which were especially open to attack, but it was a nerve wracking experience for the hard-pressed garrison, particularly those located just to the east of the main village in the so-called *Südostpark* [Southeast Park].

Wehrmann Hohmann 5th Company Reserve Infantry Regiment 27 [66]

"During the evening, towards 9.00 pm, the enemy launched an attack. Dense lines of infantry attempted to capture the park under the cover of darkness. I was sitting up on the parapet of the trench and raised the alarm. My comrades rushed up immediately and opened rapid fire on the enemy. At that they withdrew and did not attack us again that night."

Back in Cambrai and about to depart Headquarters 54th Infantry Division, Brockes decided, in view of all he had been told, not to return to Flesquières via Cantaing, but to travel via La Justice. He was directed to make contact with the staffs of the formations of 107th Infantry Division on the way and to seek assistance. Meanwhile, after hours when no further information arrived, at 8.45 pm an engineer unteroffizier got through to Flesquières from Cantaing and was able to inform Major Krebs that the troops of 107th Division which had advanced to Cantaing were digging in. He could expect no assistance from that quarter. Nevertheless, Krebs despatched a situation report to Reserve Infantry Regiment 52 at Cantaing and received this reply at

2.10 am: 'During the night 107th Infantry Division has occupied the *Siegfried II Stellung* from Anneux to Noyelles via Cantaing. Front line trace: southwest entrance Anneux – La Justice – copse to the west of Noyelles. Signed: Major Steinkopff.'[67] Less than one hour later, at 3.00 am, Leutnant Brockes arrived. In accordance with his orders, he had reported successively to Headquarters 107th Infantry Division, 213 Brigade and Reserve Infantry Regiment 52. At each place he had sought support for Major Krebs, but without success.

In view of the general confusion and the uncertain situation, this was hardly a surprising reaction, but news of it meant to Major Krebs that he was now defending a lost cause. To remain where he was would simply mean the inevitable destruction of his garrison. His men had done all that they could. Now was the time to attempt to withdraw before it was too late. Summoning his officers and directing them to maintain the strictest secrecy, he ordered a withdrawal from Flesquières to begin at 4.15 am. All preparations were to be made, but the reason behind them was only to be explained at the very last minute, in order to preserve security and to prevent panic. Krebs and his garrison, comprising a mixture of men from Infantry Regiment 84 and his own Reserve Infantry Regiment 27, had succeeded in holding onto the village of Flesquières as a bastion of the defence for far longer than might reasonably have been expected. They had played a significant role in preventing the development of the attack in the direction of Bourlon Wood but, once it was clear that support would not be forthcoming, for its hard pressed garrison to stay there any longer would serve no further useful purpose.

Landwehr Leutnant Schultz Mortar Officer 3rd Battalion Infantry Regiment 84 [68]

"Night fell on 20 November. It was dark and raining heavily. The assault led by our Hauptmann had hit the Tommies hard. They did not dare to try to push further forward and we were determined to prepare to give them as hot a reception as possible, but were we not hanging in the air? We were unable to link up [with our troops] to the right or left. We then heard that the British were already occupying Noyelles, which was a damned unpleasant surprise for us. Nevertheless, our lines from regimental headquarters to the sunken road were still firmly held. The riflemen were quickly allocated positions and the machine guns set up. Fire was opened carefully all along the line and, here and there, flares were fired to give the impression that our strength was greater than it actually was. We could still hear individual tanks as they blundered and rumbled around, but they no longer disturbed us.

"Of far greater concern were the eleven seriously wounded men who had still not been evacuated. We no longer had a doctor, just one Sanitätsunteroffizier, who courageously tended the brave lads. Some of them had been lying there for half a day, their bandages soaked in blood, feverish and delirious. Their groans cut right through us. 'Leutnant are we going to be taken to the rear soon?' 'Be patient, you will all be evacuated.' Secretly, we asked ourselves, 'How?' At 1.00 am I reported personally to the regimental commander, whose serious expression gave me pause for thought.[69] 'Leutnant, what I am about to say, you are to keep strictly to yourself. It will be necessary for me shortly to give orders that we are to break clean from the enemy. Go and discuss the necessary measures with the officers in the sector. To you I am giving the order to evacuate the seriously wounded with the help of the men of the Schleswig Regiment. The road to Cantaing is still open and the fire landing on it has slackened. See to it that you achieve it.'

"Now I sent runners left and right to round up the Schleswigers. Each wounded man was placed in a groundsheet and carefully lifted up the steep steps and out of the dugout. This was not achieved without sighing and groaning because there was no time to lose. As soon as [each man] was out of the dugout he was carried off towards Cantaing. The support posts for the telephone cables made suitable carrying poles. Anybody not actually carrying [a casualty] loaded himself down with rucksacks and weapons, and off we went through the knee deep morass and water filled holes of the sunken road. Comradely feelings lent the carriers amazing strength and endurance. Finally we reached the solid road and things went better. What did we care for the falling shells? There was no cover and nobody could avoid his fate. Individuals making their way back were pressed into service to relieve the carriers for a while. Now, if we could just avoid falling into the clutches of the enemy... Nobody knew how close to the road they had pushed their lines. A patrol moved in front, ready to shout and raise the alarm. If we bumped into the enemy there would be nothing else for it but to leave the wounded for them to attend to. We carriers amounted to a useful number of riflemen, a group with whom something could be achieved. The impenetrable darkness could only be of assistance to us. In fact our soldiers' luck held once more. Towards 4.00 am we reached the entrance to Cantaing, where we soon felt safe behind the forward detachments of the supporting division. A short time later the staff arrived, followed by the remainder of the trench garrison who, together with we carriers, were reorganised into two companies."

With the evacuation of the worst of the wounded well underway, the final scenes of the defence of Flesquières were played out.

Landwehr Leutnant Bielenberg Supply Officer Infantry Regiment 84 [70]

"A few hours after midnight we received orders to break clean of the enemy as carefully as possible at 4.45 am. Landwehr Leutnant Schultz had had to make arrangements for the difficult transportation of the wounded. Just before we pulled out, we opened fire and sent up white flares in order to demonstrate that we were still there. Then, in absolute silence, we assembled in the sunken road and set off down the Flesquières - Cantaing road, the only one which was still available to us. In Cantaing we met up with elements of the support division. That we had been able to reach this temporary goal without enemy interference still seems to me today to be a complete miracle.

"A short time later the British brought fire down on our abandoned positions in Flesquières, but the Tommies no longer had any hope of nabbing us. Leutnant Thormeyer [regimental adjutant Infantry Regiment 84] put together two composite companies from the remnants of Infantry Regiment 84 and Landwehr Infantry Regiment 384. I was put in temporary command of Landwehr Infantry Regiment 384, whilst Reserve Leutnant Ofenbrück took over what was left of Infantry Regiment 84 (about fifty men). Both companies were then moved back to Cambrai without further loss."

By the early hours of 21 November most of the fighting died away and the German defenders were able to reflect on what had been one of the most disastrous days of the war for them. The 20th Landwehr Division had been brushed aside and rolled up from the south almost to Moeuvres. Large numbers of its personnel were killed or captured; when it had been placed in the line the intention had been to provide a gentle introduction to trench warfare on the Western Front, which was a very different proposition from the conditions under which it had until very recently been operating in the east. The same applied to Landwehr Infantry Regiment 376 of 109th Infantry Division, which had been moved into the position of Reserve Infantry Regiment 27 between Infantry Regiment 84 and Reserve Infantry Regiment 90 some days earlier, so as to gain experience. Leutnant Bibeljé-Schwerin, regimental adjutant to Reserve Infantry Regiment 80, later commented that this Landwehr formation was simply not equal to the demands placed on it and its failure came as no great surprise. [71]

However, the situation was not much better elsewhere. There had been encouraging successes, such as that achieved at Flesquières. In addition Moevres, parts of Anneux, Noyelles, Rumilly, Crèvecoeur, Les Rues des Vignes and Banteux were still in German hands, but the much vaunted *Siegfried Stellung* [Hindenburg Line] had been pierced to a depth of up to seven kilometres on a fifteen kilometre frontage. The remnants of 20th Landwehr, 54th and 107th Divisions and 9th Reserve Division, severely weakened and terribly intermingled, were hanging on grimly to the perimeter of the break in, with no certainty that they could hold a resumption of the offensive the following day; a view shared by the commander of Group Caudry. Because the fighting had been very severe and the Allied counter-battery fire notably effective, only eight field batteries and three heavy batteries, all below strength and desperately low on ammunition were still in the battle. Reinforcements, such as 1st Battery Bavarian Foot Artillery Regiment 5, which had arrived in Cambrai as early as 10.30 am that day, would not be deployable until late on 21 November due to lack of ammunition.[72]

Everywhere on the German side there was a huge sense of despondency and foreboding. In many cases groups of defenders had put up stiff resistance but, so overwhelming was the tank assault that, despite all the self-sacrificial gallantry, the most that had been achieved was to minimise the scale of the set back. The Army Group Commander finally summed the day up as best he could in a situation which still defied clear definition.

Crown Prince Rupprecht of Bavaria: Diary Entry 20 November 1917 [73]

"By midday it was clear that the enemy were established in the front line of the *Siegfried Stellung* [Hindenburg Line] between Havrincourt and La Vacquerie Farm and had already advanced beyond the latter. Otherwise the attacks seem to have been beaten off or only to have achieved breakthroughs on very narrow fronts in isolated places. As far as can be judged at present, the attacks between Fontaine and Bullecourt, where the British succeeded in securing our forward trenches, and the assaults on Vendhuille and Gillemont are not especially significant, whilst the attacks directed between Havrincourt and Banteux were, according to Headquarters Second Army, launched by two or three divisions.[74]

"The attack on Group Caudry of Second Army came as a total surprise. The fog during the past few days completely camouflaged the enemy offensive preparations and the attack was not preceded by an increase in artillery fire; rather large numbers of tanks cleared the way forward for the infantry. At the precise point where the deepest enemy penetrations occurred our positions were particularly strong and, for that very reason, they were garrisoned only thinly by troops with little fighting value, who were equipped with comparatively little artillery. The speed at which the tanks were able to advance due to the dryness of the going was almost unbelievable. Even more unbelievable was the way that they made child's play of breaking through the barbed wire, which before both the Main Defensive Line and the Intermediate position, was no less than one hundred metres deep – more formidable than anywhere else [along the front]. Their sudden appearance must obviously have been demoralising to the troops and there was insufficient artillery to engage them.

"By evening the overall situation was considerably worse than might have been expected from a reading of the afternoon reports. The enemy had succeeded in overrunning both the entire *Siegfried I* lines and the Intermediate Position. The Schelde had been crossed at Masnières and the advance had reached the unfinished *Siegfried II* Position. Cavalry, predominantly Indian, appeared close up by the southern suburbs of Cambrai.[75] The accusation, delivered by telephone by General Ludendorff, that we had focussed in too narrowly on events in Flanders was quite unfounded. Because it was essential to improve the offensive capability of Second Army, both the Army High Command and the Army Group directed significant reinforcements forward. The situation appeared to improve when a report was received at 10.00 pm that Moeuvres and Rumilly were back in our hands."

There may have been little fighting during the hours of darkness, but the battlefield and rear areas on both sides was a hive of activity as positions were improved, tanks maintained, refuelled and rearmed and as frantic efforts were made by the German chain of command to get reinforcements forward, make stocks of ammunition available where they were needed and to attempt to ensure that a resumption of the British offensive as dawn broke would be met by increasingly stiff and cohesive resistance. In Cambrai, Headquarters 54th Infantry Division and its commander had been under intense pressure ever since the attacks began and this continued into the night. It was a serious test for von Watter and his staff, but they proved themselves even under the most trying circumstances to be equal to the challenge.

Major Max-Georg von Köller Headquarters 54th Infantry Division [76]

"It was already dark when I returned, having done my duty forward, from the battlefield and it was time for me to resume my work with the General's staff. Absolute calm prevailed between its members. There was much activity in all the offices as officers reported in and received orders. Runners and despatch riders hurried around, bringing the latest information from the front, whilst those who had received orders rushed out. The telephones were in use continuously, maps were spread everywhere and pencils flew over paper. With a cigarette in his mouth, the general dominated his surroundings. The apparent air of calm of this man was not due to detached unconcern; the hard, sharp lines in his face made it obvious how he, inwardly, was participating in the fate of his division; of the battle; of all his soldiers who were also his comrades.

"I had to report what was happening up front and tell him all the events of the day. He quickly built up a picture in his head, adding it to the overall, almost faultless, image he carried of the course of the entire battle. Repeatedly he bit down on his lip, concealing his inner anguish when the name was mentioned of one of his finest men who had fallen before the enemy. Then he would pull himself together once more, exude calm and his features would convey his pride in the outstanding deeds and collective courage of his division. He had an unshakeable trust in his soldiers, who had never let him down and he had never for a moment doubted that they would hold on, even when the first reports arrived of the massively superior force that was assaulting his division and threatening to annihilate it...

"He was never still. One minute he would be in the pigeon loft of his headquarters, then in the operations room. He appeared first in this office, then that: assisting, giving orders, advising and taking decisive action. His hand was continually reaching into his pocket as he offered cigarettes around. When a heavy explosion made the building rock, he just smiled. He totally rejected the suggestion from higher headquarters that he withdrew from the seriously threatened and unprotected command post and reopen it further to the rear. Neither the bad news that some British tanks and small cavalry detachments had broken into the outskirts of the town, nor the report that tanks were pushing along the roads in the direction of the divisional staff, could disturb his calm demeanour or change his determination to remain here. However, at that [report] he disappeared for a moment, returning with a pistol at his belt and giving an order to the remainder to arm themselves. He then summoned some of the staff officers who were not fully committed at that time and ordered them to move off to the places at risk with all personnel who could be spared and to halt the progress of the advancing enemy detachments.

"Gradually calm returned to the battlefield, but not to the headquarters. Haggard, hungry and thirsty, looking exhausted, officers and men sat at their work places. This had not gone unnoticed by the general as he did his rounds and he appeared in the offices followed by orderlies carrying large trays of sandwiches. Everybody was urged to help himself, whilst he personally poured glasses of port wine and handed one to each individual, speaking words of encouragement to each of them, officer or soldier alike. Although urgent matters were constantly being brought to his attention, he also made certain that everybody ate and drank then, as night fell, he directed that each in turn was to sleep for an hour. He himself gave sleep no thought – he hardly seemed to need it – and, instead, took extra care to see that the others had some rest and were refreshed by a short opportunity to sleep. He imposed his will energetically on anyone who thought he did need to follow his instructions..."

It remained to be seen if the General's own iron will would be matched by his front line infantry when the battle resumed in the morning.

Notes

1. See *General Oskar Freiherr von Watter* pp 84-85
2. Hauptstaatsarchiv Stuttgart M 33/2 Bü 373a. *Anlage 4 zum Bericht der Gr. Caudry: Fernsprech Gr.Caudry an 107.ID vom 20.11.1817, 9.40 Uhr vorm.*
3. Hauptstaatsarchiv Stuttgart M 33/2 Bü 373a *Anlage 3 zum Bericht der Gr. Caudry: AOK 2 Ia/b Nr. 232/Nov. Geheim! Armeebefehl Nr 15/Nov. vom 19/11/1917*
4. Hauptstaatsarchiv Stuttgart M 33/2 Bü 373a Bü 143 *Lagemeldung des LIR 387 vom 20.11.1917 1030 Uhr & Fernspruch der Gr. Caudry an die 107. und 54.ID vom 20.11.1917, 10.50 Uhr*
5. Before his death, Hauptmann Soltau had managed to despatch two reports to 54th Infantry Division. The first read, 'We are holding out in *Kampfstellung II* [Battle Position II] as long as possible. *Kampfstellung III* will be held at all costs. Tanks have reached our position and pressed on beyond. Six to eight tanks are pressing forward against *Kampfstellung I* to the north. The artillery must bring down fire on *Kampfstellung I* and *Kampfstellung II*. We are currently reinforcing *Stollenweg* [Dugout Way]. We shall hold out to the last man. Soltau'; the second read, 'I am holding out with the gallant lads of my battalion astride *Stollenweg*. The artillery is not engaging the numerous tanks. Support needed! Get the guns forward to Flesquières! Soltau.' See History IR 84 4.Folge Nr 6 pp 48 – 49. No more was ever heard of Soltau or his men. They fell where they had fought. Hauptmann Harro Soltau's body was recovered later and he is buried in the *Kamaradengraben* of the German cemetery, Cambrai.
6. *General Oskar Freiherr von Watter* p 86
7. *Ringkanonen* were obsolescent by 1917. The 'rings' in the name were strengthening features designed to permit the use of greater breech pressures and, therefore, larger charges. As a result useful increases in range were achieved, but this 19th Century technology had been superseded by this stage of the war. Only operational demands had caused the retention in service of these weapons for so long.
8. Kessler: History Reserve Field Artillery Regiment 9 p 219

9. Schwenke: History Reserve Infantry Regiment 19 pp 287-288
10. *ibid.* pp 288-289
11. Accusations that Allied troops in the attack here and elsewhere were drunk appear constantly in the German literature, but they are generally unlikely to have been true.
12. See footnote 11. Assertions like this crop up constantly in the German accounts. They are very improbable.
13. These two guns were later recovered.
14. According to Cooper: *The Ironclads of Cambrai* p 96, this tank was badly damaged by a German howitzer on its approach to the battery position at Lateau Wood. The crew baled out but the tank was left in gear and continued, unmanned, on its way until it collided with the howitzer and destroyed it.
15 Schwenke: *op. cit.* p 289
16. *ibid.* pp 289-290
17. *ibid.* p 291
18. *ibid.* pp 290-291
19. This statement is improbable. Either he may have been referring to the crew of a disabled or broken down tank or, more likely, that he mistook British infantry following up close behind the advance, for tank men.
20. This seems slightly confusing because 7th Company was deployed just to the east of Gonnelieu, but the entire outpost line running south from La Vacquerie to Banteux was known as the *Vacquerie Stellung*.
21. Gerth: History Infantry Regiment 395 pp 140-141
22. Schwenke: *op. cit.* pp 293-294
23. *ibid.* pp 295-297
24. It is impossible to determine the veracity of this statement. Possibly it is true, but it may also be that Höft drew false conclusions from the presence of British aircraft above the battle area.
25. This appears to be a reference to the operation which led to the capture of Quennet Farm by 6th Battalion Royal Welch Fusiliers.
26. Dahlmann: History Reserve Infantry Regiment 27 p 375
27. *ibid.* p 375
28. *Erinnerungsblätter der ehemaligen Mansteiner 4. Folge Nr 13* p 118
29. This would have been a thoroughly unpleasant and dangerous experience. The jagged wounds caused by splinters of wood are frequently worse than those inflicted by normal shell splinters.
30. *Erinnerungsblätter der ehemaligen Mansteiner 4. Folge Nr 12* pp 109-110
31. This is probably a reference to one of the Dragoon regiments which moved into this area during the afternoon, but the reference to a 'great mass' is a considerable exaggeration. The total numbers of British cavalry in the forward area that day were small.

32. Ulrich: History Reserve Infantry Regiment 52 p 400
33. Interesting to note, when the time came to write the histories of the regiments of 107th Division no mention of this confusion was included. The history of Reserve Infantry Regiment 52 (p 401), for example, merely notes, "At 9.30 the divisional order arrived, 'The regiment as Group reserve is to move immediately to Proville, Cantaing and the southern outskirts of Cambrai..."
34. Ludendorff: *Meine Kriegserinnerungen* pp 394-396. Naturally none of these reinforcements could be expected to arrive before 21 November so, in the meantime, the outcome of the battle was still entirely dependent on the defending troops in place when it began.
35. Ulrich: *op. cit.* p 401
36. *ibid.* p 401
37. *ibid.* pp 402-403
38. Giese: History Reserve Infantry Regiment 227 p 411
39. These orders were extracted in turn from an order telephoned through to 54th and 107th Infantry Divisions by Group Caudry at 10.50 am: 'It is essential that the line which we currently occupy be held come what may. The counter-strokes currently in progress are to be carried out, but no others are to be launched. 107th Division is immediately to make available Reserve Infantry Regiment 52 to 54th Infantry Division. This regiment is to be used to reinforce the garrison of the *Z[wischen] Stellung*. Reserve Infantry Regiment 232 of 107th Infantry Division is to occupy the *SII Stellung* along the line Anneux – Rumilly and is to remain at the disposal of the Group.' See Hauptstaatsarchiv Stuttgart M33/12 Bü 373a Anl.4
40. Giese: *op. cit.* pp 412-414
41. Unteroffizier Franz Bienert is buried in the German cemetery at Frasnoy Block 7 Grave 226.
42. Giese: *op. cit* p 414
43. Spitlocking a trench occurs when the turf is removed to reveal the planned shape of the excavation and the spoil is removed to the depth of one spade or 'spit'.
44. Giese: *op. cit* p 415
45. *ibid.* p 415
46. *ibid.* pp 415-416
47. *ibid.* p 416
48. *ibid.* p 416
49. *ibid.* p 417
50. This composite grouping, which was hastily thrown together under the command of Major Bredelow, commanding officer 3rd Battalion Guards Reserve Regiment 1, was made up of the first units rushed forward to Cambrai. It comprised 3rd Battalion Guards Reserve Regiment 1, 2nd

Battalion Reserve Infantry Regiment 98 and 3rd Battalion Bavarian Infantry Regiment 13. Assembled in Cambrai at 4.30 pm, it was sent forward later that evening. See *Kriegsarchiv München* 1Res Korps Bd 169: IGRD Ia. Nr 6804 vom 26.11.1917: *Erfahrung im Kampf gegen Tanks*.

51. Giese: *op. cit.* p 418
52. This is almost certainly a reference to the operations of the Fort Garry Horse of the Canadian Cavalry Brigade, whose B Squadron lost forty men killed, including its commander, Captain Duncan Campbell, during the action. The remnants of the squadron subsequently conducted a fighting withdrawal back over the canal led by its second in command, Lieutenant H Strachan, who was awarded the VC.
53. Ulrich: *op. cit.* p 404
54. Bartenwerffer: History Reserve Infantry Regiment 232 p 99
55. Ulrich: *op. cit.* p 405
56. *ibid.* p 406
57. History Field Artillery Regiment 213 pp 171-172
58. This is a further reference to the activities of the Fort Garry Horse.
59. This is a reference to the arrival on the battlefield of men of the Recruit Depot 54th Infantry Division and a draft intended originally for 49th Reserve Division.
60. Ulrich:*op. cit.* p 407
61. Dahlmann: *op. cit.* p 389
62. *ibid.* p 389
63. *Erinnerungsblätter der ehemaligen Mansteiner 4. Folge Nr 13* pp 118-119
64. Dahlmann: *op. cit.* p 402
65. Brockes explained later that he had refused a written report from Major Krebs in case he fell into enemy hands during his journey – a far from improbable fate.
66. Dahlmann: *op.cit.* p 391
67. In the confusion this report was not totally accurate. Noyelles was in British hands and was not retaken until the morning of 21 November by 8th Company Reserve Infantry Regiment 232.
68. *Erinnerungsblätter der ehemaligen Mansteiner 4. Folge Nr 8* pp 62-63
69. The timings given by Schultz vary somewhat from those of other eyewitnesses. It seems probable that his interview with Krebs happened a little later than he remembered but that his party carrying the wounded were the first to withdraw.
70. *Erinnerungsblätter der ehemaligen Mansteiner 4. Folge Nr 13* p 119
71. Pries: History Reserve Infantry Regiment 80 p 238
72. Schlörer & Schwinn *Kriegstagebuch der 1. Batterie 5. bay. Fußart.-Regiments* p 42

CHAPTER FOUR

The Battle for Bourlon Ridge

The weather during the night 20 – 21 November was dreadful. It was cold and heavy rain lashed the battlefield, driven by strong winds. This undoubtedly contributed to the ability of the German defenders at Flesquières to break clean successfully and eased the movements of the first of the reinforcements, who were fed forward as soon as they detrained in the Cambrai area; but it also meant that exhausted men on both sides had to confront another hard day hungry, wet to the skin and frozen to the bone. It had not taken long to determine that Flesquières had been evacuated and, by 6.00 am on 21 November, it had been occupied by troops of 51st (Highland) Division. It had taken twenty four hours of hard fighting to achieve but now, at last, this bastion, which had held up the advance for many critical hours, was in Allied hands. From there, as dawn broke, the dense, dark mass of Bourlon Wood could be made out, looming through the early morning mist, five kilometres to the north. This was not the sole objective for 21 November, there were to be further attempts to push the 'Right Hook' forward, but it was, nevertheless, the most important and was to remain so for the coming week.

As the units of 51st (Highland) Division shook out and prepared to advance towards the intermediate objective of Cantaing, some three kilometres away to the northeast, prior to continuing in the direction of Fontaine Notre Dame, harassing fire continued to fall all along the German lines from Anneux to Banteux. Second Army had directed that priority was to be given to building up so-called Flanking Groups - concentrations of artillery to protect the shoulders of the newly formed salient – and the first unit to arrive, 1st Battalion Field Artillery Regiment 84 of 30th Infantry Division, was immediately despatched in support of 54th Infantry Division. The southern group, which was to be based around Aubencheul, about six kilometres southeast of Banteux, was placed under command of 9th Reserve Division.

As far as the German chain of command was concerned, the situation could hardly have been more grave. General der Infanterie Freiherr von Watter, commander of Group Caudry, had already submitted an assessment of the situation to Second Army which could hardly have painted a bleaker picture: 'It cannot be denied that, if the enemy continues the tank battle before more artillery arrives, an expansion of the break in and, therefore, possibly a real breakthrough will hardly be preventable. Even after this crisis is overcome, the situation will remain serious.'[1] Unfortunately the necessary artillery build up was to prove a relatively slow process. The various units had to be transported on the overcrowded rail network so, for some time, the lack of heavy field howitzers and 100 mm shells meant that artillery support continued to be precarious in the extreme. About 7.00 am there was an increase of fire in the centre of the salient as the British attempted to establish bridges in the Masnières area as a prelude to a resumption of the attack. Group Caudry, which had already expressed its extreme concern about its ability to hold on, immediately put in a request to Second Army for the entire artillery of 30th Infantry Division and all the artillery units of 214th Infantry Division as they became available.

Initially, however, the attack did not develop from Masnières, where British preparations appeared to be continuing. It was, for the time being, relatively quiet in the 20th Landwehr Division sector, apart from the fact that Moeuvres and Anneux were under heavy fire. In the 54th Infantry Division sector, British artillery fire was coming down in the rear areas and on Noyelles. Reserve Infantry Regiment 52 had retaken La Justice and Reserve Infantry Regiment 19 had conducted successful street fighting in Les Rues des Vignes – even though it had had to summon its very last battalion in order to hold on. There was great concern amongst all units and formations of 107th Infantry Division, because of the lack of ammunition – especially of hand grenades and S.m.K. rounds, almost all of which had been left behind, in accordance with orders, at Stochod on the Eastern Front. The prospect of further tank attacks in the near future was far from reassuring to the men of Reserve Infantry Regiment 52 as they lay in their shell hole positions, covered with mud and clay, and waited for dawn.

Gefreiter Skorna 1st Company Reserve Infantry Regiment 52 [2]

"Morale during the cold and wet night was hardly rosy. Up until about 8.30 pm, when we had to report to the company commander, Büder's section had worked hard on improving the position and carrying out sentry duty. A machine gun (crew) was already there when we were ordered to advance and occupy Graincourt, so as to cover the mass of wagons, guns and limbers which were continuing to pull back through it. The following morning we were to defend the place against the British, because it was assumed that the village would be the first objective. In that event [once we had imposed delay] we were to conduct a fighting withdrawal. We all felt that it was a very tricky mission, but we set off immediately, so as to carry out our orders promptly.

"On and around a prominent crossroads in the village, which was some kilometres distant...we dug holes and mounted the machine gun. Half the section was on guard, whilst the remainder took cover in an adjacent house. Still wearing our equipment, our rifles next to us, we lay down wearily in the cellar. I fell asleep immediately, but was woken from a deep sleep at 2.00 am to be given a mess tin full of cold food – my last meal given me by the Prussians had been a midday meal of cabbage the previous day. Apparently the field kitchen had arrived at the company location at 1.00 am, so the midday meal was not served until after midnight. Despite the fact that cold food and a cold stomach did not go together all that well, it tasted really quite good.

"The section commander then informed us that we were to report to the company commander at once. Our section was, in fact, responsible for the grenade launcher. About an hour later I arrived at the company commander's location. At that time, like all other members of the grenade launcher team, I was so tired that whenever I lay down I fell into a deep sleep. What we would have given for a few hours of rest! I think that we should even have given up our iron rations for it! The company commander ordered me to collect the two grenade launchers, together with several boxes of ammunition (forty to fifty rounds per launcher) and to set them up. Gefreiter Burmeister was to take command of one launcher, whilst I set up the other in the second platoon area.

"This task was not without danger because during this, the hour before dawn, the British artillery was bringing down heavy fire on the main road, together with all the other roads in the village. The shells, which I estimate were of 150 mm calibre, were fuzed instantaneously and so did not blow large holes in the main road; instead the whole area was more or less strewn with large and small splinters. Despite this fire we brought up the launchers, together with their heavy iron baseplates and their even heavier ammunition and, much to our surprise, we got back to our dugouts unscathed. In the meantime dawn was breaking on 21 November and in the early morning a car arrived from division bringing the first resupply of ammunition. This comprised only flares and small arms ammunition, but at least it was something. During the course of the morning, trucks arrived at the eastern entrance to Fontaine carrying hand grenades, mortar bombs and small arms ammunition."

During the morning tanks were seen assembling around Graincourt and were engaged by the German artillery. Elsewhere, units arriving from 30th Infantry Division were being assembled into an *Eingreif* grouping near Esnes and Second Army subordinated about two thirds of 214th Infantry Division, deployed at Sains lès Marquion and Bourlon, to Group Caudry. This enabled orders to be given to 20th Landwehr Division to take them under command and to use them to counter the threat developing from Graincourt. About midday, battle was joined in earnest as a British attack by infantry and cavalry, supported by tanks, crashed down against Moeuvres and to the west of Bourlon Wood. There was some initial success and what was left of Landwehr Infantry Regiment 386 after the fighting of the previous day was forced to pull back on its own left flank. At that, Infantry Regiment 77, which had been concentrating on tightening its hold on the trenches between Inchy and Moeuvres, released the attached 2nd Battalion Infantry Regiment 92 to launch a limited counter-attack and so restore the link to Landwehr Infantry Regiment 386.

At the same time, speedy intervention of one battalion of Infantry Regiment 50 of 214th Infantry Division meant that the south west tip of Bourlon Wood was retained after a battle which ebbed and flowed for some time. This action also involved 3rd Battalion Infantry Regiment 77 and 1st Battalion Infantry Regiment 175 forming an *ad hoc* 'Regiment Weinlig', which was forced to conduct a fighting withdrawal and to spread its ranks ever more thinly to try to cover the gaps. 3rd Machine Gun Company of Infantry Regiment 77 fought heroically, firing no fewer than 35,000 rounds in support of the battalion. Further consolidation occurred when the remaining elements of Infantry Regiment 50 and Infantry Regiment 63, under command of 20th Landwehr Division, thrust hard towards Moeuvres and Bourlon Wood. In this critical battle the divisional infantry was led in person by the divisional commander, Generalmajor von Brauchitsch. As an illustration of the appalling state to which the defence was still reduced, the only artillery support for this crucial attack comprised four batteries, drawn from three different regiments.[3] It was a desperately close run affair and was almost the final contribution of 20th Landwehr Division to the battle. Later that day, much of its communications still cut, Headquarters 20th Landwehr Division handed over command responsibility to 214th Infantry Division and moved to Douchy, where it gradually assembled the remnants of its regiments which had survived the previous day's fighting.

The battle continued to lap around Bourlon Wood but, by that evening, it was still held determinedly, if somewhat thinly, primarily by 214th Infantry Division, but with formations of 20th Infantry Division linking to its right (west). The British assault directed against the line Anneux – Noyelles, enjoyed rather more success. Here British pressure led to a breakthrough around Cantaing and the further launch of a strong infantry thrust, supported by tanks along the line of the Cantaing – Cambrai road. In the process both Cantaing and Noyelles were lost. Men of Reserve Infantry Regiment 52 saw these attacks developing very obviously from the direction of Ribécourt.

Those present later stated that there were marvellous targets for artillery everywhere, but the continuing shell shortage, coupled with the lack of available guns lost previously to British counter-battery fire and through being overrun, meant that the response was extremely muted. The defenders watched the Scottish regiments form up relatively unmolestedin in their assembly areas along the Marcoing – Graincourt road and then saw the advance begin by company columns, with mounted officers moving in amongst the ranks. There was a gentle breeze blowing towards the German lines and, carried on it, came the sound of bagpipes playing the infantry forward into battle. For the men of Reserve Infantry Regiment 52, waiting anxiously, it was the start of a terrifying few hours of extreme danger and frustration.

Gefreiter Skorna 1st Company Reserve Infantry Regiment 52 [4]

"The tanks drew steadily closer, growing before our eyes...the company commander sent a runner to me ordering me to prepare the launchers to fire, but I had already caused this to happen on my own initiative. All the ammunition had been made ready; that is to say, the bands which held the fuze safety pins in place had been removed. Everyone was feeling the tension. Would we be able to hold out? By now the tanks had closed in to about 1,500 metres. We could make out their details with the naked eye. They were great big black objects. Now, to our joy, we heard the sound of field guns, located in the village behind us, opening fire. They appeared to be engaging the tanks, but they scored no hits. They strewed their shells all over the place as though they were simply trying to get rid of them. Rounds were landing hundreds of metres left or right and either in front of, or behind, the tanks.

"The black monsters continued calmly on their way. Now we could clearly see assault groups, eight to ten strong, following each tank. Finally, at perhaps 11.30 am, the tanks were only 700 metres away. Rapid fire was now ordered. The machine guns chattered away ceaselessly and we fired our rifles against the tanks. They, however, continued undamaged on their way. There was great consternation in our ranks. We continued to fire our rifles rapidly. The assault troops following the tanks disappeared behind them as a result of all this cross fire and apparently had gone to ground. Fire was poured at the tanks. They were now four hundred metres away. The company commander was asked if it would not be better to pull back across the canal where the tanks could not cross, because we seemed to be powerless against them.

"Our guns (truck-mounted anti-aircraft guns) fell silent at that point, but we fired without stopping. A reply came from the company commander that we were to hold our current positions, so I prepared to fire my launcher. All the men felt great bitterness towards the leadership and especially the artillery, because not one single gun of ours could be heard firing. As the rifles and machine guns continued to shoot, I fired the first round from the grenade launcher. This demonstrated that the tank that was heading directly for us was still not close enough. As the first grenade exploded, it veered to the left. I redirected the launcher in the same direction and saw once more that the tank was still moving forward, but even further to the left. It is no easy matter to hit a moving target with a grenade launcher and to conduct a successful engagement is a matter of pure chance.

"Our grenades certainly impacted close to the tank which had suddenly pulled up about one hundred metres half left of us. We thought at first that we might have hit it, but we were swiftly disabused of the notion when a round was fired by its main armament. As soon as the first round was fired, we saw that it had landed perfectly ten metres to our right, in the trench manned by the first platoon. We could hear faintly above the general racket that men had been hit and word arrived that it had cost Musketier Mayer from Alsace-Lorraine one of his arms. We now came under British machine gun fire from our front, Musketier Rautenberger from East Prussia was shot through the head and instantly killed, twenty metres to my right. Meanwhile the tanks to our right and half right had approached to fifty metres.

"However, I did not pay them much attention, concentrating instead on the tank halted half left of us and trying to hit it with the grenade launcher. It set off once more, crushing the wire obstacle as though it was made of dried grass. It was now able to cover the entire position with machine gun fire from a range of only thirty metres. To have raised our heads would have meant certain death. We could hear the dull roar of its engine, then there was a pause in its machine gun fire. Immediately some comrades opened up on it, whilst others fired to the front... I aimed directly at the tank, which was thirty metres behind us and heading for the village. The round impacted on the external armour, but the tank simply opened up a lacerating rate of machine gun fire. Simultaneously, the tank to our half right began to hose the trenches with machine gun fire. It was impossible for anyone to raise his head in all this crossfire.

"The tank to our rear now spun round and began to approach us, firing its machine guns. This forced us to seek shelter in the dugout. Taking a quick decision, I heaved the grenade launcher off its stand and covered it and its base plate with clay. The tank fired directly into the dugout and machine gun bullets clattered against its walls. It was fortunate that the dugout had both an entrance and an exit, otherwise we should probably all have been hit. We were all seized with feelings of numbing desperation. It was clear to us all that, as long as the tank covered the entrance and the exit, nobody could show himself. We were consumed with immense anger at the commanders who had left us thus totally defenceless against the tanks; at the lack of any artillery support, armour piercing ammunition or mortar fire. The mortar men were located, uselessly, back at battalion headquarters in the village, having been unable to obtain any ammunition from the 'conscientious' Group Caudry. Aside from all that, it would have been quite feasible to have pulled back one kilometre behind the canal, or at least into the village, which the tanks might well have bypassed. We tossed these questions to one another, but received no answers."

These preliminary skirmishes were already proving to be costly and, by the end of the day, Reserve Infantry Regiment 52 had suffered very badly. Its companies were severely shaken by the shock effect of the tanks and visibly angry that their weapons to counter them were inadequate. Entire platoons, neutralised by tank fire or indirect fire from British artillery, were captured by the advancing British infantry, though attempts were made repeatedly to offer effective resistance.

Leutnant Mann 1st Company Reserve Infantry Regiment 52 [5]

"Together with Leutnant Neumann I occupied a small trench on the embankment of the road to Flesquières. We brought down rapid rifle fire to our left when, suddenly, I was shot in the back. I ran down into the dugout so I could be bandaged up. The stretcherbearers took my coat and jacket off. The bullet had merely grazed my right shoulder blade and the wound was not bleeding much. I put my jacket and coat back on, fastened my equipment around me and set off up one side of the embankment – just as the British were descending the other one. The gun commander, Unteroffizier Rosenhahn of 1st Machine Gun Company, just had time to remove the working parts from his gun before he had to disappear rapidly. We conducted a withdrawal towards the right and the position of 2nd Company, but were pinned down several times on the way. We were under machine gun fire and suffered heavy losses. Unteroffizier Nehring and Musketier Rock, both of whom had been with the company since 1915 and both of whom were excellent patrollers, were killed and several other men were wounded.

"I received a blow and was bowled over. It was not for several days before I discovered that a bullet had gone through my notebook, which was in my right hand jacket pocket, without causing further damage. We took up positions on the left flank of 2nd Company, thus reinforcing it and prevented the British from advancing any closer. We were occupying a trench from which we had to fire forwards, to the right and to the rear, because British infantry and cavalry were already in Cantaing and a tank was firing at our rear from there. Another tank was set on fire by Vizefeldwebel Lohrentz of 1st Machine Gun Company . Together with Leutnant Pabst, I made an attempt to regain the line of the Cantaing – Flesquières road, but it was manned by British soldiers, packed together shoulder to shoulder, who kept us at bay.

"We continued to wait for a counter-stroke and, despite the desperate situation, we continued to hold out for another three hours. Leutnant Zumwinkel ran around out of the trench moving from man to man and firing up his company. He seemed to be invulnerable. The casualties continued to mount rapidly, because we also came under mortar fire from Cantaing. One of our own 150 mm batteries also brought down fire on our own trench. Not until we fired flares did the fire lift onto the village. British cavalry launched out from there and were heavily engaged by us.[6] If the British had acted with greater daring, they could easily have captured all of us, but they did not risk closing in. The telephone line had been shot up long since. In order to pass information to the rear, I despatched a few men bearing a map with our positions marked on it and a request for both a counter-stroke and artillery fire."

As the assault against Cantaing developed, increasingly sub units of Reserve Infantry Regiment 232 were drawn into the fighting. The right flank of 6th Company, commanded by Reserve Leutnant Hauschild, was deployed right up against the outskirts of the village. Compromised once more by the lack of artillery support and anti-tank weapons, the men were unable to prevent tanks from approaching almost to within touching distance of their positions. Destroyed by gun fire, its platoons split up and surrounded, the 6th Company front was simply brushed aside. One of its platoon commanders, who was slightly wounded, managed to break through to the rear to inform 2nd Battalion Headquarters about the situation and to request support.

Unteroffizier Feldweg Platoon Commander 6th Company Reserve Infantry Regiment 232 [7]

"I requested the services of a platoon of 5th Company in order to restore the front. When we entered the village we came under fire from two tanks. I asked for several grenades to be passed to me. Joining them together into one large charge I made my way towards one of the tanks. I made a quick decision then threw the entire charge at the tank. There was a mighty explosion then the tank disappeared behind a great black cloud of smoke. About twenty minutes later I went back to it. The charred corpses of its six man crew [*sic*] lay there.

I then observed how the British were employing the second tank. I did not delay, but prepared a second charge, crept up behind it to throwing range and hurled the charge onto the tank, which tore its petrol tank off. We took the entire crew prisoner and I sent them to the rear with a two man escort. I then directed my men to re-establish the front, but we had to evacuate it a short time later; it was impossible to hold out against the overwhelming number of tanks which came against us."

This short battle did not live up to Feldweg's hopes, but he was awarded the Iron Cross First Class for his courage and leadership that day and also promoted to Vizefeldwebel. Later, the attacks by a British cavalry brigade between Cantaing and Noyelles were much less successful. They withered away in the fire of 3rd Battalion Reserve Infantry Regiment 232 which, up until that moment, had been the least engaged unit of the regiment. This did not prevent the advance from continuing. It proved to be impossible for the units of either Reserve Infantry Regiment 52 or 232 to make a firm stand anywhere. The men were so exhausted and demoralised that they gave ground steadily in the face of the continuing advance. By mid afternoon, 12th Company Reserve Infantry Regiment 52, defending Anneux, was down to twenty survivors.

Leutnant Weßlau 12th Company Reserve Infantry Regiment 52 [8]

"We saw tanks appear at the southern edge of Anneux. We were of good courage, because we assumed that our artillery would be able to acquire a target as big as this one, even in bad visibility, and destroy it. In order to be sure I despatched a runner to the rear. We observed flashes in amongst the tanks and thought at first that they were the impacts of our artillery. We soon discovered, however, that they were the flashes of the tanks firing their own guns, seemingly completely at random. As the tanks drew closer, a lot of their fire passed very close to us, but they did not enjoy much success. However it was really unpleasant when one of the tanks crossed and re-crossed our line, engaging us at point blank range with main armament and machine gun fire. The way our trenches were laid out made it very difficult to thin out [to avoid this fire] and it was only the slightly hesitant advance of the tanks and the even greater indecisiveness of their infantry which kept our casualties within bounds.

"Almost to the exclusion of the remainder, I directed only men with telescopic sights to engage the tanks, but now and again if one appeared broadside on, I had the entire company engage it. Other than that I concentrated on neutralising the British infantry with small arms fire. We derived great amusement from the fact that a field latrine made of planks, which was located about fifty metres to our front, was surrounded and engaged heavily by artillery…unfortunately a tank made us aware once more of the seriousness of our situation. This beast drove systematically along our lines, causing Thomas's platoon heavy casualties. Four men, who found themselves right under the muzzles of the tank's guns, were forced by shouted instructions from inside to walk alongside the tank and so screen it from the the fire of our men. Amongst them were Unteroffiziers Bunzlaff and Klocke and Gefreiter Gerwig. Suddenly Klocke was killed by a shell from the tank's main armament. Bunzlaff and Gerwig managed to duck behind the tank and to make their escape. They arrived at our position happy, even though they had been wounded. In this manner the battle continued through into late afternoon."

Eventually all the German troops had to withdraw from Anneux and pressure built up against Fontaine Notre Dame. A gefreiter from 11th Company Reserve Infantry Regiment 52 later recalled[9]:

"Whilst stuck in this terrible situation, an order from the regiment reached us about 3.00 pm. It directed us to withdraw to planned positions on the south west edge of the village of Fontaine Notre Dame, where sappers of Pionier Company 213 had laid out the design for the position. The route to it, about 1,500 metres, was complete torture. We had to ascend a slight rise, which lacked any form of cover and which was swept by fire from the main armament and machine guns of ten to twelve tanks, reinforced by low flying ground attack aircraft. Because we still had our coats, which were stiff with clay up to our thighs, we had great difficulties in running. When we reached the allocated trenches we came across very few men. We worked to improve the trench for defence, but the British infantry did not follow up. That day they could have reached Cambrai without incurring very many casualties."

Be that as it may, the thinly scattered defenders were unable to hold on in this area and the village had to be evacuated, with the survivors pulling back about two kilometres to the *Wotan III* line, which, had it been constructed, was intended as the final line of resistance before Cambrai. Nevertheless, the loss of Fontaine Notre Dame proved eventually to be the high water mark of the entire British Cambrai offensive. 9th Company Reserve Infantry Regiment 52 hung on, somewhat precariously, on the western edge of Anneux until it went dark, then about sixty men, commanded by Leutnant Renkert, who had been wounded, managed to escape to the north and withdraw through Bourlon Wood. Later the commander of 20th Infantry Division summarised the day's events from his perspective:

1. The Kaiser, Crown Prince Rupprecht of Bavaria and General der Kavallerie Georg von der Marwitz at Headquarters Second Army, Le Cateau.

2. General der Kavallerie Georg von der Marwitz, Commander Second Army.

3. Generalleutnant Oskar Freiherr von Watter, Commander 54th Infantry Division, complete with a trademark cigarette. He seemed to have an inexhaustible supply.

4. Defence from shell holes near Bourlon village.

5. Field Guns in the anti-tank role firing from pits.

Generalleutnant Wellman Commander 20th Infantry Division [10]

"At 2.00 pm fighting was already taking place in Bourlon Wood.[11] Tanks pushed forward to the western edge of this wood and were engaged by our artillery...I now placed all my reserves at the disposal of Oberst Eggers [commander 40 Infantry Brigade]. My left flank was in the greatest danger...If 20th Infantry Division did not now enjoy good fortune, things could be really bad! At 3.00 pm 20th Landwehr Infantry Division reported that they had no information about their troops and that the enemy was in the process of capturing Fontaine. I ordered Oberst Eggers to deploy all available forces against it. The situation was completely desperate...I was now faced with the most difficult decision I had to make throughout the entire war: Should I, with the agreement of my right hand neighbour, pull my division back...to save it from the threat of encirclement and man a new defensive line there, or should I strain every sinew to fight for my old position?...I had to make the decision entirely alone and I decided to opt for the more dangerous...The fact that it turned out to be correct I ascribe to the enemy, whose high command showed itself here to be incompetent. They could have advanced to Cambrai without resistance and probably achieved the greatest success of the war."

Further south, the British attack on Rumilly came up against firm resistance. The first wave of tanks broke through the positions of Regiment Bredelow, but other infantry units swiftly manned a counter-penetration position behind it and, racing forward, a combination of field artillery batteries and truck-mounted anti-aircraft guns destroyed the tanks which had broken through, causing the attack to stall. Bavarian Infantry Regiment 13 later claimed at least a part of the credit for this: 'The 3rd Battalion was deployed to the south of Rumilly. A British attack was launched at 1.00 pm. Four tanks appeared initially in the battalion sector. The infantry operating with them were shot to a standstill; the tanks destroyed by machine gun, mortar and artillery fire. The actual infantry attack withered away one hundred metres before our lines. Those who were not shot down flooded to the rear.'[12]

9th Reserve Division also came under attack during the afternoon. Heavy artillery concentrations crashed down on the valley of the Escaut, infantry units could be seen gathering in assembly areas and tanks were observed moving forward. At 2.15 pm, Infantry Regiment 99 of 30th Infantry Division was subordinated to the division then, shortly after 3.00 pm, heavy attacks developed to the west of Crèvecoeur and directly against Les Rues des Vignes. In bitterly contested fighting at close quarters, the attacks were held by 1st Battalion Reserve Infantry Regiment 261 of 79th Reserve Division and 3rd Battalion Infantry Regiment 440 from 183rd Infantry Division, together with those elements of Reserve Infantry Regiment 19 which had survived the battles the previous day, and the Recruit Companies of 9th Reserve Division.

Hauptmann Kühme 1st Battalion Reserve Infantry Regiment 261 [13]

"Located on the southern edge of Rumilly was the staff of a battalion which had just arrived from Russia; I think it was from Reserve Infantry Regiment 228 [*sic*[14]]. According to a briefing given by its commander, Major Feuerstein, the British had broken through on a ten kilometre front and intended to advance to Cambrai...The British use of surprise was absolutely brilliant but, as before in Flanders, the British showed that their leaders lacked training. They had not worked out how to exploit their success and to push on to their ultimate objective until after they had broken through. By then the German line had been re-established and their further attacks were beaten off. Feuerstein's front line lay forward of Rumilly. Because it was only very thinly held and had been weakened through the fighting, he requested us to relieve his men whilst it was still dark.

"However, before the companies could get forward, it was already light and the relief impossible. A patrol was despatched to link up with the regiment to the right of Reserve Infantry Regiment 228 [*sic*] and the two companies were held back in Rumilly at readiness. Shortly after it got light, 1st Company, under the very able Nadolni, arrived, together with the brave Hämke [1st Machine Gun Company] and his twelve heavy machine guns and Humann with his mortars. Whilst these elements of the battalion were busy taking up their stand by positions, the British brought down medium calibre artillery fire on the front line and the southern edge of the village. Simultaneously, troops heading for the rear passed on the information that the British, supported by tanks, were attacking to the west of the road Rumilly – Cambrai.

"At that Leutnant Steinhäuser, commanding 1st and 3rd Companies, was ordered to bring the British attack to a halt and to throw them back beyond the German front line...The way the two companies, supported by Hämke's machine gun fire and Humann's mortars, threw back the enemy, together with their tanks, has already been described in our regimental history... [15] I recall that Humann fired indirectly at the tanks from a farmyard and that one of them was knocked out by a direct hit. I also recall that the regiment to our right was already pulling back when our companies restored the situation by their action (the heavy machine guns opened up at the tanks at a range of only a few metres). Their counter-stroke meant that matters were once more in our favour."

One unusual footnote to the fighting in Rumilly was the fact that none of its French residents had been evacuated prior to 20 November. It was thought to be so far behind the German lines that the action was not necessary. During a quiet period on 22 November, after the British had ceased operations against this sector, the inhabitants piled their possession onto wagons and, assisted by men of Infantry Regiment 99, made their way to the rear, allegedly cursing *ces maudits Anglais* [these damned English].[16] Reinforcements continued to flow in. As they arrived, Second Army subordinated the formations of 119th and 30th Infantry Divisions to Group Caudry and the specialist Machine Gun Sharp Shooter Detachment 51 arrived in Cambrai to shore up the local defence of the town. By around 9.00 pm, Infantry Regiment 99 and Infantry Regiment 143 of 30th Infantry Division, together with the commander and four batteries of Field Artillery Regiment 84, were assembled at Esnes and a further two battalions had been sent to reinforce 9th Reserve Division.

Not all reinforcements came from distant sectors. Within Group Arras there proved to be scope for internal readjustments, once the dimensions of the British attack became clear. For example, occupying positions just to the west of the main battle area were formations of 111th Infantry Division. When the artillery bombardment began on 20 November this area, too, was brought under heavy fire, disrupting communications and causing casualties. However, it was soon realised that the attack was not directed at the divisional sector and orders arrived that the resting battalions should be moved rapidly to the aid of the threatened front. At 8.00 am, 2nd Battalion Infantry Regiment 164 was alerted and ordered to be ready to move off. Three hours later, orders arrived from 221 Brigade directing the commanding officer, Reserve Hauptmann Mierzinsky, to move to Dury and remain at the disposal of Group Arras. It was the start of an exhausting period for the battalion. Reserve Hauptmann Mierzinsky had had the foresight to direct his field kitchens to accompany his companies, which meant that the men at least were able to eat hot food, before seeking shelter from the cold and wet weather in houses and barns in Dury. Very shortly, however, further orders arrived that the battalion was to march forward and occupy positions in the *Wotan I Stellung* [Wotan I Position]. Despite numerous difficulties, this was achieved by 2.00 am on 21 November. Three companies manned the first line forward of the road to Hendecourt, whilst the fourth, together with 2nd Machine Gun Company, moved into the support trench to the rear and liaison officers were despatched to link up with Infantry Regiments 470 and 471 of 240th Infantry Division, which had both been under pressure

Despite its unfamiliarity with the ground and the bad weather, 2nd Battalion Infantry Regiment 164 battled its way forward to move into support of Infantry Regiment 471. Stumbling around in the cold, wet and muddy conditions through totally unknown terrain, the companies were at a low ebb as they attempted to establish themselves in a place which had no continuous trenches, merely a few dugouts, whose locations were unknown and which was only dubiously protected by a wire obstacle. It was pouring with rain, which half filled the shell holes and isolated sections of trench in which the men were attempting to take cover. The battle situation was totally unclear but, nevertheless, as dawn broke, the battalion had managed to occupy the entire 1,200 metre frontage of Infantry Regiment 471, thanks to the subordination to it of one hundred engineers and various other surplus personnel. It was a typical example of the improvisation for which the German army was well known.

Reserve Hauptmann Mierzinsky Commander 2nd Battalion Infantry Regiment 164 [17]

> "As a result of repeated heavy squalls of rain, the men were soaked to the skin and the ground was saturated and muddy. Nevertheless, the harassing artillery fire, which continually swept the rear areas, forced everyone to attempt to obtain protection in swiftly constructed shell scrapes, which quickly filled with water and became unusable. It was no better for the staff. Initially the command post was established in the second line. As a result of our [contact] patrols, news began to filter through about a major tank battle around Cambrai.
>
> "Despite all, our men behaved splendidly, keeping calm and remaining good humoured, despite the cold and wet conditions. 'Let 'em come', they said, 'No bugger is going to get through here.'

As the defending forces built up and the general development of the battle became clearer, Second Army directed that 214th Infantry Division, which had assumed responsibility for the former sector of 20th Landwehr Division, was to come under command of Group Arras, commanded by Generalleutnant von Moser. Further artillery reinforcements, in the shape of Field Artillery Regiments 20 and 61 from 10th and 25th Infantry Divisions respectively, together with the heavy 150 mm guns of Foot Artillery Battery 10 and 3rd Battalion Foot Artillery Battalion 64 were promised to Group Caudry, with arrival times during 22 November. The defence was gradually stiffening, though much hard fighting still lay ahead. Summing up the events of the day in a letter to his wife, Commander Second Army portrayed a situation rather more under control than was reflected by the reality of the battlefield.

General der Kavallerie Georg von der Marwitz [18]

> "A great many tanks have been destroyed but, naturally, not all.

The cavalry attacked, reaching the outskirts of Cambrai, but has been more or less wiped out. The woods to the front of Bourlon and Fontaine have been lost today. Comprehensive directions, from the Army High Command, designed to rectify the situation, are underway. Attacks directed at Banteux and intended to broaden the break in have been beaten off and, overall, fire has not been excessive."

Crown Prince Rupprecht of Bavaria: Diary Entry 21 November 1917 [19]

"At 8.00 am a report arrived from Second Army stating that, for the time being, the situation around Cambrai was relatively quiet. On the other hand heavy enemy artillery fire was being directed against Group Arras. At midday Second Army was ordered to retain, without fail, the canal crossings in the Crèvecoeur – Banteux sector and to mount counter-attacks to recapture the positions lost yesterday. Once more it received reinforcements. According to an order which we captured, the aim of the British attack was to achieve a breakthrough at Cambrai. To that end, stronger forces than we had estimated were deployed: two Corps, three cavalry divisions and seven tank battalions! The truck mounted anti-aircraft guns, which were used in the anti-tank role as an emergency measure, proved to be outstanding. One of them alone knocked out seven tanks. As a result all guns of this type mounted on motorised trucks and which belong to Fourth and Sixth Armies are being rushed to Second Army.

"There were renewed attacks during the afternoon. According to Second Army our infantry performed outstandingly. We have held on to Moeuvres and Rumilly, but the enemy are advancing on Bourlon Wood, whose edge we occupy. Because of lack of troops there can be no question of counter-attacks being launched before the day after tomorrow. By evening the situation along the battle front was approximately as follows: About four divisions and the remnants of two other mauled divisions are maintaining positions along the line Moeuvres – Anneux, by the recaptured La Justice Farm, around Noyelles, along the southern edge of Rumilly and around Crèvecoeur, along the Rue des Vignes, in the three bridgeheads west of the canal and in Banteux.

"Opposing them are the six divisions of the British Third Army and three cavalry divisions with, in reserve to the rear, a further two divisions and a cavalry division. General Ludendorff has been on the telephone, pressing for all forces which can be spared from Fourth Army to be moved over to Second Army. We had already made all the necessary preparations."

As Crown Prince Rupprecht had noted, as soon as his headquarters had discerned the full extent of the crisis at Cambrai, orders were given to comb out all possible reinforcements from within Army Group resources but, so overloaded was the railway system, the moves of all these reinforcing units were far from straightforward, quick, or comfortable for those involved. Frequently orders were fragmentary or non-existent and much depended upon the resourcefulness of those charged with carrying them out.

Reserve Leutnant Wilhelm Fechner Adjutant 3rd Battalion Field Artillery Regiment 20 [20]

"During the evening of 21 November, the battalion was assembled, ready to be loaded, at the station at Mouscron. The journey, which was conducted in unheated trains, took us to the south. It lasted all that night and the following day then into the next night. There were endless halts in the middle of the countryside and at anonymous stations. Whenever I asked the station commanders about our destination, they either knew nothing or did not want to know. Finally, during the night 22/23 November, the batteries detrained in Sancourt. At long last this uncomfortable train journey was at an end and the first station commander who actually had maps and orders for us was standing in front of me. Now, for the first time, we found out about the successful surprise break in by the British around Cambrai on 20 November.

"I received the orders of the artillery commander 54th Infantry Division and passed them on to my commanding officer, Landwehr Hauptmann Röpke. Hauptmann Röpke rode on ahead with the battery commanders to meet the artillery commander in Cambrai, having ordered me to lead the batteries forward during the night to Awoingt, via Cambrai. Finding the way through unknown territory was difficult and it was impossible to obtain information from men who loomed up in the night from time to time. The answer was always the same: 'We only arrived here a few hours ago!' The night was calm; Cambrai lay before us, dark and deadly quiet. The silence was only broken by heavy explosions, the noise of which reached us from the centre of the town. The market place was under enemy long range fire. The British were firing with two heavy guns.

"In order to get to Awoingt, 3rd Battalion Field Artillery Regiment 20 had to traverse the market square in Cambrai. The leading elements having almost reached the market square, I ordered the column to halt, in order to see how the market place, which was under heavy fire, could be passed most appropriately and safely. Losses to men and equipment were unacceptable; it was my job to avoid these. I soon spotted that the friendly British gunners were observing their orders to bring down night time harassing fire very exactly. Watch in hand I worked out that the British were firing at intervals of almost exactly two and a half minutes. Luckily the danger area of the explosions was not great. The British were scoring a bullseye every time.

"I took a decision. The vehicles of the battalion would be slipped across the market place individually and at pre-determined intervals. The time of two and a half minutes was sufficient for the vehicles, moving at a fast speed, to clear the beaten zone of the guns and the ensuing shell fragments. In this way, within one hour, I had slipped twenty four vehicles through. Throughout I was tortured by the thought that the British might deviate from the regularity of their harassing fire. Had that happened, I might have despatched a vehicle to its destruction. However, gun after gun, ammunition wagon after ammunition wagon, thundered through the night, crossed the market place and disappeared into the darkness. The British gunners continued their work. After slipping them across for one and a half hours, I met up once more at the appointed assembly area. All the men and horses had made it safely."

Not all redeployments were so troublesome and, by the afternoon of 21 November, leading elements of 119th Infantry Division were arriving from the previous locations in Flanders. 1st Battalion Infantry Regiment 58 was retained to assist in the defence of Cambrai itself but, by early evening, the other two battalions were receiving orders from the chief of staff of 107th Infantry Division to advance rapidly towards Fontaine and there to cooperate with Reserve Infantry Regiment 52 and launch a counter-attack to retake the village. After all that Reserve Infantry Regiment 52 had suffered during the past twenty four hours, this was decidedly over-optimistic. Already as they approached the outskirts, the forward sub units of Infantry Regiment 58 came under heavy machine gun fire. There were several half-hearted attempts to launch attacks at various times during the night, but each foundered, because Reserve Infantry Regiment 52 was completely unable to reorganise its battered sub units and get them in position on a start line to begin. Finally, at 4.30 am, 107th Infantry Division called the whole attack off until Infantry Regiment 46 could also move to take over the positions of Reserve Infantry Regiment 52. In the event it was midday 22 November before this could be done and then the subsequent assault on Fontaine was largely thanks to local initiative.

Reserve Leutnant Torzewsky 2nd Battalion Infantry Regiment 58 [21]

"It might have been about 6.00 pm when we received the following order: '2nd Battalion Infantry Regiment 58 is to withdraw its sentries and to assemble on the main road Cambrai – Fontaine at the western edge of Cambrai and is to storm the village of Fontaine, about three kilometres away.' Moving in good order, despite the enemy machine gun fire, the companies and battalion closed in tight. Enemy machine gun bullets buzzed amongst us, snapping like vicious village mongrels. It was completely impossible to determine from which farmyards these unpleasant objects were coming. We could not even tell if the fire was coming from Fontaine itself or from positions in front of the village, but there was an incident which provided us with the answer.

"The courageous field kitchen driver of a battery asserted that his battery was occupying a fire position 1,500 metres to our front. His men, who had still not returned, wanted him to bring up their rations. He ignored our warnings and headed off with his kitchen in the direction of the enemy. We listened intently to the rumble of his wheels. Then, it could not have even been five minutes later, there was a short burst of rifle fire, a few hand grenades exploded then everything was silent again. The field kitchen was no more, but we now knew that the enemy was barely 1,000 paces away. To our great joy, our own field kitchens had arrived at the assembly area. Warm noodles, known by the slang expression of 'puttees', soon filled our empty stomachs.

"In the meantime the witching hour approached. The companies deployed, rifles were unloaded so as to ensure that no round could be fired too soon and so betray our approach. Bayonets were fixed and we were off! We crept forward like ghosts, silently, avoiding all noise, until, finally, we crawled forward and formed a large semi-circle in front of the place we were to assault. The lack of enemy machine gun fire was an extremely welcome bonus. In fact the whole business seemed to us to be like an interesting night exercise. It took a good two hours for us to get into an assault position, because we had to crawl on all fours. It was boring and hard work to have to slide forward on our stomachs across sticky clay, made worse by all the rain.

"There was still an hour before that attack was due to begin; an hour before the storm! The hands on our watches crawled terribly slowly. In addition, with the temperatures only just above zero, we had to put up with cold, saturating, sheets of rain. Nevertheless our morale reflected no lack of courage, rather it was reliable and buoyed up by the thoughts of victory. With every nerve on edge and poised to spring like cats, everybody lay there, leaders and men alike, each with a watch in his hand. It was ten minutes to four; ten minutes before the moment that would remove all this tension.

"Suddenly a murmur ran along the ranks as an order was passed around. Had we heard correctly? 'Everybody, about turn, assemble at the original starting point on the Cambrai – Bapaume road.' We were speechless and bitterly disappointed. After all the strain and tension of the past few hours, this assault would have been an enormous relief, both physically and mentally. After all, we had been on our feet, without rest for forty hours now – ever since we departed Flanders. We could not understand why the order had been given and [we pulled back], muttering and cursing hard under our breath."

Elsewhere, the battlefield was relatively quiet during the night 21-22 November but, by 6.00 am, heavy artillery fire was once more coming down on the 54th Infantry Division sector. About 7.30 am a heavy British attack was launched against Rumilly and Crèvecoeur, but battalions of Infantry Regiments 99 and 143 of 30th Infantry Division, which were holding the line there, beat it off. Precisely the same thing happened to an assault against 9th Reserve Division at Les Rues des Vignes, where men of Reserve Infantry Regiment 19, supported by 1st Battalion Pionier Battalion 18 shot it to a standstill.

Hauptmann Hollender 11th Company Reserve Infantry Regiment 19 [22]

"To the right and left my flanks were hanging in the air and I had already beaten off repeated British attacks. Twice they forced their way into the trench, but on both occasions they were driven out using hand grenades. Unteroffizier Langner distinguished himself in particular. With the fire of forty rifles and two machine guns, we forced a tank, which was heading for the *Aichweg*, to turn away."

Quite plainly the impetus was draining away from the so-called right hook, though the reduction in intensity of operations in this sector was entirely consistent with Haig's original orders to Byng, which were to plan for operations extending to forty eight hours only. From this point on, almost the entire emphasis of the British offensive would be directed against Bourlon Ridge. Both Bourlon Wood and Fontaine Notre Dame were kept under very heavy fire throughout the day. In accordance with orders given the previous day, the sector came under the orders of Group Arras from 6.00 am that day.

As has been mentioned, 107th Infantry Division spent the early morning attempting to get formations of the reinforcing 119th Infantry Division into position to bolster the defences around Fontaine and, if possible, to improve the positions there.

Gradually more and more troops were being allocated to Second Army. 34th Infantry Division was moved to Esnes to act as an *Eingreif* force and 5th Guards Infantry Division was directed to assembly areas in the general area Malincourt –Villers-Outreaux – Beaurevoir – Frémont. The number of observation balloons was increased, which enabled the defence to spot British troop build ups around Fins and Metz en Couture. There were still dangerous gaps in the defences, in particular one of two kilometres between 107th and 214th Infantry Divisions, but urgent steps were taken to close it. In order to achieve this, commander Infantry Regiment 46 of 119th Infantry Division was directed at 9.40 am by Generalmajor Havenstein, commander 107th Infantry Division, to take up positions between Bourlon Wood and Raillencourt and to probe forward towards Fontaine if possible. He was further directed to make contact with the commander of 213 Infantry Brigade if he could but, failing that, to act independently.

Moving onto the high ground at Sainte Olle, Oberstleutnant Zunehmer discussed the situation with Major Richert, commanding officer 1st Battalion, who had previously been directed by divisional headquarters to move to the area with all speed. By this stage 2nd Battalion Infantry Regiment 46 was in the process of linking with 214th Infantry Division on the right and establishing its left flank on the road Raillencourt – Cambrai. Richert had planned to use 1st Battalion to extend his line left (to the east) as far as the roughly defined *Wotan III* line which ran south from the southeast tip of Sailly, but Zunehmer decided to place the emphasis on moving on Fontaine. This was an inspired decision. Although the Germans had no means of knowing it, companies of the Argyll and Sutherland Highlanders, who had been occupying the village, were withdrawn earlier that morning, leaving the place in the hands of what was later reported to be only a few hundred exhausted men of 1/4th Battalion Seaforth Highlanders.[23]

Although men of Infantry Regiment 46 marching forward from Cambrai were harassed from the air with both bombs and machine gun fire, there was little in the way of artillery fire. There was also hardly any fire coming from Fontaine and a patrol of 1st Battalion Infantry Regiment 79 was observed moving unmolested from Raillencourt to Bourlon Wood. Zunehmer interpreted this to mean that some sort of pause in operations was being observed. He was also concerned that the gap he had been directed to close would be very wide if the British reinforced their forward positions and renewed the attack. He decided, therefore, while his men were relatively fresh, to launch an immediate surprise attack on Fontaine.

At 11.45 am, therefore, Zunehmer briefed the commanding officer of his 1st Battalion in person and despatched a written order to 2nd Battalion that Infantry Regiment 46 was to assault Fontaine Notre Dame and to push on to the crest line beyond it. The axis of advance for 1st Battalion was to be the church tower in Fontaine, 2nd Battalion was to maintain contact with Infantry Regiment 50 on its right on the eastern edge of Bourlon Wood and both were informed that 2nd Battalion Infantry Regiment 58, which earlier had pulled back to the *Wotan III* line, would follow up the attack.[24]

Reserve Leutnant Torzewsky 2nd Battalion Infantry Regiment 58 [25]

"Our period of rest was of short duration. Three hours later, about midday, orders came through. 'Make ready! Fix bayonets! Prepare to assault Fontaine!' The dazed mass of men sprang into life. Both sleep and exertion were forgotten. Let's get up and at the Tommies! As though on exercise, the battalion shook out for the attack: leaders to the front, then the lines of infantry, followed by the commanding officer, Hauptmann Scholtz. He was followed in turn by the medical officer, Dr Vogeler, and his medical orderlies. It was like a scene from peacetime and it made every soldier's heart beat faster. But what followed was deadly serious. A four kilometre advance over fairly rolling countryside lay before us. Right, advance! During the first three kilometres we had hardly any casualties from enemy machine gun or artillery fire then, suddenly, we came under lacerating fire from the rows of houses, the station buildings and from a chapel which stood on a small rise. Death was stalking us!'

Meanwhile the two battalions of Infantry Regiment 46 had deployed. Its 2nd Battalion spread out, all four companies in line, in a convenient hollow between Raillencourt and Bourlon Wood, where its 5th Company linked up with Infantry Regiment 50 on the edge of the wood, despite suddenly coming under heavy artillery fire, which appeared to have been directed from the air and which forced it to move further forward. 1st Battalion was slightly more compressed, advancing with 1st Company right, 3rd Company left, each supported by a machine gun platoon. 4th Company was echeloned in depth covering the left flank and 2nd Company formed a third wave. The regimental commander managed to make contact with the guns via the operations officer at divisional headquarters and arranged for fire to be lifted from Fontaine and on to the rise one kilometre forward of it, then the attack began. Oberst von Teichmann, commander of Infantry Regiment 77, had a grandstand view of the attack from a hill to the north of Bourlon Wood and he, no mean soldier himself, later commented that the progress of the attack as its well drilled lines pressed forward unstoppably on Fontaine was an absolutely remarkable sight.[26]

One of the reasons for his excellent view and for the smooth progress was that the ground favoured Infantry Regiment 46 for most of the advance. Only when it had closed to within 600 metres was the precise direction and strength clear to the beleaguered defenders of the village. In addition, the various preliminary moves appeared to have confused the British aerial observers. There was a response by the British guns, but it was not properly concentrated, the attackers moved swiftly and there were very few casualties from this source. The total lack of tanks available to the defence was also significant. By 1.00 pm, 1st and 2nd Battalions Infantry Regiment 46 were fighting for the northern outskirts of the village, 2nd Battalion Infantry Regiment 58 was about 1,000 metres in rear and advancing rapidly and 3rd Battalion Infantry Regiment 46 was moving to reinforce the centre of the attack.

Despite heavy fire from the northwest tip of the village, aggressive action by 2nd Battalion Infantry Regiment 46 enabled rapid progress to be made, for positions to be overrun systematically and, in the case of Fähnrich Heinz, 5th Company, a British machine gun to be captured and turned on its previous owners. The 1st Battalion, in contrast, suffered heavily during the capture of the station and railway embankment. All the officers of 1st Company became casualties in rapid succession, but decisive action by men of 4th Company Infantry Regiment 46 and the timely intervention of 2nd Battalion Infantry Regiment 58 had enabled the consequent slight check to be overcome and, by dint of further hard fighting, all resistance gradually ceased and the village of Fontaine was once more in German hands by 3.00 pm.

Reserve Leutnant Torzewsky 2nd Battalion Infantry Regiment 58 [27]

"There was no time to lose. Doubling forward, we closed with the enemy. We reached the chapel and within a few minutes had secured the railway station. The Tommies fled back behind the protective walls of the house in the village and we closed up to the railway embankment, which was located about two hundred metres from the houses. Here we paused and took cover. The enemy poured a crazy rate of fire on us from their protected positions and caused our assault to stall. Shouts of encouragement and the example of the leaders were in vain. We could get no further. My platoon was on the extreme right flank of the battalion and elements of our neighbouring regiment, *Graf Kirchbach*, [i.e. Infantry Regiment 46] moved forward as well, interspersed [amongst our sub-units].

"What was to be done? To delay would merely increase the number of casualties. Almost every round the enemy fired seemed to find a target, whereas we could not draw a bead on them in their concealed positions. My company commander, Reserve Leutnant Krüger, rushed over to my platoon, which was nearest to the houses and which, thanks to the presence of men from Infantry Regiment 46, was also the strongest. We had a quick discussion, then the two of us, together with ten fearless volunteers from Infantry Regiment 58, sprang to our feet then, brandishing spades and rifles and shouting the command, 'Everybody on your feet, double march!', we launched forward. The example worked. As one man, the entire line of 58th and 46th charged forward, oblivious of the death dealing fire, into the village street. Those enemy who were to slow to take to their heels were captured and we pressed hard up behind those who fled.

"Firing from a standing position, we sent shots whistling after them. Their captured machine guns were turned around and used against them as well. Reserve Leutnant Rossow fell at this time, cut down by a machine gun bullet.[28] We fired after them for a few moments then followed up, but heavy fire from the direction of Bourlon Wood forced us to take cover in a hollow near the railway embankment. At the same time the company on our left had stormed and captured La Folie Wood and the high ground to the right of it. This meant that contact was lost between us. Our comrades on the hill, led by the Battalion Orderly Officer, Leutnant Schulz, had had a hard fight of it and had suffered severe casualties. Shouts for help reached us and, although it appeared to be impossible to make our way upwards for three hundred metres through heavy fire, we had to respond...

"Every man who was taking cover to my right and left, about fifty men of the 58th and 46th, obeyed my order, 'On your feet! Double march!' Dashing forward in bounds, crawling at times, boiling with sweat, we worked our way forward. Out of all the brave young lads, most of whose names I have now forgotten, I can still recall the sight of the youthful Musketier Figas, barely twenty years old, keeping pace with me and frequently charging ahead, [despite the weight of] his light machine gun on one shoulder and heavy boxes of ammunition in his other hand. I gave the brave lad a hand and on we went through the murderous flanking fire. Somehow we got there in one piece and were able to both fill the gaps and ease the shortage of ammunition. Armed with this, the counter-attack of the Scottish Guards [*sic*] was nipped in the bud by our joint rapid fire. With that the main battle of the day was over. It soon went dark and the exchanges of small arms fire died away. The day was ours! A wonderful feeling of victory swelled within us."

The 9th Reserve Division area continued to cause concern because at that time there was still no way of knowing for certain that offensive operations had effectively been called off in that sector; naturally the Germans were not privy to the original forty eight hour timetable. 1st Battalion Grenadier Guard Regiment 3 and 3rd Battalion Guards Field Artillery Regiment 4 of 5th Guards Infantry Division were rushed there on arrival and leading elements of 28th Infantry Division began to arrive at various off-loading points. The defence of Cambrai was also placed on a firmer footing. Oberst Freiherr von Buttlar-Brandenfels, who was commander 9 Ersatz Brigade of 20th Landwehr Division, was formally placed in command of the town and all defending troops within the built up area came under one single headquarters for the first time.[29] On the battlefield it was a relatively calm day. During the morning there was no further action in the 54th Infantry Division area, whilst troops facing 107th Infantry Division around Cantaing and Noyelles were observed digging in and consolidating.

During the night 22/23 November there was a great deal of British artillery fire throughout the Cambrai area but, as increasing quantities of ammunition became available to the defence, for the first time serious concentrations could be brought down against British troops gathered between Le Pavé and Gouzeaucourt and around Villers Guislain. This work by the gunners was coupled with feverish activity by both sides as they sought to manoeuvre newly arrived reinforcements into position so as to be able to renew operations on Bourlon Ridge the following morning. Supported by about ninety tanks, IV British corps launched an attack with over twenty infantry battalions on a ten kilometre front from Moeuvres to Cantaing.

Anticipating a hard day ahead, at 8.30 am Group Arras had already brought to readiness one infantry regiment and two field artillery battalions from each of 30th and 119th Infantry Divisions in Cambrai. In addition, one third of 5th Guards Infantry Division and 43rd Infantry Division were directed to form themselves into *Eingreif* groups and to be on standby, ready to react, in Beaurevoir and Esnes – Walincourt. Then, in order to fill the gaps in the chain of reinforcements, one third of 28th Infantry Division was ordered forward to Esnes and one third of 220th Infantry Division, which was still in the process of arriving in the area, to Cattenières.[30] Towards midday heavy artillery fire began coming down all along the Bourlon front as far as Rumilly then, more or less exactly at 12.00 pm, the British attack, supported by tanks, was launched against the entire front from Moeuvres to Fontaine Notre Dame.

Very soon serious assaults were being reported by the defending units. For example, no fewer than twenty four tanks, leading the way for the attack of 152 Brigade, were said to be heading for Fontaine. Due to the violence and weight of the assault, there were break ins to the defences both at that place and Bourlon Wood. Infantry Regiment 46 of 119th Infantry Division (which by now had assumed responsibility for the 107th Infantry Division front) mounted a spirited counter-stroke, which enabled it to hold on against the Scottish regiments at Fontaine, but attacks by the British 40th Division at Bourlon Wood enjoyed considerable success. Once the advance had pushed north up through the wood, a further thrust by tanks against 2nd Battalion Infantry Regiment 46 in Fontaine was launched from within it. Emerging from its eastern edge, the tanks got separated from their accompanying infantry and suffered accordingly. It was later claimed that six had been knocked out by the infantry using hand grenade charges.

In fact the defenders had little choice. Their grenade launchers had still not been adapted for direct fire and no guns were on hand to take on the anti-tank role. However this regiment had practised its tactics for dealing with tank attacks. This was based around separating tanks and infantry – a task made somewhat simpler because, once more, their experiences a few days earlier at Flesquières notwithstanding, the regiments of 51st (Highland) Division hung back in the assault and left the tanks isolated. Dispersing to one side, the forward troops allowed the tanks to penetrate into the village, there to be dealt with by depth positions. In the meantime, the original front line was reoccupied, the British infantry was brought under extremely heavy fire and the assault was stopped in its tracks. Altogether, about a dozen tanks got into Fontaine and the tank hunt went on for some considerable time. A male tank, C47 'Conqueror', which featured a painting of a German soldier surrendering (presumably to encourage others to do likewise), was pursued for hours by a two-section team from 1st Company led by Feldwebelleutnant Holtzhausen. Caught in unsuitable built up surroundings, the tank crew attempted all manner of manoeuvres to escape, smashing through the cemetery wall twice, knocking over fruit trees and demolishing the wall of a house – but its efforts were in vain. Cornered and knocked out, its crew were shot down as they attempted to escape and much the same fate was suffered by the remaining armoured vehicles.[31] Out on the other flank, the attack on Moeuvres was held with relative ease.

By far the heaviest of the fighting took place within Bourlon Wood that day. Following earlier actions, Infantry Regiment 50 of 214th Infantry Division was in need of relief but, although moves were made to achieve this late on 22 November, the commander of Infantry Regiment 50, Oberst von Paszenski, had not received orders to that effect. Instead, Infantry Regiment 50 remained in command and 1st and 3rd Battalions Lehr Infantry Regiment relieved his two depth battalions. It was considered too difficult to carry out the relief of 3rd Battalion Infantry Regiment 50, which was occupying the southern part of the wood that night. The result of this was that the concentrated attack by 40th Division hit a miscellany of units, half of whom had barely had time to orientate themselves and none at all to establish links or junction points with their neighbours. Most of 1st Battalion Lehr Infantry Regiment was held back in reserve near Bourlon Chateau, or was manning positions in an old communications trench just to the south of the track from Bourlon – Sains lez Marquion. To its left it was in contact with no other unit; to its right was one company of Infantry Regiment 50. Its 2nd Company deployed to the northern section of the western edge of Bourlon Wood, with only a visual link to 4th Company Infantry Regiment 358. The 3rd Battalion was scattered around the eastern outskirts of Bourlon village and the northern section of Bourlon Wood.

To compound the difficulties even further, the two commanding officers from the Lehr Infantry Regiment were called to an Orders Group at Bourlon Station by Generalleutnant Märker, commander 214th Infantry Division, at

9.00 am. Out of this emerged an order for 3rd Battalion to begin the arrangements for relief of 3rd Battalion Infantry Regiment 50 from 10.00 am. As a result, when the bombardment of the wood and surrounding area began some time after 11.30 am, the reconnaissance group was moving forward to check out the relief. For the moment there was no link with the troops fighting on the southern edge. Faced with an attack by about fifteen tanks and supporting infantry, the greater part of 3rd Battalion Infantry Regiment 50 and three platoons of its associated machine gun company were cut off and captured.[32] Infantry Regiment 50 ordered a counter-stroke, to be carried out by its own 1st Battalion and that of the Lehr Infantry Regiment. In fact, such was the confusion that the passage of orders was extremely haphazard and, in addition, the sheer speed of the attack, coupled with the extreme violence of its accompanying drum fire, meant that many other groups were isolated and killed or captured, before the situation was temporarily restored somewhat later.

In the meantime, the defence found itself very much on the back foot. The dense undergrowth within Bourlon Wood, its hills, ravines, numerous sunken roads which criss-crossed it and the fact that many of the defenders were completely unfamiliar with their surroundings, made for an extremely difficult battlefield environment, as this account from a member of 3rd Battalion Lehr Infantry Regiment makes clear:

Sergeant Kreibohm 10th Company Lehr Infantry Regiment [33]

"Towards 10.00 am all the unteroffiziers and the company commander made their way to *Kampfbataillon 50* [3rd Battalion Infantry Regiment 50] in order to view the 'position'. Only Feldwebel Bayhinger and I remained with the company. The Tommies began to get restless, so we increased the alert state. The artillery fire became heavier and heavier and shells began to come down in our vicinity. British airmen, a whole lot of them, flew low over the wood. There could be no doubt; the Tommies were about to attack. We deployed; there were some seriously wounded men. Suddenly, coming over a rise in the wood to our front, were the company commander and the unteroffiziers. What a piece of luck! The Tommies hammered the wood madly with shells and shrapnel rounds. Trees flew in all directions then, running from the front, came some individuals who were fleeing the Tommies. They carried on until they reached the sunken road Bourlon – Fontaine. Everything was complete confusion. There were already dead and wounded.

"We got up out of the holes and lined the embankment of the sunken road, then it was a matter of firing as quickly as we could. To the left the road took a turn to the rear. It was unoccupied. If the

Tommies were to reach that point they would be able to take us from behind. I pointed this out to a feldwebel from 12th Company, which was located to our left, but he did not move to it. At that one of the feldwebels of our company ran over to the bend with five other men. The entire place was enveloped by the smoke from shells. Everyone pushed towards the village. To the left the Tommies advanced up to and across the road. Mounting a machine gun at the bend, they swept the road with fire.

"Our men had to pull back from there because the Tommies had worked their way round to our rear. Some of the company ran to man the embankment facing to the rear. Our front was still half left. The Tommies continued to advance. Making an enormous racket, a tank moved along the road. We pulled back through the wood which was under extremely heavy fire. No matter! The main thing was to get clear of the wood! British machine guns were already hammering away to our left."

In fact by this time and making use of covered approaches in the wood and high walls, the British had reached the northern edge of the wood and the brickworks near to the command post of 3rd Battalion Lehr Infantry Regiment. Its adjutant wrote a detailed account of events in a letter despatched immediately after the battle.

Reserve Leutnant Neuendorf 3rd Battalion Lehr Infantry Regiment [34]

"Our house stood where the track forked, so the British brought it, in particular, under fire. Shells crashed down in front, behind and to the sides of our home so that the walls shook and the window panes – those that were not already smashed to fragments - rattled. It was not exactly comfortable, but we settled down to finish off our midday meal from the day before. From time to time we had to dash out onto the road to keep a look out. It will bring a ray of sunshine to my twilight years to remember that nevertheless I ate my whole share. Some shells that crashed down rather too close forced us to take cover in the cellar, where there was a concrete shelter. We had not got as far as the stairs when there was a hell of a crash. A shell had smashed straight through the concrete wall without causing any more damage than a few superficial scratches on the persons of some men who were already sitting in it. What were we to do? The actions of the British forced us to consider our position.

"The artillery fire, which up until then had seemed fairly innocuous, was concentrating about one hundred metres in rear and infantry direct fire weapons were already impacting on the building. There were no reports from the front. Because of the wood to our front and the extensive brickworks we could not observe anything, but the fire made it obvious what was happening. The Orderly Officer rushed in with the order for a counter-stroke. 'Now is the time,' I said to the Hauptmann. Order: 'Everyone out! Follow me!' Taking the lead, the Hauptmann and I made our way carefully through the small arms fire that was increasing in intensity – not to the rear, but one hundred metres further to the left, to the sunken road and our reserve company. Order: 'The hill to the front of the sunken road is to be defended to the last man.'

"The company commander, Reserve Leutnant Leißner, displaying exemplary calmness and energy, deployed a few men who, despite the raging artillery fire, had held on with him in a place totally bereft of cover. The battalion staff, just the officers and a few men, took over the left flank. Our medical officer and some men who remained behind in the cellar had already fallen into the hands of the British, who were pressing up close behind. If the concrete shelter had not been pierced right in front of our noses, I should by now have been sitting in the same positions as our friendly cousins! In these situations it is better to be outside.

"We now set about defending the sunken road. To our right the British had broken through. To our left there was nobody in sight at all. There were about thirty of us to cover 500 metres. 200 metres to our front, the British were lining the edge of the wood. We now began to bring down rifle fire. Our enemy checked then stalled. Sadly we had no machine guns with us. Suddenly from the right we heard: tak, tak, tak; a tank was closing in on our right flank. Remarkable to relate, it drew off when fired at with small arms by an infantry section, which the company commander despatched to the right flank. It hauled itself around heavily and waddled off through the village. The British infantry did not advance any further.

"The British set about wearing us down with artillery fire, concentrating lovingly on our sunken road for about twenty minutes. Because our firing line was so thinly manned this gave us an anxious twenty minutes but caused no casualties. The attempted British attack which followed was immediately halted by our rifle fire. But - what terror! About 400 meters away on our left flank, the British came strolling out of the wood. The six rifles of the battalion staff first forced the forty men to take cover. Over the next two hours, having noted where the firing was coming from, one by one they crawled back on all fours. It was a jolly sight! Now the British attempted to pull their last trick against our damned sunken road: they hurled aircraft at us.

"For about half an hour six of the beasts buzzed around our heads, dropping bombs and machine gunning us. It was a bloody unpleasant situation. They flew so low that we had the feeling that they could reach out of their machines, grab us by the collar and whisk us away! We made ourselves as small as possible! At long last, after hours in our island, surrounded on all sides, relief arrived. A counter-stroke, launched by a battalion from each of Infantry Regiments 50 and 175, advanced and took the village. We had already thought about pulling back a number of times because our ammunition was running out, but there had been no prospect of success. Our battalion trumpeter, Sergeant Zimmermann, who had been wounded by the tank's machine gun, attempted to withdraw but, the moment he left the sunken road, he came under British machine gun fire from the edge of the wood and was hit three more times – luckily not mortally.

"Shortly before it went dark the edge of the wood was free of enemy. Our few men had halted the enemy attack. Of course, in rear nobody had any idea about our little band. To 'ease our existence' even more, our own artillery despatched a few shells into the sunken road. At about 4.00 pm things were relatively quiet and we were all extremely happy. Yes, it was real warfare once more! Despite the ticklish situation, it was one hundred times better than Flanders. There the artillery was much worse and there was nothing for it but to hold fast and die. Here, we were the ones dealing death."

It seemed to the defenders that the assault on Bourlon Wood broke down into two main phases and that the attack on the western section and up to the village of Bourlon itself began rather later than that aimed at the eastern part of the wood. When it came, much of the attack was met by 1st Battalion Lehr Infantry Regiment. Under the protection of smoke, a number of tanks in support of the British 121 Brigade launched an attack into the gap between 2nd and 1st Companies and on into the southwest outskirts of Bourlon. The danger spotted, there was a mad scramble as elements of 1st Company Lehr Infantry Regiment and 1st Battalion Infantry Regiment 50 rushed to man a sunken road in that sector and so attempt to halt the advance. Well equipped with machine guns, the defenders caused extremely severe casualties to 121 Brigade. In fact, by that evening 13th Battalion Green Howards and 20th Battalion Middlesex Regiment had almost ceased to exist. The tanks had also had a hard time, one of them falling to the machine guns of the Lehr Infantry Regiment.

Unteroffizier Hetschold 1st Machine Gun Company Lehr Infantry Regiment [35]

"We saw the British about 400 – 500 metres away and advancing. We held our fire, even though we had a brilliant field of fire. My Gefreiter, Bumger, manned one weapon. I wanted to fire the other one myself. We allowed the British to get to 300 metres then I gave the signal to open fire. We were on target from our first bursts. Never before had I been able to see so clearly what a well-manned machine gun could achieve. From the many who had set out, those British soldiers who could still move scattered, but they too were brought down. After about half an hour we had completely beaten off the attack. We celebrated like tiny children. We then lit up cigarettes and awaited developments. Suddenly from our left half rear came the clank of metal. A British tank was steering for us and was firing. Our comrades yelled and leapt for the sunken road.

"I heaved my gun round and loaded 'K' [i.e. S.m.K.] ammunition. There was no time for thought; the monster was within twenty metres of me. I fired at the place where I had been taught. I could hear that my gefreiter was also firing. There was a whirring noise and smoke appeared. Men jumped out of the monster and raced away. Driverless, it came past us burning. It ran into a concrete block and jammed there. Just before that I saw my gefreiter receive a direct hit, which hurled the machine gun up into the air. I yelled, but nobody was there. Suddenly, two gunners came rushing up out of a bunker, their faces as white as chalk. I thought it over. We could not stay here. We were down to two boxes of ammunition, so we had to pull back into Bourlon.

"Deciding quickly, I took up the gun, the two gunners carried the boxes then we crept back into the sunken road and headed off to the right. We then had to cross some open pastureland. I pushed forward, but the British had reached this meadow ahead of us! When they saw us, however, they broke off and disappeared off to the left. We took cover gratefully behind a barn. Our hearts were beating fit to burst and we could hardly breathe. We had to get back to the white chateau where our battalion reserve was on stand by. My two gunners carried the gun and I one of the ammunition boxes. The other one was thrown away in shock by one of the gunners when he saw the British soldiers.

"We went through a garden and pushed through a hedge. My two gunners were in the lead. Suddenly there was a burst of British machine gun fire at close range. Schütze Raschkowsky yelled out loud and collapsed, as did the other gunner. I threw myself face down behind the hedge. A few seconds passed then there was a shout and I heard one of my gunners being told to carry something. Suddenly they were pushing past me and I heard the gunner say, 'The Korporal's dead.'[36] They moved on, leaving me lying where I was. As soon as they were a little way off I sprang to my feet and hared off behind a house, where I bumped into an Unteroffizier from 2nd Company. We decided to try to break through and we succeeded in traversing the village. On the far side of the railway embankment we reached our rallying point."

Writing in his diary later that day, the commander of Group Arras neatly summarised the events of what had been a testing day for his corps and also illustrated how rapid the build up of defending troops had been.

Generalleutnant Otto von Moser Commander Group Arras [37]

"Today I have at my disposal more than six divisions (11th, 240th, 20th, 214th, 21st Reserve and 3rd Guards). In addition, the number of artillery pieces on the battlefront has risen to more than 200 and the number of flying units to seven. That makes it possible to carry on [the fight], but today has been an especially difficult and critical day. The British have introduced new forces along the Inchy – Fontaine Notre Dame front, reinforced their artillery and doubled their air attacks. It is clear that they intend today to force a breakthrough at this point. The chief of staff, recalled by telegram, arrived back and I moved my office or, more properly, my command post, into the music room on the ground floor, right in amongst my staff, where I could be reached at any time. Briefing followed briefing; decisions were given thick and fast.

"In two places the enemy hurled themselves forward with extreme violence: during the morning around Moeuvres, for which place a hard battle of ever-changing fortunes was fought. During the afternoon there were repeated attacks against Bourlon Wood then, in the late afternoon, there was yet another attack directed at Inchy. The attack against Bourlon Wood was accompanied by numerous tanks and there the fighting continued with bitter intensity late into the night. Elements of 3rd Guards Infantry Division were deployed there but, towards evening, the enemy, with vast numerical superiority in infantry, which was heavily armed with machine guns and supported by a large number of tanks, pressed on deep into Bourlon Wood and Bourlon village itself.

"A daring counter-stroke pushed them back from the northern sector of the wood into its centre and Bourlon village was recaptured. The chateau and its British garrison were completely surrounded. Heroic deeds occurred all along the front. Numerous tanks were knocked out in front of Bourlon and in Bourlon Wood itself. Losses were high and the infantry is very worn down. It is fortunate that our artillery and airmen are gradually gaining the upper hand, otherwise the situation would be almost desperate. I express words of appreciation and recognition to the troops and their commanders, but I leave no doubt that, in no circumstances, may the enemy renew their attack out of Bourlon Wood tomorrow! Counter-attacks were to be prepared everywhere. I departed for bed. My thoughts were serious, but I had trust in my courageous troops."

The fighting was renewed throughout the day. Heavy losses were suffered on both sides and more tanks were knocked out on the approaches to the village. That evening, the leading British troops having been forced back out of the village, the remnants of the Lehr Infantry Regiment and Infantry Regiment 50 were drawn in tightly to positions east and west of Bourlon. The situation was extremely critical but already, before night fell, the next of the formations of the outstanding 3rd Guards Infantry Division (which the previous year had fought with exceptional skill and bravery to hold the Ovillers shoulder, during the initial stages of the Battle of the Somme) was ready to enter the battle for Bourlon Ridge. By 3.45 pm 23 November the men of Grenadier Regiment 9 were already on the march towards Sailly-Raillencourt. The commander, Major von Seelhorst, went on ahead in order to be briefed and receive orders from the commander of 214 Brigade, Generalmajor Maercker. Here he was told:

> "The village of Bourlon has been recaptured by elements of Infantry Regiments 50, 77, 358 and the Lehr Infantry Regiment. The west and southern edges of Fontaine [Notre Dame] are being held by Infantry Regiment 46 and Reserve Infantry Regiment 46. However, the British with tanks in support, have forced their way into Bourlon Wood. There are still pockets of German troops in the wood, but their numbers are too few for them to be significant. The enemy are not firing their artillery much and ours is fairly weak at present."[38]

Generalmajor Maercker then ordered the regiment to carry out an immediate counter-stroke, aimed at recapturing the wood and adding that, if it was not in German hands by the morning, there were plans to abandon the Cambrai positions altogether. The situation in the wood was fundamentally unclear. 1st Battalion Guards Field Artillery Regiment 5 took up positions to the south of Raillencourt and Major von Seelhorst gave out his orders to his battalion commanders on the southern edge of Raillencourt:

> "The battalions are to line up in the order 1st, Fusilier [3rd], 2nd along the Cambrai – Arras road, left flank on the Raillencourt – Fontaine road. The flanking battalions are to echelon one company in rear in order to provide flank protection against any possible counter-stroke. The operation is to begin at 9.00 pm, with each battalion advancing on a 700 metre frontage. There is to be no firing, but hand grenades are to be prepared and bayonets fixed. The assault is to continue to the southern edge of the wood. Regimental Headquarters

will be established in the last house in Sailly-Raillencourt in the direction of Arras. The Regimental Pionier Company will be located there at the disposal of the regiment. Heavy machine guns are to spread all along the line."[39]

On the ground it had once more been a desperately hard day, but both the Army and Army Group Commanders, maintaining a necessary detachment from the intensity of the contact battle, were both able to summarise the fighting without indicating the slightest trace of overall concern.

General der Kavallerie Georg von der Marwitz [40]

"There has been heavy fighting around Moeuvres and, about midday, a thrust towards Fontaine, spearheaded by eight tanks, was beaten off. Later, however, the enemy succeeded in manoeuvring around Bourlon Wood and reaching the built up area. Fighting was still going on there this evening. I visited several divisions and was happy with the command and control I observed."

Crown Prince Rupprecht of Bavaria: Diary Entry 24 November 1917 [41]

"A whole series of observations and intelligence reports indicate that the enemy are transporting troops southwards from the Flanders front. Whilst the number of enemy batteries opposite Groups Lille, Aubers, Loos and Souchez has reduced, in the centre and left flank of Group Vimy there has been an increase. The enemy are likely to do everything possible to exploit the advantage they have gained at Cambrai and to try to expand on it by means of an attack against the left flank of Sixth Army, which could possibly be launched astride the Scarpe. Diversionary attacks launched simultaneously at St Quentin and to the south of that place are to be expected. At any rate there has been an increase of artillery fire against the positions there and it was especially heavy at Hancourt.

"When I arrived at Headquarters Second Army at 9.30 am, I was informed that Bourlon Wood had been completely recaptured and that rather a large number of knocked out tanks had been discovered. It is now certain that the British deployed all of their nine tank battalions and it appears from examination of captured documents that the British Fifth Army [sic] was inserted between the First and Third. General von der Marwitz stated that, as soon as the artillery had been supplied with four days' supply of ammunition, the counter-attack would be mounted; this would probably be on 27 November. It would be launched from the east and would probably extend south as far as Gillemont Farm."

At exactly 9.00 pm, the battalions of Grenadier Regiment 9 were on their start line, with their left flank anchored on the track running from Sailly-Raillencourt to Fontaine. All was relatively quiet. Artillery fire was coming down generally throughout the area, but the sound of machine gun and other small arms fire had died away. Silently, bayonets fixed, belts hung with hand grenades, the line advanced through the moonlight towards Bourlon Wood, whose silhouette could be picked out like a dark mass on the horizon. Moving forward as quietly as possible, the regiment crossed the railway embankment, to the evident relief of the exhausted remnants of Infantry Regiments 50, 77 and 358 who were clinging on to their rough positions there. Still nothing broke the silence as, through the darkness, the shape of the wood loomed ever closer. Finally, at about 10.30 pm, the companies entered the wood.

The situation was far from ideal. During the advance the 2nd Battalion got off line and became separated from the remainder, dragging 11th Company with it. It then missed the edge of the wood and moved towards Fontaine. The remainder, struggling with tangled clumps of brambles, undergrowth and boggy areas, pressed on into the wood. The alarm had still not been raised, not even when Offizierstellvertreter Hohenstein of 9th Company came across a British listening post and captured the occupants. The enemy lines were thought to be 500 metres further on and, once more, there was a whispered order to move as quietly as possible. Suddenly, there was a clash and heavy small arms fire was opened by both sides all along the line. In a thoroughly confused close-quarter battle, the dull thud of hand grenades exploding mixed with the crack of bullets and the rattle of machine guns.

There was no point in delaying further. Through the hellish cacophony of noise, the men of Grenadier Regiment 9 launched a wild charge. Eyewitnesses later spoke of the sight of shiny bayonets lit up by the flashes of exploding shells and grenades, as a running hand to hand fight for possession of the wood began in earnest. The commander of 1st Battalion Grenadier Regiment 9 reported at 12.15 am: 'Heavy small arms fire in the wood. [There are] huge areas of swamp and ravines the depth of houses in several places. To cross them is extraordinarily difficult.'[42] Nevertheless progress continued to be made. Leutnant Knecht, Fähnrich von Horn, together with a few men of 2nd Company, spotted a light at one point. Heading straight for it, they overran a broken down tank and captured it, together with those of the crew who had not been shot down. Some idea of the intensity of the battle may be gained from the experiences of a member of the 3rd Battalion.

Reserve Leutnant Bethge 10th Company Grenadier Regiment 9 [43]

"Apparently there were still some [German] troops to our front and we were supposed to incorporate them into our attack. We, however, only came across the occasional, totally exhausted individual, whom we left where he was found. Continuing to believe that we would locate a German defence line to our front, we pushed on into the wood, through the dense undergrowth. Together with my platoon commanders, all my runners and medical orderlies, I was located in front of the centre platoon and gave the order, 'Centre Platoon, make for the felled fir tree to your front.' This fir tree was about sixty metres away and around it were located – the British!

"Scarcely had I given the order than small arms fire came down, which forced the Centre Platoon into cover. The hail of fire may have only lasted about one minute, but it was the worst that I experienced throughout the war. My platoon commanders, all my company and platoon runners, my batmen (my courageous Bölke and also Böhm) were all seriously wounded. Sanitätsunteroffizier Noak was killed as he tended the wounded. By some miracle I was the only one not hit. I crawled forward a short distance amongst the dead and wounded and dug in about fifty metres in front of the British. During the night I was joined gradually by the brave Unteroffiziers Streek and Ratschinsky, together with Vizefeldwebels Genzen and Dittmar and all their men, who dug in silently. The groaning of the wounded was awful. In addition the Lewis guns continued to pour fire down at a range of fifty metres."

The further the penetration into the wood, the more the defence stiffened. It was clear that ground had been gained, pressure had been relieved and a useful buffer obtained, but it was equally obvious that large parts of the wood were still in British hands. A renewal of the attack was conducted at 7.00 am but, after the strenuous efforts of the previous night and consequent severe casualties, it was not possible to bring to bear sufficient concentrated force and the attack ran out of momentum swiftly. The net result was that it was in no position to counter the main attack of the day by the British 40th Division against the wood and the village, which developed around mid-afternoon.

Generalleutnant Otto von Moser Commander Group Arras [44]

"Already during the night I was informed to my great joy that the Pomeranian Grenadiers [Grenadier Regiment 9] had stormed Bourlon Chateau and had thrown the British back into the depths of Bourlon Wood once more. In addition Moeuvres is once more in our hands. The movement of 3rd Guards Infantry Division and 21st Reserve Division is now complete and most of their infantry is already committed to the battle. Leading elements of 221st Infantry Division are arriving, not to mention a continuous stream of fresh batteries by rail or road, together with ammunition and more aircraft. What the Army Group has achieved in terms of the supply of reinforcements all along the Cambrai battlefront ... is quite remarkable.

"Despite that the Group is extremely busy with the business of command and control. Today is the fifth day of intense battle. Above all, clear orders must be given concerning the organisation of fire missions of the artillery, which today has increased to almost three hundred guns. A Bavarian artillery commander has arrived. To him I have given orders that the railway embankment to the north of Bourlon Wood is to be prepared for defence and equipped with mortars. In addition, the poplars lining the main road from Cambrai to Douai are to be felled, so as to produce a large tank obstacle.

"In the morning the happy news arrived that fifty prisoners have been taken and a number of tanks have been captured. However, during the afternoon, once more there were heavy attacks against Inchy – Moeuvres then, towards 6.00 pm, an appalling weight of artillery fire came down, causing all the windows in the chateau to rattle. This was followed by an extremely determined attack against Bourlon Wood, launched by very strong forces and supported by thirty tanks, which forced its way to the outskirts of Bourlon once more... The situation is extremely critical because our infantry, both leaders and men, are totally exhausted through the constant fighting and the strain of the cold, stormy weather.

"Energetic measures are essential, We throw in everything we have within range to Bourlon Wood: on foot and using vehicle convoys. Commander 3rd Guards Infantry Division assumes command of the sector. I give orders for a night attack against the village, followed by an assault in the early morning against Bourlon Wood. The aim is to ensure that in no circumstances can the enemy establish a foothold to the north of the wood. The reason is that there are now about fifty German batteries in positions behind the railway embankment, which would be lost in the event of a breakthrough. At 12.30 am I telephoned all the front line divisional commanders, in order to convince myself that the line Inchy – Moeuvres – Bourlon would be held whatever might happen and that the thrust against Bourlon and the wood was being properly prepared. Once that was finished I had done everything in my power. I know that the eyes of the whole of Germany are directed via the army communiqués to events around Bourlon Wood and the threatened breakthrough. I am also well aware that if there is a serious reverse here, my name will always be coupled to it. With those serious thoughts in mind, I finally turned in to sleep."

The defence of Bourlon village had been largely in the hands of elements of the Lehr Infantry Regiment. As the attack developed, the whole western edge of Bourlon, including the station, was in British hands. From their positions the British threatened to enfilade the right flank of 3rd Battalion Lehr Infantry Regiment, which was manning the embankment with two platoons arranged one behind the other, front facing the station.

Reserve Leutnant Krümmel 1st Company Lehr Infantry Regiment [45]

"During the morning of 24 November, heavy British harassing fire began to come down. It continued until 3.45 pm when, using the same routes as the previous day and protected by smoke, seven tanks advanced against the southwest corner of the village and opened heavy fire with both machine guns and main armament against us. We responded as hard as we could and succeeded in knocking out a tank with our S.m.K. ammunition at a range of fifty metres. However, this used up our total stock of special ammunition. The entire crew of the tank was killed. Some of my men examined the tank immediately, both for rations and anything else that looked to be worth taking. We were able to capture several bars of chocolate, which we had long coveted, together with boxes of biscuits and a good compass.

"At 4.30 pm the British [infantry], which had been following the tanks, succeeded in advancing via the edge of Bourlon village to the western exit where the road to Bourlon to Sains–lès–Marquion led off. Our troops, which had been located in the village, had pulled back along the same road, but failed to conform to the positions of the 1st Company so, once more, its left flank was hanging in the air. As a result, the British forced their way into this section of trench, but were swiftly ejected by an immediate and daring attack with hand grenades by Sergeant Westphal and some determined fusilier guards. Unfortunately, Westphal was severely wounded during this action. The British troops, (as we were able the following day to verify, by examining where their dead lay) had forced their way about 800 metres along the road towards Sains–lès–Marquion and had fired at the rear of the company. Leutnant Krümmel immediately ordered two machine guns to be turned around and for the fire to be returned.

"The company now found itself in the not altogether comfortable situation of having to defend on three sides. To make things worse, two light machine guns were knocked out by artillery fire. Leutnant Krümmel borrowed one light machine gun from the reserve platoon of 2nd Battalion Reserve Infantry Regiment 88, which was located on its right flank, reported the dangerous situation of 1st Company Lehr Infantry Regiment to the commanding officer of 3rd Battalion Reserve

Infantry Regiment 88 and requested the support of one platoon of infantry. This support was refused, despite the fact that the battalion had a platoon in reserve. In view of the fact that the company was surrounded on three sides by the enemy and was running short of ammunition, it was necessary at all costs to get a report through to its superior headquarters in order to provided relief for the company in its very unpleasant situation.

"This was not just a matter of the well-being and woes of 1st Company. Because it was impossible in the darkness to establish the strength of the British detachments which had forced their way onto the road to Sains–lès–Marquion, or whether they had been reinforced, it would have been quite possible that our own troops deployed in Moeuvres might have been attacked from the rear. In order to deliver the necessary report a four man patrol, commanded by Unteroffizier Weichenhahn, was sent out, ordered expressly to fight their way through to the battalion command post and to request support. Hours went by, Unteroffizier Weichenhahn had not returned, so Vizefeldwebel Geschke, accompanied by one other man, Fusilier Guard Rösner, volunteered to try to get through to the battalion command post. He was despatched, accompanied by the blessing of the entire company.

"Suddenly Unteroffizier Weichenhahn and his daring party returned. He reported that, despite heavy fire, they had passed through the British positions and had found the battalion after a lengthy search. On the basis of his report 3rd Battalion Fusilier Guard Regiment was launched in a counter-stroke against Bourlon. Vizefeldwebel Geschke also returned safely, despite coming under fire. During his return journey Unteroffizier Weichenhahn had come across rations and equipment, which he recognised as belonging to the 1st Company carrying party. It later transpired that these men had run into the arms of the British in the dark near the Sains–lès–Marquion road. After a sharp fight ten of them, mostly wounded, had been captured. Eight men were able to make their escape. Instead of receiving a much needed hot meal, the brave fusilier guards of the company just had to go on sticking it out – and they duly did."

Had the Army Commander been aware of the ferocity with which Bourlon Ridge was being defended, he would have felt reassured. As it was, when he came to write his daily letter to his wife, it is evident that he felt pressured by the turn of events and was concerned about how the battle would develop.

General der Kavallerie Georg von der Marwitz [46]

"Once more Bourlon and Bourlon Wood are in our hands. Grenadier

Regiment 9 (Stargard) again distinguished itself there. Numerous tanks were knocked out. From midday onwards very heavy attacks were renewed all along the front, but I hope to be able to hold with the forces available. During the morning I was visited by Crown Prince Rupprecht and I outlined the plans for attack which I wish to carry out on the Banteux flank. He was in agreement. This is major battle at its most outstanding. The two Richthofens are in action here in the air and both have shot down an opponent. The French are hovering around St Quentin and appearing as though they wish to launch an attack with five divisions. If that happens I shall have a second focus of battle to deal with and everything possible is being done to counter this possibility. Stapff (Chief of Staff) and Ditfurth (Head of Operations) are performing brilliantly.

"During the afternoon it transpired that there was not in fact a major attack in progress. The report came from airmen who had mistaken knocked out tanks for serviceable ones. I have given orders that stocks of bundled grenades are to be held available for use by those manning the forward trenches, so that they can be thrown under the tanks as they approach the positions."

Summarising initially the fighting during the night 24/25 November, then moving on to describe developments during the following day, Commander Group Arras noted in his diary during the evening of 25 November:

Generalleutnant Otto von Moser Commander Group Arras [47]

"In a night attack our troops have once more ejected the British from Bourlon village and the northern part of the wood. Thank heavens! I recommend the regimental commander, Oberst von Paszensky, who directed the attack, for the Pour le Mérite – and he receives it. British strong points in the village were cleared out in wild, bloody and merciless hand to hand fighting. However the tough British did not just accept the situation. Instead they launched further attacks against Sailly and Bourlon Wood. Despite the stormy weather, once again today our airmen maintained air superiority over the battlefield and reported the move forward of forty tanks from Flesquières to Graincourt in a timely manner. This was a juicy target for our artillery which brought a torrent of fire down on them, destroying some and forcing others to turn away. By evening we had captured three hundred prisoners from four British divisions. According to their statements, yet more are available on readiness behind them. However, from about midday today most of the fears at Corps Headquarters faded; we had the feeling that the British were not going to be able to break through!

"At midday the two divisions on my right flank, the 111th and 240th, were subordinated to the newly inserted Group Lewarde (XVIII Army Corps). This was a pleasant and, increasingly, a necessary relief to us… In the meantime I have to give absolute priority to providing my increasingly tired infantry with as much help as I can. I despatched officers to all divisions in order to discover what the troops required. Following that, convoys of trucks were sent forward carrying ammunition and hand grenades, but also drinks, bacon, sugar and bread, together with woollen blankets and huts which could be assembled rapidly."

So much for the view at Corps level. The, 'wild, bloody and merciless fighting,' which had left a deep impression on all the participants and alluded to by von Moser was described in some detail after the war by eyewitnesses from 3rd Guards Infantry Division.

Reserve Leutnant Schafrinna 1st Company Fusilier Guard Regiment [48]

"On 24 November the company was ordered to advance in a west southwesterly direction as the right hand company of the battalion, with its right flank on the station, to maintain contact with the 3rd Battalion and to clear the British out of the village. I set off from my start line on the railway embankment to the east of Bourlon and, with scouts deployed, headed for the railway station which, according to reports, was in British hands. The scouts checked the station buildings and discovered that they were unoccupied. When they attempted to continue the advance, however, they came under intense machine gun fire from the loading ramp and the houses to the south of the tracks. Because the orders to 3rd Battalion had been altered and they were now approaching from the west to clear the village as far as the church; and in view of the fact that the right flank of 1st Battalion was under threat, the battalion commander ordered me to smoke out the British nest in Bourlon Station.

"One platoon, commanded by Vizefeldwebel Maushake, swung round to attack on the right, but this attempt was halted by machine gun fire. During a second attack, a platoon of 3rd Company attempted to surround the position from the rear, while two hand grenade troops of my company assaulted the loading ramp. This attack, too, failed; machine gun fire from the flank was too strong. A third unsuccessful attack was also launched. Because of the lack of exact information concerning enemy strength and the fact that the extent of their positions was unknown, there was no immediate prospect of success, so I decided to wait for morning in order to avoid unnecessary casualties. The 3rd Company platoon was withdrawn and the remainder of my company went firm by the station and the village itself.

"The following morning I orientated myself over the exact situation, the layout and strength of the British nest of resistance. I then issued the following orders: one assault troop under Vizefeldwebel Maushake, together with one heavy machine gun commanded by Vizefeldwebel Schade, 1st Machine Gun Company, was to capture the loading ramp. 2nd Platoon, commanded by Vizefeldwebel van Hoorn, was to provide fire support from a flank to aid the advance of the assault troop and was to engage any enemy attempting to escape. Despite the fact that there was obstinate defence the assault succeeded, thanks to the total commitment of the assault troop. The enemy, attempting to withdraw, ran straight into curtains of machine gun fire.

"The nest of resistance had been garrisoned by approximately 150 men and fifteen machine guns. Thirty prisoners were taken and eleven machine guns captured. About fifty were killed and the remainder, all of them wounded, moved back without their weapons westwards along a communication trench where they were processed by 3rd Battalion. Our own casualties amounted to three killed and ten wounded."

Reserve Leutnant Krümmel 1st Company Lehr Infantry Regiment [49]

"In an attempt to avoid the mopping up operation, a British company approached the left flank of 1st Company Lehr Infantry Regiment. The men deployed there immediately opened fire. Leutnant Krümmel hurried across and, accompanied by Vizefeldwebel Geschke and ten men launched an attack on the British to shouts of *Hurra!* After brief resistance, to our surprise they threw down their weapons and surrendered. It was not clear if their loss of courage to continue to resist was because they were not anticipating that we would be in that particular place; or that the extraordinary quantity of machine gun fire from Bourlon station had worn them down; or the loss of their captain, whose death was confirmed to me by a British lieutenant, 'He is killed' [*sic*].

"British artillery fire continued to come down on our positions throughout the morning. To have gathered together the prisoners for counting and movement to the rear, therefore, was hardly to have been recommended. Eventually the company commander ordered one of the unteroffiziers to establish exactly how many there were, so the unteroffizier and a few men escorted them to the rear and numbers were checked at the battalion [command post]. The count revealed that there were eight officers (two of them severely wounded) and 120 men. Naturally the entire 1st Company was delighted at this success and morale soared. It was also possible now to establish what the British losses of the previous day in the company sector had been. In the immediate vicinity of our trench there were about one hundred dead and a great many wounded. The company took great satisfaction that the British had met their fate so close to its position. The remainder of the day passed in an atmosphere of proud calm."

Later that day, once reports had been passed upwards to Second Army, it was clear that the defensive success at Bourlon was the source of considerable satisfaction to the commander and deemed worthy of inclusion subsequently in the daily Army Communiqué.

General der Kavallerie Georg von der Marwitz [50]

"*Totensonntag* [All Souls Day[51]]. The morning report contained the highly pleasing information that, at 2.00 am, two battalions of the Fusilier Guards retook Bourlon at bayonet point. It is probable that this was made possible by the outstanding performance of Grenadier Regiment 9, which has maintained a firm grip on the adjacent Bourlon Wood. Once again the regimental commanders were outstanding; leading from the front. I must obtain *Pour le Mérite* orders [for them]. The men are superb. Later I am going to visit the 3rd Guards Division. In meeting the emergency, it has worn itself right down. Today there has been no major action in the sector of the break in. It appears that the quarry position has been lost at Banteux, but we still hold the canal crossing."

Army Communiqué 25 November [52]

"After a heavy bombardment, during the evening the enemy attacked Bourlon Wood and village. Hidden by smoke they pressed forward to the village. The Fusilier Guards, launched forward in a counter-stroke, succeeded in the course of a bitter fight in the darkness with fixed bayonets in driving the enemy back to their start line. For their part, the Pomeranian Grenadiers manning the edge of the wood shot every enemy thrust to a standstill."

Following the see-saw battles of the past few days, 26 November was relatively quiet. The German defenders made full use of the pause to redeploy their forces in and around Bourlon and to improve the anti tank obstacles which had been thrown up there. It was, nevertheless, quite evident that a further major effort on behalf of the British to force a decision on Bourlon Ridge was in the offing. Despite the pressure of operations on the ground and, increasingly, in the air, there was still time for a certain amount of socialising. Profiting from the slight reduction in intensity that day, during the evening of 26 November Freiherr von Richthofen [The Red Baron] was the guest at dinner of the officers of Group Arras.

Generalleutnant Otto von Moser Commander Group Arras [54]

"There was fighting once again in Bourlon Wood during the night. During the afternoon battles with hand grenades occurred around Inchy. In the evening there was a further strong British attack against Bourlon village and the woods to the east of it. This was beaten off. On both sides there was a great deal of aerial activity and artillery fire. The enemy appears to be carrying out reliefs. Prisoners have stated that the British 40th Division has been almost completely wiped out. We have received further artillery reinforcements…

"When I retired Lessing's words about me and my staff were running through my head, 'Their efforts deserve universal praise.' Earlier I had the pleasure of the company of Rittmeister von Richthofen at dinner – despite all his fame he is of exemplary modesty and a good companion. He explained to us, in simple terms, that the entire secret of his success was his firm decision in aerial combat to approach enemies so closely that he both pressured them psychologically and was certain of hitting them with his machine guns. In other words the same principles apply in the air as on the ground! When our First Adjutant remarked to him at the table that he had now done his duty and could in future restrict his contribution to the important task of training newcomers, he replied, without a trace of bitterness, 'I am not numbered amongst those whose primary concern is to survive the war and to preserve their valuable lives for the post-war world'."

During the night 26/27 November there was considerable activity behind the British lines as the Guards Division moved into position to assault Fontaine Notre Dame and men of 62nd Division prepared to launch what was to be one final all-out effort to secure Bourlon Wood and village. Drum fire began coming down at around 7.15 am on 27 November then, at 8.00 am, the attacks began. The British 187 Brigade, supported by eleven tanks closed up on Bourlon village, where their advance was shot to a complete standstill by 3rd Battalion Fusilier Guards. The fact that the tanks arrived some hundreds of metres ahead of the infantry certainly helped. In complete contrast to the shock caused only a week previously, when surprise was on the side of the British attackers, this time, with the assistance of makeshift tank obstacles and two guns in the anti-tank role, not even the presence of tanks was able to shake the forward defenders.

In fact three of them were swiftly knocked out in front of the village, at the price of heavy casualties amongst the crews who continued to serve the guns under close range small arms fire. Men of 10th Company Fusilier Guards managed to scramble on top of two other tanks which succeeded in breaking into Bourlon village and, after a wild ride right round the village, succeeded in posting hand grenades inside them and bringing them to a halt. A further two tanks were destroyed by solo attacks launched by Unteroffizer Donath and Meißner of 9th Company with bundled hand grenades. Both were awarded the Iron Cross First Class for gallantry. Lacking intimate tank support, the infantry of 187 Brigade was abruptly halted by massed automatic fire, including that supplied by the use of large numbers of Lewis guns captured during the recent fighting.

The story was much the same for the attack of 186 Brigade in Bourlon Wood itself. Progress towards the northern edge of the wood was made, despite the heavy defensive bombardment which was brought down on it, but there can be no doubt that the defence was pressurised once more and that only good, determined leadership and courageous defensive work saved the day – as this description of the fight for the sunken road to the east of the village demonstrates. This sector was the responsibility of 11th Company Lehr Infantry Regiment under their energetic commander, Reserve Leutnant Leißner.

Reserve Leutnant Fischer Fusilier Guard Regiment [55]

"Early on 27 November the entire hullabaloo began all over again. The brickworks and crossroads came under fire from large calibre shells. Moving rapidly to the rear, wounded men and captured Tommies, their hands above their heads, told of severe losses. They were joined by men from all sorts of different regiments, streaming backwards and announcing that the Tommies were coming. The 11th Company took up positions along the sunken road and the swarm of stragglers, naturally telling their favourite tales about machine guns jammed with mud, were forced by the energetic intervention of Reserve Leutnants Leißner and Herbert to take up positions in amongst our company. Other comrades were deployed to block the routes to the rear. We let none of them through and even though we received dirty looks, it all helped somewhat.

"As we were lying there manning the embankment and adjacent

meadow we heard, coming from the wood, a strange roaring and clanking. Then, from out of a clearing, spitting fire and puffing smoke came a 'Male Tank'. Initially some men wanted to drop back into the shelter of the sunken road, but they stayed put when they saw that others were holding fast. Anti-tank ammunition was brought out, a murderous rate of fire was opened and bundled grenade charges were made ready. The British occupied positions along the edge of the wood, so some of us brought fire down on them. Rockets were fired to inform our artillery about the appearance and whereabouts of the enemy. The response from the, fortunately numerous, artillery within range, was prompt and accurate. Shells began landing very close to the tank.

"The battle continued like this for some time. It was clear to the Tommies that they were not going to get any further forward here. The tank turned around and disappeared back into the wood, at which we all breathed a sigh of relief but, simultaneously, fire came down from the brickworks to our half right rear and the meadow had to be cleared."

This action was critical for the ultimate success of the defence, a fact which was acknowledged later when Reserve Leutnant Ließner received the Iron Cross First Class for the stubborn resistance his men had mounted. There was a similar vital intervention at Fontaine at more or less the same time. Reserve Infantry Regiment 60 was at readiness in the *Eingreif* role, when information arrived from 6 Guards Infantry Brigade at 9.00 am that Fontaine had come under enormous pressure. A patrol was despatched forward but, by 9.40 am, orders arrived that a full scale counter-stroke was needed. It would coincide with a similar operation by 1st Battalion Reserve Ersatz Infantry Regiment 1 directed into Bourlon Wood. Despite the urgency of the situation, the attack against Fontaine could not simply be improvised, so it was a full two hours later that Reserve Infantry Regiment 60, advancing two battalions up, hit the northwest corner of Fontaine and made rapid progress. Three German field guns were recaptured, together with one anti-aircraft gun in use as a tank destroyer and men of 8th Company Infantry Regiment 46, who had been trapped in catacombs beneath the church, were released once more.

Within an hour the entire village was back in German hands but, as ever, a price had been paid. Leutnant Röttger, Offizierstellvertreter Drewes and nine other ranks were killed, the loss of Drewes being particularly keenly felt.[56] Despite the apparent stabilisation of the situation on the Group Arras front, its headquarters continued to redeploy its forces and to pour fire into Bourlon Wood and on the British positions before Fontaine. At the end of the day, when there had been no renewal of the British attacks, its commander settled down to summarise the events of the day.

Generalleutnant Otto von Moser Commander Group Arras [57]

"The eighth day of battle and, once again, what a hard day it was! When I awoke at 7.00 am it was still dark and I could hear the sound of an extremely heavy bombardment: a major attack was underway against the centre of my position. Supported by our artillery, the 21st Reserve Division and 221st Infantry Division, which were deployed there, beat it off. Simultaneously, however, the British launched another attack against Bourlon Wood, using strong infantry forces, accompanied by thirty tanks. This threw the very tired – in fact exhausted – garrison, back to the northern edge, captured part of the village and by midday it was pressing towards the railway embankment to the north of the wood! To our left, in the sector of the neighbouring group, Fontaine Notre Dame was lost. This was a breakthrough!

"But we did not lose our nerve, as the British had evidently hoped. I caused Bourlon Wood to be shelled from all sides by the heaviest possible artillery fire, effectively neutralising and isolating it. Rarely have I ever heard such a bombardment! Simultaneously, all our ground attack aircraft flew sorties against Bourlon Wood and Fontaine. I also sent several reserve battalions of 221st Infantry Division on foot and by truck to support the troops who were fighting so hard at Bourlon Wood. I also ordered an immediate counter-attack and despatched two officers from corps headquarters in order to bring me oral reports about the situation. Now it was a matter of remaining calm and patient and awaiting success, which could not be expected to be achieved for several hours.

"I can confirm that I had both – yes, I even found time and opportunity to send brief letters about the battle to three friends at home and also to draft the citations for the *Pour le Mérite* for the two divisional commanders who had so courageously defended the right and left flanks of my Group sector since 22 November and would certainly continue to do so. I never doubted inwardly for a single instant that I should be able to despatch both proposals tomorrow morning. In actual fact and, admittedly, not until after a bloody see-saw battle with heavy casualties all along the front, was the entire attacking line thrown back into Bourlon Wood and ejected from Bourlon village. In the same way, troops of Group Caudry succeeded in assaulting and recapturing Fontaine. I was filled with the deepest gratitude for my brave men and I spoke by telephone, expressing these thoughts to the commanders involved.

"It was necessary that night to relieve 3rd Guards Infantry Division, which had borne the main load of the battle, replacing them with the

221st Infantry Division. I now regard the attacking power of the British to be so attenuated that we shall have a quiet day tomorrow. We certainly need it if we are still to be able to summon up sufficient strength for our own assault on 29 November."[58]

His overall view was also shared by the Army Group Commander.

Crown Prince Rupprecht of Bavaria: Diary Entry 27 November 1917 [59]

"During the day there was heavy fighting for the village of Bourlon, Bourlon Wood and Fontaine. At the cost of high casualties, the enemy only succeeded in seizing the greater part of Bourlon Wood. For the time being it does not appear as though new enemy reserves have appeared on the battlefield."

Both commanders were quite correct in their assessments. In fact, once it became clear to General Byng that this latest attempt had failed, even more obviously and decisively than some of the previous assaults, he gave orders to Lieutenant General Woollcombe, Commander of the British IV Corps, to suspend offensive operations, consolidate where he was and to begin work on defensive positions. The battle for the Bourlon Ridge had frequently been a close run affair, but the German chain of command had recognised its key importance as soon as it was threatened and had strained every sinew, not only to reinforce it, but to do so with formations of the highest quality. The smoking wrecks of tanks and the enormous numbers of fallen who littered the slopes below Bourlon village and Fontaine and who lay scattered throughout the ploughed up wood bore testimony to what, ultimately, was a clear-cut German defensive victory. The development of the early stunning success of the British surprise attack had petered out into an offensive abandoned for lack of further resources.

Of course there were still small scale actions to come and it was at that stage impossible for the defence to be sure that the British offensive had finally shot its bolt, so, for the time being, Group Arras continued to maintain the pressure on the British troops within its sector. On 28 November General von Moser noted:

Generalleutnant Otto von Moser Commander Group Arras [60]

"Last night we poured gas shells into Bourlon Wood so as to spoil the British stay there. Throughout the day the engagement of the wood with high explosive continued. Apart from that there were only minor clashes. The prisoners spoke of heavy casualties and reliefs. One hundred Irish guardsmen marched past my headquarters. These were all upright, well-built men, who reacted to the words of command of their NCO by marching to attention with such precision that it could only have been achieved through lengthy practice of drill. How come all the talk of German militarism! The contrast between these guards and the scruffy prisoners belonging to the 62nd Division could hardly have been more striking."

The end of serious fighting for Bourlon Ridge meant that the whole emphasis of operations for the Germans moved from the defensive to the offensive. Some days later, when its further retention had become pointless and costly, the British withdrew. There was a remarkable amount of battlefield tourism by the Germans when the battle died down – probably because everyone was curious to examine the tanks at close quarters. Commander Second Army was no exception and, on 4 December, he visited the Group Arras battlefield, picking his way past wrecked and burned out tanks and spending some time walking through the tangled remains of the once-magnificent rides of Bourlon Wood. Writing to his wife on 5 December, he remarked:

General der Kavallerie Georg von der Marwitz [61]

"Yesterday I was in Bourlon Wood, which the British had evacuated and which looked absolutely dreadful. The British had done everything to push through the wood and, when that was unsuccessful, had to remain there. It became an evil experience for them. We drenched the entire wood with large amounts of gas. It was, in fact, the park belonging to Bourlon Chateau and contained many beautiful oaks and beeches. In a similar way to our beeches, [it] stands on rolling countryside, which is criss-crossed by numerous ravines and steep tracks. In went the infantry and in, too, went the gas. It was clear to see on the many dead that they had been using gas masks; whilst all round lay piles of equipment of the type that an infantryman will only leave behind when he is forced to. It was quite obvious to the eye that this had been pure hell..."

Notes
1.   Strutz: *Die Tankschlacht bei Cambrai* p 72
2.   Ulrich: History Reserve Infantry Regiment 52 p 409
3.   Viereck: History Infantry Regiment 77 p 476
4.   Ulrich: History Reserve Infantry Regiment 52 pp 412-414
5.   *ibid.* pp 414-415
6.   It is probable that this is a reference to a unit of the British 1st Cavalry Brigade.
7.   Bartenwerffer: History Reserve Infantry Regiment 232 p 105

8. Ulrich: *op. cit.* pp 418-419
9. *ibid.* p 420
10. Wellmann: *20.Inf Division in Ost und West* quoted Viereck: *op.cit.* pp 482-483
11. This is a reference to the first assault on the wood, conducted by troops of 186 Brigade, 62nd Division.
12. Mark: History K.B. Infantry Regiment 13 p 83
13. Reserve Infantry Regiment 261 *Nachrichtenblatt Nr 32* pp 2-3
14. The unit involved was actually part of Reserve Infantry Regiment 227 of 107th Infantry Division. Reserve Infantry Regiment 228, part of 49th Reserve Division, did not join the battle until 24 November, having moved south from Flanders and not west from Russia.
15. Apparently the attack was supported by four tanks, which caused confusion and panic, but a hail of fire from every weapon available to Reserve Infantry Regiment 261 caused it to stall on the edge of Rumilly. Here aggressive work by the German guns partly destroyed the tanks and made the remainder turn away. The two companies then launched attacks on the British infantry who were occupying heights 300 metres south of the village, in a strength of about two companies. They threw them off the heights and subsequently held them. See Schwerin: History Reserve Infantry Regiment 261 pp 166-167
16. Petri: History Infantry Regiment 99 p 101
17. History Infantry Regiment 164 p 424
18. Tschischwitz: *General von der Marwitz* p 259
19. Kronprinz Rupprecht *Mein Kriegstagebuch Zweiter Band* pp 292 - 294
20. Benary: History Field Artillery Regiment 20 pp 332-334
21. Schmidt: History Infantry Regiment 58 pp 204-205
22. History Reserve Infantry Regiment 19 pp 299-300
23. The German army later believed that they had been fighting men from two battalions – one of Argyll & Sutherland Highlanders, the other from the Seaforth Highlanders. See Zunehmer: History Infantry Regiment 46 p 336. They were also adamant that a machine gun detachment, sixteen guns strong, was involved in the defence. The truth probably lies somewhere in between. It took the attackers three hours to subdue the defence, which suggests that the garrison was of reasonable size when the operation began.
24. A chance encounter between the regimental commander and a staff officer of 107th Infantry Division had enabled the former to request this support and so prevent his left flank from hanging in the air during the attack. See Zunehmer: History Infantry Regiment 46 p 334.
25. Schmidt: History Infantry Regiment 58 pp 205-206
26. Zunehmer: *op. cit.* p 334
27. Schmidt: *op. cit.* pp 206-207

28. Reserve Leutnant Franz Rossow is buried in the German cemetery at Cambrai, Block 2 Grave 18.
29. In the circumstances this was probably the best use of what had effectively become a spare brigade headquarters. 20th Landwehr Division had been so badly smashed on 20 November that it never saw service again on the Western Front. The remnants were moved east just in time to witness the end of active operations there, then were deployed into the Ukraine, where they spent the next twelve months.
30. See *Hauptstaatsarchiv Stuttgart M33/2 Bü 373a 'Die Tankschlacht bei Cambrai' pp 15&16*
31. Zunehmer: *op.cit.* p 342
32. Vogt: History Infantry Regiment 50 p 201
33. Mülmann: History Lehr Infanterie Regiment pp 440-441
34. *ibid.* pp 441-442
35. *ibid* pp 443-444
36. Korporal is an old German rank and is the equivalent of Unteroffizier.
37. Moser: *Feldzugsaufzeichungen* p 312
38. Hansch: History Grenadier Regiment 9 p 440
39. *ibid.* p 440
40. Tschischwitz: *op.cit.* pp 259-260
41. Kronprinz Rupprecht *op. cit.* pp 295-296
42. Hansch: *op. cit.* p 441
43. *ibid.* p 443
44. Moser: *op.cit.* pp 313-314
45. Mülmann: *op.cit.* pp 447 - 448
46. Tschischwitz: *op. cit.* p 260
47. Moser: *op. cit.* pp 314 - 315
48. Schulenburg – Wolfsburg: History Garde-Füsilier Regiment pp 193-194
49. Mülmann: *op. cit.* pp 448-449
50. Tschischwitz: *op. cit.* pp 260-261
51. *Totensonntag*, the Sunday before Advent, was decreed in 1816 by King Friedrich Wilhelm III of Prussia to be a day marked by the protestant churches in general memory of the dead. It still serves a similar purpose to All Souls Day celebrated by other branches of the Christian church on 2 November each year but there are fundamental theological differences between the Calvinist and Roman Catholic approaches to its observance.
52. Schulenburg – Wolfsburg: *op. cit.* p 195
53. Tschischwitz: *op. cit.* p 261
54. Moser: *op. cit.* pp 314 - 315
55. Mülmann: *op. cit.* p 451
56. The body of eighteen year old Reserve Leutnant Theophil Röttger was repatriated after the war. He is buried at Kassel-Wehlheiden Cemetery Row 1 Grave 16. Drewes was mourned by all who knew him. His

battalion commander later wrote, 'Who of the 60th did not know Drewes! In 1914 he came as a private soldier to 5th Company. When he breathed his heroic last at the Battle of Cambrai he was an officer deputy and had been recommended for promotion to officer rank. The real worth of a man such as he, straight and true, is often only revealed during a war. He was a soldier to his fingertips; a man who knew no fear; a man who actively sought danger, because only that way could he put himself to the test.' See Zechlin: History Reserve Infantry Regiment 60 pp 144-145

57. Moser: *op. cit.* pp 314 - 315

58. This entry was made prior to the arrival of the decision by Second Army to postpone the counter-attack, at Group Caudry's request, by twenty four hours.

59. Kronprinz Rupprecht *op. cit.* p 298

60. Moser: *op. cit.* p 318

61. Tschischwitz: *op. cit.* pp 266-268

CHAPTER FIVE

A Counter Attack is Planned

No sooner had the British attack opened on 20 November than the thoughts of the higher German levels of command turned to the question of large scale counter action. As the reports from the front had flowed into the Army Group Headquarters, each more alarming than the last, the staff moved quickly into action. Under the direction of General der Infanterie Hermann von Kuhl, the Chief of Staff, staff checks quickly identified the location, availability and transport times of reinforcements and orders were issued almost immediately to ensure that Second Army resources were boosted with all possible speed. Within hours the Army Group commander was being briefed that he could expect to have sufficient resources in the Cambrai area to permit a major counter-attack to be launched in approximately seven days' time, even allowing for the pressures of the contact battle which, naturally, would absorb the early reinforcements entirely.

Responsibility for countering the evolving situation was squarely the business of Second Army and its subordinate Group Headquarters, in particular Group Caudry. Above that level the priority, as always, was on the allocation, provision and sustainment of manpower and *materiel*. Unfortunately, the Army Group was not left in peace to concentrate on its main task. By autumn 1917, Ludendorff had been carrying an impossible workload for more than a year and the strain was beginning to tell. In addition he had had to come to terms with a series of rude shocks during the course of that year – especially at Vimy Ridge in April and Messines in June - and this had had a negative effect on his command style. Always inclined to interfere, finding it impossible to delegate sufficiently, he had taken to fighting one fire after another and, in the process, tended to get bogged down in unnecessary detail.

Relations between Crown Prince Rupprecht and he had been under strain for some time. It was, perhaps, the most senior manifestation of the tension between commanders and the General Staff. It certainly irked the Crown Prince greatly, wasted his time and that of his staff and did nothing for overall efficiency. Matters did not improve on 21 November as the British continued with renewed vigour to attempt to broaden the break in and force open the way to Cambrai. The news was grave and it called for cool heads at the highest level if the tank attacks were to be held and the situation restored. The Army Group Commander, although always relatively restrained in his recording of events, captured the pressures and the atmosphere well that evening.

Crown Prince Rupprecht of Bavaria: Diary Entry 21 November 1917 [1]

"The necessity to relieve four of the divisions of Second Army is most awkward. However, according to its headquarters, it will in any event not be possible to go over to the counter-attack before 27 November, because insufficient fresh troops are on hand and, in particular, because the artillery reinforcements are only arriving in dribs and drabs. One of the greatest disadvantages of conducting defensive operations is the fact that there are almost never sufficient troops available to launch an immediate counter-stroke against the enemy and so prevent them from becoming established in the positions that they have captured. Only in the rarest of cases is it possible for the defender to wrest the initiative back. On the basis of several indicators, Sixth Army is expecting an attack against its left flank south of the Scarpe. This would certainly be the most effective way of supporting the continuation of the British offensive at Cambrai.

"General Ludendorff was very nervous today. He was continually on the telephone demanding information about a thousand small details, which was extremely disruptive. Despite his constant urgings, we cannot simply weaken Fourth Army, because in [Flanders], even at times of low battle intensity, relief in the line has to take place more frequently than on other fronts. Nevertheless, and here I must give praise where it is due, it did its utmost to meet our wishes, despite the difficulties that arose for them as a result.

"During the evening Second Army reported that on the far bank of the canal they have a firm grip on five crossing places and that the recapture of Fontaine succeeded without heavy fighting. The noting of increased railway traffic south and Army southwest of St Quentin has given us food for thought. It caused the Army High Command to place one division from Seventh Army and an artillery regiment from Army Reserve behind Group Quentin. By December Ludendorff hopes to be able to transport four or five divisions across from the East."

As early as 21 November, Army Group Crown Prince Rupprecht, having already received the acquiescence of Supreme Army Headquarters, issued a preliminary order to Second Army:

"The positions which were lost yesterday are to be retaken by means of a counter-attack. As far as possible the reinforcements which have arrived and those still to be transported [to the area] are to be moved to where they can be deployed in flanking manoeuvres from the north and the east.

"It is of particular importance that crossings over the canal in the sector between Crèvecoeur and Banteux are retained or recaptured as soon as possible by the leading elements of reinforcements as they arrive.

"In addition to the reinforcements directed to [Second] Army on 20 November, the following are also to be made available: three Army Field Artillery Regiments and several battalions of long-range, low trajectory guns from Supreme Army Headquarters; 28th Infantry Division and, in addition, 21st Reserve Division from Fourth Army will be moved to cover behind the left flank of Sixth Army.

"Headquarters Second Army is to report shortly how it intends to conduct the counter-attack." [2]

Unfortunately, for the time being, such plans as were developed had to remain a future aspiration, because the formations of 214th, 30th and 119th Infantry Divisions had to be rushed to the defensive front as soon as they arrived, so as to plug gaps and relieve the original hard-pressed defenders of Group Caudry. However, such was the perception of the crisis and the desire to conduct a counter-offensive, that reinforcements were soon pouring into the Cambrai area.

By 22 November, in addition to 3rd Guards Division, 119th and 214th Divisions, found from within the resources of the Army Group, Supreme Army Headquarters allocated 5th Guards Division, 30th and 34th Infantry Divisions and these were followed up swiftly with two additional Corps Headquarters (XVIII Army Corps and XXIII Reserve Corps). 220th Infantry Division and 21st Reserve Division were found from within the resources of the Army Group and 28th Infantry Division was directed to move by Supreme Army Headquarters.

Crown Prince Rupprecht of Bavaria: Diary Entry 23 November 1917 [3]

"During the evening Second Army reported that the British, with tanks in the lead, had thrust through Bourlon Wood and had forced their way into Bourlon. At this point the tanks turned back but several remained there damaged. The British who had got into Bourlon Chateau were now surrounded and the wood has been recaptured as far as its central section. Originally Second Army had wanted to counter-attack attack from both north and east, but anticipated wastage prior to the start time only permits an attack from an easterly direction. Second Army now shares this view. Today there was another stream of enquires from General Ludendorff which, for the most part, concerned totally inessential matters."

General der Infanterie Hermann von Kuhl Chief of Staff Army Group Crown Prince Rupprecht Diary Entry 23 November 1917 [4]

"As swiftly as possible, we must attack on the left flank near Le

Pavé with everything we have got. This would be the best way of relieving Bourlon. I briefed this to the Crown Prince, told Stapff [Chief of Staff Second Army] this over the telephone and will drive tomorrow to Le Cateau [location of Headquarters Second Army]. I believe that this is a good idea. In all the battles we have never managed to mount a good counter-attack."

On 24 November, Crown Prince Rupprecht and General von Kuhl visited Second Army Headquarters. For the first time, the plans for the counter-offensive had been expanded to include an element taking the British salient in the flank from the north though, with the battle for Bourlon Ridge still raging, it was not entirely clear at this stage if this refinement would be possible. However, there was unanimity that a surprise attack from the east, supported by a massive concentration of artillery would definitely be conducted and that, if necessary, the attack frontage would be extended to the south as far as Vendhuille. In fact, closer study led to increased enthusiasm for operations in the extreme south. It was felt, for example, that an attack to the south of Banteux offered good chances of success, because the British, whose positions were protected to some extent by localised flooding around the Escaut, would not be expecting an attack there.

Their positions in that sector were known to be less well developed than elsewhere and the trench garrison was far weaker than was the case further north, where the going against a stronger defence would be further complicated by cratering and the existence of a maze of old trenches. Initially, and so as to exploit the opportunity of the moment, Army Group Crown Prince Rupprecht informed Supreme Army Headquarters that the counter-attack was planned for 26 November, but that it was more likely that the date would slip to 27 November. This was still extremely optimistic; over-optimistic as things turned out, because arriving troops continued to be swept up in the defensive battle in the Group Arras area, which had to take priority in the short term.

Report of the Conference of His Royal Highness the Crown Prince of Bavaria at Headquarters Second Army 24 November [5]

"The divisions which have arrived have been so deployed that the attack can be launched from both north and south. Whether it is actually going to be possible to mount the attack from the northern front remains questionable. Here the British are continuing to press their attacks and the reinforcing formations are required to hold the thrust. Regardless of that, the attack in the south must be carried out.

"The following consideration is of importance regarding its launching: As soon as the attack makes progress in a northwesterly direction, it will be threatened by the flanking fire of enemy batteries located to the south of Havrincourt Wood. It is necessary, therefore, for the attack to be extended more to the south. To that end, the boundaries of 183rd Infantry Division must be made narrower by the introduction of 5th Guards Infantry Division on its southern flank. Heavy howitzers will take the lead in preparing the assault of 183rd Infantry Division.

"The attack is to be based on surprise and favourable flanking positions available to the artillery. 26 November has been ordered as the day of the attack, in order to ensure that preparations are conducted with maximum energy, [but Second] Army Headquarters believes that it will be impossible to carry it out before 27 November.

"Currently (24 November a.m.) fifteen reinforcement battalions are in place. There is a further requirement for four days supply [of shells] to be available; two on the battery positions, one loaded on supply columns and one in the ammunition dumps. Enemy battery positions are to be gassed.

"Even though high speed action is essential in the current situation, nevertheless a reasonably solid foundation is required. This cannot be expected before 27 November."

Much of the thrust of this message was repeated by the Army Group Commander that night in his diary.

Crown Prince Rupprecht of Bavaria: Diary Entry 23 November 1917 [6]

"A whole series of observations and intelligence reports indicate that the enemy are transporting troops southwards from the Flanders front. Whilst the number of enemy batteries opposite Groups Lille, Aubers, Loos and Souchez has reduced, in the centre and left flank of Group Vimy there has been an increase. The enemy are likely to do everything possible to exploit the advantage they have gained at Cambrai and to try to expand on it by means of an attack against the left flank of Sixth Army, which could possibly be launched astride the Scarpe. Diversionary attacks launched simultaneously at St Quentin and to the south of that place are to be expected. At any rate there has been an increase of artillery fire against the positions there and it was especially heavy at Hancourt.

"When I arrived at Headquarters Second army at 9.30 am, I was informed that Bourlon Wood had been completely recaptured and that rather a large number of knocked out tanks had been discovered. It is now certain that the British deployed all of their nine tank battalions... General von der Marwitz stated that as soon as the artillery had been supplied with four days' supply of ammunition the counter-attack would be mounted; this would probably be on 27

November. It would be launched from the east and would probably extend south as far as Gillemont Farm.

However, it was one thing to will the means; quite another, as the Army Group report indicated, to receive and deploy all the extra forces and equipment. Meanwhile, not having yet read the report, Ludendorff became impatient, contacting Major Stapff directly at 8.00 am on 25 November and learning that the earliest possible date for the operation would have to be postponed to 27 November, due to the slow arrival of artillery assets and ammunition in particular. According to the telephone log, the substance of this exchange was as follows:

> "Stapff: The [delay] will probably not lead to a worsening of our situation. The enemy will be unable to advance any more without pushing out the shoulders of the break in further. Around Banteux we are so strongly and tactically favourably placed – as the recent battles have shown – that the enemy will have to stand on the defensive there. They lack the necessary forces to attack against both Moeuvres and Banteux. So their assault will continue to concentrate on the Moeuvres – Bourlon front. The more they pressurise this front, the more artillery they deploy there, the weaker they will be on the other front and the more effective will be the main thrust. I guarantee that everything will turn out well, provided that we are permitted time for the build-up'
>
> "Ludendorff: I am not pressing you, Stapff. When do you want to carry it out?
>
> "Stapff: I cannot give precise timings, because it all depends on the arrival of the artillery and mortars; but, I think, not sooner than 27th and not later than 29th."[8]

Although there was still emphasis on an early start date, it was equally clear that Ludendorff had to be realistic about what was possible. It also seems that he accepted the argument that the more British forces were drawn into intense fighting for Bourlon Ridge, the more the way was clear for the main thrust eastwards, even if the contribution of Group Arras were to be compromised somewhat.

General der Infanterie von Kuhl, who had accompanied the Army Group Commander on his visit to Le Cateau, commented: 'The Army Headquarters exhibited an air of calmness. I am now somewhat better pleased with Stapff.' Coming from him and bearing in mind that he had been instrumental in having Stapff removed from Fourth Army five months previously, this was high praise. In the wake of the conference of 24 November and receipt of an Army Group Directive,[9] Second Army issued the first of the orders for the counter-attack. Groups Caudry and Busigny (the latter based around Headquarters XXIII Reserve Corps and commanded by General der

Infanterie von Kathen) were to drive hard for the main objective of Metz en Couture, whilst Group Arras, whose right flank formations were to be moved across to the new Group Lewarde (Headquarters XVIII Army Corps), was simultaneously to drive southwards along the line Fontaine – Moeuvres. It was also intended that minor operations would be conducted on both flanks, partly to disguise the width of the attack and partly to protect its extremities. It was stressed that all preparations were to be completed with the very least delay, because surprise was paramount.

On the basis of the Second Army Order, the Groups moved fast to prepare their own orders. Group Caudry had already issued the first version of its plan for the operation, codenamed *Götterdämmerung* [Twilight of the Gods], by 4.30 pm 25 November. This was very much a warning order; the conduct of the attack and all coordinating instructions and other details were discussed orally with the divisional Heads of Operations later. Group Busigny was also swift to issue an order to its two divisions earmarked for the main attack; *viz*, 34th and 183rd Infantry Divisions. This detailed their main missions and tasks within the context of the overall operation, laid down the broad outline of the use of artillery and mortars and stressed the need for the greatest possible acceleration in the speed of preparation, consistent with the need to maintain strict operational security. However, this first set of orders for Operation *Winter* was soon overtaken by events. A meeting between the Corps Commander and General der Kavallerie von der Marwitz, who was accompanied by his Artillery Commander, Oberst Krenski, was quickly followed by a second version of Operation *Winter*, which reduced the widths of the divisional frontages and shifted the *Schwerpunkt* [point of main effort] to the right flank.

Group Arras, too, spent much of the day working out its orders (which soon turned out to be nugatory) for the thrust from the north, which was codenamed *Sturmflut* [Tidal Wave]. An initial staff check revealed that, of the five divisions under command of the Group, only two (21st Reserve Division and 221st Infantry Division) could be regarded as fully battleworthy. To attempt an attack against an enemy of at least equal strength, whose troops would most probably be fresh, offered no prospect of success. Whilst the planning went ahead, a request was placed with Second Army for the subordination of 49th Reserve Division and for the use of 119th Infantry Division (the right flank division of Group Caudry) to secure the left flank of the operation, despite the fact that the 119th was somewhat worn down by the fighting around Fontaine Notre Dame. Through the issue of Order Ia 539 Secret Headquarters Second Army, this was approved:

"119th Infantry Division will be subordinated to Group Arras for the day of the offensive. Generalleutnant von Moser is granted the right to influence the preparations of 119th Division for the attack. The southeastern boundary of the sector of 119th Infantry Division will run from Moulin de Catigneul -

north of Noyelles – Centre of Beaucamp. 49th Reserve Division will be allocated to Group Arras, provided that the situation does not force its prior deployment elsewhere. The necessary preparations are to be made." [10]

It is clear that the provision of additional forces was foremost in the mind of the Group Commander as he made his entry for that day in his diary.

Generalleutnant Otto von Moser Commander Group Arras Diary Entry 25 November [11]

"An Army order arrived [today]. According to this, on order of higher authority, all preparations are to be made for a major counter-offensive to be launched from the entire Cambrai salient. This means, in addition to the conduct of the defence, that we have much to consider and to do. On the other hand it is hard to think of a more serious and therefore fascinating leadership task... I place a request to have the 49th Reserve Division, which has arrived at Group Lewarde [sector] and the 119th Infantry Division, which is occupying positions along the line Fontaine-Notre-Dame – Noyelles, placed under command of Group Arras for the counter-attack." [12]

In support of the plans, the Army Group directed that Fourth Army up in Flanders was to release two more divisions and so further reinforce the southernmost thrust.

"From 27 November the Army Group will transfer to Second Army from Fourth Army the 9th Bavarian Reserve Division and 185th Infantry Division – both of them strong and battleworthy – with the aim of making the left flank of the offensive as strong as possible. Accordingly, both divisions are to be moved up and to be made ready to act as Army Group reserve. In addition it is probable that the 208th Infantry (which up to now has been in Army Group reserve) will be made available for this purpose, provided that the situation around St Quentin does not make this impossible. [13]

"Furthermore, the transportation away of 107th Infantry Division is to be postponed for the time being. Its use may become possible in the event of the need to exploit success. The use of 16th Bavarian Infantry Division for possible strengthening of the right flank is also under consideration. To that end it is to be held in readiness by Sixth Army behind Group Vimy, but it is there primarily to provide security against possible minor attacks against the south flank of Sixth Army. It will not be possible to withdraw it until after the Second Army attack has begun." [14]

During all this period of preparation, most of the fighting was taking place on

Bourlon Ridge. This did not mean, however, that the remainder of the battlefield was completely quiet. On the Group Caudry – Group Busigny front there were constant exchanges of gunfire, which at times rose to extremely heavy harassing fire on the trenches and the rear areas. Cambrai itself was often under fire, with particular attention being paid to the railway station in an effort to disrupt the arrival of German reinforcements. This was not particularly successful and, in any case, use was made of a number of off-loading points in the Cambrai area, in order to speed up the process. Along the forward areas there were occasional attempts at local attacks, which often degenerated into close quarter clashes with hand grenades. In general these were driven off or nipped in the bud by extensive use of the increasing amount of artillery which was arriving in the sector.

There was one more serious attempt at an attack on 24 November. Probably mounted to provide a diversion from the heavy fighting for Bourlon Wood, following a short, but very heavy, bombardment, troops of the British 12th Division launched an attack either side of the Le Pavé – Le Catelet road against the positions of 9th Reserve Division. Some ground was taken by men of 35 and 36 Brigades, but action by Infantry Regiment 395 restored the front line and there were no more British attacks worthy of the name throughout the remaining period until the beginning of the counter-offensive a few days later. Nevertheless the 24 November attack had been a cause of concern while it lasted and the Divisional Commander was quick to issue a laudatory Order of the Day the following day. 'Enemy assaults to the north of Banteux were broken up as a result of a counter-stroke by 10th and 11th Companies of the courageous Infantry Regiment 395. It must be assumed that there will be further attacks tomorrow. The retention of the bridgeheads is of the utmost importance.'[15]

During the morning of 26 November all the Chiefs of Staff of the divisions which would be involved with *Sturmflut* were summoned to a conference at Headquarters Group Arras. The aim and objectives of the Group were briefed in detail and the participants were directed to return to their own headquarters, there to brief their commanders and, in accordance with von Moser's consultative style of command, were to return later in the day to Group headquarters with all requests for additional support or clarification. Later that morning the Army Commander arrived for talks.

General der Kavallerie Georg von der Marwitz [16]

"The enemy have once again made all necessary preparations for an assault on Bourlon, but nothing had happened by evening. It is said that between sixty and seventy tanks have been spotted, but they have not attacked. I believe that they are moving their artillery forward; without its mass effect there can be no expectation of renewed success. May we be ready first to counter them. I had lengthy discussions with Groups Caudry and Arras. [Group]Arras is so far out on a limb that hours are taken up getting there. On the way back I traversed Cambrai, which is not under fire from the British because it still has civilians living there. The streets are largely empty; only now and again does one meet up with one of the traumatised inhabitants as they seek shelter in a cellar. The windows to the cellars have all been carefully blocked up with stone against the effect of flying fragments. It could, at a stroke, become a dead town, as so many others in northern France already are. I hear that a further two divisions are on their way, but I have not yet decided how to use them."

Although von der Marwitz did not go into detail about the matters discussed at the 11.00 am meeting, it seems that it was conducted amicably and that it broke up in general agreement.[17] The overall objective was to be the regaining, within boundaries, of the original German First Position and the Army Commander accepted the timings proposed by Group Arras: destructive fire from 7.30 – 7.45 am, followed by the assault. The objective and timings were all confirmed during the second conference of the day for divisional Chiefs of Staff, held at 5.00 pm, then the Group Arras staff worked straight through the evening in order to complete the written orders and distribute them to the divisions.

Generalleutnant Otto von Moser Commander Group Arras Diary Entry 26 November [18]

"Today was filled until late into the night with the mental preparation for the attack. If it was my decision, I should launch it as soon as possible, namely on 28 November. [The reason is that] my artillery build up will be complete by the evening of 27 November and every additional day that my poor infantry has to hold out on the defensive against an enemy, superior in numbers and repeatedly boring in, is expecting a lot of it. Today it has already proved necessary to withdraw 214th Infantry Division from the front line and replace it with 21st Reserve Division. However, we heard during the course of the day that the offensive preparations of our neighbouring groups cannot be completed until the evening of 28 November. In consequence the Army has fixed the attack for 29 November, so we have to hold out for two more days. This is no small responsibility for us!

"There is little time for lengthy consideration or pondering what to do. All our thoughts have been directed and occupied with consideration about how best to organise and deploy our artillery and infantry for the attack. The ground over which we shall be attacking has become very well known to us as a result of the battles of the past eight [*sic*] days, but there are numerous difficulties to be overcome. The first point arises from the size and strength of the troops under command for the operation. There are seven divisions; from right to left: 49th Reserve, 20th, 21st Reserve, 214th, 221st, 3rd Guards and 119th. There are 508 guns (118 heavy and 390 light). Together the total ration strength is about 130,000 men. I cannot get out of my head the fact that the numbers of divisions and guns is almost identical with the [strength of] the German troops at the Battle of Wörth on 6 August 1870. It is both an uplifting feeling and a demonstration of the enormous increase in scale of this war.

"One staff officer after another briefs me: attack boundaries; frontages; deployment in depth; infantry objectives; placement, organisation and tasks of the field artillery and heavy artillery; tasks for the eleven air detachments subordinated to me; communications and reporting; supply of all types; care of the wounded and much more besides. On the basis of my decisions it will be possible during the night 26/27 November to finish and print off the Group Orders for the attack. This means that they can be got to the divisions as soon as possible and so give them sufficient time to think them through, discuss them with their subordinates and then make their own dispositions.[19] That said, these orders must remain secret from our subordinates for as long as possible. The codeword I have chosen for this operation is *Sturmflut* [Tidal Wave]."

Crown Prince Rupprecht of Bavaria: Diary Entry 26 November 1917 [20]

"The Counter-attack, scheduled for 29 November is planned as follows:

"A powerful strike force will be launched to the south over the line Moeuvres – Fontaine Notre Dame. The main thrust of the divisions assaulting from the east will be aimed in the direction of Metz-en-Couture. In order to achieve this aim, the emphasis of the assault divisions of Group Caudry is to be maintained to the left. The terrain between the Arras and Caudry thrusts is to be rolled up by weak forces turning gradually inwards. In order to protect the left flank of the main attack, 185th Infantry Division is to break through via Vendhuille and Gillemont Farm then, with flank protection posted against Epéhy – Lempire, is to roll up the British front in the direction of Villers Guislain. As a diversion, the enemy front line is to be captured at Malakoff Farm. Second Army is to hold 208th Infantry Division east of Honnecourt in readiness to renew the assault. The direction of its advance will be as ordered by Army Headquarters.

"Apart from the troops allocated for the assault, 49th Reserve Division, which is currently located behind the right flank of the frontage of the offensive, can be moved forward if it is not required in Sector Lewarde and, in addition, 18th Infantry Division and 9th Bavarian Reserve Division are expected to arrive north and south of Le Cateau by the evening of 28 [November]. The last two have already been earmarked by me to continue the advance, so it is perhaps possible that we shall be able to achieve a great success and roll up the enemy front to the area of Croisilles and, perhaps, further to the north."

Whilst all the staff work was being completed at the various levels, it is clear that there was still concern at Supreme Army Headquarters that there was risk of a further slippage in the start of the offensive. Once more bypassing the Army Group, Ludendorff telephoned the Chief of Staff Second Army at 7.00 pm 26 November.

"Ludendorff: We have got to launch on the 29th.
"Stapff: I shall go through the calculations in the morning.
It is on a knife edge.
"Ludendorff: No, it must be. The British divisions are worn out and there are no reserves. It has got to be the 29th." [21]

It is clear that up until the morning of 27 November, all commanders and staffs involved were in agreement that the offensive would open on 29 November and that all three Groups would launch their attacks as soon as it was light enough to permit accurate gun fire. However as the hours ticked by, doubts crept in at Supreme Headquarters and at the Army Group concerning aspects of the plan. As a result, an extremely significant conference attended by Ludendorff and all the principal figures was called for on 27th at Headquarters Second Army. For some reason when the Official History for this period came to be written, none of the files relating to this meeting could be discovered, so even the official historians had to depend primarily on the recollection of Crown Prince Rupprecht in his published diaries. [22]

A special train carrying Ludendorff and five officers from his operational staff arrived at 8.00 am at Le Cateau. Army Group Chiefs of Staff, General von Kuhl and Oberst Graf von der Schulenburg, arrived simultaneously and the discussions began. Crown Prince Rupprecht arrived at 10.00 am and the conference finally broke up at midday. Both Ludendorff and General der Infanterie von Kuhl expressed doubt about whether Group Arras, realistically, could be expected to participate in a meaningful way and actually carry out the difficult operation that had been planned for it in the timeframe previously agreed. The point was made strongly that no attempt was to be made to assault Bourlon Wood; instead the attack was to pass to the west of it. That was not the only alteration to the plan, Ludendorff also demanded that Group Busigny not only fight its way westwards, but also expand its attack, with the aim of rolling up the British lines to the south and so open up the possibility of further divisions being introduced, in the event of the successful conduct of the operation. Major Stapff, during a detailed presentation, succeeded in proving that the offensive could not begin until 30 November. Interesting to note, his overall performance during this conference was described later as *mässig* [mediocre] by one of the staff officers from the Army Group, despite the fact that he had gone on to make a very sensible suggestion during it regarding the deployment of the heavy artillery at various stages of the planned battle.

Crown Prince Rupprecht of Bavaria: Diary Entry 27 November 1917 [23]

"During the morning I attended a conference at Le Cateau with Ludendorff, who had ordered the chiefs of staff of Army Group German Crown Prince and that of Seventh Army to be in attendance. I am now pleased that, despite the initial doubts of my chief of staff, I directed the accelerated move forward of 9th Bavarian Reserve Division and 185th Infantry Division. This got the ball rolling, in the sense that Ludendorff has now warmed to the plan to turn the Cambrai counter-attack into a rolling up of the British front to the north. Not for years has such an opportunity presented itself to prepare at the very least a painful partial defeat for the British.

"It is a matter of regret that, according to Headquarters Second Army, we must wait until 30 November to launch the offensive. This certainly offers the advantage that further significant reinforcements can be moved up. On the other hand it must be borne in mind that by that time the enemy may have been able to push back our detachments which are holding out on the far bank of the canal between Crèvecoeur and Banteux, which would certainly make the later crossing of the canal during the attack extremely difficult. Luckily, in their attacks, the British keep flogging a dead horse by pressing between Fontaine and Bourlon and I hope that, despite having once bitten off more than they can chew there, they continue in the same way for a few more days. The fact that so far we have not attempted to reply with any sort of counter-attack worth the name will serve us well. They will assume that we have no offensive power available and, in that assumption, they will be quite wrong."

In an expansion of these remarks, published in the third volume of his diaries, Crown Prince Rupprecht added:

"Commenting on the Second Army [counter-] attack proposals during the 27 November conference, General Ludendorff remarked that it seemed to him to be questionable if it would in fact be possible for Group Arras to go over to the advance. It would be difficult to attack Anneux and Cantaing and the fight for Bourlon Wood, where the enemy were continuing to press, would result in especially heavy casualties. Generalleutnant von Kuhl, sharing this view, felt that because the duration of enemy attacks against Group Arras could not be predicted, it was impossible to say of it would be in any position on 30 [November] to participate in a counter-attack. At that I stated that, whatever the situation, this Group must make the attempt and that Group Busigny had also to make an impact with its attack.

"Depending on how the situation develops, it might, perhaps, be possible to transfer over one or two divisions of Sixth Army to support the Group Arras attack. The main thrust must, nevertheless, be conducted by Group Busigny and every effort had to be made, not only to throw the enemy back across the *Siegfried Stellung* [Hindenburg Line], but also to roll them up to the north and so cause the entire front to become unstable. General Ludendorff stressed that under no circumstances was Bourlon Wood itself to be attacked; rather the assault was to be directed along both sides of the wood, so that it could then be cut off from the rear. The main effort of Group Arras was to be transferred to its right flank. A subsidiary attack could then be launched from the east against Anneux and Cantaing and would probably prove not to be too difficult. As far as the attack of Group Busigny was concerned, it was desirable that it was not continued by its main forces in a westerly direction but, instead, should concentrate on rolling up the enemy to the south and leaving their flank hanging in the air.

"I answered affirmatively when asked if it would be possible to withdraw more troops from Fourth Army, but qualified this by saying that it would be feasible to remove two further divisions for a short period but then [the Army] would have to be reinforced, otherwise the extraordinarily bad conditions of the forward positions would place far too great a burden on the troops and would wear them down badly. If Fourth Army were to be weakened, it was possible that the loss of Westrozebeke would have to be accepted.[24] General Ludendorff decided that Army Group German Crown Prince was to earmark an additional three divisions, ready to be inserted along the left flank of the offensive if its progress was favourable. To the same purpose, some divisions were to be withdrawn from the East and all the reserve artillery formations of the Army High Command, including those which were only just forming up back in the Homeland, were to be made available. In other words, everything would be done to help bring about the break through for which I had been pressing.

"Major Stapff, Chief of Staff Second Army, then made an excellent proposal, which was approved by General Ludendorff. He pointed out that due to restrictions of space, after the initial stages of the attack, a considerable proportion of the heavy artillery would not be usable. At that moment the superfluous batteries should be moved to the sector to the north of St Quentin, where the enemy had only stationed weak forces. By reducing the salient there, we should be expanding the frontage of our offensive and, simultaneously, be in a position to halt in its tracks any French attack on St Quentin or to the south of it." [25]

Once the conference at Headquarters Second Army was over, Crown Prince Rupprecht noted what happened next that day. This was yet another example of tension within the chain of command – in this case between Ludendorff and Crown Prince Rupprecht - who clearly resented the fact that Supreme Army Headquarters had issued orders directly to Second Army and only included Army Group Headquarters as an information addressee.[26] This he regarded as unwarranted interference with his area of responsibility and it did not leave him in a happy frame of mind.

Crown Prince Rupprecht of Bavaria: Diary Entry 27 November 1917 [27]

"From Le Cateau General Ludendorff, accompanied by General von Kuhl, drove to Headquarters Sixth Army at Tournai, where the chief of staff of Fourth Army, General [*sic.* - Generalmajor] von Loßberg, had been summoned to meet them. That evening he released the following order to Headquarters Second Army:

1. The attack is to take place on 30 November.
2. The main thrust is, as envisaged by the Army, to be carried out by the Eastern Group attacking in the direction of Metz en Couture. The capture of the heights around Flesquières and Havrincourt Wood, in order to be able to thrust against the main British forces in the flank and rear, is decisive for overall success.
3. The attack from the north (Group Arras), provided that the way the situation develops permits it to occur, is to be so timed that it is not launched until the main thrust of the Eastern Group has become effective. It is to be conducted in a southerly direction, west of Bourlon Wood, by all the force which can be made available. It is recommended that early artillery bombardment and simulated attacks on adjacent sectors be used as a means of fixing the enemy forces in position.
4. In order to be able to exploit a major success, Army Group Crown Prince Rupprecht and the Supreme Army Command will hold divisions ready to be transported. Headquarters [Second] Army is to prepare for

their unloading, accommodation and move forward.

5. Preparations are to be made for the secondary attack north of St Quentin proposed by Headquarters Second Army to be launched in the event of a major success.

"In fact, of course, the preparation of the order should have been the business of the Army Group..."[28]

None of these frustrations affected the Commander Second Army, who that night confined himself to a simple outline of the facts of the day.

General der Kavallerie Georg von der Marwitz [29]

"Ludendorff arrived today at 8.00 am and had the attack plans of the Group Commanders briefed to him in fullest detail. He suggested a few minor alterations, which I duly noted. The artillery will not be in its forward locations before 29 November, so I have decided not to attack until 30 November. In the meantime the British have intensified their attacks in the north. Provided only that my troops can hold on, that suits me well. Ludendorff stressed the overall significance of the operation and wished me the best of soldierly good fortune."

During the evening all the changes were issued by Second Army to Group Arras. The news was extremely unwelcome, but von Moser and his headquarters simply had to make the best of a bad job. Specific guidance included,

"The more the enemy establish themselves in Bourlon Wood, the more the decisive thrust to the west of the wood gains in significance. It is a case, therefore, as much as possible to avoid being drawn into fighting in built up areas or woods and so to arrange the operation plan that the thrust from the north is *only* conducted to the west of the wood by the forces which have been brought together. Even in this case, however, the planned attack by 119th Infantry Division between Anneux and Cantaing is to be retained. Neutralisation by the artillery of the garrisons of Graincourt, Anneux and Cantaing is of the utmost importance.[30]

Generalleutnant Otto von Moser Diary Entry 27 November 1917 [31]

"During the night a message arrived from the Army. Because the preparations of the neighbouring groups cannot be completed any earlier, the attack has had to be postponed until 30 November! The news hit us hard; some of my men were almost in despair, but there could be no question of that. We should have to make a virtue of necessity and try to ensure, as much as possible, that the troops allocated for the attack on 30 November were given maximum opportunity to rest on 28 and 29 November, to ensure that they were well fed and had deficiencies in their equipment made up."

It is worth pausing for a moment here and considering what Moser is saying. His troops had been engaged in the intense fighting for Bourlon Ridge for a week by then. Every twenty four hours of battle was exhausting his men more, causing a mounting toll of casualties and reducing measurably his ability to participate effectively in the counter-attack. But he was not simply concerned with the effect on his troops, though all his thoughts and actions indicate that they, quite rightly, were his highest priority. His own headquarters, upon which so much depended and which was very small in size compared with its modern equivalent, had been handling a span of command far in excess of the normal and in a desperate crisis - with all that that implies in terms of the load on the various staff branches.

Alongside all the increased routine staff work and the demands of the contact battle, his operational staff had had to make an almost superhuman effort on top of everything else to devise a plan, work through all the attendant staff checks and, against the clock, produce a finished, polished, written product complete with all necessary traces, overlays and annexes. They finally finish their work, breathe a collective sigh of relief and hope to be able to snatch some food and a short rest, when news arrives that the entire effort was for the waste paper bin. No wonder he talks about 'despair' and goes straight on to say, 'there can be no question of that'. At times such as this, all involved turn to the leader for an example and for encouragement. Moser turned in that night absolutely determined to provide just that; the Army Commander, for his part, faced the prospect of digesting the new written directive and communicating the changes to his corps commanders the following morning.

General der Kavallerie Georg von der Marwitz [32]

"The battle for Bourlon Wood continues. Ludendorff has consolidated his philosophical thoughts into an Army High Command directive. According to this Group Arras is only to launch its attack, assuming that it is in a position to do so, once the main thrust by Groups Caudry and Busigny has begun to take effect. Unfortunately this directive arrived so late that it could only be evaluated by means of a conference called for 10.00 am in Caudry. It was a hard task to make each individual grasp the main threads but, finally, it was successful and I was able to drive away at 1.00 pm with the hope that I had set everything to rights. There was little fighting throughout the day. A total of about seventy tanks was reported as moving forward from the sector of the break in and these were brought under fire. It is obvious that they might well be used in other places – perhaps south of St Quentin or around Bellicourt, which is manned by the fought-out 5th Division."

At least one participant in the Caudry conference was extremely displeased by the turn of events. Generalleutnant von Moser took it as a personal affront that he had not been involved in the consultation process and that the changes compromised the surprise upon which his plan of attack had been based.

Generalleutnant Otto von Moser Diary Entry 28 November 1917 [33]

"Last night we fired great quantities of gas at Bourlon Wood, in order to make life as difficult as possible for the British who were occupying it. During the day the wood was kept under heavy bombardment with high explosives. Otherwise there were only minor clashes...But today brought an entirely unexpected and serious surprise. The Army Commander informed his corps commanders, who were assembled in Caudry, that the attack planned for 9.00 am 30 November by Group Caudry (General der Infanterie Freiherr von Watter) and Group Busigny (General der Infanterie von Kathen) would not involve my Group Arras until midday. The thinking was that the enemy would be obliged, due to the attacks of Groups Caudry and Busigny, which were to begin three hours earlier, to withdraw troops from the Group Arras front and so make our attack easier to mount.

"Deployment of the assault forces of Group Arras was to be made possible through the production of an enormous smokescreen, which would prevent the enemy from observing it. Given that this had never been tested and in view of the enemy superiority in observation from aircraft and balloons, this was an extremely risky directive. Nevertheless the Army Commander ordered it to take place, without permitting any sort of discussion. It was a new, striking and very dubious example of how blind obedience of direction from above has evolved into standard procedure. The new order meant that we had to rework the orders that we had only just released for *Sturmflut*. Up until now our plan had been predicated on the deployment of our attacking forces in the early dawn, coupled with a short, sharp artillery barrage, then launch of the operation: in other words it had been based on surprise. Now, because our troops had to deploy into attack formations during daylight, the entire artillery plan had to be altered; not to mention the need to earmark numerous batteries to fire smoke.

"We had to get down to the new work immediately. There was

simply not a minute to lose, because the divisions had to be in receipt of the new orders as soon as humanly possible. To begin with the divisional General Staff officers were summoned and briefed orally about the most important points. Then, once again, came a series of briefings, one after the other. During the afternoon the new Army Order for the attack was issued. Its first paragraph read: 'During the course of daily heavy battles against heavy odds, Group Arras has continued to hold its positions; only in Bourlon Wood were the enemy able to establish themselves.'

"The start time for the attack by Group Arras has finally been ordered for midday, 'as far as that is still possible'. That, too, is my concern. My troops have been performing almost superhuman feats during nine days of battle. But I base my hope that my Group may yet be able to participate in the attack on the thought that the opportunity to take the offensive once more against the arrogant British will motivate not only the commanders but also the troops.

In fact, to be fair to von der Marwitz, it is quite evident that concern about the ability of Group Arras to play a full part in the forthcoming offensive had led to this change of plan and, indeed, that the pressure for the alteration had come from above Second Army. Crown Prince Rupprecht, perhaps sensing a chance of a great encirclement, was in favour of a continuing role for Group Arras; his Chief of Staff far less so and he had the ear of Ludendorff, who, effectively, had the last word on the matter. It is perfectly possible, in any case, that the Army Commander was given no leeway over the application of the alterations, though it was, perhaps, unfortunate that the information concerning the changes was not made available until this conference and that the manner in which it was communicated (though we only have Moser's account of how it was done) clearly wounded his *amour propre*. As Moser states, the changes undoubtedly created a great deal of extra work for his Group, then further alterations were made to the overall plan during the night 28/29 November, when Second Army changed the boundaries of Groups Caudry and Busigny.

Crown Prince Rupprecht of Bavaria: Diary Entry 28 November 1917 [34]

"An extract from the Second Army Order of 28 November 1917:[35]
'The Army offensive will begin on 30 November. Groups Caudry and Busigny will attack at 'Y Hour'; Group Arras at 'Y + 2'. As far as possible the attack of Group Arras is to be conducted to the west of Bourlon Wood. The initial aim is to capture our old positions west of Graincourt, together with the heights around Graincourt. Thereafter the right flank is to be protected to the west by means of follow-up divisions wheeling gradually outwards.

'In order to protect the left flank and to ease the progress of forces advancing to the west of Bourlon Wood, 119th Infantry Division is to be launched at Ferme de la Justice. Group Caudry is to direct its main thrust between Villers-Plouich and Gouzeaucourt in the general direction of Metz en Couture. In so doing, it is of decisive importance that the high ground by Beaucamp and Trescault is captured. In order to achieve these tasks, Group Caudry is to deploy its forces so as to achieve mass on its southwest flank and is to strive to push forward with strong forces between Gouzeaucourt and Villers-Guislain in the direction of Fins. The aim will be to link up with its forces thrusting to the south of Honnecourt to the west of Villers-Guislain. Group Busigny is responsible for maintaining the link between its own formations and those of Group Caudry. The deployment of the Army Group reserves (185th Infantry Division and 9th Bavarian Reserve Division) will be at the direction [of the Army Group]. The first named is to be moved forward under arrangements made by Group Caudry on 29 November to the area Esnes-Selvigny-Caullery-Cattenières-Wambaix; whilst the latter is to be moved by Group Busigny to the area Walincourt-Villers Outréaux-Prémont-Maretz-Clary.'

"Various regroupings have made it possible to station sufficient forces behind Sixth Army to meet any contingencies and, in addition, to make 49th Reserve Division available to Group Arras by 10.00 pm to carry out an attack on its right flank."

It is easy to forget that the last time the German army had launched a major assault on the Western Front was eighteen months earlier at Verdun. Some experience in the necessary techniques had been gained on the Eastern Front and, more recently, in Italy, but the lessons did not transfer readily to the situation at Cambrai, where the geography was difficult. For example, methods had to be devised to pass large numbers of troops through the Escaut valley, where the river and the canal, located so close together, formed a major obstacle. Very few roads led east-west and most of the main routes at the time were orientated north – south, which presented the logisticians with a planning problem of the first order, given that the objectives – Metz en Couture and the high ground around Flesquières - were a good ten kilometres behind the British front line. Nevertheless, having wrestled with all these difficulties, on the eve of the counter-offensive there was an almost tangible air of confidence amongst the formations and units of the attacking corps.

What a force had been improvised during these last few hectic days! No fewer than eighteen divisions had been transported, equipped and deployed for battle. As they waited to go into battle, they were organised as follows:

Group Caudry (General der Infanterie Freiherr von Watter) 107th,

30th, 220th and 28th Infantry Division in the first wave, with 9th Reserve Division in support, together with 111 heavy artillery pieces and 284 light field guns.

Group Busigny (General der Infanterie von Kathen) 34th, 183rd and 5th Guards Infantry Division in the first wave, with 208th Infantry Division in support, together with 121 heavy artillery pieces and 216 light field guns.

Group Arras (Generalleutnant von Moser) 20th Infantry Division, 21st Reserve Division, 3rd Guards and 119th Infantry Division holding the front line. 214th and 221st Infantry Division following up, with 118 heavy artillery pieces and 390 light field guns in support.

Of this great array of forces, ten divisions were rated as fully battleworthy. The remainder, especially within Group Arras, which had borne the brunt of the recent battles, were more or less worn down by the heavy fighting of the previous days. Had the need arisen, 79th Reserve Division, located behind Group Quentin and acting as Army Reserve, could have been called upon, as could a further six divisions from the Army Group Reserve and two more at the disposal of Supreme Army Headquarters. There was also a generous allocation of air force units, though their operations were severely hampered by bad weather.

In order to ensure surprise, there were strict limitations on the amount of ranging in that was permitted and the preliminary bombardment was also to be of short duration. Part of the artillery plan was to drench all known battery positions with gas, whilst all guns within range would fire at intense rates for one hour once the light was good enough for accurate shooting. This period of destructive fire was to be followed by a rolling barrage to cover the advance of the forward divisions of Groups Caudry and Busigny. There were separate arrangements for Group Arras, which was not to launch its operation until three hours later. In one of the earliest attempts at a large scale infiltration attack, there were strict orders that Bourlon Wood and similar locations were to be neutralised with fire and gas, but that the advancing infantry was to press on and avoid as far as possible becoming embroiled in fighting in built up areas or woods.

As far as the main thrust was concerned, Group Busigny in the extreme south was to attack from a previously quiet front, which had not been involved in the British attack. It was directed to maintain very close contact with Group Caudry on its right, but to drive hard westwards towards Fins. General der Infanterie von Kathen elected to advance with 183rd Division left and 34th Division right, linking with 28th Infantry Division of Group Caudry. Leading elements of 208th Infantry Division were intended to be inserted between the two leading divisions as required. 5th Guards Division was given an independent role. It was to attack Gillemont and Malakoff farms. To its north, Group Caudry was entrusted with the advance on Metz en Couture, though it was stressed that the capture of the high ground around Beaucamp and Trescault was of the first importance. General der Infanterie Freiherr von Watter decided to push forward, two divisions up, with 28th Infantry Division left and 220th Infantry Division right. 9th Reserve Division, which was somewhat worn down after days of fighting (even though for some days past the intensity had reduced), was intended to pass through between the leading divisions in due course and to take the Trescault heights. 107th Infantry Division, which was effectively already fought out when the counter-attack began, was directed simply to conform to the moves of its neighbours left and right. Its ultimate objective was the crest line northwest of Marcoing.

Group Arras was allocated as objectives the former German position west of Graincourt and the heights around Flesquières. Following additional direction, Generalleutnant von Moser placed his main effort to the west of Bourlon Wood, with his left flank passing through Anneux. Of his long-suffering divisions, 214th had been the worst affected by the desperate battles of recent days. It was not included in the overall assault plans, but 20th Infantry Division and 21st Reserve Division were earmarked to advance either side of Moeuvres and so secure the right flank of the operation. 3rd Guards Division had the task of sealing off Bourlon Wood from the north, whilst 119th Infantry Division covered its left flank and advanced via Cantaing.

At Headquarters Group Arras, the wounded feelings of its commander notwithstanding, work went ahead in a professional manner and at breakneck speed throughout the rest of 28 November. By midnight the amended order for *Sturmflut* was in the hands of the divisions, having been preceded by a verbal orientation about the changes a little earlier. With its distribution the ultimate shape of the northern thrust was finally determined. It envisaged four divisions advancing in the first wave and one in a second. Its main objective was to secure the line Moeuvres – Orival Wood. The primary individual divisional missions and the orders relating to the artillery are of particular interest:[36]

> "49th Reserve Division is to roll up, within boundaries, the old German trenches from the north and is to advance to a line from where the old position crosses the Cambrai-Bapaume road to the *Solmstellung*, 200 metres east of the Sains lès Marquion – Havrincourt road... Contact is to be maintained with 21st Reserve Division and 214th Infantry Division.
> "214th Infantry Division is to roll up, within boundaries, the old German positions from the north, is to capture the sugar refinery to the north of Graincourt and is to advance to the line *Solmstellung*, (linking up with 49th Reserve Division) to the track Graincourt –

Havrincourt.

"221st Infantry Division is to provide flank protection against Bourlon Wood, to capture Anneux and Graincourt and to advance, linking with 214th Infantry Division, to the line of the track Graincourt – Havrincourt to Orival Wood.

"21st Reserve Division is to facilitate the movement of the attacking divisions – 49th Reserve Division, 214th and 221st Infantry Divisions through its positions and is to follow up the advance of 49th Reserve Division as it progresses, in order to occupy our old First Position from the current divisional right flank to the Cambrai – Bapaume road, where it is to link up with 49th Reserve Division.

"3rd Guards Infantry Division is to screen off the heavily gassed Bourlon Wood from the *SII Stellung* to the Cambrai-Bapaume road.[37] If tactical considerations or the way the gas cloud moves demands it, the division can redeploy to Bourlon village and the railway embankment between Bourlon Station and Fontaine, but the northern part of Bourlon and the railway embankment must be held firmly.

"119th Infantry Division is to screen off Bourlon Wood, occupy Cantaing and provide flank protection in the area of La Justice Farm, whist maintaining contact with107th Infantry Division."

As far as the artillery was concerned, a smokescreen was to be fired from X [i.e. H Hour] - two hours to X - 30 minutes to cover the movement in broad daylight of large numbers of assaulting troops. At that moment, whilst the divisions shook out along their start lines, the priority was to shift to the firing of destructive fire to the front. From X, the assaulting infantry was to be protected by a rolling barrage lifting one hundred metres every five minutes. The assault troops were to be urged to keep hard up behind it. 'It is to be impressed on the infantry that the rolling barrage is their best friend, because it will keep the heads of the enemy down. Any delays in the advance will permit the enemy to come to battle readiness.'[38] The use of infiltration tactics and how the guns were to support it were also discussed at paragraph 16 of the Group Order.[39]

"The built up areas [original emphasis] and the sugar refinery to the north of Graincourt are to be engaged by high angle fire in accordance with divisional arrangements. The leading waves of infantry are to by-pass these places whilst they continue to be engaged by high angle fire. Not until the arrival of later waves are these places to be surrounded then, once an agreed signal has been given and fire has been lifted, they are to be assaulted from all sides. Any remaining resistance is to be broken by means of direct fire at close range from the field artillery of the assault divisions.[40]

"Whilst the follow up waves are conducting the battle for the built up areas, the leading waves are to press on towards their objectives. Resistance encountered during the future course of operations, which will be based mainly around the infantry and artillery dugouts of the old German positions, is to be broken by means of the mobile field artillery and the exploitation of every other possible means of envelopment."

The final section of the order stressed:

"The objective of the Second Army operations, that is to say an encircling attack, designed to cut off enemy troops in Bourlon Wood and around Marcoing, can only be achieved if the infantry and its accompanying artillery drive forward with gusto and if all commanders do everything in their power to help neighbours under pressure by means of thrusts against the enemy flanks and rear. This is particularly important in terms of support of 221st Infantry Division by 214th Infantry Division.'[41]

Although it was the corps most obviously affected, it was not only Group Arras that had to absorb alterations to the plan as a result of the Le Cateau conference. Group Caudry had to issue amended orders for *Götterdämmerung 3* at 5.40 pm 28 November. This replaced *Götterdämmerung 2*, which had only been completed and sent out to divisions on 27 November. It was altogether shorter than the Group Arras orders, because it was concerned primarily with changes to boundaries. Detailed instructions concerning infiltration tactics and the employment of artillery were the subject of separate documents, but the revised divisional tasks were covered in full.[42]

"9th Reserve Division is to be ready from Y Hour [Group Caudry version of H Hour] with two main start points around Seranvillers and Esnes Mill. It is to cross the St Quentin canal at several points near Crèvecoeur and Rues des Vignes as soon as the progress of the attack permits this. It is then to move to occupy the boundaries allocated to it between 30th and 220th Infantry Divisions. Mission: To capture the high ground around Trescault and Beaucamp.

"30th Infantry Division is to screen Les Rues Vertes and Marcoing with light forces, whilst carrying out its main thrust towards the heights at Ribécourt.

"220th and 28th Infantry Divisions are to neutralise the strong defences of Le Pavé and are to keep them under constant heavy bombardment with artillery and heavy howitzers. It is essential, however, that the mass of these divisions drives forward, ignoring all else, with the aim of reaching the main objective at Metz en Couture.

Only an absolute minimum of forces is to be used to seal off villages along the way. 28th Infantry Division has the permanent responsibility of maintaining contact with Group Busigny.

"107th Infantry Division is to provide flank protection for the Group and is to advance at Y+1 [Hour] against Noyelles. As soon as the way is cleared by the advance of 30th Infantry Division, it is to advance to the heights northeast of Marcoing, secure the right [flank] and support the assault of 30th Infantry Division."

The situation was much the same with Group Busigny. The main point that the revised orders for *Winter* had to convey were the alterations in the divisional boundaries.[43] Space was at a premium at the southern end of the battlefield, so formations were directed not to expect to find billets or other accommodation easily. Cover from view from the air was also in short supply, as was road capacity, so there were also strict instructions to minimise on the number of vehicles or rear echelon units brought into the forward area.

"34th Infantry Division The former German trench system west of Banteux will be captured by 28th Infantry Division. The boundary with Group Caudry, whose main forces will break through between Villers-Plouich and Gouzeaucourt, will be the [forward] extension of the line crossing through the northwest corner of Dessart Wood... 34th Infantry Division is responsible for maintaining contact with 28th Division of Group Caudry.

"208th Infantry Division The boundary with 34th Infantry Division runs from the northwest corner of Gauche Wood via the northwest corner of Heudicourt to the church in Sorel le Grand. Elsewhere it is unaltered. The division is to echelon its main forces on the right flank in order best to be able to support the deep thrust of 34th Infantry Division towards Fins.

The Group was informed that 185th Infantry Division, which was the Army Group reserve, would be held in assembly areas in rear of Group Caudry, ready to move. The order also made the point, 'The faster 34th and 208th Infantry Divisions thrust towards Fins, the better for us. There is to be concentration on seeking contact with the formations to the right, but this procedure is not to be allowed to lead to the situation where one division awaits the advance of its neighbours.' Whilst slightly clumsily stated, at least this had the merit of emphasising the need for decisive forward movement throughout the operation. Orders for the reception of 9th Bavarian Reserve Division were also given and, with that, apart from small last minute adjustments, the orders for the offensive were finalised.

There remained much to arrange at all levels. In order to assist Second Army in the fulfilment of its mission, on 28 November the Army Group issued a directive to the headquarters of its other armies: 'In [support] of the overall situation, it is desirable that Fourth and Sixth Armies fix the enemy to their front during the afternoon of 29 November and the morning of 30 November by use of appropriate measures. Increased artillery activity to simulate the preparation of attacks (ranging in, gassing etc) as well as local assaults will best serve the purpose. It is recommended that locations be selected where the enemy would expect us to attack.'[44]

Responding to an earlier Second Army written request for additional forces, the Army Group responded formally late on 28 November:

> "From yesterday's discussions, Second Army is acquainted with the forces available to the Army Group, together with their intended employment. The situation on the Fourth and Sixth Army fronts rules out immediate [original emphasis] transfer of further divisions. The requested reinforcement of the northern flank can only occur at the cost of the eastern grouping. Bearing in mind the terms of Army Group Ia Nr 4610 Secret, a weakening of the eastern grouping is unacceptable. That being the case, for the time being only 49th Reserve Division and 214th Infantry Division may be considered. The consequent weakening of the northern attack is less disadvantageous than a weakening of the eastern group and, if necessary, must be accepted. The arrival of further divisions cannot be anticipated before 30 November. Where and how these may be deployed is entirely dependent on the situation as it develops."[45]

If the logic of the balance of advantage between the attacks from the east and the north had been followed through to a conclusion, it is slightly difficult to see why the German chain of command persisted with launching a full-scale assault from the north at all. Had the role of Group Caudry been reduced to fixing British troops to its front and had 49th Division been available to reinforce the main thrust, the overall outcome might have been far more favourable to the Germans. It is hard to escape the conclusion that there was insufficient time to overcome differences of opinion at high level and that the ensuing compromise had a negative effect on the outcome of the counter-attack. Meanwhile, despite their guarded response, it was clear that the question of follow-up forces was both important and squarely the job of the Army Group to attend to. In yet another directive distributed on 28 November, the matter was addressed:

> "It is possible that the Second Army attack on 30 November may bring us a great success. In that case there would be favourable preconditions for an immediate exploitation of the success by developing it into a more ambitious offensive operation. Great success by Second Army will force the enemy to transfer stronger forces there.

This will lead to a fundamental easing of the situation for Fourth and Sixth Armies and, that being the case, we shall be able to withdraw additional forces from those Armies and exploit the success.

"The most important precondition for a successful continuation of the offensive, however, is that we must complete all possible preparations for further transfers of forces, in order that we may surprise the enemy by the speed of the transfer and the violence of the operation. Because there are limits to the capacity of the railway transport system, Fourth and Sixth Armies will have to cooperate by fixing the enemy forces opposite them, making use of the troops remaining to them.

"The following troops are earmarked as initial reinforcements [original emphasis]: From Fourth Army, 24th Reserve Division ; from Sixth Army 50th Reserve Division and, possibly, 234th Infantry Division. There will, in addition, be two to three divisions from Army Group German Crown Prince. Special orders to govern this and other formations which may have to be prepared will be issued later."[46]

Once Second Army Order Ia 631 had been despatched during the evening of 28 November, Major Stapff conducted a lengthy conversation with the Chief of Staff of Army Group Crown Prince Rupprecht. It shows how broad the responsibilities of Stapff were and what a crushing responsibility he, as a relatively junior officer, had to bear as the moment of the counter-offensive approached.

"Stapff: Tomorrow will be used to brief the three chiefs and the heads of operations of Groups Caudry and Busigny. I am now confident that everything is clear. The intervention was necessary to deal with the boundaries between Groups Caudry and Busigny and 220th and 28th Infantry Divisions. Everything is now arranged. The matter which was concerning Your Excellency, just prior to your departure, has been emphasised distinctly.[47]

Kuhl: You do share this view, don't you? We are of the same opinion? I mean, I have not pressurised you into it?

Stapff: No, absolutely not. Mende has the sketch.

Kuhl: Send it to me, please.

Stapff: By all means. It is a simple diagram, with not much to it.

Newly added today are the areas to be gassed, intensively, tonight and during the night 29/30 November. In the final stages we shall drench Bourlon Wood with *Gelbkreuz* [Yellow Cross = mustard gas]. I believe that everything has been done which could be done. The Heads of Operations make a good impression too. They are all greatly enthusiastic..."

Stapff went on to point out that on 30 November, after the advance of 49th Reserve Division, there would be no more reserves on the right flank of the Army and went on to request the simultaneous move forward to the south of 16th Bavarian Infantry Division. Kuhl replied that he would receive orders to that effect in due course.

> Stapff: The number of firing batteries in the Croisilles salient has increased. There are still battery positions there from the Battle of Arras. All that has to be done is for them to be occupied and immense drum fire could result. A major battle could break out there overnight and not just minor tank attacks as is the case now. I believe that a division is needed to cover it. About seventy tanks are located on the roads Ribécourt - Beaucamp, Marcoing – Villers-Plouich and Masnières – Le Pavé. This means that the British are regrouping. I estimate that they are moving towards [St] Quentin, in order to take part in an operation.
>
> Kuhl: I believe that they are heading for Croisilles.
>
> Stapff: That is also possible. Perhaps it is just a diversion. The tank battle of Cambrai is over.
>
> Kuhl: Yes, the [movement] of the tanks is certainly striking...

Von Kuhl then asked if Stapff had sufficient artillery and ammunition, to which Stapff replied affirmatively. Finally Kuhl stressed, 'Above all be careful over ranging in, so that they do not notice anything.' Stapff replied, 'The worst thing is the telephone. You never know who is listening in.'[48]

The following day, General der Infanterie von Kuhl was as good as his word. During 29 November, the Army Group issued order Ia Nr 4622 Secret. Although the wording was somewhat laboured, its meaning was clear and Second Army must have been relieved that one of its major remaining concerns had now been overcome.[49]

> "During the evening of 29 November, after nightfall, 16th Bavarian Infantry Division is to move into the area currently occupied by 49th Reserve Division and is to be briefed about the current tasks of 49th Reserve Division. 234th Infantry Division is to move during the evening of 29 November, after nightfall, into the area currently occupied by 16th Bavarian Infantry Division and is to be briefed about the current tasks of 16th Bavarian Infantry Division. Both of these divisions are Army Group reserves."

Only after these orders had been issued, the various alterations had been incorporated into orders right down to company and battery level and the immense mass of men and *materiel* had been moved into position, were the preparations for the counter-offensive complete. It was an enormous scramble to have everything in place, even for the amended 30 November start date. The movement control staffs and all the rest of the logisticians had worked minor miracles. Ever since 20 November, an average of 160 trains per day had poured into the Cambrai area, discharging reinforcements, equipment, ammunition and stores of every kind but, even so, it had proved to be impossible to move all the supporting services or to build up the ammunition stocks to the levels ideally necessary to support such an ambitious attack. It was largely due to the limitations of the transport network that the date had had to be slipped, but there came a point when Supreme Army Headquarters and the Army Group were no longer willing to concede to the representations of the Groups and Second Army itself.

The view at the highest level was that it was impracticable to await the arrival of all the specialist troops or every last round of ammunition because the success of the operation was likely to be less dependent on perfect preparation than the maintenance of operational security, use of surprise and the exploitation of the tactical situation on the ground, which was assessed to be extremely favourable as the British began to move equipment and men out of the area. There was also considerable concern that the massing of so much artillery and so many troops in virtually open terrain was effectively impossible to conceal from British reconnaissance aircraft and balloon crews. The longer the delay, the greater the risk of compromise and the less the chance of the attack falling on largely weakened and fought out British divisions.

Inevitably, however, the time compression had an effect on preparedness; it is simply difficult to quantify what difference the deficiencies made to the conduct of the actual operation. Group Caudry later listed some of the difficulties.

"It was not possible to place all artillery batteries and mortars optimally. Junior commanders and troops had insufficient time to study and rehearse their tasks fully and it was not possible to conduct reconnaissance of every detail of the enemy positions. Bearing in mind that, after three years of trench warfare, the troops were not used either to mobile operations or offensives, allowing adequate time to prepare was even more important... Tactical preparations were also rendered more difficult when, on 28 November, substantial changes were made to the boundaries of the four southern divisions. This meant that almost all Corps and Divisional Orders had to be cancelled and new ones prepared. Only through the most strenuous efforts could it be achieved that the Group was ready on 30 November to carry out its tasks... reinforcements of mortars and flamethrowers did not arrive until the very last day before the offensive and, to begin with, the flamethrowers had no oil..."[50]

The other Groups also had their concerns. On the eve of the offensive, for example, the war diary of Group Busigny recorded, 'Because of transport difficulties, ammunition stocks available to the divisions have not reached the necessary quantities. This is a situation which may have serious consequences. At 6.45 pm the facts were reported to Army Headquarters, together with a request for continued efforts to make up the deficiencies.'[51] It will be recalled that Major Stapff had assured General der Infanterie von Kuhl earlier that, even if stocks of ammunition were not optimum, nevertheless Second Army had sufficient for its purposes. This view was maintained later when the headquarters reported up the chain of command that, although there had been sufficient ammunition on hand, the divisions had failed to get it distributed to where it was actually needed.[52] Apart from a seemingly endless series of similar requests and queries which flowed into Headquarters Second Army in Le Cateau day and night, by 29 November matters were largely out of its hands. It could only wait and see how its plans would play out when the offensive opened.

General der Kavallerie Georg von der Marwitz [53]

"Today the British were quieter. Apart from some clashes with Group Arras, there was hardly any other warlike activity. The preparations for 30 November are complete. I shall be thrusting forward in the south with the following divisions: 30th (Graf Lambsdorff), 9th Reserve (General Hildemann), 220th (Graf Bassewitz) and 28th (Langer). So much for Group Caudry. The adjacent Group Busigny will attack with 34th, 208th and 183rd Divisions. In reserve I have 185th, 9th Bavarian and 79th [Reserve]. Group Arras, deploying 49th, 221st, 21st and 119th, will attack from the north. The wood to the front is under gas attack and will continue to be. Artillery fire begins at 7.50 am and the offensive at 8.00 am."

Crown Prince Rupprecht of Bavaria: Diary Entry 29 November 1917 [54]

"General von der Marwitz has issued the following Commander's Guidance to the Army Order dated 28 November 1917:

'1. For the break in battle, the boundary between Groups Caudry and Busigny is to be moved south, sufficient that the built up areas of Bantouzelle and Banteux are inclusive to Group Caudry.

'2. Artillery formations and mortars which have already been allocated by Group Busigny to prepare and support the attack on the enemy positions west of Banteux are to continue with these tasks.

'3. I wish to stress the importance I place on a simultaneous break in by 28th and 24th Divisions, advancing due west shoulder to shoulder.'

"For the purpose of deception, Fourth Army has ranged its guns in on numerous points and has brought down long range fire on the enemy approach routes and other transport links. In consequence the enemy artillery has sprung into action all along the front in Flanders. Tomorrow the deception plan will continue there and Sixth Army will do likewise.

"In preparation for tomorrow's attack, today the batteries of Group Arras have already begun to bring down heavy fire; whilst those of Group Busigny are carefully ranging in on particular points. Tomorrow at 8.00 am artillery fire will start coming down all along the front. The artillery of Group Arras will drench Bourlon Wood and the battery locations near Lagnicourt with gas; whilst the newly arrived reinforcing batteries of Groups Caudry and Busigny will range in. At 8.30 am drum fire will come down all along the front then, at 8.50 am, protected by this fire, which will be shifted forward gradually, the attack from the east will begin. At 11.50 am the attack by Group Arras will be launched from the north. Second Army hopes to advance at least as far as the railway line at Fins."

So much for the commander's guidance; the final order by Second Army, as issued down the chain of command, read as follows:[55]

1. As far as possible the inner flanks of 28th and 34th are to remain linked tightly together and are to push forward in a westerly direction.
2. Carrying out the role of flank protection, but also attacking are, in the south, the 208th and 183rd Infantry Divisions of Group Busigny; in the north [the same tasks are being conducted by 220th and 30th Infantry Divisions of Group Caudry. Following up is 9th Reserve Division.
3. Once the attacks have made progress, strong assault forces from Group Arras will advance south in the direction of Havrincourt – Flesquières.
4. By these means the enemy will be cut off along the baseline of the salient and destroyed."

In issuing this order, von der Marwitz was confirming that the two divisions on the inner flank were to concentrate exclusively on the main thrust and were to drive hard west, whilst the other two divisions were also to ensure flank protection. Only once this thrust had made clear and definable progress was the assault from the north to be launched. Geographical considerations probably forced this solution on Second Army, but it is as least questionable if it was entirely wise to entrust the main thrust to two divisions from different corps. All boundaries tend to be weak points, either in attack or defence so, from the outset, this plan ran the risk of communications difficulties between the divisions and, with that, scope for misunderstanding. It is true that in the aftermath of the counter-offensive, post-battle analysis stressed that there had been perfect understanding and harmonized movement between the two divisions concerned, but there will always be a lingering suspicion that a main thrust under unified command might have achieved more.

Just as the main tasks of Second Army were complete on 28 November, so they were the following day for the Groups. That evening Generalleutnant von Moser reviewed the events of the day, outlined his concerns for the following day and mentioned in passing the toll the strain of the past nine days had taken on him personally.

Generalleutnant Otto von Moser Diary Entry 29 November 1917 [56]

"During the early morning there was another thorough and critical check of the draft orders, which had been prepared during the night, then officers of the staff took them to the divisions by car. To the front there were very heavy exchanges of artillery fire; we, for our part, concentrating on keeping Bourlon Wood under constant fire. At 8.00 am there was yet another enemy thrust against our centre, but it was beaten off. Nevertheless it showed that the enemy were still attempting to cling on to their idea of breaking through. I summoned all seven divisional commanders of the formations which were to be subordinated to me for tomorrow's attack to a conference at Marquette Chateau at midday, in order to discuss once more the main points of tomorrow's attack. It is well known that the transition from defensive to offensive operations is numbered amongst the most difficult of tasks. For us here there were several reasons why it was exceptionally hard.

"The first reason was that our infantry was very worn down by the heavy casualties of the strenuous battles of the past few days. As a result I paid great attention to ensuring that the artillery, which had suffered less, was to strain every sinew to ensure that the preparatory bombardment and supporting fire was absolutely beyond reproach. Of course the tasks of the artillery are also far from simple as the defensive switches to the offensive. It calls for the greatest possible care and for the batteries to work hand in glove with one another.

Other factors are the unavoidable mixing of the formations and the necessity for some of my attacking troops to launch forward through the garrisons holding the trenches, because they were too tired to be placed in the front line tonight.

"The 49th Reserve Division was only subordinated to me at 5.00 pm today. Not only that, but there will be a further problem if the enemy infantry, which is stronger than us numerically, simply goes over to defence on Hill 100, southwest of Bourlon Wood, and elsewhere along the front, where former strong German trenches, complete with many dugouts, form very powerful positions. On the other hand, they may launch another attack tomorrow, either before us, or simultaneously and, if this does happen, doubtless it will be in cooperation with numerous tanks. In any case the highest standards of comradeship and support between the brigades and the divisional commanders will be paramount. Finally, the shortness of the winter day will leave us barely five hours to achieve our task of throwing the enemy back out of Graincourt. A speedy, decisive, advance will be essential.

"On the positive side we have great superiority in artillery and in the air. I have stressed this to all the men by means of a Group Order, which has just been printed and which is to be read this evening in all companies and batteries:

'Group Order

Tomorrow morning a major offensive launched by Second Army will finish off the enemy and deny them their hope of capturing Cambrai. Massed artillery support will prepare the attack with one immense concentration of fire and precede it with a rolling barrage. Strong formations of aircraft will take the lead and the remainder will be achieved by the courageous infantry in a dashing assault, which will have the intimate and comradely support of our accompanying field guns.

Up and at the enemy! The Corps Commander'

"I had the satisfaction at the end of the conference with my divisional commanders of receiving a resounding 'no' to my question if anybody had any doubts about the attack orders they had been given and this afternoon we have received not one single query. That is a good sign that everything has been clearly and efficiently worked out. Now it is all down to the Lord's will and soldierly luck – and, above all, the courage in battle of the troops. Incidentally, today I really could do with a break. Working almost all of the past eight days and nights in a small, generally overheated room, I have caught a heavy cold and a most unpleasant side effect. The nerves in my neck, which give me constant pain, have become inflamed. The pain reaches deep down into my left shoulder and I can hardly turn my neck. However, the feeling that an enemy breakthrough on a front which is so important [to them] and which they have attacked so obstinately, has been thwarted from 22 to 29 November, enables me to rise above all physical difficulties and fills me with confidence for tomorrow.

"The past week of battle has highlighted clearly once more the tasks and contribution made by the higher levels of command. Supreme Army Command, the Army Group and Army have allocated the missions, despatched forward the necessary troops and *materiel* and, in so doing, have put in place all the elements necessary to conduct a battle. The entire load of the hard-fought battles; the difficult tactical leadership of the very variable divisions in terms of quality and battleworthiness and the great artillery formations; the overcoming of almost daily crises concerning personnel or practical matters and the complete responsibility for the outcome of the fighting devolved where it naturally belongs: on the corps commander. This meant that I was at long last able, for once, to regard myself as an independent support and pillar, rather than a clamp and an anvil. I am already deriving great pleasure from the fast-approaching, marvellous role as a hammer.[57]

"Throughout the night Bourlon Wood, to the west of which the attack of Group Arras will pass, is being drenched heavily with gas once more. This is intended to damage and handicap the enemy who have established themselves there."

It is only right to note that this extensive use of gas, especially the persistent blister agent, mustard gas, was not regarded as an unmixed blessing by German troops in the vicinity. 237 Infantry Brigade of 119th Infantry Division felt compelled to issue special precautionary orders to its units and formations late on 28 November, in case they became affected by rogue shells or the associated downwind hazard.

"1. Bourlon Wood is going to be attacked with mustard gas tomorrow. This calls for the greatest care. The highest gas alert state is to be maintained, because mustard gas is colourless and odourless.

2. Prisoners wearing contaminated clothing who emerge from Bourlon Wood, are not to be permitted to approach. They must be directed to throw away their clothing!

3. 3rd Guards Division, deployed around Bourlon Wood on its eastern and northern sides, is permitted, should prudence dictate, to withdraw behind the railway line. It must be assumed

that moves to the rear will have to be carried out.

4. Entry into Bourlon Wood is forbidden during the coming days. In due course special permission to enter will be granted in particular circumstances."

There was a verbal addition to these orders. Any British soldiers who refused to conform to the directions in Paragraph 2 were to be shot, because any contact with contaminated soldiers brought danger to those involved.[58]

All manner of Orders of the Day were written and distributed during these final hours. That of the overall commander read,

"Soldiers of the Second Army!

Following the surprise deployment of large numbers of tanks, the British achieved success near Cambrai on 20 November. Thanks to the brilliant resistance offered by the troops placed there for that purpose, they did not succeed in their aim of forcing a break through. Our aim now is to launch an encircling counter-attack and to turn their initial success into defeat. The eyes of the Fatherland are on you. It is expected that each and every one of you will do his duty. So, let us go to it, with God's help, to victory!

The Commander in Chief von der Marwitz General der Kavallerie and Generaladjutant"[59]

For his part, the Army Group Commander noted what, for him, was the minimum acceptable return for all the effort which had gone into preparing the counter-attack.

Crown Prince Rupprecht of Bavaria: Diary Entry 29 November 1917 [60]

"The minimum outcome of the offensive which begins tomorrow has to be the recapture of Second Army's *Siegfried I* Positions."

The staff work was long since complete; the commanders had issued their Orders of the Day. It now remained for the multiplicity of formations and units to ensure that their members were fired up for the challenge the morning would bring. Major Kuczkowski, commander Infantry Regiment 395 of 9th Reserve Division, which would be returning to the front after a few days rest in Cambrai, chose to inspire his men with the words, 'I am sure that every member of the regiment will be highly delighted with the marvellous task we have been given for the first time since we embarked on trench warfare. I do not have the slightest doubt that we shall easily achieve our objective. With God's help we shall overcome any possible difficulties. I wish you the best of luck for tomorrow and the days which follow!' [61]

It was a fervent wish, one shared by all involved. It had not been possible to disguise all the forward movement of troop concentrations and additional guns and aircraft from the British but, on the ground along the front line, operational security had been preserved and surprise was going to be virtually complete. In Havrincourt village, during the afternoon of 29 November, Brigadier General Elles conducted a final review of the survivors from the tank brigades, who had paraded assuming that the tanks had fully proved their worth and that their work was complete. The parade over, completely oblivious to what was looming up, the tank men continued the process of backloading their tanks. Mentally, with the exception of Major Generals Scott and Jeudwine, commanders of the British 12th and 55th Divisions respectively, who held urgent talks that day at Villers-Guislain to discuss what they took to be a serious threat, the remainder of the British army had consigned the battle of Cambrai to the past.

However, when darkness fell, the German rear areas were a hive of activity, as strenuous efforts continued to complete the final build up. All along the line, assault troops moved into position and, having done so, tried to catch a few fitful hours of sleep wedged uncomfortably into damp forward dugouts or wrapped in their groundsheets. The night of 29/30 November was quiet and relatively peaceful throughout the area and the attackers drew collective strength from the realisation that there had still been no alarms and that even the weather was on their side.

Notes

1. Kronprinz Rupprecht *Mein Kriegstagebuch Zweiter Band* pp 294 - 295
2. *Heeresgruppe Rupprecht Ia. Nr. 4517 vom 21.11.17 Aktenauszüge aus OHL O Ia 'Operationen West 1.-30.XI.1917' BA.-MA. RH 61/51716*
3. Kronprinz Rupprecht *op. cit.* p 295
4. See: *Persöhnliches Kriegstagebuch des Generals der Infanterie a.D. von Kuhl BA.-MA. RH 61/50652* p 97
5. *Besprechung S.K.H. des Kronprinzen von Bayern beim A.O.K. 2 Aktenauszüge aus OHL O Ia 'Operationen West 1.-30.XI.1917' BA.-MA. RH 61/51716*
6. Kronprinz Rupprecht *op. cit.* pp 295-296
7. Tschischwitz: *General von der Marwitz* p 260
8. *Die Deutsche Gegenangriff bei Cambrai 1917 BA.-MA. RH 61/51507* p6
9. *Heeresgruppe Rupprecht Ia Nr 4579 vom 25.11.17 Die Deutsche Gegenangriff bei Cambrai 1917 BA.-MA. RH 61/51507* pp 6-7
10. *AOK 2 Ia Nr 539 vom 26.11.17 Die Deutsche Gegenangriff bei Cambrai 1917 BA.-MA. RH 61/51507* p 10
11. Moser *Feldzugsaufzeichnungen* p 315
12. This request was granted but, so tight were the timings of the arrival of

reinforcements, that the 49th Reserve Division did not move to under command Group Arras until 5.00 pm 29 November.

13. This is a reference to a report by an agent received a few days previously by Headquarters Army Group Crown Prince Rupprecht, which stated that two French divisions, supported by tanks, were poised ready to launch an attack in the St Quentin area. *Die Deutsche Gegenangriff bei Cambrai 1917 BA.-MA. RH 61/51507* p7

14. *Heeresgruppe Rupprecht Ia Nr 4719 vom 26.11.17 Die Deutsche Gegenangriff bei Cambrai 1917 BA.-MA. RH 61/51507* pp 10-11

15. Gerth: History Infantry Regiment 395 p 148

16. Tschischwitz: *op. cit.* p 261

17. The war diary of Second Army was no help either. It merely noted, 'The Commander and Chief of Staff drove during the morning to a conference with Group Caudry.' There was no mention of the Group Arras meeting or if discussions took place with Group Busigny that day. *Die Deutsche Gegenangriff bei Cambrai 1917 BA.-MA. RH 61/51507* p 11

18. Moser *op. cit.* pp 315-316

19. Here Moser is demonstrating his sense of responsibility as a higher commander. In operational planning the so-called 'Rule of Thirds' applies. This means that each successive layer of command should not exceed its 'ration' of one third of the available time. If, say, three days were available to plan a German corps level operation, the corps headquarters would take twenty four hours for its work and divisional headquarters sixteen hours, leaving thirty two hours. Of these the brigade would have eleven hours, the regiment seven hours and the battalions five hours. This would leave only nine hours for the troops at company level and below to complete preparations and move into position in time for the start of the operation. Frequently this would be insufficient, so all armies developed battle drills and used a system of warning orders, so as to permit valuable time to be gained and for best use to be made of it by means of concurrent activity.

20. Kronprinz Rupprecht *Mein Kriegstagebuch Dritter Band* pp 181-182

21. *Die Deutsche Gegenangriff bei Cambrai 1917* BA.-MA. RH 61/51507 p 12

22. *Der Weltkrieg, Dreizehnter Band* pp 132-133

23. Kronprinz Rupprecht *op. cit.* pp 296-297

24. Westrozebeke is a village located three kilometres north of Passchendaele.

25. Kronprinz Rupprecht *Mein Kriegstagebuch Dritter Band* pp 182-183

26. *OHL Ia Nr. 5510 op.geh. vom 27.11.17 Aktenauszüge aus OHL O Ia 'Operationen West 1.-30.XI.1917'* BA.-MA. RH 61/51716

27. Kronprinz Rupprecht *op. cit.* pp 297-298

28. In fact the proprieties seem to have been observed to the extent that the

Supreme Army Headquarters directive was passed down to Second Army by Army Group Crown Prince Rupprecht as its *Ia Nr 4610 Die Deutsche Gegenangriff bei Cambrai 1917* BA.-MA. RH 61/51507 p 13

29. Tschischwitz: *op. cit.* p 261
30. *Die Deutsche Gegenangriff bei Cambrai 1917* BA.-MA. RH 61/51507 p 13
31. Moser: *op. cit.* p 317
32. Tschischwitz: *op. cit.* pp 261-262
33. Moser *op. cit.* pp 318-319
34. Kronprinz Rupprecht *Mein Kriegstagebuch Dritter Band* pp 183-184
35. This is reference to Second Army *AOK Ia 631 vom 28.11.17 Die Deutsche Gegenangriff bei Cambrai 1917* BA.-MA. RH 61/51507 p 18.
36. *Gruppenbefehl Ia 8283 vom 28.11.17 Die Deutsche Gegenangriff bei Cambrai 1917* BA.-MA. RH 61/51507 pp 22-27
37. Without access to the original map overlay, this wording seems a little strange, because the *SII Stellung* ran north south to the west of Bourlon Wood. The interpretation has to be that the division was being directed to screen eastwards north of the wood, then south to the Cambrai - Bapaume road near Fontaine.
38. *Die Deutsche Gegenangriff bei Cambrai 1917* BA.-MA. RH 61/51507 p 25
39. *ibid.* p 26
40. This is a reference to the batteries which actually accompanied the advancing troops to provide intimate support.
41. *Die Deutsche Gegenangriff bei Cambrai 1917* BA.-MA. RH 61/51507 p 28
42. *Gruppe Caudry Gen. Kdo. XIII Chef/Ia. 78 op geh. 28.11.17 5 Uhr 40 nachm. Hauptstaatsarchiv Stuttgart M33/2 Bü 374* pp 13-14
43. *Die Deutsche Gegenangriff bci Cambrai 1917* BA.-MA. RH 61/51507 p 33-35
44. *Heeresgruppe Rupprecht Ia Nr 4613 vom 28.11.17 Die Deutsche Gegenangriff bei Cambrai 1917* BA.-MA. RH 61/51507 p 15.
45. *Die Deutsche Gegenangriff bei Cambrai 1917* BA.-MA. RH 61/51507 p 15.
46. *ibid.* p16.
47. The nature of this 'intervention' is not known.
48. *Die Deutsche Gegenangriff bei Cambrai 1917* BA.-MA. RH 61/51507 pp 20-22
49. *ibid.* p 36
50. *Die Angriffsschlacht bei Cambrai Hauptstaatsarchiv Stuttgart* M33/2 Bü 374 p 1
51. *Die Deutsche Gegenangriff bei Cambrai 1917* BA.-MA. RH 61/51507 p 39

52. *Bericht der Gruppe Caudry über die Angriffsschlacht bei Cambrai vom 9.12.17 Hauptstaatsarchiv* Stuttgart M33/2 Bü 374 p 4
53. Tschischwitz: *op. cit.* p 263
54. Kronprinz Rupprecht *Mein Kriegstagebuch Dritter Band* pp 184-185
55. Voigt: History Füsilier Regiment 73 p 612
56. Moser *op. cit.* pp 319-321
57. This metaphorical reference to hammer and anvil was common currency in Germany during the early part of the 20th Century and was used, most notoriously, in respect of Germany's place in the world. Was it to be a hammer, or an anvil?
58. Zunehmer: History Infantry Regiment 46 p 358. This is a very rare reference in the German literature
59. Christian: History Infantry Regiment 418 p 114
60. Kronprinz Rupprecht: *op. cit.* p 298
61. Gerth: History Infantry Regiment 395 pp 152-153

CHAPTER SIX

30 November 1917: Hopes Raised

Leutnant von der Goltz Field Artillery Regiment 14 [1]

"Today, we are doing the drumming!

It is the early morning of 30 November 1917. Normally, each day begins as the gunners emerge, creeping out of their dugouts, drunk with sleep. They leave behind the smoke of the stove and the harsh glimmer of the acetylene lamp and their red-rimmed, swollen eyes accustom themselves to the daylight. The gun layer staggers, with limbs stiffened from lying on hard boards and goes over to lift the tarpaulin, stiff with frost, off the sleeping gun. Taking a soft white cloth he wipes the dew, which is threatening to cause rust, off the grooves in the breech, then he stands up straight, still stiff from the night before and blinks reproachfully at the sun, which is dispersing the early morning mist and prays, 'Stay away, cruel, inquisitive sun! You are betraying our location. You are enabling the enemy to train his telescopes on us. For the one thousand and twenty seventh day you are bringing forth a day full of noise and fumes.' Then the old gun layer would sit with his gasmask, damp from the night, brooding on top of the shell baskets, shuddering at the thought of the first shell which would tear through the silence...

"But today is different. Today is our day. Today it is we who are doing the drumming...

"7.50 am. The order to fire flies from the observation post to the guns. It passes along the chain of relays like a flat pebble skimming along the surface of a pond. The battery commander has lit a living time fuze.

"Rumm... rumm... rumm... rumm... and simultaneously angry streams of flame belch out from behind hedges and bushes, from hollows and the ruins of houses. It is as though in the dead of night a dog has begun to bark, then all around, in the surrounding farms and villages, alert guard dogs reply, until the entire darkened valley is full of the weird echoes of howling and barking – that is the effect rising above the steaming St Quentin Canal, of the racket of the German bombardment.

"Next target 3,000! From the right, fire! Rumm... rumm... rumm... rumm... (That is revenge for the naval guns firing on the Lorette Spur, which ploughed up our cemeteries.)

3,500! Fire! Rumm... rumm... rumm... rumm... (That is for the autumn battles in Champagne. Now the Tommies are picking up the bill for the French.)

3,700! Rumm... rumm... rumm... rumm... (Go on, crawl away into the earth, duck down low. Revenge for the whimpering of the helpless comrades buried alive on the Somme.)

3,900 Rumm... rumm... rumm... rumm... (Great fun, eh, Tommy? Swallow the gas and choke out your death rattles. That is for Verdun.)

Rolling Salvo!

4,000! ... Rumm... Revenge for Vermelles!

3,900! ... Rumm... Revenge for Givenchy!

3,800! ... Rumm... Revenge for St Hilaire!

3,700! ... For Fontaine!

3,600! 3,500! Revenge for Wavrille and Herbebois!

3,000! Rapid fire!

What fun Tommy! We are taking our revenge for the dismal years when we had to be patient. Long, long years of being on the receiving end of drum fire, helpless. Today we are drumming. Clouds of fog hang far and wide over the trenches but, through the smoke, flash the death-dealing bayonets of the grenadiers and fusiliers crouched down, waiting to storm forward. Rumm... rumm... rumm...rumm...

Today we are doing the drumming!"

This was a day of intense fighting, with a great many units and formations moving simultaneously and deeply echeloned, on a battle front between thirty five and forty kilometres long. In order to keep the description of the events of the day as straightforward as possible, the operations of each of the Groups will be described separately, commencing in the extreme south.

In an attempt to conceal the precise extent of the counter attack, formations of 5th Guards Infantry Division, deployed just to the south of the Group Busigny boundaries and occupying the so-called *Bellicourtstellung*, were involved on 30 November with the conduct of diversionary attacks, the main one of which was directed at Gillemont Farm and conducted by assault troops of Infantry Regiment 184.[2] To facilitate this, Mortar Battalion 8 was allocated to the division, its weapons being divided up between the forward regiments, with Grenadier Guard Regiment 3 holding exposed forward trenches near to Malakoff Farm receiving four heavy, six medium and three light mortars.[3] The mortars brought down heavy fire when the remainder of the artillery opened up and British battery positions were gassed, but there was very little response, either at the time or later. Nevertheless, two light field guns in the anti-tank role arrived to assist in flank protection should it have been necessary. To the right of Grenadier Guard Regiment 3, Footguard Regiment

3 managed to obtain more of a reaction, though how great a contribution to the overall operations of the day was made is hard to estimate.

Hauptmann Egon von Loebell Footguard Regiment 3 [4]

"At exactly 7.50 am the heaviest mortar fire imaginable came down on the farm with a sudden crash. The word 'heaviest' is thoroughly justified because we used the new, really unpleasant, finned mortar rounds. At 8.00 am the assault troops of Infantry Regiment 184 attacked the farm and were simply beaten back.[5] The enemy who, it seemed, assumed that a large scale attack was underway, brought down heavy fire into the hollow behind our forward position, presuming that it contained attacking forces which had so far remained under cover. Meanwhile we had begun to bring down unusually heavy fire on the main break in point further to the right; gas was then brought down on the enemy batteries.

"The British trench garrison assumed that it was one of the usual fire concentrations and sought shelter in the dugouts, where they were quickly surprised by the assaulting infantry. The German attack made brilliant progress. From the *KTK* dugout we watched the entire military pageant unfolding. At first, we exercised the normal care, but then we were able to cast caution to the wind, despite the fact that we were only 300 metres from the enemy front line, because the result of the gassing was that all the enemy artillery in our area ceased firing. It was a fantastic military sight! Everywhere the infantry was advancing, sometimes in very large formations. Very soon our artillery began changing locations and moving forward. Batteries in harness were on the move everywhere. Most of them were moving at a sensible pace, so as to spare their horses and some were trotting, whilst the occasional one risked a short gallop. The whole thing was reminiscent of the mobile warfare we all longed for.

"Everywhere there were smiling faces, hardly any wounded seemed to be making their way back, so casualties must have been few. Stragglers, the well-known 'last men of their companies', or 'affected by gas', were nowhere to be seen. According to reports from our neighbours, Infantry Regiment 440, the whole thing was going brilliantly and, according to plan, forwards. From early morning a detachment of Stendal Hussars[vi] was on stand by. In response to our questions, they explained that they were there to escort groups of prisoners to the rear, which seemed rather unlikely to us. In the end there were nowhere near enough of them to cope with the task."

Group Busigny: General der Infanterie von Kathen

Operating on the left flank of the Group were the regiments of 183rd Infantry Division. The attack was mounted with Infantry Regiment 440 left forward, Infantry Regiment 418 right forward, with Infantry Regiment 184 deployed initially in reserve, its 1st and 2nd Battalions being located near Gouy. Infantry Regiment 440 did not produce a history post war and that of Infantry Regiment 184 is extremely sketchy. Fortunately the history of the short period of existence of Infantry Regiment 418 is very detailed and, in the case of Cambrai, one of the surviving officers wrote a full and atmospheric account of the events of the day on this southern sector. The divisional mission was to protect the left flank of the entire enterprise and, to that end, during the course of the day it assaulted (mostly against very light opposition) several British positions and occupied trenches stretching as far forward as a point one kilometre southeast of Villers Guislain, where it linked up with 34th Infantry Division, which was responsible for the southern sector of the main thrust.

Leutnant W Koch 12th Company Infantry Regiment 418 [7]

"Whilst the defensive battle was still raging, the Army High Command directed the mounting of a powerful counter-stroke to be launched by twenty divisions and which was known as the *Angriffsschlacht bei Cambrai* [Cambrai Offensive]. Our sector was to be included on the extreme left flank of the offensive front. 30 November was selected for the start of the operation. The tense atmosphere was felt by all. This was, after all, the first major German offensive on the Western Front for a very long time and, in addition, it was being launched on the back of a defensive operation and with an extremely short period of preparation.

"Orders: 'At X-90 10th and 12th Companies are to be on standby in the Hohenzollern Strongpoint and are to work their way forward to the Offus Position [one kilometre northwest of Vendhuille] by X+60. At about X+90 10th Company is to take over the positions of the 1st Battalion and 12th Company, those of 2nd Battalion. Whilst those two battalions storm the enemy second line trenches and clear them, 10th and 12th Companies are to close up and take up positions on the right next to 2nd Battalion, ready to continue the attack. Company frontages are to be two hundred metres. The Assault Troops of 3rd, 2nd and 1st Battalions are to fight their way forward independently. The remainder of the companies are to follow up in accordance with the progress of the attack.' This, more or less, is how the orders for the attack were couched. Although they were quite clear, they possessed the disadvantage that they did nothing to familiarise us with the ground [over which we were to attack]. The previous evening we were informed that X [H Hour] was to be 7.50 am.

"During the night, at about 3.00 am, we moved up, filled with the usual uncertainty of every front line soldier when confronted by the start of a new day of battle. Nevertheless, we were confident and had the light of battle in our eyes. It soon became clear that all the roads were jammed with marching and waiting troops, ammunition columns, field kitchens etc. Time and again the roads had to be cleared for motorised convoys carrying forward gas shells which were needed for the preparatory bombardment. As a result, we were forced to move across country, negotiating wire obstacles, firing batteries, trenches and dugouts. Sweating profusely, the crews of machine guns and grenade launchers toiled forward under the weight of their heavy equipment and ammunition boxes. They were certainly unaware that it was a chilly night. Fortunately it was also a clear, starry night so, aided by our compasses, we were just able to reach the Hohenzollern Strongpoint at the appointed time. To our front the canal banks and bridges were under heavy fire. Could the British have found out about the attack or noticed something?

"After a short pause we pressed on. Now, with the front line trenches of the Offus Position looming up to our front, there were no more convoys to block our way. The narrow temporary bridges were crossed at the double under shrapnel fire. Meanwhile our own drum fire had begun. Shells roared forward over our heads to be answered by the hasty harassing fire of the British batteries. As it became light we reached our jumping off point and advanced into the morning mist, just as the companies of the first and second waves stormed the first British positions. The first consequence of the bad visibility, which made orientation in this unknown landscape, cut by numerous ravines, extremely difficult, was that the 11th Company, charged with making and maintaining contact between us and the neighbouring division, disappeared into the fog without a trace. It was not until late evening that they were discovered after a lengthy search.

"We had traversed No Man's Land and the First British Position and moved into a carefully repaired communication trench, equipped with duckboards, in order to conform to the advance of the neighbouring battalion, when the fog cleared suddenly and we were able to observe the 2nd Battalion, which was heavily engaged as it attempted vainly to dislodge the British from their position on some high ground that they were defending stubbornly.[8] We rushed forward and were soon established on the British flank. Two machine guns were brought swiftly into action and rapid enfilade fire was directed at the British. Their surprise was great, as was the effect of the fire. Some made for the rear, whilst others directed their fire at us. With loud shouts of *Hurra!* The 6th Company stormed forward. Delighted with this initial success, we stormed on and shortly a sunken road, complete with dugouts, opened up on our left.

"It was crammed with British reserves – Scottish troops dressed in kilts; tough-looking lads – who were attempting to prepare the sunken road for defence. Once again our appearance was a surprise and a scene of utter confusion unfolded before our eyes. Very little fire was directed against us, so I gave orders for the capture of the sunken road. This was achieved with only light casualties, especially because the 6th Company advanced at the same time. I ordered a brief pause to permit the company to reorganise and to prepare for a further advance within our allocated boundaries. But which was our area? In reality this hilly countryside looked nothing like it did on the map and as for the 10th Company, with which I was supposed to be cooperating, it had suddenly disappeared off the face of the earth.

"Whilst we were engaged with the enemy on the left flank, it had possibly been marching forward unopposed. This was a pretty kettle of fish! Our right flank was hanging in the air, so it was impossible to know if the British were threatening our flank or rear. A reconnaissance patrol despatched to the right finally returned with a report that they had made contact with advancing troops from the division to the right. In addition and this was of far greater importance to our men, in a quarry which Leutnant Weber and 3rd Company had taken in a *coup de main* operation, a British depot had been found. It contained woollen underwear, coats and large quantities of rubber boots. In the meantime we continued the advance. Fire from concealed enemy forces caused a considerable number of casualties. When the firing died away, I held a short council of war with my platoon commanders and decided to exploit the possibilities of the moment and to push on with the considerably reduced remnants of the company. Unopposed, we arrived at a reinforcement holding area, which also appeared to have provided a battalion command post.

"The British could only just have left because we discovered two very large dixies of cocoa and tea - hot and ready to drink - in a dugout. Beef was stewing on top of a stove in another dugout, eggs and bacon were in a frying pan and there were entire cases of eggs stacked up next to the stove. It made a marvellous meal for our famished men, who had been on the move with nothing hot to eat since 3.00 am and on whom the strain of this day of battle was beginning to tell. We found other treats such as cigarettes, ham and jam. It was only by taking a great deal of care that we ensured that we maintained the necessary sentries in order to be sure that we did not receive an unpleasant surprise.

"In the dugout the telephone still rang, but nobody responded when we answered it. From captured British maps it became clear that we were located immediately in front of a fortified strong point. It was also soon confirmed that it was strongly held, when our meal was interrupted by the arrival of rifle grenades and when a patrol, despatched forward, was greeted by grenades and machine gun fire. An attempt by 1st Battalion to outflank the strong point and to assault a weak point failed. By now it had gone dark so, with heavy hearts, we had to abandon any thought of continuing the advance that day. The following morning an assault troop from Infantry Regiment 184 captured it very early. The assumption that it was heavily garrisoned was confirmed. Enormous heaps of fired cartridge cases next to two machine guns knocked out with artillery fire showed how stubbornly it had been defended.

"Later we examined a large dugout carefully. The company commander had been occupying a niche in it. There we found all his possessions. These included his smart Scottish uniform, his letter and map cases, his sleeping bag etc. As was clear from photographs on the wall, this was a Captain Brown. One of my platoon commanders, who until the outbreak of war had lived and worked as a businessman in London, seized the uniform and examined the letter case. He stated that he recognised Captain Brown from the photograph and that he had been together with him in London. We assumed that he was making it up, but suddenly he pulled a photograph of a swimming club out of the letter case and, unmistakably, there was my platoon commander in a swimsuit standing near to Captain Brown.

"Suddenly shouts and the noise of battle were heard coming from the trench above. A voiced yelled excitedly into the dugout, 'Get out, get out, the Tommies are coming!' Rushing out, we saw a large mass of enemy cavalry charging straight at our position. Everybody who could hold a rifle poured fire at the swarms of riders who were closing in with their lances at the ready. Soon our machine guns joined in as well at the rapid rate. Above us, unnoticed amidst the general excitement, shrapnel rounds burst above the strong point. It made for a breathtaking scene of intense battle and the excitement levels were high. A cavalry attack on the Western Front. That was absolutely unknown, unbelievable almost! The attack withered away under the weight of fire. The entire ground to our front was littered with dead and wounded riders and their horses. The losses amongst the cavalry were simply dreadful. Two unwounded riders, one of them leading a wounded horse, were captured and brought to me. To our amazement we saw that they were Indian. One was an officer of noble appearance, his pale face surrounded by a full black beard and the other a corporal of his squadron. Both stood before me dressed in turbans. Bitterly they informed me that the British had held back their own cavalry and, instead had despatched an Indian cavalry brigade on this idiotic attack, which had ended with the complete destruction of the Indian regiments.[9]

"We rated their disregard of death with which they had hurled themselves forward at our trenches very highly and gave them due recognition, but this did nothing to ease their sorrow and their anger at the British chain of command. These events marked the end of our short but remarkable involvement in the Cambrai Offensive. An Indian lance and a long dagger, which I still possess, bear silent witness to that day."

As has previously been mentioned, at X Hour two assault groups and supporting mortars of Infantry Regiment 184 were in position near to Gillemont Farm, which was almost the most southerly tip of the entire operation. During most of the day the various units followed one tactical bound behind the main advance, but later in the day 6th and 8th Companies were involved in a hard fight for a British strong point. On 1 December the assault on the strong point continued and 6th and 8th Companies succeeded in capturing thirty prisoners and several machine guns. Consolidating on the position, 5th and 7th Companies were involved in beating off an attack by a number of cavalry squadrons. Allied losses were high and Infantry Regiment 184 captured a further twenty five prisoners, twenty horses and one machine gun.[10] It then moved forward to reinforce the final line reached, which Infantry Regiments 418 and 440 were working hard to develop.

Just to the north and forming the southern part of the main thrust, were the regiments of 34th Infantry Division, to which 1st Company Jäger Storm Battalion 3 had been attached and then, during the night 28/29 November, a further regiment – Infantry Regiment 25 of 208th Infantry Division, the Group Reserve, was also inserted into the front line on the left flank, with prime responsibility for the capture of Villers Guislain. As a result, space for each regiment to shake out fully in the advance was severely limited. Nevertheless, it provided considerable strength in depth on the right flank of the Group. *Königs-Infanterie-Regiment* [King's Infantry Regiment] 145 advanced to the left of Infantry Regiment 67, which was charged with maintaining close contact with 28th Infantry Division on its right and Infantry Regiment 30 followed up a tactical bound behind Infantry Regiment 67. The objectives for the two leading 34th Infantry Division regiments were: King's Infantry Regiment 145 (Gauche Wood, then main thrust towards Sorel le Grand); Infantry Regiment 67 (Gouzeaucourt then further advance on Fins).

These aims, which were not totally defined in advance, implied a very long advance into the depth of the British positions of between eight and eleven kilometres. It was obvious from the start that these regiments would be fought out long before final objectives were reached but, as events were to prove, neither the required reinforcements nor the key decision makers were well placed to react to the situation as it evolved.

1st Company Jäger Storm Battalion 3 was also set ambitious objectives by commander Infantry Regiment 67. It was to break into the old *Siegfriedstellung* and then to clear the way up to and including Gonnelieu, at which point it was to link up with Infantry Regiment 67 once more and go firm to prevent the defenders of the British position to the north of that place from interfering with the further advance. After a strenuous march through the night, 1st Company was ready on the start line for the bombardment to lift. Such was the aggression shown by the officers and men of the company, that it was not long before the assault groups, impatient with the speed of advance of the rolling barrage, were pushing on through gaps in the fire and bringing the fight to the British defence forward of the German artillery cover. There was stout British resistance in places, but the effect of operating in advance of the barrage was that surprise was considerably enhanced and the overall early pace of the advance in this sector rapid. Meanwhile, out on the left flank, following a vicious fight at close quarters, Infantry Regiment 25 succeeded in taking the forward British positions and capturing 200 British soldiers, together with two field guns and nine assorted machine guns.[11]

Following up and benefiting from the fire of the infantry support batteries of Field Artillery Regiment 70, the forward units of King's Infantry Regiment 145 and Infantry Regiment 67 surged forward in long, widely spaced lines and discovered to their great satisfaction that, in contrast to the situation elsewhere, in their sector at least the artillery had done a good job of destroying the British wire. There were numerous gaps in it and although there were anxious moments from time to time, in case there were machine guns trained on these gaps, the leading companies managed to pass through it in quick order and to discover that the forward British positions were only lightly held. Pressing on rapidly into the *Wettermulde* [Banteux Ravine] 34th Infantry Division threatened for a while to achieve the precise aim of the operation; namely, to cut a swathe right across the base of the British salient. Standing in their way were the men of the already weakened 1/5th South Lancashire Regiment holding a hopelessly wide two kilometre front in section and platoon posts. Despite fighting to the last, this battalion was utterly annihilated. Not one man returned, though a few wounded men, including the Commanding Officer, Lieutenant Colonel James, were captured. The remaining scattered units of the British 55th Division were also smashed or brushed aside, surprised by the high speed of the advance.

Pushing on rapidly, leading elements of the division were reporting little or no resistance as they closed in on Gonnelieu, Villers Guislain and Gouzeaucourt. The regimental historian of Infantry Regiment 67 later described the scene as, 'being like the war of movement during August 1914. Hauptmann Steinbricht stood, swinging his stick and calling out, 'Now, isn't this fun today! Keep pushing on as hard as you can!' Far and wide there were no British soldiers to be seen...'[12] There was then a check. The advance had moved so quickly that the regiments had got ahead of their own barrage, which now began to crash down among them. Frantically, green flares were fired to get the gunners to increase the range, but it was all in vain. The signals were not seen, or discounted. The attackers suffered casualties and men dispersed left and right, becoming entangled with other units. It was a hard price to pay for advancing a complete kilometre in ten minutes.

However, even this difficulty did not succeed in halting the advance, which continued as planned. Pockets of resistance were quickly dealt with; the occupants either surrendering promptly and being sent to the rear, or being shot down. In fact there was a more serious check when 34th Infantry Division overran numerous field kitchens located in the sunken roads around Gonnelieu. Many of them had meals cooking on them or hot drinks being kept warm. There was no stopping the advancing troops gobbling down what they could and making off with the some of the copious supplies of biscuit, tinned foods, jam, rum and whisky which were stacked everywhere. Pockets, pouches and stomachs full, however, they pressed on; Infantry Regiment 67 helping King's Infantry Regiment 145 deal with a stubborn strong point in Gauche Wood. It was still only mid morning. The advance was still way out in front of the artillery support, so there was a pause of a good thirty minutes just east of Gouzeaucourt. This enabled stragglers to close up and the artillery fire to lift further forward.

The leading regiments had covered about four kilometres in little over an hour – an astonishing rate of progress. Direct aimed fire was poured into tents and vehicles parked beside or moving along the Gouzeaucourt – Heudicourt road, then the entire line stood up and pressed on westwards. It really did seem to be a return to a war of movement. Horse lines and columns of wagons were overrun and ever-increasing streams of British prisoners were making their way to the German rear. The regiments closed up to the road, dealing with several machine guns firing from the edge of Gouzeaucourt and the nearby railway embankment by bringing the guns of the direct support batteries into action. A concentrated effort by Infantry Regiments 30, 67 and King's Infantry Regiment 145, enabled the division to move into Gouzeaucourt but, very significantly, not to clear it of numerous machine gun crews and, meanwhile, British emergency counter action saw the 20th Hussars moving against the village, together with tanks of D and E Battalions I Tank Brigade, which did not actually arrive in time to intervene when the first counter-attack was launched.

Whilst the British manoeuvred, the 34th Infantry Division was overrunning even more attractive supplies of food and drink, which was too great a temptation for men denied such luxuries for months on end. Only with great difficulty did their officers re-establish control and even then command was rendered difficult because the mixing of units and sub units was now even worse than it had been previously. Without any doubt this would have been the moment for German reinforcements to arrive and to press on towards Metz en Couture and Fins, now a mere three and a half kilometres distant. But the advance had been so rapid, far quicker than anticipated, that there was no question of that. For a moment, whilst the advance hesitated, it seemed that the chance of a genuinely significant break through was there to be seized, but the impetus had gone out of the attack. Patrols pushed forward were already having to deal with stiffening British resistance then, out to the right, columns could be seen approaching.

For a short while it was thought that they might be German but, to general dismay, they turned out to be British. Instead of troops coming to their assistance, a bold, hasty counter-attack launched by the British 1st Guards Brigade at about 2.00 pm succeeded in retaking the village. As the British battalions bore down on the village, the local commander, Hauptmann Thosehrn, having briefly attempted to organise a firing line, ordered a rapid withdrawal to the Gouzeaucourt – Revélon road. His aim was to hold this new line against further British advances, but the setback of having to yield one thousand metres of ground was a bitter blow to the 34th Infantry Division, during a day which had promised so much. There were some slight attempts to move back in the direction of Gouzeaucourt, but the British had fully recognised the danger; the moment had passed. Now, as British attacks built up against the new line, the more pressing question was if the weakened, disorganised troops could hold out if a more deliberate attack was mounted.

Towards 4.00 pm tanks were seen closing in slowly, but surely. Initially they were sighted at a range of 2,000 metres, but that reduced fairly rapidly. A British cavalry brigade appeared on the scene and German accounts also mention the presence of British infantry in some strength. Taking on the advancing armour, once the range had closed somewhat, the accompanying guns in the direct fire role knocked out five tanks in rapid succession and forced the remainder to turn away. Fire of all kinds was then brought down against the other British troops in the vicinity, Infantry Regiment 67 claiming that it beat off repeated assaults launched by the 'bullheaded British', who formed up between the railway embankment and the road, attempted to advance, suffered heavy losses and scattered, only to form up once more and repeat the operation – with exactly the same results.

Be that as it may. Both sides were running out of daylight and for the men of 34th Infantry Division it was time to take stock. The troops were utterly exhausted due to a combination of the demands made on them during the past few days and the stress and strain of the day's offensive operations. Losses by the end of the first day were heavy, especially – and this was generally the case on 30 November – in junior leaders, both officers and NCOs. Strenuous efforts were made to ensure that a more or less continuous defence line was manned. Outposts, sentries and patrols operated between the various regiments and there were constant attempts to open and then maintain some form of communication back to Brigade and Division, which had been interrupted for most of the day. The mood was subdued. The unexpected check had taken its toll on all ranks and there was real concern about what the morning of 1 December might bring. Would the British be reinforced? What would the tanks do next? Could they hold a concerted armoured thrust and what was to be done about the need to push on further in to the depths of British position? With these thoughts racing through their heads, all of them, officers and men, all who were not on duty, lay down on the ground and, despite the cold, slept the sleep of the dead.

Group Caudry: General der Infanterie Freiherr von Watter

During the late evening of 29 November, the formations of Group Caudry, which were to be responsible for the main thrust west towards Metz en Couture, began their march forward. Men of Leibgrenadier Regiment 109, for example, advanced into position during a strenuous march via Walincourt, Malincourt, Villers-Outréaux (where they were issued with hand grenades and flares) to Aubencheul and Rancourt Farm. After a brief pause, they moved straight into the attack, allegedly singing, *Die Wacht am Rhein*.[13] Given the immense noise of the bombardment, it would appear to be a matter of historical indifference whether they were or not. 28th Infantry Division attacked from south of Le Pavé [located just south of the modern N44 and D 917 road junction], with formations of 220th Infantry Division on their right. Their advance, initially with Füsilier Regiment 40 right, Leib Grenadier Regiment 109 left and Grenadier Regiment 110 in reserve back in Banteux, led west via the *Friedensberg* [Mountain of Peace = modern Hill 133] towards La Vacquerie. Fusilier Regiment 40 was in trouble from the start, with British counter-attacks being mounted with artillery support from 10.00 am. The fact that all contact had long since been lost with the left flank of 220th Infantry Division soon meant that the situation was becoming critical. Deployment of all the reserves and desperate close-quarter fighting allowed some progress to be made eventually.

Vizefeldwebel Engesser 9th Company Fusilier Regiment 40 [14]

"In no time at all we were in possession of the first enemy positions. Without pausing we assaulted the next hollow, where we came across numerous dugouts. We had soon cleared the enemy out of them. Up to this point, about two hundred metres, we had doubled forward. I commanded the light machine guns, whose crews found the advance exceptionally strenuous because of their heavy loads. Despite the great effort involved, we stormed forward onto the hill to our front and, once again, we soon broke the tough defence of the enemy. We took numerous prisoners. We continued on unstoppably through the next dip, clearing the dugouts by the use of hand grenades and were on our way to assaulting the next hill when we came under heavy small arms fire.

"Our ranks had already been thinned. From the crew of the machine gun which was following me, only the gunner was still on his feet. The two of us took up a position in a shell hole and began engaging the enemy to the left. We had intended to remain there until the companies to our left and right had closed up. Suddenly I heard shouts from my right, 'Here come the British!' and everyone was streaming backwards. The two of us were well to the fore and entirely alone. We turned our machine gun around and engaged the enemy, who were pushing forward in dense ranks to our half right, causing them heavy casualties. Our company commander, Leutnant Motsch, rallied the men who had pulled back and led them forward in a fresh attack.

"The British, for their part, attempted to get clear, but they did not succeed because they ran directly into our line of fire. Hit simultaneously frontally and from a flank, they were completely wiped out. We caused them so many casualties that the company to our left was also able to advance and break the resistance [to their front]. The entire front began to advance and soon the hill was in our possession. We dug in on the far slope of this hill and, having prepared it for defence, held it for the entire night."

Leib Grenadier Regiment 109, in common with most other first wave formations, had led off with two battalions: 1st and 2nd, both reinforced by a company of the 3rd Battalion and, in addition, a specialist company of Jäger Storm Battalion 3 operated with the regiment. The layout of the front line trenches left them at an awkward angle to the opposing ones, which complicated the start of the attack and affected its momentum somewhat. The regimental task was far from straightforward. From a start line about 400 metres west of Banteux, the first requirement was to break through a tangle of old trenches and obstacles constructed on rolling countryside, incised with ravines, to a depth of two kilometres. Destructive fire hammered down on the enemy positions from 8.20 to 8.50, the local mortars joining in for the final ten minutes, prior to the start of the rolling barrage which lifted on to the enemy rear positions during the final moments before the infantry assault. The minute that the infantry began to storm forward, only to be greeted by enemy fire, it became clear instantly that the rolling barrage in the depth of the British positions had been insufficient to neutralise all the machine guns and artillery pieces. Pushing forward in rushes towards the trenches opposite, the leading assault groups of Jäger Storm Battalion 3 were greeted by showers of hand grenades, which meant that they had to begin fighting for every traverse. This would normally have been a slow and costly procedure but the regimental commander, Oberstleutnant Freiherr von Forstner, sensing the intensity of the fight, ordered the leading companies of Leib Grenadier Regiment 109 to launch attacks across open ground. These were able to threaten an outflanking movement and the defenders ultimately withdrew, having taken a considerable toll on the assault troops.

There can be little doubt that these forward British positions, which had proved to be so difficult to take out, would have presented an even bigger problem had it not been for the presence of 2nd Company Jäger Storm Battalion 3, one of the first and most experienced of these specialised units. As usual, it had been necessary for its commander, Major von Hohendorf, to engage the commanders of the regiments to whom the companies were allocated in intense, forceful discussions, in order to ensure that the special skills of his sub units were deployed correctly and not frittered away by his men being employed on tasks which normal infantry could carry out. Once that was clear, constructive work was done between commander 2nd Company and the regimental commander of Leib Grenadier Regiment 109 and it was decided that the specialists would spearhead the attack and be responsible for attacking and clearing British positions to a depth of 1,700 metres. There were three areas of trenches to be tackled, so the task organisation reflected that.

Storm Group Right under Reserve Leutnant Vensky had four assault troops armed with two 08/15 machine guns, two grenade launchers and a flamethrower troop. Storm Group Left, under Reserve Leutnant Linder, was similarly equipped, but was slightly smaller and the so-called Security Group, commanded by Vizefeldwebel Demmin, had none of the specialised weapons, but was available to reinforce either group as necessary.[15] At Y Hour [H Hour], the groups stormed forward in typically aggressive fashion and very swiftly broke into the position. However they did not have it all their own way. Bitter hand to hand fighting broke out right across the regimental sector. The British defenders were thrown back, but made use of the labyrinth of saps to infiltrate back in to the battle. Grenades flew in all directions, extensive use was made of flamethrowers and casualties mounted on either side. However, a combination of the fighting power of the storm groups and the manoeuvring of Leib Grenadier Regiment 109 meant that the outcome was inevitable and the surviving defenders had to pull back hastily. This short engagement had cost 2nd Company Jäger Battalion 3 one officer and nine

Jägers killed, with 24 more wounded. These were serious losses and the regimental commander, not wanting to risk a prized asset wasting down, held them back as a special reserve for the next two days. They were not used again before the offensive was scaled back, but there is no doubt that their expertise had played a crucial role in the opening round of the counter-attack.

At this point, rapidly reinforcing his forward elements with 11th and 12th Companies, Oberstleutnant Freiherr von Forstner restored essential impetus to the advance and, overcoming a series of machine gun posts and other pockets of resistance at further painful cost, they closed in on the *Siegfriedstellung*. Here they were greatly concerned to find that, for all its weight, the preliminary bombardment had failed to neutralise the sector they were to attack. Both trenches and wire were largely intact and, as the regimental historian of Leib Grenadier Regiment 109 made clear, 'the defensive position was eminently defensible; the high courage of its garrison quite unbroken.'[16] The artillery barrage was falling far away. It could not be recalled and there was nothing for it but to mount an attack with the assets that were on hand. Having gained 1,500 metres quite quickly, the attack was now in danger of stalling. It was 9.45 am.

Initial attempts by 5th and 6th Companies to get forward under the covering fire of the 2nd Machine Gun Company failed to gain ground and casualties were high due, at least in part, to lack of experience in the attack of the sub units involved. One hour later 2nd Battalion Grenadier Regiment 110 was introduced into the attack and 5th Company, in an action to be described later, provided stout support. Overall, however, progress was not satisfactory and Oberstleutnant Freiherr von Forstner had to resort to sending for his mortars, which were located back in Banteux, in an attempt to neutralise some of the strong points. All this took time but, gradually, one after the other, these places: *Filseck, Wilhelmsburg, Krähenhaus, Donaufeste*, fell to determined assault by all parts of the regiment. By 2.00 pm, they had fought through the depth of the old German positions and were beginning to bear down on Gonnelieu, located behind the original British front line. Those of the British defenders who were not killed were all captured.

By now, however, the cumulative effect of continuous heavy fighting over several hours was taking a toll. Losses, especially amongst the most experienced, most forceful junior leaders, both officers and NCOs, had been severe and all the sub units were tangled up as a result of battlefield confusion. Oberstleutnant Freiherr von Forstner was already aware that Gonnelieu was effectively undefended, because a patrol despatched forward under the command of Reserve Leutnant Hermann, the regimental orderly officer, early in the afternoon whilst the fighting continued within the *Siegfriedstellung*, had passed through it undisturbed. The British 12th Division had given orders earlier that 36 Brigade was to arrange for the defence of the village, but there was no time and or resources available to achieve that. A few sappers from 70th Field Company RE did attempt to man a trench just north of the village, but could achieve nothing. Later, fire from 377th and 379th Batteries RA proved troublesome, but the main reason for lack of further progress on this front during the first day was exhaustion, heavy losses and a confused intermingling of the attacking troops.

All in all, the situation for the advancing troops was critical. They were extremely vulnerable to British counter-attack, so attempts were made to reorganise the scattered companies of Leib Grenadier Regiment 109 in and around Gonnelieu, as quickly as possible. Whilst this was happening, its commander, Oberstleutnant Freiherr von Forstner, discussed the situation with the commanders of Infantry Regiments 30 and 67 of 34th Infantry Division, who had had a somewhat easier time of it so far. As a result of these conversations, 3rd Battalion Infantry Regiment 67 was despatched to Leib Grenadier Regiment 109 to reinforce it. Infantry Regiment 30 had already occupied the line of the former British second position from the heights east of Gouzeaucourt to Gonnelieu and now Infantry Regiment 67 could do much the same thing as far as the Villers-Guislain – Gouzeaucourt road. As the daylight began to fade, all three regiments of 28th Infantry Division also went firm along the line they had achieved and made certain that, in the event of British counter-action, they could present a reasonably coherent, unbroken defensive frontage. That was fine as far as it went, but the situation on the right flank, where contact with Füsilier Regiment 40 had been lost, remained completely unknown. Reinforcements were rushed into position from various sources, to bolster 2nd Battalion Leib Grenadier Regiment 109, held back in Gonnelieu in regimental reserve and, at 6.00 pm, Bavarian Reserve Infantry Regiment 14 of 9th Bavarian Reserve Division (which, controversially, had been made available earlier) arrived to plug the gap. The troops were able to stem their hunger with supplies taken from the British positions but, during the bitterly cold night which followed, they missed hot drinks and warm food from their field kitchens, which had been unable to get forward.

Bringing up the rear of 28th Infantry Division when the advance began, Grenadier Regiment 110 had followed one tactical bound behind the advance. Its 1st Battalion, reinforced by two companies of the 3rd Battalion, was deployed in rear of Füsilier Regiment 40 and its 2nd Battalion behind Leib Grenadier Regiment 109. As casualties amongst the junior commanders began to mount, elements of Grenadier Regiment 110 began to be deployed forward to deal with particular problems. Following on from an attack on Le Pavé by 1st Battalion Füsilier Regiment 40, 3rd Company captured two field guns, whilst, to the south, the companies of the 2nd Battalion took part in several minor actions.[17] Of these, by far the most outstanding was an attack launched by 5th Company Grenadier Regiment 110 east of Gonnelieu and later described by the battalion commander.

Hauptmann Schede Commander 2nd Battalion Grenadier Regiment 110 [18]

"It was late morning on 30 November. The German counter-attack against the break in achieved by the British west and southwest of Cambrai during the tank battle was making victorious progress. The 28th Division from Baden, which had proved itself in heavy fighting around Verdun during 1917, was deployed on the flank of the southern pincer movement. Headquarters Second Army had designated the built up area of Gouzeaucourt as the first objective of the southern wing, but standing in the way were the British positions around Gonnelieu. With exemplary dash the Baden Leibgrenadier Regiment 109, commanded by Oberstleutnant Freiherr von Forstner, had already thrust forward into the German *Siegfriedstellung* on the west bank of the Schelde [Escaut], which had been in enemy hands ever since the British attempt at breakthrough. In order to break down the bitter British resistance, it had been necessary to send all three battalions into action. Weakened by heavy losses, especially amongst leaders, its sub-units mixed up following the trench fighting, the Leibgrenadiers came up against additional British pockets of resistance to the east of Gonnelieu. It was impossible for them to tackle these from their own resources; fresh forces had to intervene.

"The 2nd Battalion of the Baden Kaisergrenadier Regiment 110 from Heidelberg was quickly on the scene having, in accordance with orders, followed up a tactical bound behind the Leibgrenadier Regiment [109]. After the battalion had moved under artillery and machine gun fire, first along the narrow track through the marshy margins of the Schelde then across the Schelde canal by means of half-destroyed crossing points – fortunately with only slight casualties – it kept close up behind its sister regiment as it drove forward, in order to be able to support it whenever and wherever it was required. With the Leibgrenadiers stalled in front of Gonnelieu, the moment had arrived.

"Hauptmann Schede, commanding officer of the 2nd Battalion, hurried forward to join the commander of Leibregiment in the front line, who was conducting a reconnaissance. One heavily defended enemy strongpoint located along the Banteux – Gonnelieu road had so far beaten off with bloody losses every attempt to capture it. The light machine gun sections of Unteroffiziers Alexander and Seuffert, which were amongst the leading elements of 5th Company, thrusting forward under its daring commander Reserve Leutnant Kempf,[19] were already engaging this enemy nest of resistance. Swift action was needed. It was essential that the British were not allowed time to reorganise their resistance within and to the west of Gonnelieu.

"The commanding officer ordered Reserve Leutnant Kempf to capture the strongpoint with his company. After brief preparation in the available trenches and shell holes, the company launched an attack on a broad front with exemplary daring. Heavy machine gun fire brought down by the British, some of whom were firing from the cover of knocked out tanks, forced the company into cover after the initial dashes forward. However the example shown by their platoon commanders, Landwehr Leutnant Geiges and Vizefeldwebels Heinzler and Hermann, together with other courageous men, kept the platoons moving forward unstoppably. It proved possible to force a way in to the densely manned position at two different points. The British defended desperately and the trenches had to be wrested from them bit by bit using grenades. Quickly the cry went up, 'Grenades forward!' and every single available grenade was taken forward to 5th Company along communication trenches by carrying parties from the other companies. It was effectively impossible to attempt to cross the open ground around the maze of trenches because of the enemy machine gun fire which swept it.

"Right at the front stood the platoon commanders, providing their grenade teams with a superb example of coolness under fire. However it was not long before Leutnant Geiges was mortally wounded during this determined advance. He was swiftly followed by both Vizefeldwebels Heinzler and Hermann, who were both killed by enemy grenades. The very youthful Fähnrich Heizler, who had been with the regiment since Verdun, rushed up to replace them. He pressed forward but also met a hero's death.[20] Others stepped into the breach and took the lead. There was no hanging back. Above all it was thanks to the energetic and exemplary forcefulness of the daring Unteroffizier Gersbach that the enemy was forced back more and more. After two hours of bitter trench fighting, which cost the lives of many brave grenadiers, the enemy resistance collapsed.

"The remnants of the garrison of the strongpoint attempted to escape across the open ground to Gonnelieu, but machine gun fire cut down the would-be escapers. A surprise attempt at a counter-stroke withered away in the fire of a light machine gun which the watchful Unteroffizier Gersbach had brought into action. The way to Gonnelieu was open. The attack gathered momentum once more and, by early afternoon, the trenches to the west of Gonnelieu were firmly in German hands. The battle for the strong point had cost the courageous 5th Company sixteen killed, including four platoon commanders and a further sixteen wounded, most of them seriously, but the company had shown what iron willed Baden grenadiers could achieve. The exemplary daring and death-defying courage involved in the capture of this strongpoint means that it will ever remain one of the laurel leaves in the wreath of fame of the Baden Kaisergrenadier Regiment."

Although there was still a long way to go to Metz en Couture, as darkness fell the men of 28th Division were reasonably happy with what they had achieved. To the victor, the spoils. Officers doing their rounds and checking on their men in the forward companies of Füsilier Regiment 40 as they dug in and consolidated their gains, noticed that almost every man had managed to acquire a warm British leather jerkin and was wearing it. Some were devouring stocks of corned beef, biscuit and other tinned rations they had come across, whilst others were enjoying smoking English cigarettes that they had found in the trenches and dugouts (and probably on the bodies of the fallen). The success had been bought dearly, however. The 1st Battalion was no longer a fighting force. It had suffered crippling losses and was virtually devoid of junior leaders. It had to be withdrawn from the battle. The other battalions had suffered badly as well. Half their officers were casualties and they were both severely weakened. However, under the energetic leadership of Oberleutnant Buch and Rittmeister von Diersburg respectively, they reorganised and prepared for what was to come the following day.

Back near Banteux, the medical services were at full stretch. Reporting up the chain of command, their problems were laid out in graphic detail:

Feldunterarzt Schweitzer 3rd Battalion Füsilier Regiment 40 [21]

"In the house located by the sugar refinery to the west of the point where the road Le Catelet - Le Pavé crosses the canal (about 300 metres north of Banteux) are located about one hundred severely wounded men, ninety percent of whom belong to the regiment. The Regiment is asked to request the Division to despatch motorised ambulances to the sugar refinery to evacuate the wounded. In addition the permanent use is requested of at least three motorised ambulances, each capable of carrying four stretcher cases, to be sent to the quarry, approximately 800 metres west of the sugar refinery. The stretcher bearers should be supplied with copious quantities of dressings, anti-tetanus vaccine, morphine and camphorated oil, because the current stocks are running out rapidly."

This message was reinforced by another from Rittmeister von Diersburg to the regiment: 'The conditions in which the wounded are currently being tended here are indefensible...' A carrier pigeon was immediately flown back to Divisional Headquarters and hundreds of wounded fusiliers were soon evacuated to hospitals in the Cambrai area. With that, for the northern sector of the main thrust, relative quiet descended on the battlefield.

Having begun moving south from Flanders on 23 November, the regiments of 30th Infantry Division began to relieve forward elements of 220th Infantry Division on 28 November. But they were not to spend long in static positions and nor were the men they had relieved, all of whom were destined to participate in the forthcoming attack. Within 220th Infantry Division detailed orders were issued early on 29 November down to all the battalions and the day was spent in a frenzy of preparations and adjustments to deployments, so as to ensure that the leading waves were positioned and supported optimally as Y Hour approached. A moonlit night and the fact that the British lines were completely quiet assisted in this process. Particular attention had been paid to maintaining the momentum of the attack and to monitoring progress. Reserve Infantry Regiment 99, for example was directed, once initial progress had been made, to 'Fire the pearl type white flares, so that the artillery fire can be lifted forward. Should the assault stall in one place, the line achieved is to be marked with red flags. The attack is to be pressed without regard [to any other factor]. There is to be no waiting for neighbouring units. In the case of resistance, reserves are to be directed against the flanks and rear. It must be assumed that there will be counter-attacks involving tanks. Light security forces are to be left behind when the *Siegfriedstellung* is crossed. Entry into the dugouts is to be avoided. If their occupants do not surrender, they are to be smoked out...'[22]

With two hours to go before the start of the operation, liaison officers were exchanged with neighbouring units and the final preparations were made. Then, once the preliminary bombardment lifted, the first waves set off from their start line between Les Rues Vertes and Les Rues des Vignes, heavily reinforced with machine guns and heading off westwards with all possible speed. As soon as they set out they came under fire. Initially this was light but, as soon as the British defenders got organised, the volume quickly grew as first machine guns and then artillery joined in. Very sensibly, the defence in this sector comprised a forward, thinly held line, which had attracted a great deal of the preliminary fire, but it was soon clear that this was backed by a network of machine gun positions, each of which had to be reduced separately – a slow and costly business. In some sectors, especially to the east of the Masnières – Le Pavé road, some attackers felt that they were actually outnumbered locally by defenders.

Nevertheless, progress was satisfactory and there were certainly places where a combination of surprise, speed and aggression in the attack made it easy at times to capture prisoners and equipment. Prisoners were despatched to the rear in fairly large numbers and it certainly appeared during the early stages of the attack that there was every chance of it achieving its aim. All along the divisional front the new tactics appeared to be working. Wherever possible, strong points were rushed. If this proved not to be practical then flanking sub units duly launched attacks from unexpected directions, but very quickly problems arose. Command and control became exceedingly difficult, because units and sub-units became mixed up and, because speed was of the essence, no sooner had a pocket of resistance been taken than all involved, regardless of unit, pressed on again westwards. It was also proving to be very costly in terms of junior officer casualties. Leading from the front, a great many company officers were killed or wounded and, given that most companies had only one officer or, at best, perhaps two, there were soon large groups of leaderless, rudderless infantrymen advancing without proper coordination.

There was one other unforeseen difficulty, which led to much ill-feeling after the battle. Leading elements, in reducing numerous defended localities, captured significantly large numbers of Lewis and other machine guns. These were highly prized items, because a bounty was paid for their recovery. The leading waves could not possibly carry them with them in the attack, so reserve units and formations, with more time and less pressure on them, made a great deal of prize money at the expense of the forward units. In the greater scheme of things this may seem a small point, but it was not to those involved.

Despite the early momentum, all these different sources of friction began to take a toll, so both time and momentum were lost as the day wore on. Coming under the flanking fire of 6th Battalion Royal West Kent Regiment from Lateau Wood, 3rd Battalion Reserve Infantry Regiment 99 mounted an attack which ejected the defenders and cleared the way for a continuation of the attack by Infantry Regiment 190, but it all took time and did not, in fact, lead to the hoped-for collapse in the British defences. In fact resistance around Quennet Farm mounted by the remnants of the British 37 Brigade was such that the advance juddered to a halt in heavy fire about mid morning, whilst leading elements were still about one hundred metres short of the Masnières – Le Pavé road. In addition to the original garrison of the farm, on the heights around it were gathered the survivors from the front line. Supported by artillery and numerous machine guns, a sharp check was imposed, despite intense efforts by German aircraft flying low and pouring machine gun fire down on the defenders. One of the participants in these attacks later wrote a detailed account of the events of the day.

Leutnant Steller 1st Machine Gun Company Reserve Infantry Regiment 55 [23]

"During the night 29/30 November, Reserve Infantry Regiment 55 moved into position in Les Rues-des-Vignes. 1st Battalion was located forward left in contact with Reserve Infantry Regiment 99. 3rd Battalion was deployed right forward, with 2nd Battalion in reserve. The British were to be attacked and driven back to their start line. Previously the regiment had been engaged almost everywhere where there had been intense fighting on the Western Front. It was only a few short weeks since [it had experienced] hard bloody days of battle, but it faced the new fighting in a superbly calm spirit. At precisely 8.00 am on 30 November the German preliminary bombardment crashed down with unparalleled violence. At 8.15 the artillery and mortars began to combine to throw their huge shells into enemy territory. Smoke, dust and fog blanketed the entire front in such dense clouds that it was impossible to see anything. From the rear areas came the noise of the propellers of German aircraft which were closing in. Suddenly they appeared out of the mist, moving slowly and deliberately, like a flock of giant birds over the enemy lines.

"8.20 am, 8.25 am; still five minutes to go. Muttered conversations died away and here and there men were taking deep breaths. Friends shook hands once more. 8.30 am. Suddenly choked off, the artillery and mortar fire ceased. There was a signal and, as one, the first wave launched out of the ruined houses, scrambled over hedges and trenches and stepped out calmly into the open ground. A few metres in rear came the second and third waves with the machine gun platoon sandwiched in between them. In this way the 1st and 3rd Battalions stormed forward; in their midst their commanders. Landwehr Hauptmann Kuhne led the 3rd Battalion; whilst the third was commanded by the tall Kürassier, Major von Holtzendorff, standing a head higher than all around him.

"Immediately the enemy machine guns opened up, pouring fire into the ranks of the assault troops. Leutnant Alt, adjutant of 1st Battalion, was one of the first to be wounded; his duties being assumed, in addition to his own, by the commander of 1st Machine Gun Company, Leutnant Steller. Here and there one of the attackers went down like a felled tree, but the waves continued to surge forward in perfect order. The early morning battlefield teemed with grey steel helmets, under which burning eyes had only one thing in sight: the objective, the objective to the front. The first prisoners were directed on their way to the rear, happy to be able to depart the hell of this battle. Then the attack stalled. A strong bulwark, Quennet Farm [this appears on the modern map as Le Quesnet Farm] prevented all further movement forward.

"Machine guns to the front line! On your feet! Double march!' Sweating profusely under the weight of their equipment, the four machine gun crews of 1st Machine Gun Company, under their platoon commander, Vizefeldwebel Cellarius, moved forward. From terrain devoid of cover, they sent down curtains of fire of all types at every target, at every gap in the wall from which death-dealing bullets could be directed at the gallant attackers. Death reaped a rich harvest. One gun crew after another was knocked out and the platoon commander, too, Vizefeldwebel Cellarius, who had been awarded the Iron Cross First Class at the beginning of 1915, died a hero's death. So as not to yield [to the pressure] new crews rushed forward. Suddenly, with a great crash which sent clouds of red dust skywards, the artillery joined in. The infantry stormed forwards using hand grenades. Hand to hand fighting broke out, then the farm fell into German hands.

"One of our finest was carried back from there. He was Leutnant Rödlingshöfer, commander 1st Company. Seriously wounded in the head, he lay dead still on the stretcher. Nevertheless everything continued as before. Leutnant Anhalt,[24] previously an Unteroffizier and promoted to officer as a result of bravery in the field, raced ahead, leading 11th Company from the front when he was killed; whilst the commander of 10th Company, Leutnant Hollmann, was seriously wounded. Then the first British trenches were reached. Those of the enemy who did not surrender were hacked down. Enemy machine gun nests in No Man's Land were surrounded and taken out to shouts of *Hurra!* The wild hunt continued across the Cambrai – Le Pavé road as the men in clay-coloured uniforms were chased.

At a very early stage, formations of 9th Reserve Division, following up the advance, were introduced into the battle; officially, 'between 30th and 220th Infantry Divisions,'[25] but this turned out to be an overoptimistic view by the planners of what was possible on the ground. Nevertheless, it followed up the forward divisions with Reserve Infantry Regiment 6 right, Infantry Regiment 395 left and Reserve Infantry Regiment 19 bringing up the rear. The commander of Reserve Infantry Regiment 6 later described the scene in his diary entry for 30 November 1917:

Major Alexander Schwencke, Commander Reserve Infantry Regiment 6 [26]
"We crossed the start line to the west of Revélon Chateau [situated on the northern edge of Les Rues des Vignes], where Reserve Infantry Regiment 55 had begun its attack. In the British trenches 200 metres further on lay enemy dead and wounded, together with weapons and equipment. Prisoners and British wounded approached in ones and twos, making their way bareheaded towards the rear. The wounded helped each other along. Two of them were carrying a third and another carried a wounded man on his back. A *Feldgrau* was also assisting a man in khaki as they limped, arm in arm, towards the rear.

"Forward, in the area of the Cambrai - Le Pavé road, the lines of infantry of our regiments could be seen advancing one behind the other, with the occasional rider in between them. Moving across country, a battery of Reserve Field Artillery Regiment 9 appeared and began bringing fire down on Masnières. An artillery staff appeared mounted high on their horses. It was a new, rather strange sight, this open battlefield. It was something that had not been seen for years; not since the war ossified into positional warfare."

It is impossible to say which battery of Reserve Field Artillery Regiment 9 he was describing. 3rd and 6th Batteries advanced in direct support of Infantry Regiment 395 and Reserve Infantry Regiment 6, but only a short time later, the 3rd, 5th, 8th and 9th also moved to engage a range of targets from this area.[27] As the move forward of 9th Reserve Division continued, so confused was the situation and narrow the divisional boundaries, that there was considerable overlapping and crowding in the forward area, with the result that Infantry Regiment 395 became directly involved with the battle for an area of trenches just south of Quennet Farm and other regiments of 9th Reserve Division were also engaged close by.[28] The intention and expectation had been that this formation would fight through the two forward ones in pursuit of the main objectives. The regimental history of Infantry Regiment 395 later noted,

"As a direct result of the direction of higher authority that 9th Reserve Division was to be inserted between the 30th and 220th Infantry Divisions, so as to continue the attack, there was an utterly extraordinary mixing of formations, which rendered normal command and control completely impossible. Once the [Masnières – Le Pavé] road had been crossed, the troops suddenly came under heavy, well-aimed machine gun fire from the front, the flanks, and even partially from half right in rear of us in the direction of Les Rues Vertes. This immediately caused us casualties. We took a short break in the Rendsburg Hollow, then the attack continued..."[29]

One of the casualties of the machine gun fire was an officer of Reserve Field Artillery Regiment 9, designated artillery liaison officer to Infantry Regiment 395.

Reserve Leutnant Hellmuth Heinze 1st Battery Reserve Field Artillery Regiment 9 [30]

"Between 8.00 and 8.30 am we marched off via Lesdain for Les Rues des Vignes. There we paused in amongst the ruined houses so that the companies could shake out. The enemy artillery was quiet; only the occasional heavy shell was directed against the canal bridges and the nearby pontoon bridge, constructed by the engineers. We then ascended the hill. The first line had been overrun by the newly deployed divisions. A great many dead British soldiers lay in and behind the position. There was heavy enemy machine gun fire from

Masnières, but the advance continued without significant casualties.

"In the meantime our batteries and those of Field Artillery Regiment 51 had crossed the canal and had driven up onto the heights. Around midday I linked up with our artillery group, which I found at Quennet Farm after a long search. There I orientated myself about the situation of our infantry. On the way to my 1st Battery, to which I was bringing a fire order, prior to returning to 2nd Battalion Infantry Regiment 395, I was caught in a burst of enemy machine gun fire and wounded in the knee. I limped to the battery firing position where I was soon bandaged up. That was the end of my involvement in the tank battle [strictly speaking this is the German designation for the first part of the battle when the British were attacking] and I was admitted to hospital.

"As far as the activities of our batteries are concerned, I can report that they drove up onto the heights and took up firing positions in the open without casualties. It was a marvellous sight. Retreating British infantry offered worthwhile targets, as did machine guns, which were scattered around in every bump and dip, causing us a considerable number of difficulties throughout the day. Enemy artillery fire was slight.[31] In all events, 30 November 1917 was a great day for our 9th Reserve Division."

Near to Quennet Farm, in order to inject new life into the attack, the various regimental commanders got forward and urged their units to greater efforts, but this crucial area of resistance was only gradually subdued over the next four or five hours by the combined efforts of Reserve Infantry Regiments 55, 99 and Infantry Regiment 395 and the casualties were very high. By the end of the first day of fighting, for example, Reserve Infantry Regiment 99, with only two of its three battalions in the forefront of the attack, had lost one battalion commander and six company commanders killed or wounded out of total officer losses of seventeen. Here once more, as it began to go dark, the attackers were hopelessly intermingled. Reorganising and digging in to the west of the Masnières – Le Pavé road were men of Infantry Regiments 40, 99, 190 and 395, as well as Reserve Infantry Regiments 55 and 99.

Getting rations and ammunition forward was intensely difficult, whilst distributing orders and preparing for a coordinated continuation of offensive operations the following day was almost impossible. Major von Holzendorff was nominated *Kampftruppenkommandeur* [KTK = Commander of the Forward Troops] of all these disparate elements and spent the entire following night trying to re-establish coherent command and control of this important sector of the front.[32] The commander of 1st Machine Gun Company Reserve Infantry Regiment 55 left an equally vivid picture of the closing phases of the battle.

Leutnant Steller 1st Machine Gun Company Reserve Infantry Regiment 55 [33]

"The assault fell like a storm between the corrugated iron huts where the British support troops were accommodated. The enemy even forgot to buckle on their equipment. Steaming coffee and white bread were still laid out on the tables. Hey, that made a tasty meal; just the thing to give us renewed strength. In the sky above, our pilots buzzed around swooping down to a few metres and showering the fleeing [British troops] with bullets. Artillery shells began to land very close, in amongst the assault troops. Sure enough a battery was in position close by and was firing like mad. It was knocked out from close range with hand grenades and nine guns were captured. Suddenly murderous machine gun fire opened up from close range, forcing 1st Battalion and elements of 2nd Battalion to halt. It was now about midday. Full of anger they had to dig in on the heights to the west of the Cambrai – Le Pavé road.

"To the right, 3rd Battalion pressed on. There was already a gap on the left flank. Mortars were dragged forward. Then suddenly, like a scene from 1914, artillery arrived at full gallop. The bodies of the horses almost touched the ground, the drivers used their whips and the gunners hung on tight. Officers and section commanders out in front were killed. Hard up behind the front line, the battery of Leutnant Wendemuth of Field Artillery Regiment 51 unlimbered then, with flash and crash, fire was opened and the first shells began landing in the enemy trenches. A short time later six batteries were pouring fire and iron into the enemy machine gun positions.

"At about 3.00 pm the assault was renewed and we pushed through the flooded hollow and its wire obstacles up onto the heights. The resistance of the enemy was broken. Weapons were captured and prisoners were taken. On the right flank, against the frontage of 3rd Battalion, the British attempted to counter-attack. The utterly worn out troops defended themselves, even though they were so exhausted that they could hardly grip their weapons. Help came from the 9th Company led by Leutnant Dieckmann. This commander, who had survived unwounded at the front ever since the outbreak of the war, fell mortally wounded just in front of the trenches. The enemy was beaten off and, at that same moment an enemy observation balloon, which had been engaged with incendiary bullets by a German pilot, was shot down. Loud cheering broke out as this spy [in the sky] fell to the earth in flames."

Off to the south of 220th Infantry Division, to the left of Infantry Regiment 190, the Saxon Infantry Regiment 105 of 30th Infantry Division was involved in brutal, unsuccessful, fighting throughout the day. Linking with Infantry

Regiment 143 from 30th Infantry Division on its left, it pushed forward hard at Y Hour for the north and northeast edge of Masnières, with its 3rd Battalion aiming to take out Mon Plaisir Farm. The regiment was quickly in trouble, being caught by unbroken barbed wire under heavy machine gun fire, soon after the first British positions were captured. Yet again, it seemed, the hurricane bombardment had not been fully effective in neutralising the defence and destroying wire obstacles and strong points. This was in sharp contrast to the situation on 20 November when, with relatively few exceptions, the predicted fire of the Royal Artillery came down with great precision. Possibly this was an example of the German techniques trailing those of the Allies, whose own gunnery was improving rapidly by this stage of the war.

Pressing on, with difficulty, eventually all three battalions of Infantry Regiment 105 were caught in cross fire from British positions near Mon Plaisir Farm and Masnières and were cut to pieces. Theirs was one of the least successful attacks of the entire day. As their casualties mounted and they vainly tried to salvage something of the attack, they could only watch as Infantry Regiment 99 to their left pushed on across the Masnières - Le Pavé road. In an attempt to rectify the situation, 220th Infantry Division ordered a deliberate attack against Masnières for 3.00 pm. According to Infantry Regiment 105, the bombardment of this place had not been particularly heavy earlier in the day and now, at the critical moment, the priority for the divisional gunfire was elsewhere, so the bombardment could not be fired.[34] Reasoning that advances elsewhere would render the retention of Masnières by the British impossible anyway, Divisional Headquarters cancelled the attack and, as soon as it could be relieved by Reserve Infantry Regiment 227 of 107th Infantry Division, Infantry Regiment 105 was temporarily withdrawn from the battle, moving back to Crèvecoeur to recuperate.

Regiments of 107th Infantry Division, which had been involved in the battle as early as 20 November and at periodic intervals ever since, were very worn down by the end of November but, nevertheless, were incorporated in the plans for the counter-attack. Located on the northern flank of Group Caudry, it was intended that it should cooperate with 119th Infantry Division just to the north and drive west, first to surround, then to capture, Cantaing. As will be seen later, the assault of Group Arras ran into major difficulties early. Its divisions located to the west encountered immense difficulties in getting forward, which in turn degraded the ability of the weak 119th Infantry Division to move. Operating on the extreme right of Group Caudry, the battalions of Reserve Infantry Regiment 232 waited to see when Reserve Infantry Regiment 46 would advance and stood by to take their cue to move from it. Unfortunately the latter regiment was slow in getting into position and late to start, which meant in turn that men of 3rd Battalion Reserve Infantry Regiment 232 in particular were exposed to shelling for a protracted period.

The complete assault group of 10th Company was knocked out by a single shell whilst they were waiting, which was exceedingly bad for morale and damaging to the prospects of a successful attack.[35] The intended start time of 11.50 am came and went, German artillery fire continued to fall on Cantaing, but hours later the British defenders were still holding out. Eventually, following a very heavy bombardment lasting from 4.30 to 4.45 pm, a force comprising Reserve Infantry Regiment 46, 2nd Battalion Reserve Infantry Regiment 232, one battalion from Reserve Infantry Regiment 227 and Machine Gun Detachment 15 began their assault. After an extremely difficult period of fighting, Reserve Infantry Regiment 46 was pinned down in a sunken road north of Cantaing and the remainder had only reached the *SII Stellung* northeast of Cantaing, which remained garrisoned by the British, who were plentifully armed with machine guns.

An attack by other elements of 107th Infantry Division against Noyelles also ground to a halt in the face of determined defence. Near Rumilly Reserve Infantry Regiment 52, in a very weakened state after the casualties it had suffered earlier, had to be reinforced by elements of Reserve Infantry Regiment 227 to enable it to hold on whilst, on the northern flank, 119th Infantry Division withdrew from its exposed positions near Cantaing. This left Reserve Infantry Regiment 232 out on a limb and, at 9.15 pm, orders arrived that the survivors were to pull back to their original start line. Reserve Infantry Regiment 232 felt that more could have been done to hold forward and that withdrawal meant that all the casualties had been for nothing.[36] Nevertheless, leaving a small bridgehead party on the western side of the canal, the remainder pulled back to Proville.

Reserve Infantry Regiment 52, operating on the left of Reserve Infantry Regiment 232, was also involved in various efforts to push forward towards evening, though it later described them as 'patrol actions'. It too, got as far forward as the *SII Stellung* but, in contrast, assisted by Reserve Infantry Regiment 227, it clung on to its gains, digging furiously throughout the night 30 November/1 December to improve the trenches, because the *SII Stellung* had never been continuous and there were far too few dugouts to hold all those seeking shelter. It had not been a successful day for the attackers in this sector and its positions left much to be desired. The *KTK* of Reserve Infantry Regiment 52 later outlined some of the difficulties.

Hauptmann Wesemann Commander Composite Battalion Reserve Infantry Regiment 52 [37]

"The battalion staff was co-located with the centre battalion in a cavern near the platelayers' shed by the railway line leading to Marcoing. On the way to this cavern we had to pass through heavy artillery defensive fire, which was coming down between the regimental command post and our own, but we got through without loss. The regimental command post was located in a mined dugout near Mont sur l'Oeuvre [about one kilometre northwest of the centre of Rumilly]. In daylight it was not possible to move between the platelayers' shed and the regiment or the forward positions. To begin with individuals moving about were not always shot at, but later every movement attracted heavy machine gun fire from the British.

"The cave was a good twelve metres deep. A shaft dug by the northern gable of the platelayers' hut dropped vertically and was descended by means of an iron ladder. At the foot were the infantry and artillery telephones and to one side was a sleeping area, which was particularly damp and contained several half-rotting mattresses where weary heads could be laid. The central corridor of the cavern was the working area, separated from the other alcoves with beams and laths festooned with grubby pieces of cloth and sacks. On one occasion I counted and noted that in a space about two metres by four metres there were sixteen individuals. Traffic within the dugout and, at night, to the outside world was always busy... The Tommies took great pleasure in frequently bringing down fire on one or other of the entrances...

"The battalion received two field guns to provide anti-tank defence. Leutnant Kittel was our artillery liaison officer with Foot Artillery Regiment 65. He was a very calm individual who, by dint of tireless efforts, maintained good contact with his regiment and obtained constant fire support – it was brilliant cooperation! Our position was only spitlocked and it was difficult to dig, because it was solid chalk covered by a thin layer of top soil. The obstacles to the front comprised nothing much more than supports, with no wire."

Group Arras: Generalleutnant von Moser

The commander of Group Arras was up and about early on the morning of 30 November. Describing the extraordinary physical and mental tension of the moment, he later recorded his relief that his divisions had all reported that they were ready for action. At least his attack could be launched as planned. However an operation by his troops was dependent on progress being made to the south, so it was an anxious time as he sat in his operations centre and monitored the incoming signals and telephone traffic.

Generalleutnant von Moser Diary Entry 30 November 1917 [38]

"From 8.00 am the thunder of guns could be heard throughout the Cambrai salient. Around 9.00 am my attack divisions which were not in the front line, namely the 49th Reserve Division, 214th and 221st

Infantry Divisions, began to move into position under the protection of a wall of smoke, which was fired by all my heavy howitzer batteries, but which was in no way free of gaps. About 10.00 am the first information came in, stating that Groups Busigny and Caudry were making progress forward. Thereafter the stream of reports never ceased all day. Towards 11.00 am all observers and one divisional commander who had gone forward into the battle area reported unanimously that the move forward of my divisions from their assembly areas into their forming up places had passed off as though it had been conducted on a parade square; this despite the fact that an enemy balloon had spotted our lines of infantry and directed heavy fire on them, causing quite serious casualties. As had been predictable, the wall of artificial smoke was dispersed here and there by the wind.

"I was sorely tempted to go forward and observe for myself what was the first major attack for a long time, but duty held me back in the place where all the command links from the flanks and the front came together. By 11.20 am the start lines had been reached and now the fire of my 500 guns rose to hurricane force. At 11.50 am all the divisions set off simultaneously, just as our ground attack aircraft appeared over our infantry and brought machine gun fire and bombs to bear on the enemy. However, the enemy, whose numbers were strong, resisted desperately. Despite this, 20th Infantry Division ejected the enemy from their first position, the previous German First and Second trenches; 21st Reserve Division pushed forward south of Moeuvres; 49th [Reserve] and 214th Infantry Divisions threw the enemy back almost to the main road in a continuous hard fought battle.

"After their first assault was beaten off, 221st Infantry Division stormed the important and dominating Hill 100, southwest of Bourlon Wood, after 3.00 pm and pushed on; whilst 3rd Guards Infantry Division sealed off Bourlon Wood from the north and east and 119th Infantry Division advanced to the line Fontaine – northeast corner of Cantaing. When, at about 5.00 pm, darkness began to fall and brought hostilities to a close, reports and prisoner statements yielded the following picture: The enemy had introduced their 2nd Division and elements of their 47th Division into their northern front, in order to continue their attack [sic]. Our attack had prevented that; but also explained their stiff resistance. Despite this, they had been ejected from their front line trenches along our entire front and pushed back, with extremely bloody casualties, about one kilometre to a point near the main Cambrai – Bapaume road.

"In addition, 450 prisoners have already been captured, along with numerous machine guns, two field guns and four tanks. One enemy captive balloon and five aircraft have been shot down on my front. The eastern front has succeeded in pushing deep into the enemy positions in the direction of Gouzeaucourt and there have also been large captures of prisoners and guns. 30 November has been a brilliant success for German arms, demonstrating before the eyes of the entire world that the German army has lost none of its attacking powers, despite apparently being completely worn down by trench warfare. I thank God and my amazing troops for the fact that I have been able to live to experience this wonderful day."

This account, written in the confused aftermath of a day of close-quarter, serious battle, took an altogether too sanguine a view of progress on this front which had, in fact, not achieved anything like what had been hoped for before it was launched. Earlier in the day, not being bound by the demands of high command, or required to participate in the initial assault, the commander of Reserve Infantry Regiment 80 was able to watch what happened:

Oberstleutnant Breitenbach Reserve Infantry Regiment 80 [39]

"About 8.00 am I went together with my staff to the dugout of the *Kampftruppenkommandeur* [Commander of the Forward Troops]. I was there by 9.00 am. Everything began at 9.50 am. Initially there was artillery fire on the enemy positions. Two hours later, our infantry began to attack. Because my regiment was to follow in the second wave, I was able to observe the advance of the others in peace. Heavy artillery fire was coming down on the lines of infantry to my left. Gradually there was a change of behaviour. In contrast to the previous momentum, hesitation and reluctance [to move] occurred. On one occasion there was a move to the rear. This was an unsatisfactory sight which made the blood in my veins run cold.

"But, at precisely this unpromising moment, one of our batteries (2nd Battery Reserve Field Artillery Regiment 21) rushed up at the gallop with its commander in the lead. This was a wonderful sight; it might have been an exercise, but this was war and it was as heroic an act as may possibly be imagined. The battery arrived in the middle of the men who were fleeing, unhitched and went into action. The commander fell, but it halted the stream of men [heading for the rear]. This hero had paid for the success with his own life. To the front there was nothing but wild disorder. The British seemed to be sitting tight, right under our noses."

The men of 49th Reserve Division, operating out on the right flank of Group

Arras, had been given a difficult mission to perform. Had the assault gone in on 28 November, it was to have been reinforced by the 2nd Battalions of Infantry Regiments 76 and 164 of 111th Infantry Division, but the delay made that impossible. Attacking with Reserve Infantry Regiment 225 on the right, Reserve Infantry Regiment 226 left (followed a tactical bound in rear by Reserve Infantry Regiment 228) it was given objectives well behind the British front lines. In order to achieve a final line in the former front line of the *Siegfriedstellung* southwest of Lock 3 and west of Lock 4 on the Canal du Nord, an advance of around four kilometres would be necessary. Although 1st Battalion Infantry Regiment 76 and Reserve Pionier Company 49 were placed under command, this was an extremely ambitious plan.

The regiments were all on the start line more or less as directed and set off promptly at 11.50 am behind a rolling barrage which, in this sector, lifted one hundred metres every three minutes. This was also an ambitious timetable, allowing for very little in the way of enemy interference with the advance. Even during the move forward from the assembly areas there had been difficulties. Reserve Infantry Regiment 226 later noted, 'Our own batteries were supposed to cover this movement by firing a smokescreen. In reality they only fired a few smoke shells and the protection they provided was illusory, because the wall of smoke was very quickly dispersed by a strong wind.'[40] As the units marched past Sains-lès-Marquion, artillery fire began to come down and, by the time they were within 800 metres of their start lines, they were, effectively, having to pass through an artillery defensive fire zone.

Three hundred metres short of their forming up places, they also came under machine gun fire and units got mixed up. Elements of Reserve Infantry Regiment 226 found themselves alongside men of Reserve Infantry Regiment 228 and Infantry Regiment 363 (from 214th Infantry Division), whilst the reinforcing 1st Battalion Infantry Regiment 76 veered off to the east and lost contact for the time being. This was not a good start and, even though there was a certain amount of time in hand, it proved to be impossible, despite a great deal of energetic action from officers and NCOs on the scene, to unscramble even the worst of the problems. In addition, the fact that the troops had to spend an hour exposed to heavy artillery, mortar and machine gun fire, which caused heavy casualties before the actual operation began, did nothing to enhance their offensive spirit.

Nevertheless, according to 49th Reserve Division, promptly, at the appointed time,[41] they all went over the top in three waves, supported by no fewer than fifty ground attack aircraft which, in an innovation for the Germans at least, continually swooped and dived on British pockets of resistance, forcing the defenders into cover and enabling the advancing troops swiftly to gain about three hundred metres of ground, without incurring many additional casualties. Then, in an incident which was an echo of how handfuls of courageous German machine gunners had wreaked havoc on the approaches to Passchendaele during the desperate fighting of the past few weeks, the assault suddenly came under heavy fire. No barrage or suppressive fire of this era ever succeeded in neutralising all resistance and Vickers and Lewis gunners now began to make inroads into the German ranks. Forced to switch to the use of short bounds forward under covering fire, some progress was made.

2nd Battalion Reserve Infantry Regiment 226, for example, claimed to have advanced a total of 900 metres in the next fifteen minutes, but elsewhere the impetus was already going out of the attack. Part of the reason was the mixing of units, which was still not fully resolved when the attack began. Infantry Regiment 76 later blamed this for some of the problems, 'Enemy action, coupled with over hasty movement, had led to a serious mix up of units and made command and control extremely difficult.'[42] Delay was being imposed; the rolling barrage was disappearing into the distance and could not be recalled. In many cases the British positions were located on reverse slopes. Subject to heavy frontal fire and machine guns in defiladed positions on the right flank of the German assault, progress faltered then stalled. There could be no question of driving on to anywhere near Locks 3 and 4 until the Lock 2 area was secure and precisely there the position was held stoutly by teams of British machine gunners. It was the responsibility of Reserve Infantry Regiment 225 to break this resistance and to secure the way forward for the rest of the planned advance, but it failed to do so – either when contact was first made, or throughout the day when they launched repeated, fruitless attacks across open ground towards it.

One of the airmen operating over the Moeuvres battlefield left a vivid account of his part in the day's events:

Fliegerleutnant Johannes Fischer Field Flight Detachment 8 [43]

"Hardly one hour after having landed, we took off on an infantry cooperation flight in support of 32nd Reserve Division [*sic.* either 49th Reserve Division or 20th Infantry Division; probably both]. The entire area of Moeuvres was in complete chaos. There was talk of treachery, of the attack, which had begun so well, becoming stalled in the face of pre-positioned enemy troops. To the south the German infantry was still storming forward with undiminished impetus. Our task was simple and straightforward: to determine the German line of advance to the south and west of Moeuvres. Keeping a sharp look out, we glided down over the battle area and fired flares. We could not see any form of acknowledging signal. We glided lower. Were we already beyond the British lines? Why were we still getting no response? We dropped down until we were just above the ploughed up ground, searching in vain for any signs.

"Suddenly splinters from an exploding shell hit our right wing and the force of the explosion threw the aircraft onto its side. Shortly after that we spotted steel helmets and we flew backwards and forwards over the steel-helmeted heads, so low that flares which Knerlich was firing upwards fell to the ground and continued to burn. In several places our signals were returned by waving or laying out white cloths. Here and there we fired flares at the parapets of wrecked positions and turned to see if our efforts had been understood. At long last we had established communications.

"Southwest of Moeuvres, on the other hand, it was only the movement of individuals or groups which betrayed the current battle situation. There was an immense muddle as battles were fought with hand grenades and bayonets. There the battle was raging around the former German lines. Despite the noise of our aircraft, the sound of intense firing echoed in our ears. Repeatedly flying up and down, we buzzed around the battle area until we had drawn the line definitively on our map. Further to the east, the roads leading south and southwest from Bourlon, which were under fire, were overflowing with German reserves moving forward. Now and then a rider would hurry by the advancing troops.

"Enemy air activity had increased significantly. We had to keep extremely alert to ensure that we were not surprised by half a dozen British fighter aircraft and we saw how a number of British and German fighters had just clashed over Moeuvres. This situation was favourable for us and we soon found ourselves, too, above the ruins of Moeuvres and continuing to communicate with the infantry by signal. Four hundred metres above us an air battle was in full swing whilst, right beneath us, hundreds of brave soldiers were going down, killed or wounded. Whilst we occupied ourselves confirming the line we had established, we kept one eye open for enemy aircraft, because not all of them had an opponent. There were too few German aircraft as far as we were concerned. It would only have taken the enemy aircraft about three seconds to swoop down on us.

"When I looked up almost vertically from my seat, I could see the small fighter aircraft which, a few days earlier, had brought us the decision concerning the use of the airfield at Avesnes-le-Sec. In it, Rittmeister Freiherr von Richthofen [The Red Baron] was flying in the same direction as us: due south. He was being pursued and attacked by a British fighter flying in the same direction. Immediately my observer swung his machine gun up vertically and the first shots cracked out. In a flash Knerlich had to cease firing, in order not to hit the German fighter. Like lightning it had banked steeply round to the right and was now at the neck of the enemy fighter which, for several heartbeats, continued to fly straight on as though it was searching to its front for its opponent.

"Barely three seconds later the nose of the enemy fighter dipped forward emitting a cloud of black smoke. Wreathed in flames, it fell vertically straight at us. As though piloted by the Devil, it roared at us at head height, spitting out a constant stream of green flares. With one hand I released my seat harness. Get out! No parachute, but jump! That was my only thought. Already I was standing with one foot on the seat, with one hand grasping one of the struts and ready to jump, whilst the other held on to the joystick and my other foot remained on the rudder bar. There was still thirty metres to go; this was the moment! Suddenly the aircraft, which was one mass of flames, sheared away. Climbing like a flaming arrow into a steeply banked turn, it then skidded around violently, nose downwards and roared past our right hand side in the opposite direction at a sharp angle towards the ground, whilst a wave of heat flashed past the right hand side of our faces.

"It smashed hard into the ground just forward of a German reserve position where a mass of steel helmeted heads, packed tightly together, could be seen looking out. For a split second it seemed to be locked in its crash position as though it was trying to carry on with its dive. Then a thick black cloud of smoke mixed with green flares and sparks shot upwards and the wreckage collapsed totally as a result of the high speed of the impact. The wreckage of the British aircraft was still smoking when, towards 3.00 pm, we left the desolation of the battle area, which was littered with several smashed aircraft, lying on their backs with broken wings or strewn around like half-burnt moths under the lamplight.[44]

"The counter-offensive had had success. In the south of the British break in, the enemy had been pushed back ten kilometres in less than a day [*sic*.], but in our northern sector the enemy had been able to mount strong counter-attacks. But even here large amounts of terrain were won and painful gaps were torn in the ranks [of the enemy]."

That is one way of describing the situation, but only an optimist would describe the ground gained here as 'large amounts'. Meanwhile, more and more British weapons were brought into action, until the troops of 49th Reserve Division were coming under fire from their right rear, which was causing casualties to the follow up waves and to which they could make no reply. This same fire also affected the regiments of 20th Infantry Division, who were not involved in the main Group Arras assault, but who had been ordered, 'In accordance with special instructions, 20th Infantry Division is to distract the enemy by carrying out a mock attack.'[45] Most of the effort came from Infantry Regiment 77, but elements of Infantry Regiment 79 were also involved:

Reserve Leutnant Karl Eggers 11th Company Infantry Regiment 79 [46]

"From time to time enemy counter-action with machine gun fire and shrapnel became noticeably unpleasant. Bourlon Wood, looking totally dead, lay off to our left flank. Outside the wood there were still British machine guns which, operating from a flank, interfered with the progress of the attack and caused awful casualties. This was how Oberleutnant Schierenberg was killed. He had only just returned to the regiment after a long period of convalescence following a serious wound he had suffered in August 1914. Towards midday we reached the start line. Drum fire from our batteries was coming down on the enemy lines. When it lifted we went forward. The 92nd and 79th were all tangled up because Infantry Regiment 92 arrived too late.

"By now the British had recovered their senses and we were subject to lacerating fire. The attack of Infantry Regiment 92 appeared to be stalling then, at the decisive moment, Oberst von Heynitz, fearlessly ignoring the bullets, rushed to the head of his battalions. Mortally wounded, the courageous commander of the Braunschweigers [i.e. Infantry Regiment 92] collapsed but, inspired by the example of their commander, his men renewed the assault. Despite the heaviest of defensive fire we succeeded in gaining the dominant high ground and throwing the British back."

This makes a good story, but on the ground it did not amount to much. Furthermore, the situation became increasingly critical for 49th Reserve Division when, suddenly, a failed attack out to their left led to a swift withdrawal and left the divisional flank hanging in the air. There was nothing for it but to extend out in that direction and to dig in where they were, a long way short of their objectives. The attack had degenerated into a messy close quarter battle in the confusion of old trenches. 'During the afternoon the situation was completely unclear; the chaos of battle rendering any coherent oversight impossible.'[47] For the time being, no more progress could be expected on the right and the attackers were still at least one kilometre north of the Cambrai – Bapaume road at this point. This created something of a problem for the ground-holding troops of the battered 21st Reserve Division, whose orders had been, 'to facilitate the advance of 49th Reserve Division, 214th Infantry Division and 221st Infantry Divisions through their lines and to follow up the line of advance of 49th Reserve Division as it progressed, so as to reoccupy the old First Position up to and including the Cambrai Road and link up with 49th Reserve Division there.'[48]

Now that it was obvious that the attack had all but failed, it was time for some sort of action by 21st Reserve Division. Reports from the front brought by contact patrols it had sent forward began arriving, stating that a sunken road south east of Lock 2 had been reached, so the decision was taken to move forward in that direction. Shortly after 1.00 pm, all the troops which could be mustered by 2nd Battalion Reserve Infantry Regiment 80 were sent forward, supported by the 2nd Machine Gun Company in the usual way. This move was followed forty minutes later by the 3rd Battalion, also complete with its machine gunners. They soon found that progress had been completely stalled. Individual companies became involved in the fighting, despite the fact that their earlier losses had meant that they were not meant to be directly engaged on 30 November. They enjoyed no more success than the men of 49th Reserve Division. 5th Company attempted to launch an attack against the British machine guns at Lock 2 in mid afternoon, but it was no more successful than earlier assaults had been.

Unteroffizier Paul Schlegel 8th Company Reserve Infantry Regiment 80 [49]

"From off to the right and moving above cover, came Feldwebel Hagen, who, as commander 8th Company, was killed in September 1918. He said to the company commander, who was a few paces away from me, 'Battalion order! All 2nd Battalion companies are to attack immediately!' Leutnant Cunz, walking stick in one hand and pistol in the other, immediately ordered, '8th Company, follow me!' At that, he leapt up out of the trench. I raced up after him and joined the other members of my company in an attack against a British position to our half right. We were met by a hail of machine gun fire and a number of men on either side of me threw themselves down in a large shell hole. I avoided this, because it contained a seriously wounded man and, instead, pressed on with the leading group of the company as far as a narrow, but deep, British communication trench which we then used to get forward to the left.

"There in the middle lay a British machine gunner, still twitching, next to the remains of his gun and, a few paces further on at a trench junction, we met up with a young soldier from Reserve Infantry Regiment 225, who stood there without equipment or rifle, with no helmet or cap, sweating profusely with his jacket open. With a broad, beaming smile, he told us how he had just dealt with the British machine gun which had been causing our men considerable casualties with its enfilading fire. A few metres further on, we came across an empty machine gun nest. We had barely entered it, when we came under very heavy rifle and machine gun fire from a British trench which ran about fifty metres to our right. The trench was packed with British soldiers who poured fire at us.

"Leutnant Cunz bawled, 'Machine gun over here!' I raced back down the communication trench and got hold of Gefreiter Barry and his light machine gun. He had hardly put the gun in position than he went down backwards like a stone. He had been hit by a British bullet in the middle of his forehead and two or three other men were wounded simultaneously. Nevertheless, the twelve or fifteen of us traded shot for shot with the British, but it was obvious that we could not stay in this exposed position; we had to get back to the cover of the communication trench. The British had set up a machine gun where the machine gun nest met the communication trench and it was sending up continuous sprays of earth. We had to duck down and cross the field of fire of this gun in order to reach the trench. Making myself as small as I could, keeping my head right down, I crawled between two of my comrades, who were lined up one after the other, back to the trench.

"I suddenly saw a steel helmet come clattering past me. Amazed that anybody would throw his steel helmet away in this situation, I turned and saw to my horror that its wearer, Trumpeter Schubert from Meiningen, had gone down. He had probably not ducked down enough and he had been shot through both temples and killed outright. Straight afterwards Gefreiter Karl Weg, who was behind me, asked me if I had been lying with my equipment on top of a dead man. I denied it and took off my equipment, seeing, to my horror, that the sandbag which I had attached to it to carry my mess tins and bread ration, was full of blood, brains and other filth. Schubert had been right behind me and it appeared that he had been shot through the head by a ricochet, which had sprayed his blood and brains on my equipment. As a result of this gruesome incident, I lost my appetite completely."

Once it was clear that there would be no more progress that day, the remnants of Reserve Infantry Regiments 80, 87, 88 226 and 228, together with Infantry Regiment 363, went firm where they were. Disentangling them would be left for later. Oberstleutnant Breitenbach, commander of Reserve Infantry Regiment 80, later recalled,[50] 'Night brought an end to all heavy fighting, but there could be no thought of sleep. In a small dugout, full of the fumes of paraffin and coal, were about thirty men and more and more arrived all night: wounded, stragglers, perhaps even shirkers. The dugout was soon crammed full; even the stairs were occupied. Then someone came stumbling down them in haste, bawling like a madman, 'Orders from Division! Orders from Division!' I waited until the bringer of orders made his way over to me and lit up a cigarette. That is the way to stay calm...'

Immediately to the left of 49th Reserve Division, 214th Infantry Division set out with the objective of capturing the sugar refinery on the Cambrai – Bapaume road and pushing on to take Graincourt. As the smoke screen was being fired, the regiments made their way forward at about 10.00 am from their assembly areas to the east of the Canal du Nord near to Marquion. There was plenty of air cover and, until they pushed on to the south of the Bourlon – Sains–lès–Marquion road, they were little troubled by British counter-action. However, at this point difficulties arose. Exploiting a moment when German air patrols were changing over and there was a gap in the cover, British aircraft appeared overhead and a captive balloon was launched. This immediately led to accurate artillery fire being directed onto the advancing troops, a development made all the worse due to the fact that the smokescreen in this area, too, failed to live up to expectations.

Coming under fire from the artillery and machine guns, casualties began to mount amongst the advancing columns and, shortly before midday, the attack began. Once more, within moments of the start of the attack, British small arms fire became very troublesome; machine guns firing from Hill 100, southwest of Bourlon chapel, in particular causing heavy casualties as they fired into the flank of the advancing troops. Despite all this resistance, the first British positions fell and prisoners were captured. When attempts were made to extend the attack forward towards the sugar refinery, '...it was halted by extraordinarily heavy machine gun and artillery fire and the troops, who were being led forward with great dash, suffered heavy casualties.'[51] Neither the main German batteries, nor the accompanying infantry support field guns managed to silence British batteries near the refinery. Despite the fact that Generalleutnant Moser had 500 guns, many of them heavy, at his disposal, such was the need for fire support that he still lacked sufficient numbers to make a decisive difference to the outcome of this battle. This attack, too, stalled and the regiments had to dig in and consolidate their gains, all the time under heavy fire.

The last of the Group Arras divisions which took a direct part in *Sturmflut* was the 221st Infantry Division, whose left hand boundary was drawn as close to the western edge of Bourlon Wood as was practical. In the event, as it became light on the morning of 30 November, the nearest regiment, Reserve Infantry Regiment 60, could see clearly that, despite the immense weight of artillery fire which had been brought down, despite the extensive use of mustard gas, there were still British troops holding out against the odds in the wood. This complicated the business of getting into the forming up places prior to the attack and the solution chosen was to call for drum fire on the wood and to supplement this by the mass application of rifle, machine gun and mortar fire from within regimental resources. Once again there was air support as the regiments manoeuvred into position.

Fliegerleutnant Johannes Fischer Field Flight Detachment 8 [52]

"On 30 November 1917, at exactly 9.30 am, [we] linked up with 10 Squadron of the Richthofen Wing over the battle area. Simultaneously the guns brought down heavy fire. The area where the drama of battle was about to unfold was overlaid with a blanket of dense cloud. This provided a natural obstacle against enemy aircraft which were flying much higher. However this cloud cover also reduced considerably the freedom of manoeuvre of the two wings. Soon, in order to complicate the work of the anti-aircraft defences, the wings broke up and patrolling by individual aircraft or small groups began. The view that there was sufficient airspace and that there was little risk of a collision was disproved yet again on this occasion.

"The aircraft had to manoeuvre within strict limits above the battlefield in order not to compromise the air defence. That being the case, the enemy opened heavy fire against the mass of aircraft. Large numbers of gas shells directed against Bourlon Wood, which burst prematurely, further reduced the room for manoeuvre. Ignited at various heights, these shells traced arcs like smoking rockets through the sky before they impacted. The blue-white clouds, which hung around in plumes afterwards, poisoned the air more and more. Holding our breath ever more frequently we flew through hundreds of these comet-like smoke formations. Frequently an aircraft would appear suddenly out of the smoke, then collisions were only avoided by means of lightning-fast manoeuvres. We saw, more clearly than ever before, what a hail of shells we [normally] flew through over the battlefield; our airspeed concentrating them enormously

"In the meantime Bourlon Wood had disappeared under a huge cloud of gas; it was impossible to see anything of it. Down amongst its splintered tree trunks, more than 2,000 British soldiers battled against suffocation. They were later discovered [dead], their faces blue. The noise of the bombardment, which had increased to drum fire, could be heard in the aircraft. It sounded like the rumble of a massive kettledrum. [Looking down] it seemed as though the German artillery, packed together wheel to wheel, like a huge version of an infantry firing line, was taking part in a great parade. Without pausing for breath, the gunners thrust shell after shell into their guns and fired them as fast as they could towards their targets. The guns were being fired to the limit; small wonder that the almost red hot barrels were causing prematures amongst the gas shells.

"We swooped low frequently, almost to ground level, in order to determine the extent of the infantry advance and to convince ourselves that the reserves were moving up correctly. On the roads in Fontaine and to the south of Bourlon we spotted a number of knocked out British tanks, some of which were almost hidden within Bourlon Wood. To the south of this wood, protected by a sunken road, we spotted large numbers of British soldiers who were, in many cases, gathered around the entrances to their dugouts. Towards 10.00 am a group of enemy batteries, located to the south of Orival Wood, began firing rapidly. In the meantime British aircraft arrived over the battle area then, a little later, two of them were seen to fall to the ground to the west of Fontaine. By the time we flew low over the spot, our advancing infantry had just arrived there. At 11.31 am we returned to our airfield."

From about 10.00 am Reserve Infantry Regiment 60, especially its left flank, was kept under heavy artillery fire by British batteries. Battalion commanders continued to despatch reconnaissance patrols in the direction of the wood, but it was quite clear that the entire western edge was still occupied by British troops, a few of whom, possibly in about platoon strength, attempted to launch an attack against the German positions.[53] Needless to say it was beaten off, but there can be no doubt that the courageous action of the surviving British troops in Bourlon Wood totally inhibited the planned advance of Reserve Infantry Regiment 60, which fizzled out almost before it began. Infantry Regiment 41, operating slightly further west and thus not so much affected by direct fire from Bourlon Wood, did at least get across the start line but, having thrust forward onto and just beyond the slopes of Hill 100, this attack too faltered badly.

The weakened Infantry Regiment 92 was closely involved with this part of the attack. Reserve Ersatz Infantry Regiment 1 of 221st Infantry Division was tasked with taking over the German forward positions nearest to Bourlon Wood and Infantry Regiment 92, reinforced by 3rd Battalion Infantry Regiment 79, participated in the attack. Once more the outcome fell far short of expectations. As soon as its troops began to close up on the start line, it took heavy casualties from flanking fire originating in Bourlon Wood, the regimental history later noting that, 'the two enemy front line trenches were located further forward than the artillery had assumed. As a result, enemy machine guns were not destroyed. We did not see the rolling barrage having any effect either.'[54] This last problem may have been due to a decision not to follow the bursting shells any closer than two hundred metres, a caution which betrayed lack of experience in the attack. In contrast, by the latter stages of Third Ypres, Allied units were 'leaning on the barrage' as they advanced, often closing to within twenty five to fifty metres of bursting shrapnel pots. The net result of this tactic here was that the attack failed within two hundred metres of the start line.

It is true, however, that here and there throughout the day, determined junior leadership meant that slight (and usually temporary) gains were made but, despite more outstanding work from the direct support batteries of Field Artillery Regiment 273, the results were disappointing and casualties among the junior leadership were high. At a cost of six officers and fifty four other ranks killed and a total of 224 wounded, Infantry Regiment 41 admitted that, 'The day's success had been slight. True, we had thrown the enemy completely off Hill 100, but we were completely unable to break through to Graincourt – Anneux'[55] Not only had the regiment little to show for its sacrificial efforts, as night fell, the situation along the front line was chaotic. Flanking fire by British forces in and around the wood and amongst the tangle of old positions, meant that the thrust of the attack had deviated somewhat towards the west. As a result, at nightfall, sub units and isolated groups from Infantry Regiments 41, 79 and 92 were hopelessly intermingled. Resupply was exceedingly difficult to arrange, as was every form of administrative action and, which was worse, there was no possibility of simply renewing the assault the following morning.

On the left flank the part played by 3rd Guards Infantry Division and 119th Infantry Division was extremely limited. Both had been badly worn down in the previous fighting and neither was in any real shape to make a major contribution. In the event the regiments of 3rd Guards Infantry Division merely held their positions. They were not attacked, but lost some casualties to artillery fire. The advance of the 119th Division was very much dependent on progress being made to the west by the remainder of Group Arras. When that first faltered and then stalled, it was inevitable that the 119th would not be able to make much progress either. Once Hill 100 was seen to fall, an attempt was made later in the day to advance, but with rifle company strengths already as low as sixty riflemen in some cases and casualties occurring as soon as the attack began, it was inevitable that only a few hundred metres were gained.

Losses in Reserve Infantry Regiment 46 alone amounted to twenty six killed, with a further one hundred and twenty wounded and missing. The after action report of the 3rd Battalion summed up the dismal results succinctly: 'The order to attack on 30 November arrived too late, so that it was not launched until forty five minutes after the artillery bombardment had ended. The British, therefore, were given plenty of time to re-establish their defensive lines and to pour an appalling weight of machine gun and rifle fire against our weak lines of infantrymen.'[56]

Throughout the Second Army area nightfall brought a reduction in the intensity of the battle and time to reflect. The Army Commander summed up the battle from his perspective in a letter to his wife written that evening. His thoughts were clearly flitting from one part of the battlefield to another, so his narrative appears somewhat disjointed:

General der Kavallerie Georg von der Marwitz [57]

"I drove to the command post of 9th Reserve Division, but it was difficult to see much because everything was cloaked in smoke. The thunder of the guns was so intense at times that it was necessary to shout loudly to one another, even though we were still one kilometre from the front line. As the hour for the assault approached, the airmen appeared. They approached in two majestic swarming wings and began to orbit the lines, in order to be able to report immediately the line of advance of our infantry. I had made a firm promise to [my Chief of Staff] Stapff that I would drive back at 9.00 am and so I did. Arriving back at my headquarters, I was greeted by favourable news; particularly from Group Busigny. Several villages had been captured, the most significant of which was Gouzeaucourt. The situation was not as good for Group Arras. 220th Division was unable to make much progress, which meant that the 28th had to stretch itself thinly to cover the gap as it advanced. The advance of 30th Division moved forward well but the surrounding of the large village of Moeuvres, which was not to be attacked, consumed large numbers of troops.

"At midday the northern Group Arras attacked as planned, got forward to some extent and captured some valuable pieces of ground. During the evening the bad news arrived that Gouzeaucourt had been lost. That was serious because its possession was necessary for the continuation of the attack the following morning. The great aim which we had sought to bring about, namely, 'to cut off the enemy who had broken in,' was unachievable, therefore. Nevertheless, I gave orders for the continuation of the attack on 1 December, made available 185th and 9th Bavarian Divisions, and directed that 79th Reserve Division was to be moved closer."

The Army Group Commander also confided his impressions to paper that evening in a lengthy entry, recorded within two volumes of his diaries which he published after the war.

Crown Prince Rupprecht of Bavaria: Diary Entries 30 November 1917 [58]

"By 9.30 am our troops were across the Schelde [St Quentin] Canal and the first enemy lines had been thrown back. We stressed that, during the attack, the main effort was to be devoted to taking the area of Metz en Couture. The army order for today visualised advancing in the direction of Trescault, in order to stretch out a hand towards Group Arras, instead of adhering to the originally intended and much more effective direction of attack aimed at Metz en Couture. At 9.00 pm I directed that Second Army was to be reminded that the aim was to get forward to the south of Havrincourt Wood.

"Although the success is nowhere near as great as we might have expected, nevertheless a painful blow has been struck against the enemy and so far 2,500 prisoners have been captured... By midday the attacks of Groups Caudry and Busigny had made excellent progress. As far as was known the 30th Division had reached Marcoing, 9th Reserve Division to the south of that place, the 220th Infantry Division was at [actually short of] La Vacquerie, the 28th in Gouzeaucourt, the 34th in Villers Guislain, with the field artillery to the east of that place and 183rd was at Petite Priel Farm. As evening approached, it became known that the really problematic attack of Group Arras had only made slight progress and, advancing either side of Bourlon Wood, had not advanced much further than its hilly southern extremity. Group Busigny had lost Gouzeaucourt once more to an enemy counter-attack. Our line now ran from Marcoing south of the Schelde via La Vacquerie and Gonnelieu along the line of the railway embankment east of Gouzeaucourt then via Vancelette Farm to Vendhuille.

"Altogether approximately nine divisions had been deployed. There were still British forces north of the Schelde, but they had little chance of avoiding capture. The loss of Gouzeaucourt was highly regrettable. Despite repeated reminders by the Army Group, Second Army had failed to shift its point of main effort to the left flank of the attack. 185th Infantry Division was moved forward via Crèvecoeur; that is to say too far to the north. One of its regiments has been deployed to a sector of the front that in my considered opinion is too densely manned. During the night the remainder of the division will move into assembly areas around Bantouzelle. The 79th Reserve Division is located east of Honnecourt, which is also too far to the north."

It was clear that, though hopes were not yet entirely dashed, by the evening of the first day of the counter-attack, expectations had been considerably dampened down.

Notes

1. History Field Artillery Regiment 14 pp 224-226
2. Men of Footguard Regiment 3 watched as assault groups from Infantry Regiment 184 tackled Gillemont Farm. Their history later noted simply, 'The assault troops were beaten back; surprise was not achieved against the British at this place.' Naumann: History Footguard Regiment 3 p 82
3. Rosenberg-Lipinsky: History Grenadier Guard Regiment 3 p 540
4. Loebell: *Mit dem 3. Garde Regiment z.F. im Weltkriege* 1914/18 pp 320-321
5. The actual point assaulted was Fleeceall Post, held by 1/5th Kings of 165 Brigade.

6.   This must be a reference to the *Magdeburgisches Husaren-Regiment Nr. 10*, originally raised in 1813, whose garrison town was Stendal.
7.   Christian: History Infantry Regiment 418 pp 238 - 242
8.   This refers to the assault of 6th Coy Infantry Regiment 418 on an intermediate position, located along the line of a sunken road about 300 metres in rear of the British front line, which was held up by the action of advanced British machine gun nests.
9.   This appears to be a reference to the attack made by the Ambala Brigade of 5th Cavalry Division. It should be noted that the eyewitness account in this case contains considerable exaggeration. The Ambala Brigade was mixed. It had both British and Indian regiments within its ranks. In addition, the total casualties for the whole of 5th Cavalry Division from 20 November – 8 December 1917 only amounted to thirty five officers and 376 other ranks. We can, therefore, dismiss references to the destruction of entire regiments as simply wrong. BOH *The Battle of Cambrai* p 382
10.   Soldan: History Infantry Regiment 184 p 64
11.   Hüttmann: History Infantry Regiment 25 p 156
12.   Simon: History Infantry Regiment 67 p 100
13.   Freydorf: History Leibgrenadier Regiment 109 p 475
14.   Führen: History Fusilier Regiment 40 pp 485-486
15.   Lattorff: History Jäger Battalion 3 p 183
16.   Freydorf: *op. cit.* p 478
17.   Schede: History Grenadier Regiment 110 pp 80-90
18.   Müller-Loebnitz: *Die Badener im Weltkrieg* 1914/1918 pp 301-302
19.   Leutnant Kempf was later killed near Chilly on 26 March 1918
20.   Of the four, only Vizefeldwebel Alois Heinzler and Fähnrich Wilhelm Otto Heizler, who are buried close together in the German cemetery at Selvigny Block 4 Graves 1387 and 1383 respectively, have known graves.
21.   Führen: *op. cit.* 488-489
22.   Müller: History Reserve Infantry Regiment 99 p 171
23.   Müller-Loebnitz: *Das Ehrenbuch der Westfalen* pp 448-449
24.   Leutnant Otto Anhalt is buried, like so many other German casualties from the Battle of Cambrai, at Selvigny German cemetery Block 2 Grave 92.
25.   Hauptstaatsarchiv Stuttgart M33/2 Bü 374 *Die Angriffsschlacht bei Cambrai* p 19
26.   Schwenke: History Reserve Infantry Regiment 19 p 308
27.   Kessler: History Reserve Field Artillery Regiment 9 p 226
28.   Wißmann: History Reserve Infantry Regiment 55 p 214
29.   Gerth: History Infantry Regiment 395 pp 154-155
30.   Kessler: *op. cit.* pp 227-228

31. Heinze could only have made that statement because he left the battle area relatively early. In fact one of the major causes of the hold up here for the German advance was the heroic work done by 179 Army Brigade Royal Field Artillery firing in support from positions near La Vacquerie.

32. Wißmann: *op. cit.* p 215

33. Müller-Loebnitz: *Das Ehrenbuch der Westfalen* pp 449-450

34. Glogowski: History Infantry Regiment 105 pp 218-219

35. Bartenwerffer: History Reserve Infantry Regiment 232 p 111

36. *ibid.* p 112

37. Ulrich: History Reserve Infantry Regiment 52 pp 438 – 439. Because of serious losses during the earlier part of the Cambrai fighting, 1st and 3rd Battalion Reserve Infantry Regiment 52 were temporarily amalgamated on 27 November under the command of Hauptmann Wesemann.

38. Moser: *Feldzugsaufzeichnungen* pp 322-324

39. Szymanski: History Reserve Infantry Regiment 80 pp 267-268

40. Rohkohl: History Reserve Infantry Regiment 226 Teil II p 82

41. Note that other units in a position to judge disagreed. Reserve Infantry Regiment 80, of 21st Reserve Division, holding the forward positions, claimed that units of 49th Reserve Division arrived hopelessly jumbled together because of the fire and that 'elements of Reserve Infantry Regiment 226 arrived very late on the start line'. History Reserve Infantry Regiment 80 pp 256-257

42. Sydow: History Infantry Regiment 76 p 160

43. Fischer: *Zwischen Wolken und Granaten* pp 185-186

44. The aircraft shot down by von Richthofen over Moeuvres was his 65th victory. The pilot of this S.E.5a of 41 Squadron RFC, Lieutenant D.A.D.I. MacGregor, was killed.

45. Szymanski: *op. cit.* p 254

46. Brandes: History Infantry Regiment 79 pp 460-461

47. Sydow: *op. cit.* p 161

48. Szymanski: *op. cit.* p 254

49. *ibid.* pp 273-274

50. *ibid.* p 268

51. Vogt: History Infantry Regiment 50 p 206

52. Fischer: *op. cit.* pp 185-186

53. Zechlin: History Reserve Infantry Regiment 60 pp 146-147

54. Sobbe: History Infantry Regiment 92 p 445

55. Bülowius: History Infantry Regiment 41 pp 226-227

56. Puttkamer: History Reserve Infantry Regiment 46 p 171

57. Tschischwitz: *General von der Marwitz* p 264

58. Kronprinz Rupprecht *Mein Kriegstagebuch Zweiter Band* pp 298-299 and Dritter Band pp 185-186

CHAPTER SEVEN

December 1917: Hopes Dashed

Despite the setbacks of 30 November, as the main thrust from the east faltered then stalled and was thrown back, all the German senior commanders shared the view that another effort had to be made on 1 December. Having absorbed all the reports concerning the first day of the counter-attack, Ludendorff made contact early on 1 December with General der Infanterie Hermann von Kuhl at Headquarters Army Group Crown Prince Rupprecht, 'Another attempt must be made to attack today but, if this does not produce success in the form of a breakthrough, we must take a decision tonight...'[1] At this stage neither 185th Infantry Division or 9th Bavarian Reserve Division had been committed to the attack, 79th Infantry Division was moving up from St Quentin and further divisions were en route to the Cambrai area.

Against that background and the result of the fighting of the previous day, Commander Second Army, doubtless influenced by previous direction from Ludendorff, decided to press on with his offensive on 1 December, but adjusted its *Schwerpunkt* more to the north and gave orders for the capture of the high ground around Trescault, with a view to swinging north subsequently to occupy the heights around Havrincourt, as a preliminary to linking up with Group Arras.

Second Army Order Ia 752/November Secret 30 November 1917 [2]

"The attack launched by the Army between Moeuvres and Graincourt has reached the Cambrai – Bapaume road. 119th Division has made progress in the direction of Cantaing. The thrust from the east has reached the line of Depot Wood, south of Marcoing – western edge La Vacquerie – western edge Gonnelieu – passing to the west of Villers Guislain and Vendhuille. Over 3,000 prisoners have been counted so far.

"The Army is to continue the attack on 1 December. Initially, the most important objective is the high ground of Beaucamp and Trescault. Thereafter, the aim is to capture the heights either side of Havrincourt from the south in order to link up with Group Arras.

"Group Arras is to hold the line it has reached and is to attempt to establish links with the forces fighting around Graincourt and

Cantaing. The bombardment of Bourlon Wood with gas shells is to continue, so as to isolate it. The security of the advanced flank to the south of Moeuvres is of special importance.

"Group Caudry, whilst holding on firmly to the line reached on its right flank and centre, is next to capture Villers Plouich. The enemy in Masnières is to be cut off.

"Two thirds of 185th Infantry Division is to be placed by Group Caudry in the Escaut Valley round Vaucelles and Banteux, so that it may be deployed to develop the thrust between Villers-Plouich and Gouzeaucourt. One third of 185th Infantry Division is to be retained by Group Caudry as a reserve [Infantry Regiment 65]. The field artillery belonging to 185th Infantry Division is to take up silent positions east of the St Quentin Canal.

"Group Busigny is to outflank Gouzeaucourt on both sides and capture it. It is then to support the attack of Group Caudry by advancing northwest between Villers-Plouich and Gouzeaucourt. Group Busigny is responsible for maintaining the junction points.

"The attacks against Villers-Plouich and Gouzeaucourt are to be launched simultaneously at 9.30 am 1 December.

"79th Reserve Division is to be at my disposal, ready to move in two columns, with leading elements at Bantouzelle and Honnecourt, from 8.00 am. Its artillery is to be located in silent positions to the east of the canal. It will receive its orders directly from Headquarters Second Army.

"The newly arriving divisions will be deployed as follows: a. 24th Reserve Division in Cambrai (Army Group Reserve); b. 16th Reserve Division as Supreme Army Command Reserve between Lesdaine and Caudry; c. 10th Infantry Division, Supreme Army Command Reserve in the area Ramicourt – Fresnoy–le–Grand – Bohain.

Signed: von der Marwitz
General der Kavallerie and Generaladjutant"

Unfortunately for Second Army, the British Third Army had issued orders to all three of its corps to launch attacks from 7.30 am. These have been criticised[3] as amounting to nothing more than hasty, ill coordinated thrusts, but they had one great merit from the British perspective: they pre-empted the planned Second Army attacks, threw the timetable out and forced the Germans to use their fresh divisions in support of the troops holding the front line positions and thus, in bolstering other formations, to dissipate their attacking power. When further, better organised and stronger British attacks developed later in the day, the German assault lost its entire impetus.

East of Gouzeaucourt troops of 34th Infantry Division spent a disturbed night attempting to disentangle mixed up units and to improve their positions. There had been one disturbance. At about 2.00 am there was a sudden wave of heavy machine gun and rifle fire all along the sector front, but it soon died away. There were burning tanks scattered across the whole front, their silhouettes standing out ghostly against the flames and smoke. From time to time there were explosions as ammunition 'cooked off' in the interiors and this is thought to be what caused the firing to break out. In the relative quiet of the early dawn, Hauptmann Thosehrn of Infantry Regiment 67 despatched a contact patrol to link up with Königs Infantry Regiment 145 out to the left, but there was no trace of any troops manning the railway embankment. It was a worrying start to a new day of battle.

At 6.30 am there was a sudden, violent artillery concentration which crashed down on the German positions. Then, shortly after 7.00 am, panicky shouts, of 'Here come the tanks!' were heard.[4] These were from the British 2nd Tank Brigade. Seemingly silently, the armoured vehicles had manoeuvred into position and had managed to advance almost up to the German front line in places. The alarm was raised immediately and exhausted men reached for their weapons and equipment, prior to manning their fire positions. Already at least one tank had crossed the improvised trenches and others followed. There then began a wild close quarter battle as machine gun and rifle fire was directed at the tanks at short range and hand grenades were thrown in large numbers. Most of this seems to have been ineffective and the tanks, turning left and right having crossed the trench, began to pour fire down on the defenders.

Tank machine guns firing down the length of the trenches caused mayhem, just as they had back on 20 November. Within a short time, the position of Infantry Regiment 67 was threatened from the rear and enemy infantry could be seen crossing the railway embankment left undefended after the withdrawal of Königs Infantry Regiment 145 earlier. With casualties mounting and total destruction threatening, Hauptmann Thosehrn ordered a withdrawal, just as Reserve Leutnant Page collapsed right next to him, mortally wounded. A number of men were killed or wounded during the race to gain a sunken road three hundred metres to the rear, but it was fortunate for those involved that it was still not fully light. Had the visibility been better it is hard to imagine that the withdrawal would have been possible at all.

Back at the sunken road, which led down towards Villers-Guislain, the officers succeeded in rallying their men then, just as it was getting light enough to see clearly, one of the infantry support batteries which had been involved in the advance the previous day was able to engage the advancing tanks. This intervention came just in the nick of time; the first of the tanks had managed to get onto the high ground between Gouzeaucourt and Gonnelieu. The very first round was a hit and the tank caught fire. Subsequent shots led to its total destruction. Three or four other tanks were similarly dealt with. Amidst all the confusion of battle, some individuals behaved with exemplary calm and used their initiative to good effect. Reserve Vizefeldwebel Hock of 3rd Machine Gun Company Infantry Regiment 67, for example, came across an abandoned British battery position which had been overrun the previous day. He happened to be a trained gunner so, aided by two others, he succeeded in turning one of the field guns round, then loaded, aimed and fired at an advancing tank from only fifty metres range, destroying it with his first shot.[5] Unfortunately for him, machine gun fire from other tanks was too heavy and he was forced to pull back hurriedly. The overall anti tank defence also faltered, because there had been no ammunition resupply to the infantry support battery the previous night and its guns were soon out of ammunition. They, too, had to leave hastily, abandoning two guns in the sunken road, though they were recovered two days later.

Meanwhile to the south in *Gauche Wald* [Bois Gaucher], other tanks had got forward and were bringing down fire, in association with further heavy British artillery concentrations, which forced the men of 34th Infantry Division back yet again. The situation for the defence was suddenly absolutely critical. The defenders were flooding to the rear almost uncontrollably. Had there been a further British thrust at this precise moment it is hard to imagine that anything could have stopped it, especially because artillery fire was already falling on Gonnelieu. However, just at that precise moment, troops of 9th Bavarian Reserve Division began arriving. For the time being all thoughts of continuing with their original mission were set aside, as 2nd Battalion Bavarian Ersatz Regiment 3 and 3rd Battalion Bavarian Reserve Infantry Regiment 11 launched an immediate limited counter-attack, whilst their artillery engaged the British tanks. This bought sufficient time for Königs Infantry Regiment 145 to go into hasty defence along the western edge of Villers-Guislain and the remnants of Infantry Regiment 67 to take up positions north and west of Gonnelieu.

Although important ground had been yielded, the fall back positions dominated the low ground as far as *Gauche Wald* and the road Villers-Guislain – Gouzeaucourt. In any case the British did not seem to wish to press forward any further and the attacks here petered out more or less at this time. Some felt that the destruction of several of the dwindling number of tanks may have had something to do with it. A bold move forward by the infantry support battery of Königs Infantry Regiment 145 towards the armour near *Gauche Wald* led to the destruction of four more tanks in quick succession so, as the momentum went out of the British attack, there were nine burning tanks on the 34th Infantry Division/9th Bavarian Reserve Division front. It was just as well that the attack had died away here because, by mistake, a mounted Jäger arrived and spread the word that 9th Bavarian Reserve Division was going to relieve 34th Infantry Division. Needing no second bidding, an almost precipitous pull out began.

The troops withdrew via Banteux to Rancourt Farm three kilometres to the southeast and some were even directed back to Villers-Outréaux before the move could be countermanded. Trickling somewhat unenthusiastically back to the forward area, the survivors returned to the line between Gonnelieu and Villers-Guislain where the positions were held, in what was becoming almost a trademark situation for the German counter-attack, by a tangled garrison comprising Bavarian troops, as well as men of Infantry Regiment 30 and Königs Infantry Regiment 145. It had not been a good day in this sector but, just to the north, the combined efforts of other formations of 9th Bavarian Reserve Division had enjoyed slightly more, though nevertheless modest, success; the British troops being forced back to the railway embankment 500 metres east of Gouzeaucourt in places.

About 10.00 am, Bavarian Reserve Infantry Regiment 14 and the two uncommitted battalions of Bavarian Reserve Infantry Regiment 11 launched themselves forward from a start line to the north of Gonnelieu. Led by their commanding officer, Major Bolz, Bavarian Reserve Infantry Regiment 11 clashed with British troops who had advanced to the northwest edge of Gonnelieu and pushed them back, overrunning a British battery as it did so. The attack was pressed forward as far as the Gouzeaucourt – Le Pavé road, but there a halt had to be called. The attack on La Vacquerie had failed – in fact it never got off the ground - so there was no possibility of linking up with the formations of 185th Infantry Division.[6]

Having moved from Army Group Reserve to the command of Group Busigny, the regiments of 185th Infantry Division, which had been moved south from Flanders a few days previously, spent much of 30 November attempting to move forward to assembly areas around Bantouzelle and Banteux. After a brief rest, orders arrived for Infantry Regiment 161 and Reserve Infantry Regiment 28 to move forward to holding positions in the old *SII Stellung* at 6.00 am. 1st Battalion Reserve Infantry Regiment 28 was detached at 9.00 am to the command of Infantry Regiment 65, meaning that the divisional reserve, charged with providing flank protection to the south in Banteux Ravine, now had four battalions at its disposal. Fully expecting to be committed to an enveloping attack against Gouzeaucourt, the remaining battalions of Reserve Infantry Regiment 28 and Infantry Regiment 161 moved forward, still in reserve, at about 10.00 am.

The British counter-attacks, mentioned above, which had thrown German designs into fatal confusion, continued. Oberst Schütz, the commander of Infantry Regiment 65, was placed in temporary charge of 29 Infantry Brigade, but there were still no clear or timely orders with which to work. Reserve Infantry Regiment 28 later commented that, 'there was an unmistakeable air of nervous haste'.[7] Advancing over the high ground one and a half kilometres east of Gonnelieu [modern Hill 135], the move of 185th Infantry Division was totally dislocated when it came first under heavy German artillery fire and then unpleasantly accurate long range British machine gun fire. Shaking out, the regiments continued the advance by platoons and sections, moving in short bounds covered by mutual fire support until, eventually, they became embroiled in a messy battle to the north of Gonnelieu, where Leibgrenadier Regiment 109 and Grenadier Regiment 110 of 28th Infantry Division were already tangled up with Bavarian Reserve Infantry Regiment 11 and Bavarian Ersatz Regiment 3 of 9th Bavarian Reserve Division.

In accordance with Group Busigny orders, the intention had been for 28th Infantry Division, deployed with all three regiments in line (from right to left, Fusilier Regiment 40, Grenadier Regiment 110 and Leibgrenadier Regiment 109) to continue to attack towards Villers Plouich and subsequently Trescault but this, too, was knocked off course by the early morning British counter-attack. Fusilier Regiment 40 was to have attacked La Vacquerie from the southeast, but the orders were changed and responsibility was given to 220th Infantry Division, with Fusilier Regiment 40 dropping back into divisional reserve.[8] However, not only were the troops of 34th Infantry Division repulsed, so too were formations of 28th Infantry Division, which explains the chaotic situation encountered by 185th Infantry Division as it arrived at Gonnelieu. Fusilier Regiment 40 of 28th Infantry Division was even more scathing about how the situation developed once the original orders were overtaken by events: 'One order after another was rushed out. Right up until midday the situation was unclear, indeed thoroughly muddled. There was no general plan of attack and no unity of command. All the formations were thrown together in complete confusion.'[9]

It is small wonder, therefore, that so little progress could be made. The British attacks had played an important part in bringing this about, but much of the problem was entirely self-inflicted by the Germans. After the dash in the attack shown the previous day, this was a considerable disappointment. Unsurprising to note, little could be done to turn this disastrous situation around. A more deliberate attack, ordered for midday, had to be postponed until 3.00 pm, in order to ensure that there would be artillery fire support and, as has already been mentioned, lack of success against La Vacquerie meant that the advance on the right was limited to the line of the road Gouzeaucourt – Le Pavé whilst, on the left, British pressure, during an afternoon of changing fortunes, caused the German line to be pulled back towards the end of the day to positions just to the west of Gonnelieu. It proved to be impossible to recover the guns of a British battery overrun only one hundred metres to the west of the village, so the bounty available for their recovery went unclaimed. It was a day of relatively modest casualties for the 185th Infantry Division, but there was also much annoyance at the way the British counter-actions had frustrated their plans for a further general advance. The Army Commander himself summed up the situation succinctly in a letter written during the evening of the second day of the counter-attack.

General der Kavallerie Georg von der Marwitz [10]

"The night passed fairly quietly, but the British had spotted the danger. Before our attack could get going, they attacked aggressively, with tanks, cavalry and infantry. The tanks threw the divisions into disorder and managed to reach our artillery. Ten were knocked out, one of our batteries was overrun and the guns lost. There is no more prospect of success for the offensive at this point; that is quite clear. Nevertheless, we have captured 4,500 prisoners and forty guns and, above all, have launched an attack once more."

This heavy, confused fighting had left its mark on the area. A letter from an officer of Reserve Infantry Regiment 262 described the situation after the battle had moved on. 'Forward, the situation was amazing! Gonnelieu was still full of heavy British guns, equipped with plenty of ammunition. There was also a British ambulance and many bodies. Gonnelieu itself was just a heap of ruins.'[11]

Here and there, despite the generally unsatisfactory way the day unfolded, some minor attacks were carried out successfully. Realising, eventually, that 220th Infantry Division was not in fact going to move that day against La Vacquerie, the commanding officers of 2nd and 3rd Battalions Fusilier Regiment 40 decided to attempt to roll up the line of the *SII Stellung* towards La Vacquerie on their own initiative. This they achieved by means of an attack which they launched at about 3.00 pm. Off to their left, Grenadier Regiment 110 also attempted a similar operation, which made no progress, but nothing in their history confirms the view expressed by the British Official Historian that this was an attack pressed with great determination after a heavy bombardment. Such differences of view are not uncommon. According to the British, the trench clearance conducted by Fusilier Regiment 40 against 9th Battalion Royal Fusiliers of the British 36th Brigade was, 'beaten off until the British supply of bombs was exhausted. A withdrawal across the [La Vacquerie – Villers Plouich] road was then carried out.' [12] The German account simply states that the British were forced out of their positions until a point one hundred metres north of the road was reached. Regardless of the exact situation, the advantage to the German attackers was that from these new positions they were able the following night to link up with Infantry Regiments 99 and 190 of 220th Infantry Division.

Meanwhile, in accordance with its orders, 79th Reserve Division moved forward as Army Reserve behind 185th Infantry Division and then advanced further in the direction of La Vacquerie. In the event, its regiments were not committed to the counter-attack but, in an incident which illustrates the random nature of death and destruction on the Cambrai battlefield, just as 7th Battery Reserve Field Artillery Regiment 63 was advancing in column near Bantouzelle, a single heavy shell, fired as part of a harassing fire programme, landed in amongst it. The resulting explosion killed twenty three other ranks and thirty horses, whilst a further one officer, twenty two men and four horses were wounded. For the time being the battery was unable to continue until it had cleared up the resulting carnage and reorganised itself.[13] Whilst this work was being carried out, the other troops of the division continued on their way and were established by about midday in positions astride the Banteux – Gonnelieu road, where they remained in Army Reserve.

Füsilier Möbius 10th Company Reserve Infantry Regiment 262 [14]

"Due to the direct hits of our artillery the battlefield was littered with enemy tanks. It was simultaneously a tragic and a beautiful sight. The stomachs of we soldiers were yearning for the delicious things that a search of the tanks would reveal. The excellent gun oil was also in great demand. Everybody will remember the *ersatz* oil we had to make do with. Picking our way through the positions previously occupied by the Tommies, we came across a deep dugout which had been collapsed by a 210 mm howitzer shell with a delay fuze. It contained men of the Irish-Royal-Regiment [*sic*]. Seven were dead and one was still alive. We established ourselves in what had been a Tommies' canteen in the front line, but we were only able to enjoy it for one day before we had to move on..."

In accordance with orders, there were no major operations on the Group Arras front on 1 December. Nevertheless, pressure was maintained in other ways. Aircraft dropped bombs on British troop concentrations along the sector frontage and Bourlon Wood continued to be bombarded with both high explosives and gas, as were Cantaing, Anneux and Graincourt. About 500 prisoners were moved to Marquette, where Generalleutnant von Moser had his headquarters. Interrogation reports indicated that the obviously high morale of British soldiers captured in the first few days had given way to a much more sombre outlook as a result of the German surprise counter-attack and the realisation that many of the gains made so painfully during the past few days had been lost once more. 214th Infantry Division was finally pulled out of the line that day and arrangements were also made for the relief of the fought out 3rd Guards Infantry Division. There was one British attempt late in the day to storm Hill 100, but it was beaten back without any particular difficulty.

Crown Prince Rupprecht of Bavaria: Diary Entry 1 December 1917 [15]

"Despite the fact that as good as no information arrived during the morning, I avoided driving to Le Cateau in order not to disrupt the conduct of the battle. When, by 8.00 pm, no information concerning progress had been received, it had to be assumed that no further success worthy of the name was going to be achieved. The attack had run its course. This seemed to be the view of Second Army as well, who decided against any further advance towards Gouzeaucourt and, just in case it was not possible to get to Trescault, at least to capture Vacquerie Farm, and so to content themselves with possession of a line to the east of the railway Marcoing – Villers Guislain.

"Following the capture of Masnières and the clearance of Bourlon Wood, a further attempt was to be made from the northeast to push on via Cantaing and Noyelles, in order to reduce the salient in our lines to the greatest extent possible. We had to concur in this reduction in the aims of our offensive."

Ludendorff telephoned General von Kuhl towards the end of the day, as it became clear that the chances of success were receding rapidly, 'We must decide tonight what is to be done, selecting a good position, which can be gradually improved. The reserves are not to be thrown recklessly into the battle. It is not going to achieve very much more.'[16] Kuhl later noted the main events of the day in his diary.

General der Infanterie Hermann von Kuhl Chief of Staff Army Group Crown Prince Rupprecht [17]

"It has become quite obvious that the attack of the Northern Group enjoyed no success at all. I had always advocated simply holding firm here and leaving the entire attack in the hands of the Southern Group, especially in the decisive direction of Metz en Couture. This was where the British were most vulnerable and precisely here they launched strong counter-attacks. I decided, therefore... to report to Ludendorff that we simply had to call a halt. If it was not possible for us to achieve a breakthrough when we had surprise, it was certainly not possible now that the British had apparently brought up strong forces. There are no more troops available to us... In the evening, therefore, I drove to Le Cateau, agreed all this with Marwitz and Stapff and reported to Ludendorff, who was in agreement."

Following on from that meeting, von der Marwitz issued the following order, 'The attack will not be renewed on 2 December. The ground gained is to be held. Group Caudry is to capture Masnières and La Vacquerie by means of deliberate attacks.'[18] At his headquarters that evening, the Army Group Commander expanded his earlier diary entry, with a fuller review of the events of the day.

Crown Prince Rupprecht of Bavaria: Diary Entry 1 December 1917 [19]

"By midday the situation was as follows: attacks against our left flank from the direction of Epéhy had been beaten off. The enemy had also attacked from Gouzeaucourt and against Gonnelieu where, making use of their tanks, they managed temporarily to thrust forward to our gun lines. La Vacquerie Farm is in enemy hands and was apparently yesterday either never in our hands or only briefly. Our troops had pushed forward into Les Rues Vertes, a suburb of Masnières, but the British were still holding out in Masnières, Marcoing and Noyelles. Detonations could be heard coming from the two last named places. It was probable that the enemy were blowing bridges or dugouts. The report by [Second] Army Headquarters that heavy howitzers need to be redeployed against Masnières and that that place cannot be captured for two to three days, produced the response directed by me that there was no requirement to capture Masnières; rather that every effort should be made to cut off the Masnières salient to the east of Marcoing.

"The 9th Bavarian Reserve Division was sent into action this morning and is currently near Gonnelieu and attacking towards Gouzeaucourt. One regiment of 79th Reserve Division has been pushed forward, but the remainder is in reserve behind the left flank of the offensive. All appears to be calm on the Lewarde sector. In other words the 16th Bavarian Division, the reinforcement by which was demanded urgently yesterday by Second Army and approved, has not been sent into action. The strong resistance which has met our attacks can only be explained by the fact that the enemy had just finished its reliefs in the line and that, therefore, the troops which had just been relieved were still in the area.[20]

"Yesterday ammunition expenditure corresponded to thirty train loads and Second Army has placed ammunition demands for the next few days which are so high that they cannot be met. Once the attack had stalled, the situation before the other Army Groups argued against its continuation. Army Group German Crown Prince has provided its two best assault divisions.

"Despite my direction yesterday, Masnières was attacked and the enemy have now evacuated it.[21] Had the attack taken place further to the west, withdrawal from the place would hardly have been possible. Regardless of continuing gas shoots against Bourlon Wood, the British are still holding out within it. It may be that strong winds have substantially reduced the effect of the gas. It appears that the extreme right flank of the British, Epéhy, is only being held by cavalry. Because of the sharp increase in size of Second Army, the introduction of another Group Headquarters between Groups Arras and Caudry should be considered. On the other hand, now that it has become rather quieter along the battlefront, thoughts should be turning to a gradual withdrawal of some divisions."

Although 2 December was to be a relatively quiet day after all the heavy fighting of the past two weeks, there were still minor operations up and down the line. Out on the northern extremity of the battlefield, the regiments of 111th Infantry Division continued to harass the opposing British units. One such raid took place during the early hours of 2 December. For the men involved, it was almost business as usual once more.

Vizefeldwebel Specht 12th Company Infantry Regiment 164 [22]

"At the evening Orders Group on 1 December, I was given the task by the company commander, Reserve Leutnant Paetz, of commanding an officer's patrol at about midnight. One section of the regimental assault troop was to be put at my disposal for the purpose. The mission was more or less as follows:

'To advance along the line of the embankment which ran at ninety degrees towards the enemy position, in order to determine if an advanced post about 150 metres forward of our position was occupied and, if so, to push on further and attempt to capture prisoners.'

"Because of the non-appearance of the assault group, I was forced to make use of men from my own platoon. This caused a delay in the departure of the patrol. At about 1.30 am, I set off with two gefreiters and four men. The night was calm; the moon had already risen, but was hidden behind clouds. The first objective of the patrol was soon achieved. The advanced post, as had always been the case previously, was unoccupied. From this point an overgrown, partially collapsed trench, which was about knee deep, ran along the base of the embankment towards the enemy position. I made use of this to advance. Keeping low, repeatedly crawling then pausing, checking from time to time from the top of the embankment that we were not under threat, we made steady progress.

"The biggest obstacle we had to overcome was the British wire, but we were in luck; there was a gap by the embankment. Creeping forward carefully and lying down on the far side, we crossed the obstacle noiselessly. A few more metres and we found ourselves immediately in front of the British trench. The helmet of the sentry could be seen plainly sticking up between the piles of chalk which had been thrown up. It was now essential to act decisively before the sentry, who had his back to us and who we later discovered to be asleep, sitting in front of a dugout, spotted us. To the right of the embankment the trench did not continue, but branched off into one of the dugouts located under the embankment. To the left the trench was not continuous either.

"The sentry post was located behind a parapet, about three to four metres from the dugout. I had the four men take up positions in a half circle round the sentry post and ordered them to secure the left flank and to be ready to intervene in the expected fight if necessary. I had to forego security to the right but, after a quick reconnaissance, found I could do so without concern. I decided that the two gefreiters and I would attack the sentry, from the section of trench to the right of the parapet and we entered the trench completely unnoticed. We slipped off the safety catches of our pistols and prepared our hand grenades. I shouted *'Los!'* [Go!] and we charged. This was followed by a yell from the sentry who, when he saw us, must have thought his time was up. He leapt up, attempting to release the safety catch of his rifle and point it at us. I ripped his rifle off him so that he could do us no more harm but his shouts had woken some men who were resting to his left in a roughly covered section of trench. As I struggled with him I could feel that someone was trying to use my back as a target for bayonet practice, but the narrowness of the trench, however, hindered the attempt. I broke free of my first opponent and faced the new one, tearing his rifle with its fixed bayonet from him and so removed the immediate threat to me. My two gefreiters were now struggling hand to hand with the first opponent and, because the remainder of my men had arrived, I left the second opponent to them and turned my attention to those still sheltering in the covered trench.

"They had had no time to prepare for a fight; perhaps they had hoped that having covered the entrance with a blanket they would not be noticed. In the moonlight I could make out that there were three of them. I grabbed one and hurled him back over the other two, which made serious resistance difficult. Threatening them with the pistol, I demanded their surrender. The response was wild shouting. I kept my pistol trained on them for about a minute, when suddenly a hand grenade exploded outside. My pressing question was what had happened; had the other two managed to hold out? I left the three men in the dugout and exited. The two British soldiers stood there, resigned to their fate, but my courageous runner, Gefreiter Knöllke, was moaning from the pain of a serious wound.

"In the struggle the British had torn one of the grenades off his belt, had pulled its cord and thrown it at his feet. Apparently the two gefreiters in the trench had noticed this too late or had been unable to prevent it due to the narrowness of the trench. They were also too late to throw themselves clear of the trench. As a result of the explosion of the grenade in the trench, Gefreiter Knöllke's feet were quite badly injured. However this also marked the final extinguishing of the British resistance. I directed them out of the trench, as I did the three in the dugout and despatched them back to our lines under the control of my four other men. Helped by Gefreiter Heuer, I lifted the wounded man out of the sentry position. Heuer lifted him on to his back and carried him back like that.

"I myself looked in vain for some time for my cap which had been lost in the heat of battle then, taking the Lewis gun which lay on the parapet, together with the two weapons belonging to the gefreiters, I was the last to make my way back under the full moon, feeling calm and serene. When I arrived, the prisoners were already lined up in front of the company headquarters dugout. They comprised one corporal and four men of the [Royal] Dublin Fusiliers. They were young men who did not seem to have suffered much in being captured; rather they were pleased that their war was over. As a reward for the successful outcome of this patrol, the two gefreiters were promoted to Unteroffizier, the other four members received the Iron Cross Second Class and I the Iron Cross First Class."

There was special mention of this successful patrol action in the Corps Routine order issued by Group Lewarde on 2 December 1917.

"At 1.30 am 2 December 1917, a patrol of 12th Company Infantry Regiment 164, commanded by Vizefeldwebel Specht and carried out west of Fontaine le Croisilles, overwhelmed an enemy post and, following a short battle, captured a corporal and four men of the British infantry regiment Dublin Fusiliers (X Company) 48 Brigade, 16th Division, together with a Lewis gun. Excellent leadership, dash and energy led to this shining success. I wish to express my special recognition to the brave commander, Vizefeldwebel Specht, as well as the other participants: Gefreiters Heuer and Knolke and Musketiers Elsserling, Schwarten, Hild and Bendix for their courageous conduct.

Albrecht

Corps Commander" [23]

During the day, Commander Second Army took advantage of the lull in operations to spend the entire day visiting the corps and divisional commanders who had been responsible for the thrust from the east.

General der Kavallerie Georg von der Marwitz [24]

"I drove to each of the seven divisions of Groups Busigny and Caudry, expressing my appreciation and recognition of all of them.

The figures for captured men and material have increased substantially. They have now reached 6,500 prisoners and about one hundred guns. We have had a local success, but it is not going to be possible to develop it into a lengthy offensive operation. But how have we fought the British up to now? - just defence and more defence. Nobody ever came around to the view that attack was the best form of defence. Who since the beginning of positional warfare, for that matter, has ever captured 6,000 British soldiers? The prisoners have stated that they were totally surprised by this attack."

Elsewhere, bombardments continued and there were localised attempts to improve particular positions, or to eject parties of British troops from sections of trench which provided observation or defiladed firing points, which threatened the German advanced posts. One such operation was mounted by elements of 220th Infantry Division. Commanded by Major von Holtzendorff, commanding officer 1st Battalion Reserve Infantry Regiment 55 and involving assault groups from Infantry Regiment 395 and Infantry Regiment 190, it aimed to storm and capture the third line of the *Zwischenstellung*, just to the east of La Vacquerie and its southern extension, the *Sonderburgerweg*, which led right up to the southeast corner of La Vacquerie. Writing after the war, the commander of 1st Machine Gun Company provided a somewhat overblown account of the operation. Nevertheless it was a well-worked initiative and the ground gained proved to be useful when a deliberate attack went in against La Vacquerie the following day. Once it became clear during the course of the fighting that progress was being made and that a little more effort would probably pay dividends, 4th Guards Infantry Brigade committed its own reserve. The additional forces enabled the attackers to roll up the trenches a considerable way in each direction.

Leutnant Steller 1st Machine Gun Company Reserve Infantry Regiment [25]

"On 2 December, the order arrived that the attack was to be continued. After a short artillery bombardment, the attack began at 3.00 pm. Once more the gallant men of Reserve Infantry Regiment 55 stormed forward from the shattered trenches towards their objective. In front of 3rd and 6th Companies the British position was protected by a strong obstacle. Leutnant Wittich of 3rd Company and his assault group smoked them out and, shortly after the German artillery fire fell silent, it was captured and we pressed on. Two British machine guns prevented a further advance. Gefreiter Ohm and Musketier Mathies crept up to one of them and, before the British realised what was happening, grenades thrown by the daring lads were exploding around their ears.

"Gefreiter Bramkamp of 1st Machine Gun Company was unable to silence the other gun with his machine gun. Crawling forward alone along a sap, he worked his way forward towards the British, but then he was spotted. A shot went through his gas mask, but then his pistol cracked. The enemy gunner collapsed and the remainder of the crew pulled out. Putting the enemy machine gun across his shoulder, he crawled back to his gun. With that, the way was clear. Driving the British before them like hares, the assaulting troops gained the third trench, but then machine gun fire from the right came down amongst the ranks of the attackers, forcing them to halt once more. It was now certain that the British would launch a counter-attack against this much-weakened first assault wave.

"Spotting the danger and despite ever increasing casualties, Leutnant Eble manoeuvred his machine gun platoon right into the front line, so as not to leave his infantry comrades in the lurch. Already the British had launched a counter-stroke from north to south in order to cut off the trench garrison. As though he was running for his life, Leutnant Staarmann, commander of 3rd Company, raced to the rear to summon help, which he duly received. With great spirit and energy he led the reinforcements forward and reorganised the defence, so that the various British attacks were beaten off with bloody casualties. The explosion of hand grenades could be heard coming from the north. The 2nd Battalion was pushing forward, in order to roll up the trench from that direction and the men of 1st and 2nd Battalions greeted them with thunderous *Hurras*.

"A shining victory had been achieved. The old aggressive attacking spirit of 1914 was still alive within the regiment, enabling it to achieve such successes. Twenty two guns, numerous machine guns and hundreds of prisoners[26] were a measure of the success of this assault. However, it was victory bought at high cost."

The Army Group Commander, whose own thoughts and efforts were already concentrating on the operations which were to follow, drew the main threads of the counter-attack together in his diary that evening. For him the entire conduct of the battle since 20 November had been marred by interference from Ludendorff and annoyance at the way his level of command was bypassed regularly by Supreme Army Headquarters. It is, of course, far from certain that had the Crown Prince's wishes been followed exactly the German army would have enjoyed any more success, but it is clear from his words that he, for one, was of that opinion.

Crown Prince Rupprecht of Bavaria: Diary Entry 2 December 1917 [27]

"Because of the possibility of a renewed tank attack Second Army is going to place its main line of resistance as close to the *Schelde* [St Quentin] Canal as possible, in order that artillery support may be provided from the other bank.

"The results of our attack south of Cambrai have not been completely satisfactory. The main effort was not placed on the left flank. As late as yesterday morning the opportunity would, perhaps, have arisen to obtain a great success, had reserves been available at the decisive point: but they were lacking. In addition several of the divisions which arrived later were spread along the front. A minor setback at an unimportant point is of little consequence if it means that a decisive advantage can be pressed home at a more important place.

"The fact that the Second Army offensive did not unfold in the desired manner can in part be traced back to the fact that at the Le Cateau conference General Ludendorff stressed the importance of the Flesquières heights and, making a bold line on the map with a charcoal pen, indicated how the heights were to be seized. At this General von der Marwitz stated, 'I shall pay particular attention to this curve.'

"As a result Second Army placed the main emphasis on the direction of Trescault instead of Metz en Couture. Had the latter taken priority, the problematic attack on Flesquières would have been superfluous.

"The question as to whether we had suspended the attack too soon is explained by the fact that we could not have made available any fresh divisions to carry on the attack before next morning, because they only arrived gradually by rail. Even though there could have been greater success, nevertheless it is the greatest we have achieved over the British since the gas attack of Fourth Army in Spring 1915 at Ypres. Their future plans have been painfully disrupted and they have suffered serious casualties in the narrow salient southwest of Cambrai. 6,000 prisoners and seventy guns have been captured."

There was an interesting footnote to the events of the day on 2 December, which occurred during a telephone conversation between Ludendorff and General von Kuhl as they discussed some of the reasons for the failure of the counter-attack to achieve all its ambitious aims.

General der Infanterie Hermann von Kuhl Chief of Staff Army Group Crown Prince Rupprecht [28]

"This evening Ludendorff asked my opinion about Stapff and I expressed my doubts. We ought to have been able to achieve much more on 30 [November]. The situation was so favourable and we can expect no [such opportunity] again soon. Along the canal the British presented a virtually open flank. They had been careless, over confident and were surprised. With the strong forces [at our disposal] we should have done more. [Stapff is] clever, but insufficiently resolute. He does not have a firm grip of events."

It is significant once more to note the drift of this conversation. Possibly the performance of General der Kavallerie von der Marwitz featured but, if it did, von Kuhl did not see fit to mention it at the time in his diary. It is clear that both men held Major Stapff more or less solely responsible for the planning, conduct and outcome of the counter-attack. It is quite possible that the peevish tone of the diary note was born out of frustration at the way hopes of a great victory were dashed. Post war, von Kuhl did soften his judgement somewhat, writing in *Der Weltkrieg 1914/1918* that, given the circumstances of its launch, 'the performance of Headquarters Second Army, its commander, General der Kavallerie von der Marwitz and its chief of staff, Major Stapff, together with that of the Group Headquarters and all troop commanders merited the highest recognition.'[29] He also added a comment to his original diary entry on 14 August 1932, 'It must be borne in mind [how] extremely difficult it is to launch swiftly and correctly such an improvised counter-attack, with reinforcements being drawn in from all sides!'[30]

At 8.30 am on 3 December, troops of the British 183 Brigade of 61st Division attempted to retake the trenches to the east of La Vacquerie, which had been captured the previous afternoon. The attack, which was actually launched by only two companies of 2/5th Warwickshire of 182 Brigade, was far too weak to achieve anything and, sure enough, it was easily beaten off by troops of 28th Infantry Division, who were waiting to launch their own assault on La Vacquerie. It was almost the final set piece attack of the German counter-offensive and was pressed home after a short bombardment at 9.30 am by 2nd Battalion Fusilier Regiment 40 and 3rd Battalion Grenadier Regiment 110, with the remainder of the two regiments being fed into the battle as it progressed. Following the preliminary moves the previous day, the attackers had a very good idea about the defensive layout. They devised a simple plan and carried it through, rapidly pushing men of the Gloucestershire Regiment out of the village, though at a high cost in casualties. Writing home after the battle, one of the fusiliers described what happened.

Füsilier Karl Felber 6th Company Fusilier Regiment 40 [31]

"The village was to be stormed in the morning. I prepared myself for the attack then, about 9.30 am, our drum fire began to come down. A few minutes later the enemy artillery opened up in reply. It was dreadful. The enemy artillery fire was very accurate and a shell soon burst against the wall of the trench. Luckily only one of our comrades was wounded. I rushed round to another traverse with my mate. There was another direct hit on the trench and three of my pals lay dead around me. This was anything but the way to boost our courage. Soon we got the order, 'Up and out of the trench!'

"I leapt up with my other comrades and we raced towards the village, By the time we reached it, a few moments later, we were completely out of breath. There were already bullets whistling past our ears, but nothing could stop us. In La Vacquerie itself, the British fought desperately, but a few well aimed grenades brought them to their senses or disposed of them. Moving through the village, I bumped into four gunners, who simply wanted to get clear of the clouds of dust and dirt. They were not particularly courageous, because, as soon as they saw me, they raised their hands and started jabbering away nineteen to the dozen, but I could not understand what they were saying. Together with some of my mates, I pushed on.

"We arrived at a large and deep dugout which housed about thirty Tommies. They were still wearing their equipment and were carrying their weapons in their hands, but we only had to reach for our belts where our grenades were hanging and they raised their hands to the sky and begged for their lives. Once the last of them had left the dugout I went inside and found so many cigarettes that I had supplies to last until Christmas. We then pushed on further. Our own gunners were still bringing fire down on the village, which cost several fusiliers their lives. This fire did not slacken off for some hours, then we all took up fire positions, because we expected a counter-attack. Then came the order for our relief, but it was not until 3.00 am that the 65th arrived."

In fact Felber had been extremely lucky to survive. This was a costly attack, pressed home in the teeth of heavy British artillery and machine gun fire and numerous counter-attacks. To the north, the worn out 220th Infantry Division had already been relieved by 9th Bavarian Reserve Division now, around 2.00 am, units of 185th Infantry Division arrived at La Vacquerie to take over from 28th Infantry Division. The two day battle turned the village into a Valhalla for the men of Fusilier Regiment 40. They regarded its capture subsequently as one of their most outstanding achievements of the entire war, which also says much about the tenacity with which it was defended. On arrival there, 3rd Battalion Infantry Regiment 65 was strong enough on its own to take over from the entire regiment. This was just as well, because the threat to the northern flank was such that 1st Battalion Infantry Regiment 65 of 185th Infantry Division had had to be moved from reserve and placed under commander of Grenadier Regiment 110 just before it went dark on 3 December.[32]

Moving back to Walincourt, the men of Fusilier Regiment 40 were a sad, badly hit remnant. Field Hospital 262 was full of wounded men and the adjacent cemetery was a sea of freshly dug graves. Nine officers had been killed and ten others wounded. 126 other ranks were dead, 416 were wounded and sixty six were missing – virtually all of them killed or wounded. One consolation was the number of prisoners they and Grenadier Regiment 110 took. In all there were about 900 and they also recovered twenty guns, two hundred light and heavy machine guns and much other *materiel* besides. When they and the other formations of the reinforcing divisions left Group Caudry, they received a special mention in an Order of the Day issued by the commander.[33]

> "After the enemy's attempts at a breakthrough on 20 November was wrecked by the tough defence put up by troops under my command, the enemy has gone on to suffer additional severe blows in the course of bitterly fought battles. Displaying irresistible attacking zeal, all arms and service on land and in the air have vied with each other to throw themselves at the enemy, who defended themselves obstinately. Several thousand prisoners and the capture of a large number of guns and machine guns are outward, visible signs of our success. To all troops, units and formations involved I express my thanks and recognition and to our fallen go my honoured thoughts. The days of Cambrai will live on, shining brightly in military history. This is the heaviest blow delivered to the British since the days of victory at Le Cateau and St Quentin.
>
> "My deepest thanks go to all commanders and their staffs who, through tireless work, prepared the operations and saw them through to a victorious conclusion.
>
> "Following these glorious but difficult days the 28th and 220th Infantry Divisions leave the ranks of the Group. To them fell especially difficult attacking tasks [after] 30 November. They can look back with pride on the days [they fought] at Cambrai and La Vacquerie. I send them and their battle-proven commanders comradely greetings and my best wishes for the future. May you be granted further future brilliant successes.
>
> The Corps Commander
> Freiherr von Watter
> General der Infanterie"

Continuing on from his tour of Groups Caudry and Busigny the previous day, commander Second Army spent 3 December along the northern sector of his front. He had expressly forbidden Generalleutnant von Moser, the Group Commander, to be present for his visits to the divisions, causing the latter to make another bitter entry in his diary about what he considered to be his inappropriate treatment and incorrect working methods.[34]

General der Kavallerie Georg von der Marwitz [35]

"I drove to see the divisions on the northern flank, where they had fought courageously but not with the same success the southern flank had enjoyed. The performance of 20th Division was heroic, as was that of 3rd Guards Division especially. Grenadier Regiment 9 and the *Maikäfer* [Fusilier Guards] were quite outstanding.[36] The situation on the flanks of the main thrust is far from simple, because the canal runs directly behind. Although we have numerous bridges, the enemy, naturally, can keep them under heavy fire and drench them with gas. That has to be borne in mind. It was bitterly cold, because of a combination of frost and strong winds. However, furs and travel rugs proved to be effective."

The favourable views of the Army Commander were echoed a little later in a letter home written by one of the company commanders of the elite Lehr Infantry Regiment. There is little doubt that the performance of 3rd Guards Infantry Division was one of the primary reasons why, during the most critical days, the British army was unable to gain possession of Bourlon Ridge.

Reserve Leutnant Krümmel 1st Company Lehr Infantry Regiment [37]

"It is necessary to add a few words about the spirit of the men, the unteroffiziers and platoon commanders that I had the honour to command. It is true to say that when we saw, in most cases for the first time, the feared tanks, we were more or less terror struck. Once we realised, however, that we could successfully counter tanks with machine guns, they lost their shock effect. In fact these latest weapons did very little damage to us at that time. The great danger of being captured by the enemy imbued the troops with desperate courage. Only soldiers who were in total harmony with their superiors could have survived these trying times so well. Each wanted to outdo the other in terms of courage so, when the enemy attacked, the majority left the protection of the trenches and engaged them in the open from a standing position. In this respect, too, the officers and NCOs provided the men with a brilliantly daring example.

"Despite the awful surroundings – during this especially cold period we lay out in the open with no shelter whatsoever – there was not a word of complaint. It was accepted as a necessary evil. The fact that the food did not arrive on time (and sometimes not at all) was most unpleasant, but everyone could see that nothing could be done about it. I received especially strong support from the platoon commanders: Landwehr Leutnant Grensing and Vizefeldwebels Geshke and

Scheffler. The same was true of Sergeant Westphal and Unteroffiziers Weichenhahn and Schlüter. The success that the company achieved made heroes of even the most faint hearted. Every member of the company who experienced these days, can look back with pride and satisfaction on Bourlon."

The words of the Army Commander, just quoted, form an altogether more charitable overall view of events on the Group Arras front than that expressed by Generalfeldmarschall von Hindenburg in a formal note to Ludendorff on 11 December 1917 concerning the events of 30 November. 'From my reading of the report, it seems to me that the attack did not make the progress that would have been desirable because, from the start, the *Schwerpunkt* was not placed on the capture of the dominant Hill 100. The local Group and Divisional Commanders ought to have been able, based on their knowledge of the terrain, to recognise those points whose possession were of decisive importance for the success of the attack and, on that basis, to have organised and conducted the tactical battle. I cannot avoid drawing the conclusion that these principles were not given clear expression by Group Arras. I request your comments to these remarks.'[38]

It is not known how Ludendorff phrased his reply. It is clear, however, that the official historian did not share Hindenburg's view, blaming instead the delayed H Hour and the gaps in the concentrations of smoke and gas, which meant that there was absolutely no surprise in the north.[39] Nevertheless, the fact that doubts were being expressed up the chain of command about Generalleutnant von Moser after Cambrai may well have been a factor in his handing over command of his corps early in 1918. He was far from well and not even a lengthy period of home leave at the end of 1917 had restored his health and energy. Moser does not explain the full circumstances of his departure, so it is difficult to assess if he asked to be relieved or was forced to go. Possibly he was told that no objections would be raised if he requested to hand over command. During a period of three and a half years he had served Württemberg and the wider German army with distinction and his handling of the critical fighting for Bourlon Ridge throughout most of the Battle of Cambrai was an achievement in which any general would take pride.

Whilst Second Army Commander had been touring the northern front on 3 December, General von Moser of Group Arras had submitted a detailed plan to attack Bourlon Wood on 4 December, reasoning that, after a bombardment which still continued day and night, a surprise attack would be likely to succeed. It seems that there was knowledge of this plan all the way up to Army Group level, because Crown Prince Rupprecht commented on it in his diary entry for 3 December.

Crown Prince Rupprecht of Bavaria: Diary Entry 3 December 1917 [40]

"Numerous enemy machine guns are still firing from Bourlon Wood. Because enemy troops are not actually holding the edge of the wood but are operating from positions further back, Group Arras hopes to advance from the west and southwest edges of the wood and also from the gravel pit at Fontaine and so gradually retake it. There has been some progress at Marcoing and the same applies to 28th Division at La Vacquerie. Once the heights there have been captured this division is to be withdrawn from the line then, together with the 34th, it will be returned to Army Group German Crown Prince. Altogether six divisions are to be extracted from the Second Army front. Preparations for this are already under way. On the enemy side of the lines a great deal of activity has been detected in the Havrincourt area. The great mass of enemy artillery is concentrated around Graincourt and can be engaged there successfully."

The Group Arras aim was to launch an assault during the afternoon of 4 December from the east, north and west, preceded by a four hour intensive bombardment. Moser's thinking was that it was probable that the British would at some point decide to withdraw from Bourlon Wood, so his attack would provide a final chance to deliver a morale-sapping blow and to capture a large numbers of machine guns and other *materiel*. Whilst the plans for a preliminary bombardment by thirty six batteries of all calibres of artillery piece from heavy howitzers to light field howitzers were being set in train and Moser had departed for discussions with his divisional commanders who were due to carry out the attack, his proposals were rejected by Second Army.

Moser was furious. Convinced that someone on his staff had been in discussion with Major Stapff at Headquarters Second Army behind his back and had put forward a view of the feasibility of the attack at variance to his own, Moser contacted Stapff himself to be told that attacking Bourlon Wood with the means at his disposal would be like launching an assault on, 'the fortified positions at Verdun.' [41] Moser disagreed strenuously, but it made no difference. The following day the Army Commander drove to Moser's headquarters for talks.

General der Kavallerie Georg von der Marwitz [42]

"I drove to Group Arras for lengthy discussions concerning our plans for the coming days. General[leutnant Otto von] Moser possesses boundless energy, but he has to be reined in, otherwise he tends to launch into things which cannot be justified. During my return journey I passed through Caudry, where forty four guns had been brought together on the market place. The British paint their guns to camouflage them. The base coat is grey then shades of red blue and green are applied on top. This is to make aerial observation more difficult. The greater proportion of guns could not be recovered. We could not spare the necessary teams of horses and it was too far forward for towing vehicles to be employed. I think that we shall still be able to bring in at least some of them, but the remainder will have to be blown up...Some of the guns were turned round and used against the British, so as to ensure that the munitions, which were very numerous, were delivered to the correct address."

That same evening the Army Group Commander set out his personal assessment of the situation, which is of particular interest, because it is probably a more accurate reflection of his real views than those which appeared in an Army Group order prepared only the previous day, in which the emphasis was placed on ensuring that none of the armies under command were surprised by possible British counter-action.

Crown Prince Rupprecht of Bavaria: Diary Entry 4 December 1917 [43]

"In view of the heavy casualties which the British suffered, the terrible situation in which they find themselves southwest of Cambrai, together with the fact that currently they only have eleven divisions in reserve, some of which are required for purposes of relief, the British will have to set aside any thoughts of attack for a considerable time. It is even feasible that they will be forced by our concentrated artillery fire to evacuate the salient which juts out to the southwest of Cambrai.

"Thus far the British army communiqué has remained silent about the defeat at Cambrai, only announcing the capture of some German machine guns near Bourlon between the 2nd and 3rd. Our victory at Cambrai is extremely timely and of great significance when considered in conjunction with events in Italy and Russia. The fatal outcome for them of the battles around Cambrai will no doubt give the British pause for thought and is bound to reduce their belief in ultimate victory. So I can go and spend a few carefree days in the Homeland."

Headquarters Army Group Crown Prince Rupprecht Ia Nr. 4679 Secret 3.12.17 [44]

"Our success will force the British to bring up strong reserves. They will have to secure their difficult situation in the Flesquières salient and assume that we intend to continue our operations. It is to be expected that the British will attempt to improve their situation by means of counter-attacks. The extent and duration of battles arising from that cause cannot be determined. At any rate the attack launched by our Second Army has certainly brought about an easing of the pressure along the remainder of the British front. As soon as the situation in the Second Army sector becomes calm, it must be assumed that the British will conduct other limited surprise attacks – using tanks wherever possible – at other places...

"All armies are to carry out detailed checks and reconnaissance urgently – especially along so-called quiet fronts – in order to check on readiness to respond to surprise attacks and to be certain that suitable arrangements are in place to facilitate the call forward of reserves. Anti-tank defences are to be put in place. This includes quiet fronts. All terrain over which tanks can operate is to be subject to detailed reconnaissance and is to be prepared to counter any such attack."

As he prepared to depart for two weeks leave in Germany, it is obvious the future potential of the tanks to cause major problems for the German defences was high on the Army Group agenda. Before departing for Munich, the Crown Prince signed off additional guidance on the subject to all of the armies and groups under command. [45]

"Wherever the ground offers suitable going for tanks, surprise attacks like this may be expected... It will not be possible to provide all such sectors of the front with the most important defensive materiel. It must, therefore, be established in which places tank attacks are possible. Bogs, swamps, riverbeds and canals more or less rule out the use of tanks, as do very steep slopes, deep railway cuttings and high embankments. In the case of watercourses, checks must be made to ensure that they offer sufficient protection. Bridges must not be able to bear the weight of tanks. If necessary stronger bridges must be replaced with others of lighter wooden construction or drawbridges must be substituted. Routes into villages and other choke points are to be barricaded in such a manner that tanks cannot simply drive in, but space must be left for normal vehicles to negotiate them. Tank traps are only useful if it is impossible to divert around them."

Already before the fighting had died away completely, the Army Group was demanding after action reports from all formations concerned in both the defensive and offensive operations in the Cambrai area. [46] Whilst his staff was hard at work collating replies and beginning the preparation of its major after action report, the Second Army Commander took the opportunity in a letter home to reflect on the outcome of the counter-attack from his personal perspective.

General der Kavallerie Georg von der Marwitz [47]

"Nowadays a victory looks entirely different to the way it used to. Moltke encircled then trapped his enemy. In the age of trench warfare and tanks this is no longer possible. The resistance generated by trench lines and the great, tangled obstacle belts in amongst which the enemy takes cover in numerous *Stollen* (and not the edible kind),[48] is extraordinarily great and can only be overcome gradually. However, the attritional power of the offensive, even against an obstinate opponent, gradually takes effect. This is the way it was here. The shining success of 30 November and 1 December paved the way to today's victory.

"The broad salient , running from Moeuvres – Bourlon – [Bourlon] Wood – Cantaing – Noyelles – Crévecœur – Banteux is that which the British captured on 20 November (and the days which followed). Our former line ran direct from Moeuvres to Banteux. The arrows[49] indicate how the shape of the salient changed, which meant that from all sides enfilade fire could be brought against it. Today I was just about to organise the preparations for the recapture of Bourlon Wood but, at about midday, a report arrived stating that the enemy was withdrawing and that several villages were in flames. How far that will be continued cannot be determined at present. It is probable that the British will occupy a position which we had prepared previously and which runs more or less past Flesquières. In my opinion this retreat amounts to an acknowledgement that a complete defeat was inflicted on 30 November.

"A very large number of prisoners were captured: 7,500 for certain, together with well over one hundred guns, of which thirty were blown up. The greater part was recovered or will be soon. I drove out to see what was happening, but was overtaken by darkness and could only establish that the British fire directed at us was very weak. I passed one place where very many horses were lying around and discovered that it was where the British had launched a mounted attack, which ran into machine gun fire. Here and there, riders lay next to their horses. They were Indians who, back in their homeland, could hardly have imagined that they would give their lives for the British in northern France. There were also many tanks scattered about...

It was obviously hell in Bourlon Wood and that is the reason why the British have given it up. Relinquishment of the adjacent terrain was the necessary consequence. I then drove to Group Arras. Whilst I was still in the wood, heavy fighting was going on nearby; the Saxons were moving their positions further forward, but the British did not fire on the wood itself. I have a very exact knowledge of

Bourlon Wood. There was an army observation tower there which I frequently visited. How different it all looked now. At the front I met up with an independent machine gun company, which was just about to move forward and I was able to give the men some cigars."

As active operations on the Cambrai front drew to a conclusion, following the British withdrawal from the vulnerable and virtually indefensible Bourlon – Noyelles – Marcoing salient, the Saxon 24th Reserve Division was involved in a final attempt to recapture Flesquières. This involved it in clashes with the British 59th Division, which was temporarily holding the so-called Covering Position. Arriving from Flanders as a reinforcing formation, originally it was planned that it would relieve units of 119th Infantry Division southwest of Cambrai. These orders were changed twice. On 4 December a warning order arrived that 24th Reserve Division, in association with 221st Infantry Division, was to clear the British out of Bourlon Wood. Orders having been given, this operation was first postponed by order of Second Army and then rendered superfluous when the British army accepted that in this sector it was deeply outflanked on both sides and withdrew from the wood. The final hours for the British had been a terrible experience. The wood had been kept under very heavy bombardment for hours on end and a great deal of gas was mixed in with the high explosive. Witnesses later described traversing the wood to find it littered all over with the bodies of the fallen; many of whom had succumbed to gas poisoning and had died in appalling circumstances. Some claimed subsequently that the dreadful effect of gas shells was more apparent here than on any other battlefield of the war.

Meanwhile orders arrived for the regiments of 24th Reserve Division to move forward to assembly areas around Anneux, prior to launching an assault on 6 December towards the south on a two thousand metre front from Graincourt to La Justice towards Flesquières. Reserve Infantry Regiments 104 (right) and 107 (left) deployed in readiness for the attack. Reconnaissance patrols pushed forward that morning established that the enemy was holding the area of La Justice Farm and the hills to the west of it. 3.45 pm was selected as the start time for the attack, which was preceded by an intense thirty minute artillery bombardment. Punctually at the appointed hour, the waves of attackers set off. Supported by artillery fire and an overhead machine gun barrage, Reserve Infantry Regiment 104 on the right near Graincourt had captured its first objectives by 4.00 pm, Leutnant Schütze succeeding in taking out a gun, which was bringing down heavy destructive fire, by means of an attack with hand grenades. Unfortunately, as the advance continued towards Flesquières, British machine guns began to take a heavy toll of the assaulting troops and the leading companies were soon pinned down and unable to advance. Some progress had been made but, later that day, Reserve Infantry Regiment 104 had to withdraw about

500 metres to a more defensible position and begin to dig in. The attack had cost the lives of Leutnants Gille, Wagner, Weidemüller and Säuberlich, together with Feldwebel-Leutnant Mehnert, Offizierstellvertreter Härtel and forty nine other ranks. The numbers wounded were correspondingly high. For the time being there could be no question of a resumption of the assault on Flesquières from that direction.[50]

Meanwhile, to their left, Reserve Infantry Regiment 107 had been fighting for the possession of La Justice Farm. The adjutant and commander of its 3rd Battalion both left vivid accounts of the events of the day:

Reserve Leutnant Hiecke Adjutant 3rd Battalion Reserve Infantry Regiment 107 [51]

"There was no argument, the first attack wave of the battalion raced away from the start line near Anneux, the Rittmeister [Gelpke] in their midst, as though the Devil was at their heels. The second wave followed up and then the third, with which the adjutant was to advance. Still located in the sunken road Anneux-Cantaing he saw the ghostly forms of the British through the fog and the smoke as they pulled back from Flesquières and over the heights. The first prisoners arrived, declaring solemnly that German prisoners would be treated like gentlemen in England. They would be able to swim and play lawn tennis. Our comrade, who was accompanying the transport, seemed to have taken that to heart, because he disappeared for days and, when he finally returned to the company, he had so stretched his orders to get the prisoners to the rear that he had brought his beloved gentlemen in a series of daily stages all the way to the Lille area. All the papers were perfectly in order.

"The first of the wounded began arriving, then more and more; one of whom had clearly seen that the Rittmeister had been wounded in the hand and that the blood was dripping down. At that the adjutant could delay no longer. He handed over command responsibility to the nearest officer and hurried forward with his runners. The farm had just been captured. British hurricane lamps were still alight in the cellar. Evening had fallen, the front line was just in front of Orival Wood, held by a mixture of troops from the 3rd and 1st Battalion, together with Prussians from the neighbouring regiment to the left. Leutnant Unger took over command and, when the adjutant returned to the farm, which doubtless was to become the *KTK*,[52] there was no sign of the Rittmeister. The Machine Gun Company, under Oberleutnant Hetzschel, had taken up positions there and the cellar was crammed with the wounded.

"Fortunately our gallant signaller had already laid a cable to the rear and when we inaugurated it, we were greeted by a friendly voice: 'This is Gelpke.' Hurrah, he is still in the land of the living, bless him! Fit, well and, apparently, unharmed. He had searched the length and breadth of the battlefield and having established the new front rushed to the nearest telephone to report in to the regiment. He had probably gone to Anneux, not realising that the signals detachment had worked so fast."

It remained only to find out how the commanding officer came to be 'wounded.' He later explained it as follows:

Hauptmann Gelpke 3rd Battalion Reserve Infantry Regiment 107 [53]

"The attacking waves advanced by the book, as though they were on the parade square; whilst the continual drum roll of the rapid overhead machine gun fire promoted an acceleration of the speed of movement. It was not long, however, before the British became aware of the attack and they began to bring their own machine gun fire down over the open ground. Suddenly I had the sensation in my left thigh that somebody was trying to apply a wet compress to it and liquid was running down my leg. I had heard that in the first instant after wounding nothing was felt, so I thought that I had better check if I was wounded. I threw myself down and discovered, after opening my outer clothing, that my undergarments were coloured blood red. Despite a thorough examination, I could find no sign of wounding, not even a superficial scratch. It was not the moment to continue to get to the bottom of this peculiar event and I gave the matter no more thought. So I pressed on with the loyal members of my staff, less Gefreiter Reichel, who was a runner, whom I had to leave behind because he had received a bullet through the heel.

"In the meantime, the courageous assaulting companies, with their commanders Leutnants Wildenhayn (9th Company), Müller (10th Company), Unger (11th Company) and Hutschenreuter (12th Company) in the lead, had reached the British front line and, as I pushed forward to join them, I succeeded in extracting from the trench a British soldier, who fell to his knees begging for mercy. A few hundred metres before Flesquières the battalion attack had to be halted. In view of the approaching darkness of the short December day, a battle in a built up area appeared to offer no prospect of success and the enemy had now brought to bear all means at their disposal to defend themselves. Apart from heavy artillery fire, they engaged us with mortars and aircraft, which dropped bombs on us from a height of barely fifty metres. I myself had jumped down into a shell hole and, from there, despatched my last remaining runner with an order to the companies to consolidate in the positions they had gained.

"The hours had flown by and now a degree of exhaustion and need for refreshment made themselves felt. To meet that situation I always carried a small glass bottle containing the blackcurrant schnaps which my kind mother had sent to the field for me. I went to reach for it but, when I put my hand in the left hand pocket of my tunic, I felt nothing but fragments in it. It was now clear where the red liquid running down my leg had come from and, feeling sad because of the lack of schnaps and happy because I had not been wounded, I noticed that the machine gun bullet had only passed through the pocket of the tunic and my trousers. There was nothing else for it but to make my way without its stimulation back to the regiment to report. It was a journey in a pitch black night, lit only by the flashes of exploding shells and shrapnel pots; without landmarks, where here and there could be heard the moans of the wounded, sounding like the siren voices of ghostly apparitions. But in the darkness I had no way of locating them or bringing them aid."

In the confusion caused by the heavy fighting, it was difficult both for the commander of Reserve Infantry Regiment 107 to furnish 48 Reserve Brigade with an accurate situation report before darkness fell completely, or for the commanding officer of the reserve battalion to know what likely tasks might come his way during the night. As a result, a small contact patrol was despatched forward and was later described by the commander of the reserves.

Major Keil 2nd Battalion Reserve Infantry Regiment 107 [54]

"...On 6 December , whilst the 1st and 3rd Battalions at about 4.00 pm were throwing back the enemy from ground they had won by means of a powerful assault, 2nd Battalion remained at readiness in reserve in the sunken road which ran between Cantaing and Anneux and from which the attack had been launched. The enemy artillery had immediately brought down destructive fire throughout the entire sector of the attack by guns of all calibres. Nevertheless we had pushed our front forward about two kilometres. It had so far proved possible to watch the advance of the assaulting waves from the observation post of the support battalion, but now darkness was falling and a critical moment had arrived, as it did so often in battle: lack of contact with the fighting troops. Observation was not possible and no reports had been received from the front; what was the situation there?

"The gaze of the battalion commander fell on the short, wiry figure of Reserve Leutnant Schmidt. 'Leutnant Schmidt, you have the mission of taking two runners and establishing contact with the commander of the battalion in contact, in order to orientate yourself with the line reached so far and battle situation!' A short, 'Yes Sir!', a brief repetition of the mission, and Leutnant Schmidt and his two runners disappeared into the gloom of the winter evening. In a short while it would be completely dark. The distance to be covered was about two kilometres. Including the return journey, that meant four kilometres, to be traversed through ceaseless artillery defensive fire. Forwards could be heard the endless rattle of enemy machine gun fire. What it means to carry out a task like that in the darkness of night, over completely unfamiliar ground and under the heaviest possible fire can only be appreciated by a front line soldier. But it had to be done. 'Right lads, keep close to me and let's go!'

"Off they went forwards, moving by bounds, one minute tripping over shell holes; the next cowering in a crater for a few moments to take a breather. To the front the unmistakable silhouette of La Justice Farm on the heights provided a definite aiming mark. Extremely heavy fire was coming down on this place which, as recently as this afternoon, had been strongly held by the enemy. After a short pause to catch breath it was, 'Now, direction half right and head for the farm. Go!' As the three brave men were stumbling forward a heavy shell came growling and roaring. The force of the explosion hit the officer and his companions like a whirlwind, hurling them in all directions. The blood froze in their veins.

"Thank heavens that passed off reasonably well!' grunted the officer, 'but what has happened to the men?' One was groaning quietly and gesturing at his left leg, the other felt his way along his left arm. 'Get your field dressings on then head back!' There was nothing for it but to continue alone. The further the Leutnant went, the more obvious the crack and whine of rifle and machine gun bullets became. But he was in luck, this daring Leutnant. Uninjured, he finally arrived at the forward firing line where a start was being made to dig in. There he met the adjutant, helped to reorganise the jumbled sub units and reported to the battalion commander who, 'slightly scratched', as he put it, was sitting in a hole in the ground and then by the light of a pocket torch swiftly sketched out the line which had been captured. It was then a matter of retracing his steps, negotiating the same difficulties.

"After an absence of two hours he reappeared, with reddened cheeks and smiling with satisfaction in front of the commander, reporting that the advance had gone beyond the ordered objective and that there was contact on both flanks. Producing his marked map, he clarified the situation in a few short words. The reply was, 'I thank you', but the quiet joy and recognition shining in the eyes of his commander showed that the next time medals were distributed the daring fulfilment of their duty by the courageous little Leutnant and his two companions would not be forgotten."

With the end of the major attacks at Cambrai came the time of reckoning. On the British side, the overwhelming feeling at the time and later appears to have been one of severe disappointment. The bells which were rung out in the United Kingdom on receipt of news of the initial advances were not replaced by the tolling of a funeral knell, but they might as well have been, if only as a warning against premature jubilation. The German view, on the other hand, was much more positive. Although the ambitious aims of the counter-attack remained unachieved, nevertheless the operations had been a success and their outcome a considerable boost to morale. In accordance with usual procedure, they took stock, being brutally honest about their failures and drawing lessons for the future from the way events had unrolled. The Army Group Commander set the tone for this work in his description of how the battle had begun.

Crown Prince Rupprecht of Bavaria [55]

"The [British] offensive achieved complete surprise. It was directed against a strongly fortified, but weakly held position, which was defended partly by Landwehr units. It was a 'quiet front.' There was no artillery preparation; success was going to be obtained through the use of *over three hundred tanks* [original emphasis]. We knew almost nothing about preparations for an offensive. On 16 November, a statement by a prisoner described the move of 210mm and 300mm howitzers, towed by motorised vehicles along the roads Ervillers - Mory and Ervillers – St Leger towards the front. On 18 November prisoners from the British 36th Division, were captured north of Trescault. Analysis of their statements revealed [the fact that] there might be an intention by the British to push forward in the Havrincourt area; of which there had already been several instances against particular points along the British front.

"Our forces discounted the imminence of a major offensive because there had not been any increase in artillery fire. Not until 19 [November] did a few rounds fired in the Havrincourt area or to the east of it suggest that ranging in was occurring. Without a heavy artillery bombardment it seemed that an attack could be ruled out completely, because in the Havrincourt - Gonnelieu sector of the main thrust our positions had been prepared superbly and were undamaged. In particular it was felt that the numerous rows of barbed wire, some of them over one hundred metres thick, would provide insurance against surprise. Furthermore, up until 19

November, no increase in aerial activity had been detected.

"Corresponding to the strength of the positions in those sectors, the garrison itself was weak. The divisions guarded frontages of seven to eight kilometres and the defensive fire zones of each [four gun] battery were 900 – 1200 metres wide. In addition, in some cases the fighting strengths [of the units] were low, because losses suffered in Flanders had not been made good in all cases. The allocation of field artillery and heavy guns was also poor."

The jury, however, was still out concerning the overall value of the tanks as demonstrated during the Battle of Cambrai. Commander Second Army definitely had doubts about them.

General der Kavallerie Georg von der Marwitz [56]

"I was back in Bourlon today. In one place five [knocked out] tanks were right next to each other and three or four [more] were quite close by. Two had caught fire and the men within them were burnt to death – a dreadful sight! I cannot help it, I do not regard these things in their current form as battleworthy. Of the approximately 300 which attacked us, seventy five were knocked out and are still within our lines and a further thirty are located to our front. A large number also ditched, but were subsequently towed away. If, when deployed, over one third of them are knocked out, this becomes unsustainable in the long term. If we were to lose one third of our artillery in every battle, we simply could not continue. However, perhaps they can be improved."

Hindenburg, on the other hand, was concerned about the effect that they had on the morale and will to resist of the defending troops.

Generalfeldmarschall von Hindenburg [57]

"The British Cambrai offensive was the first appearance on the scene of a major surprise attack using armoured vehicles. We were already familiar with this form of battle equipment from [their use during] the spring offensive, when they did not make much of an impression on us. The fact that they had now been perfected to the extent that they could cross our undamaged trenches and obstacles meant that they did not fail to have a serious effect on our troops. It was not so much that the machine gun and small calibre shellfire sprayed from these steel colossi was physically destructive; rather it was their relative invulnerability that was damaging to morale. Against their armoured walls, the infantryman felt himself powerless. If these machines broke through the trench lines, the defenders believed themselves to be threatened from the rear and they abandoned their positions."

The German army had originally set out in 1917 determined to remain on the defensive in the west, as a statement defining its criteria for success that year made plain. 'It is essential that we win the 1917 campaign, which we shall do if we succeed through defensive battles in holding on to what we currently have.'[58] There had been setbacks: the withdrawal to the Hindenburg Line, then reverses at Arras, Messines and Third Ypres, for example, but, overall, the aim had been achieved. Particular pride was taken from their performance at Cambrai. Starting from the most unpromising of positions, they had improvised a powerful riposte which had come as a rude shock to the British. Naturally there were mixed feelings about the overall outcome. This was no Cannae; the attempt to encircle the British troops in the Cambrai salient failed, but the counter-attack did enough damage to boost German morale, even though the pincer movements on the flanks failed to meet up and the British were able to withdraw later to a suitable winter line.

The northern counter-attack mounted by Group Arras, being met by strong forces, achieved little and even the main thrust from the east, which enjoyed surprise, first faltered, then stalled in the face of increasing opposition. The consensus of opinion in the post-battle analysis was that the outcome of Cambrai underlined once more the near-impossibility in practice of achieving a smooth transition from defence to counter-attack, which is one of the central tenets of military theory. Recent experience in Flanders had also demonstrated that, even where forces had been assembled with a view to mounting a counter-attack, pressure elsewhere often meant that the troops had to be deployed elsewhere to shore up the defence so, either they were unable to attack at all or, even if they were, they were worn down before they ever attempted to advance. This was undoubtedly the case at Cambrai and was certainly one of the reasons why impetus was lost so quickly at various points along the front on 30 November.

It was not only the assembly of troop reinforcements that caused difficulties. Every aspect of the counter-attack had to be improvised from a standing start and there were absolutely no contingency plans available to ease the work. Without any sort of coordinated transport plan, troops, command headquarters, weaponry and combat supplies of all kinds had to be gathered in from places all along the Western Front, moved to Cambrai and placed ready to launch the attack. Speed was of overriding importance, otherwise the opportunity to exploit surprise would have been lost. Naturally this meant that corners were cut, which probably influenced the impact of the operations but, in the final analysis, the mounting of the operation was a triumph for the logistic staffs and troops in general and the railway movement staff in particular.

The latter were under absolutely immense strain. Under normal circumstances they would have concentrated headquarters and signals elements, together with advance parties, following this with pioneer, supply and transport units to handle artillery reinforcements and ammunition resupply in particular. The fighting infantry would have been the last to arrive, by which time the entire infrastructure would have been in place. At Cambrai such a build up was completely impractical. Everything had to be moved simultaneously. It was just as well that rail links into the area were good because, in transporting thirteen divisions there between 20 and 30 November and a further four by 2 December, no fewer than 1,163 trains were marshalled, loaded, moved to Cambrai and unloaded. It was an extraordinary performance and one which, quite rightly, was praised highly by Crown Prince Rupprecht.

In view of their offensive plans for the coming year, a great deal of attention was paid to an examination of how surprise had been achieved by the British army prior to 20 November. A subsequent report by Army Group Crown Prince Rupprecht drew heavily on prisoner interrogation in its assessment of operational security and the same subject was given prominence in the final published assessments.

Headquarters Army Group Crown Prince Rupprecht 1c No 4703 Secret 4.12.1917 [59]

"The enemy exploited every conceivable measure in order to maintain security: There were no changes to the garrison holding the forward positions. The newly arrived divisions were kept separate, so that none learned of the existence of the others. Their presence was carefully hidden from the ground holding divisions. The men of these divisions were briefed that they were located in a quiet sector where no operations were envisaged and that, in order to reassure them, they could inform their relatives at home of the fact in their letters. Once the order for the attack had been issued to commanders, the telegraph system could not be used for messages further forward than brigades and headquarters of corps, divisions and brigades could only communicate with each other using codes. The wires leading forward to advanced exchanges were cut. Finally, the orders for the attack were not issued to the troops until a few hours before the assault.

"Infantry and cavalry divisions conducted their moves forward almost exclusively by night and the assembly areas for the attack were not occupied until the night before it was launched. In the case of the cavalry this was delayed until the morning of the attack itself. Loading and unloading and the shipment and drive forward into concentration areas of the tanks all occurred at night. The use of lights and lighting of fires was strictly forbidden. Fires for cooking were only permitted during daylight hours, their number was kept to a minimum and, as far as possible, smoke was not to be produced (Tommy cookers with solid fuel [were generally used]). The tanks were camouflaged against aerial observation and kept hidden away from the troops as much as possible. Fire by artillery and machine guns was used to mask the noise of the tanks moving up to their start lines."

Use was to be made of all these methods and more besides during the preparations for the German offensive in March 1918.

Naturally many lessons connected with anti-tank tactics, equipment and methods were studied, absorbed and converted into doctrine for use during 1918 but, because already prior to the Battle of Cambrai it was clear to the German High Command that there could be no question of remaining on the defensive into 1918, by far the greatest effort was placed on assembling the lessons learned from the German counter-offensive. It was believed that the particular circumstances were unlikely to be replicated precisely in future but, nevertheless, a number of thoughts connected with the preparation of major operations were derived from the experience. It was felt, for example, that although the speed with which the operation had been mounted was commendable and had contributed to the surprise effect, there had also been significant disadvantages.

It was decided that sufficient time had to be allowed in future to ensure that all levels of command had time to study their missions and to conduct detailed reconnaissance of the terrain over which they were to operate. For high operational tempo to be developed from the start a detailed knowledge of the opposing positions was essential. This would enable the orders process to be improved and rehearsals to be more effective. It was felt that this lack had led to casualties that were far too high amongst the junior leaders, as a result of the need for them to be constantly at the forefront of the battle. Problems had also been caused by last minute changes to the plans and, in particular, the boundaries between the attacking formations, which meant that, shortly before the battle, all orders at corps level and below had to be totally recast at high speed, placing an almost intolerable burden on the planners and preventing them from turning their attention properly to the multitude of final arrangements which were always required before the launch of major operations.

There was also considerable concern about the physical demands on both men and horses during the period leading up to H Hour. It was felt that everything possible had to be done to ensure that attacking troops were in their final assembly areas two full days before the start of any attack. On 30 November, many of the assault troops, having been travelling or marching for several days before the beginning of the attack, were tired out before they ever crossed the start line and, as was demonstrated before Gouzeaucourt, were rapidly unable to continue the thrust with the same determination. Many of the horses were overworked and this led to heavy losses when they had to absorb the extra strain of offensive operations. Group Caudry made the point in their after-action report: 'If the horses were in good condition, they were well able to cope with the extraordinary demands placed on them. A large proportion of the teams from the field and foot artillery, the ammunition and supply columns arrived in the operational area already completely exhausted. The consequence was high losses amongst the horses. This could have been avoided if the armies which furnished them had supplied fully fit horses.'[60]

One of the problems which arose out of the deficiencies of the horses was that of supply and, especially, ammunition resupply. The attack on the 30 November had been begun before ammunition stocks were fully replenished, but the Artillery Commander at Second Army was satisfied that there were sufficient stocks available in the operational area. The main problems arose in the forward battle area, where batteries and regiments did face shortages from time to time, but this was ascribed to bottlenecks on the routes forward, shortages of ammunition columns and the weakness of many of the horses. It was considered, therefore, that better preparation could overcome many of these problems. Overall there does seem to have been adequate ammunition to support the offensive operation. Group Caudry reported that it had had at its disposal for each type of weapon: field guns 800 rounds; field howitzers 800 rounds; heavy field howitzers 500 rounds; super heavy howitzers 400 rounds; 100 mm guns 600 rounds; heavy low trajectory guns 400 rounds; old and obsolescent types 300 – 400 rounds. This amounted to four days of supply for each gun, three days of which were held forward by the divisions and the remainder in Group reserve.[61]

Of the three days of supply, two were forward on the gun lines or held nearby. The third was meant to be held on wheels, but such was the demand for transport that this could not be achieved. The regrouping the day before operation began meant that a great deal of ammunition had been dumped in the wrong places and had to be moved, whilst the need for batteries to change positions to support the advancing infantry meant that there was even greater pressure on the ammunition wagons. All these problems were exacerbated by the fact that many of the reinforcing artillery units had arrived with neither ammunition nor the columns necessary to transport it. As a result, resupply had had to be improvised; frequently this meant that shells had to be transported by formations and handed to units in other divisions or even corps, which was a thoroughly inefficient way to conduct the logistic support of complex operations. The speed at which the preparations had been conducted was a major contributory factor; but so too was the fact that the German army by this stage of the war lacked first hand experience of conducting mobile offensive operations.

In order to overcome some of the main difficulties, Group Caudry recommended the following points:

"- Each Group must have exclusive use of at least one railhead where ammunition can be unloaded.

- On the opening day of the offensive only sufficient ammunition to support the initial phase should be dumped on the gun lines. As far as possible the remainder should be on wheels.

- During changes of position, each battery should ensure that, as far as possible, it covers its new ammunition requirements from shells stored on the position it is leaving. [i.e. batteries should not move and simply abandon shells which are already a long way forward].

- Artillery reinforcements should report for duty complete with full ammunition columns.

- The supply of ammunition to divisions which do not belong to the Group should be avoided.

- Daily ammunition reports at specified times are absolutely essential, in order that the artillery commander can maintain an overview. If exact figures are not possible, then estimates which are as accurate as possible should be provided." [62]

Army Group Crown Prince Rupprecht, having studied all the reports and forwarded its own assessment to Supreme Army Headquarters, was not long in outlining the main issues which were to be addressed in Second, Fourth and Sixth Armies during the winter, as preparations were made to go on the offensive the following March.

Headquarters Army Group Crown Prince Rupprecht I b d No. 4781 Secret 11.12.17 [63]

"The Cambrai counter-offensive of 30 November has shown that the current organisation and equipment of our Army on the Western Front does not in all respects correspond to the demands of mobile warfare. The deficiencies would have been brought into even sharper relief if our operations had been pressed forward over a larger area for days at a time. In that situation, changes or expansion of our organisations etc. may be necessary. The mobility of all formations and resupply of ammunition are of prime importance. All the accumulated ballast of trench warfare must be reduced or even - at least temporarily – be dispensed with, in order to afford these the priority they require. A comprehensive study of these questions by all arms and services is required. By the end of the month reports are required as follows:

"Second Army: infantry, machine gun units, engineers and technical formations; Fourth Army: transport columns and [all aspects of] supply; Sixth Army: artillery. Specific proposals are to be made. Extensive improvements will not be possible, largely due to the lack of horses. The desirable is to be renounced in favour of the essential. The judgement of experienced field officers is likely to be valuable and discussions… will enable paperwork to be minimised."

Equally as interesting is the guidance provided with this tasking, on the basis of experience gained at Cambrai, because it highlights some of the major points raised at divisional level after the battle. It seems clear, for example, that the biggest concerns related to infantry equipment and ammunition and its carriage:

"Infantry… The normal battle loads of ammunition as allocated for trench warfare proved insufficient in the offensive battle. On 30 November there was a major shortage of ammunition within the divisions thrusting forward around the Gouzeaucourt area.[64] It would seem necessary for the infantry and machine gun formations to transport forward an initial replenishment (Ammunition wagons at company level? Allocation of elements of the ammunition columns to particular formations? Requirement for ammunition vehicles?). The former tasks of the infantry ammunition columns can be taken on by the new style ammunition columns. Carriage of S.m.K ammunition is desirable.

"Mobility Are there sufficient horse teams for the vehicles of the fighting echelons and the supply officers' vehicles? Can machine gun detachments be employed in mobile operations?

"Close Quarter Battle and *Materiel* Should the infantry carry forward light machine guns and grenade launchers in mobile operations? One division has suggested that only two light machine guns per battalion be carried into the attack, with the remainder being held in reserve and transported in the lightest possible hand carts. Another division wishes to renounce the use of the light machine gun once a breakthrough has been made, to hand them over to the divisional mortar companies and to reincorporate their crews into the infantry [sections]. There are also differing views with regard to the carriage of grenade launchers. What other close range weaponry should the infantry carry (hand grenades, flares etc)? Are special vehicles for this purpose required in infantry formations or should the pioneer companies be given additional stocks? Should there be separate columns to carry close quarter battle *materiel*, just as there is for the infantry and artillery? Is the mobility and equipment of the pioneer companies, mortar companies and divisional bridging columns [adequate]?

"Artillery The subordination of the light mortar company to the field artillery detachment in accordance with its war establishment was proved to be necessary at Cambrai and will now be introduced. It was also shown that the ammunition wagons of the field batteries and light mortar companies had to be pulled by six horses. It is to be verified if the carriage of necessary equipment [undefined] by the artillery is likely to cause problems.

"Transport Columns and Supply The organisation of the transport columns and supply arrangements for mobile warfare requires special examination. The battles around Cambrai provided no worthwhile guidance in this matter. It seems that motorised vehicles convoys on as wide a scale as possible will be necessary. The mobility of the horse drawn columns (as well as the artillery) can only be improved in particular cases due to the horse situation.

"The results of these investigations into organisations and mobility should provide the High Command with the means to judge if our army on the Western Front is fit to meets the demands of wide-ranging mobile warfare, or if it is sufficient only for operations on a limited scale. Even after a breakthrough, we must reckon on having to deal with other enemy positions, albeit less strongly developed. We must bear this factor in mind when we consider what, in the event of mobile operations, has to happen with the specialised trench warfare *materiel*."

Although matters concerning organisation and equipment in the broadest sense were important, it is equally clear that the chain of command was becoming extremely concerned about the ability of the human and animal material at its disposal to cope with the entirely foreseeable strain of offensive operations during 1918. Fodder was in short supply for the horses and mules and losses had been enormous during 1917. In addition, the quality and quantity of reinforcing manpower was causing alarm. It was essential, therefore, that everything was done to ensure that existing units and formations were given every opportunity to recuperate after the strain of the 1917 battles and train to take on the demands that mobile warfare would present in the coming year. Already, by mid December 1917, Ludendorff was addressing this major source of concern.

Supreme Army Headquarters O Ia 5655 Secret 9.12.17 [65]

"In order to permit the troops the absolutely essential [period of] rest and training required, it is necessary to ensure that the divisions held in rear in reserve – and this applies also to *Eingreif* divisions –

are kept together and that individual elements of them are not detached and thus subject to unequal demands. I therefore request that Supreme Army Headquarters be informed in advance prior to the deployment in the front line of elements of divisions located in the rear area. The move forward of *Eingreif* divisions is also to be subject to the closest supervision by the Army Groups, who are to apply the above criteria.

Signed: Ludendorff"

Ludendorff returned to this same theme only five days later, with directives which laid down that the minimum period each division was to be allowed out of the line for rest, recuperation and training was three weeks and that priority was to be given to those divisions which had not actually been granted a break that long throughout 1917. There were also special instructions concerning training and the handling of recruits, especially the class of 1899 which, with considerable reluctance, Supreme Army Headquarters would begin to employ during the winter 1917 – 1918.

Any objective assessment of the Battle of Cambrai has to conclude that it ended more or less honours even. Casualties were practically identical at something over 40,000 suffered by each side though, in the usual way, the British Official History chose to inflate the German losses to more than 53,000 for no good reason.[66] Gains and losses in territory roughly cancelled each other out as did captures of prisoners, guns and other war *materiel*. The boost to German morale came at a welcome time and the experience gained was of the first importance in the planning and preparation of the spring offensive of 1918, but the surprise and shock effect of the mass tank attack, with its novel use of predicted artillery fire, had one lasting effect which worked very much against the Germans for the remainder of the war. It may not seem obvious, but possibly the greatest short term gain for the Allies was the fact that the continuing threat of large scale use of tanks and the new tactics dominated German thinking from then on. In practice this meant that precious resources had to be devoted to the preparation of anti-tank defences and weaponry and to ensuring that never again could artillery cover and ammunition stocks be neglected anywhere along the Western Front. Never again could a major attack be allowed to go in against a division such as 20th Landwehr, with its rifle companies down to around seventy men strong and, of those, a high proportion who had no business in the front line. 'Wherever the ground offers suitable going for tanks,' wrote Crown Prince Rupprecht after the battle, 'surprise attacks like this may be expected. That being the case, there can be no more mention, therefore, of quiet fronts.' The resulting massive diversion of resources this caused was possibly the greatest legacy the tanks of Cambrai gave to the Allied war effort. That fact alone justified the entire effort and sacrifice.

Notes

1. *Persöhnliches Kriegstagebuch des Generals der Infanterie a.D. von Kuhl BA.- MA. RH 61/50652* p 98

2. *Hauptstaatsarchiv Stuttgart M33/2 Bü 374 'Die Angriffschlacht bei Cambrai'* p 21

3. Hammond: *Cambrai 1917* pp 389-390

4. Simon: History Infantry Regiment 67 p 109

5. *ibid.* p 110

6. Unfortunately none of the regiments of 9th Bavarian Reserve Division produced a history post war, so the outline of the events in this sector has had to be based on the sparse account in *Die Bayern im Großen Krieg 1914-1918* pp 413-415. There are suggestions in the literature that this division, leaving aside the difficult tactical situation, did not perform particularly well.

7. Peters: History Reserve Infantry Regiment 28 p 159

8. It is far from clear that the passage of orders was achieved successfully. Reserve Infantry Regiment 55, for example, spent almost the entire day digging in along the line reached the previous day. Wißmann: History Reserve Infantry Regiment 55 p 216. Reserve Infantry Regiment 99 only mentions minor trench clearing operations in the *SII Stellung* east of La Vacquerie. Müller: History
Reserve Infantry Regiment 99 pp 174-175

9. Führen: History Fusilier Regiment 40 p 491

10. Tschischwitz: *General von der Marwitz* p 264

11. Fischer: History Reserve Infantry Regiment 262 p 195

12. BOH *The Battle of Cambrai* p 243

13. Fischer: *op. cit.* p 193

14. *ibid.* p 194

15. Kronprinz Rupprecht *Mein Kriegstagebuch Zweiter Band* p 299

16. *Persöhnliches Kriegstagebuch des Generals der Infanterie a.D. von Kuhl BA.- MA. RH 61/50652* p 98

17. *ibid.* pp 98-99

18. *Der Weltkrieg Dreizehnter Band* pp 142-143

19. Kronprinz Rupprecht *Mein Kriegstagebuch Dritter Band* pp 186-187

20. This assessment does less than justice to the stout resistance put up by British formations and units under attack and certainly downplays the extraordinary performance of the tank crews who motored forward into battle with such effect between Gouzeaucourt and Gonnelieu.

21. This comment must have been added slightly later. The British 86 Brigade withdrew during the night 1/2 December; the operation being conducted so skilfully that its departure was not noted for some hours, when patrols despatched forward by Infantry Regiments 105 and 143 of 30th Infantry Division at dawn discovered that the defenders had

withdrawn from Masnières and the western sector of Les-Rues-Vertes.

22. History Infantry Regiment 164 pp 426-427
23. The details of this raid are confirmed by an entry in the War Diary of 1st Battalion Royal Dublin Fusiliers, 'At 2.00 am enemy made a silent raid on a post of the right front company (X Company). Missing 1 NCO and 4 ORs. The post was at the end of a T Sap and the enemy must have gotten in behind the garrison unknown to them. By blood and bits of clothing it would appear that the enemy must have suffered casualties. On patrols going out no trace could be found of the raiders. Only thing heard by posts a short distance away on either flank was a shout 'Stand To!'. Two men of the raided post, at the time off duty, were asleep in a shelter beside the post and never woke up during the occurrence. An officer had visited the post at ten minutes to 2.00 am and everything was all right then.'
24. Tschischwitz: *General von der Marwitz* pp 264-265
25. Müller-Loebnitz: *Das Ehrenbuch der Westfalen* pp 449-450
26. Fifty one prisoners and three guns, according to Wißmann: History of Reserve Infantry Regiment 55 p 217
27. Kronprinz Rupprecht *Mein Kriegstagebuch Zweiter Band* pp 299-300
28. *Persöhnliches Kriegstagebuch des Generals der Infanterie a.D. von Kuhl BA.- MA. RH 61/50652* p 99
29. Kuhl: *Der Weltkrieg 1914/1918 Band II* p 232
30. *Persöhnliches Kriegstagebuch des Generals der Infanterie a.D. von Kuhl BA.- MA. RH 61/50652* p 99
31. Führen: *op. cit.* pp 494-495
32. Piedmont: History Infantry Regiment 65 p 273.
33. Führen: *op.cit.* pp 496-497
34. Moser: *Feldzugsaufzeichnungen* p 326
35. Tschischwitz: *op.cit.* p 265
36. The Fusilier Guards had been nicknamed the *Maikäfer* [Cockchafer or May Beetles] back in the 1830s. Raised in 1826 as a two-battalion Guards Reserve (Landwehr) Regiment, its 1st Battalion was stationed in Potsdam and its 2nd Battalion in Spandau. In early May each year the 2nd Battalion used to march to Potsdam to join the 1st Battalion for joint exercises and was regularly jeered at by local urchins as *Maikäfer*. Initially this was a source of irritation to the regiment but, when in 1831 the Crown Prince of Prussia (later King Friedrich Wilhelm IV) began to use the nickname, regimental attitudes to it changed and, from the moment when King Friedrich Wilhelm III greeted the regiment, drawn up in review order, with the words 'Good day, *Maikäfer*', the name, with its royal approval, became a source of great pride to this elite regiment ever after.
37. Mülmann: History Lehr Infantry Regiment pp 455-456

38. *BA.-MA. RH 61/50652 Aktenauszüge aus: OHL O Ia 5680 geh. op.'Operationen West 1. – 31.XII.1917*

39. *Der Weltkrieg Dreizehnter Band* pp 144-145

40. Kronprinz Rupprecht *Mein Kriegstagebuch Dritter Band* pp 187-188

41. Moser: *op. cit.* pp 324-326

42. Tschischwitz: *op. cit.* pp 265-266

43. Kronprinz Rupprecht *Mein Kriegstagebuch Zweiter Band* p 301

44. *BA.-MA. RH 61/50652 Aktenauszüge aus: OHL O Ia 5598 geh. op.'Operationen West 1. – 31.XII.1917*

45. Kriegsarchiv München: 1 Reserve Corps Bd 169: HGr Rupprecht 1c No 4703 geh, H.Qu. 4.12.1917

46. Moser: *op. cit.* p 326

47. Tschischwitz: *op.cit.* pp 266-268

48. This is an untranslatable pun. *Stollen* means both 'mined dugout' and a type of cake containing marzipan and dried fruits and coated with icing sugar, which is traditionally served in Germany at Christmas.

49. The word 'arrows' clearly refers to an appended sketch map on the original letter, which does not appear in the published version.

50. Braun: History Reserve Infantry Regiment 104 p 108. Of the named casualties, the body of Feldwebel-Leutnant Alban Gustav Mehnert was repatriated later. He is buried near his home town in Zwickau-Planitz and Reserve Leutnant Rudolf Gille is buried in the German cemetery in Cambrai Block 2 Grave 22. The remainder have no known grave.

51. Anspach: History Reserve Infantry Regiment 107 pp 408-409

52. *KTK:* In this case, this refers to the command post of the commander of the forward troops.

53. Anspach: History Reserve Infantry Regiment 107 pp 409-410

54. *ibid.* pp 411-412

55. Kriegsarchiv München: 1 Reserve Corps Bd 169: HGr Rupprecht 1c No 4703 geh, H.Qu. 4.12.1917

56. Tschischwitz: *op.cit.* p 268

57. Hindenburg: *Aus meinem Leben* p 210

58. See Heeresgruppe Kronprinz von Bayern Oberkommando Ia Nr. 2026 geh. *Operationen auf dem französischen Kriegsschauplatz im Frühjahr 1917* H.Qu., 15. Januar 1917. Quoted in Kronprinz Rupprecht *Mein Kriegstagebuch Dritter Band* pp 120-126

59. Kriegsarchiv München: 1 Reserve Corps Bd 169: HGr Rupprecht 1c No 4703 geh, H.Qu. 4.12.1917

60. Hauptstaatsarchiv Stuttgart: M3/2 Bü374 p 5: Gruppe Caudry Genkdo. XIII.(K.W.) Ia Nr. 850 op. 9.12.17 *Die Angriffsschlacht bei Cambrai.*

61. *ibid.*

62. *ibid.*

63. *BA.-MA. RH 61/50652 Aktenauszüge aus: OHL O Ia 'Operationen West*

1. – 31.XII.1917

64. This is an extremely interesting observation, which does not emerge from an examination of the relevant regimental histories. It certainly goes some way to explaining the loss of momentum at that point in the advance.

65. *BA.-MA. RH 61/50652 Aktenauszüge aus: OHL O Ia 'Operationen West 1. – 31.XII.1917*

66. BOH *The Battle of Cambrai* p 272

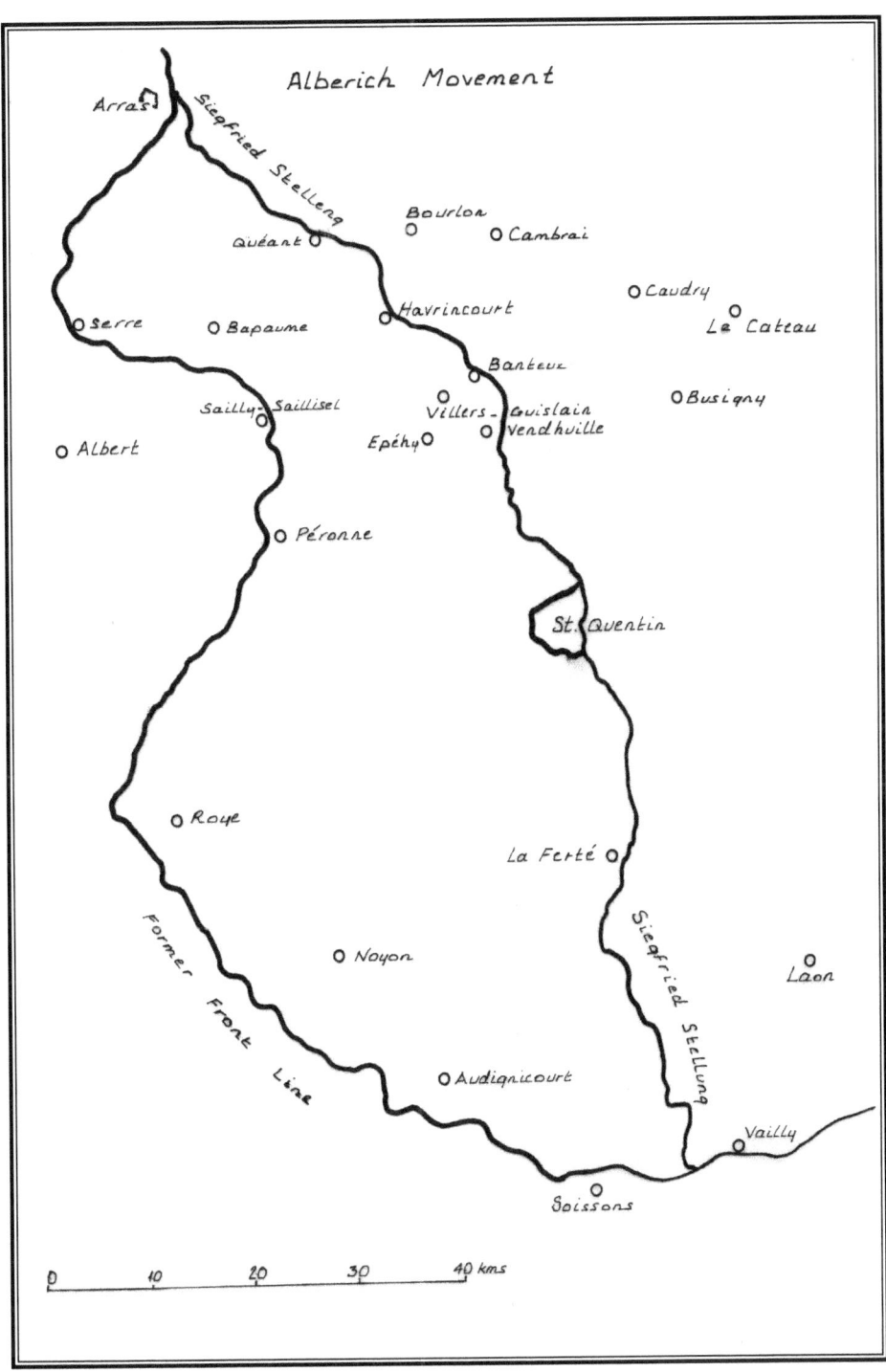

Alberich Movement

Arras

Siegfried Stellung

Bourlon

Quéant

Cambrai

Caudry

Serre

Bapaume

Havrincourt

Le Cateau

Banteux

Sailly-Saillisel

Villers-Guislain

Busigny

Albert

Epéhy

Vendhuille

Péronne

St. Quentin

Roye

La Ferté

Former Front Line

Noyon

Siegfried Stellung

Laon

Audignicourt

Vailly

Soissons

0   10   20   30   40 kms

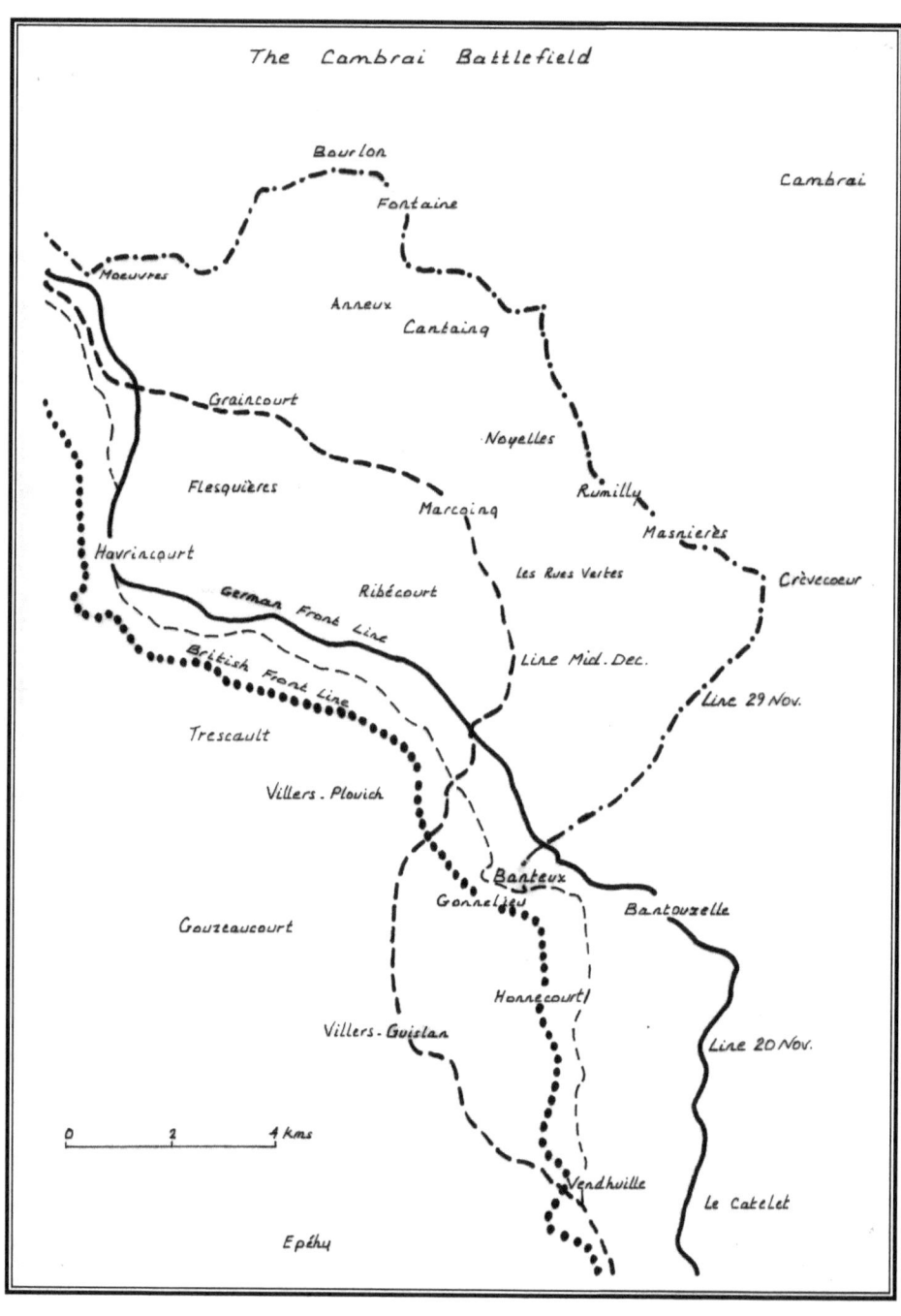

The Cambrai Battlefield

Bourlon

Cambrai

Fontaine

Moeuvres

Anneux

Cantaing

Graincourt

Noyelles

Flesquières

Rumilly

Marcoing

Masnières

Havrincourt

Ribécourt

les Rues Vertes

Crèvecoeur

German Front Line

British Front Line

Line Mid. Dec.

Trescault

Line 29 Nov.

Villers . Plouich

Banteux

Gonnelieu

Bantouzelle

Gouzeaucourt

Honnecourt

Villers . Guislan

Line 20 Nov.

0   2   4 kms

Vendhuille

Le Catelet

Epéhy

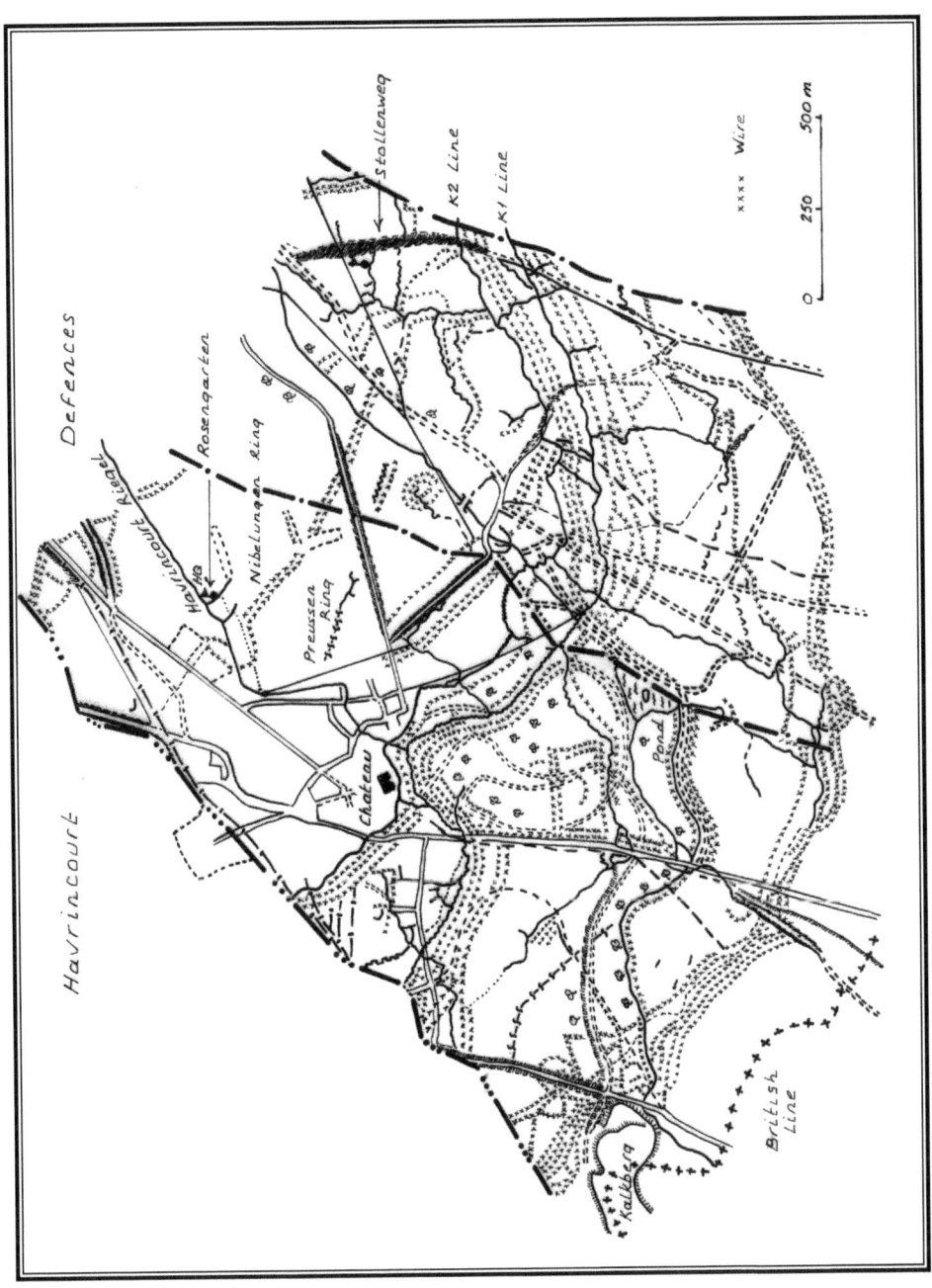

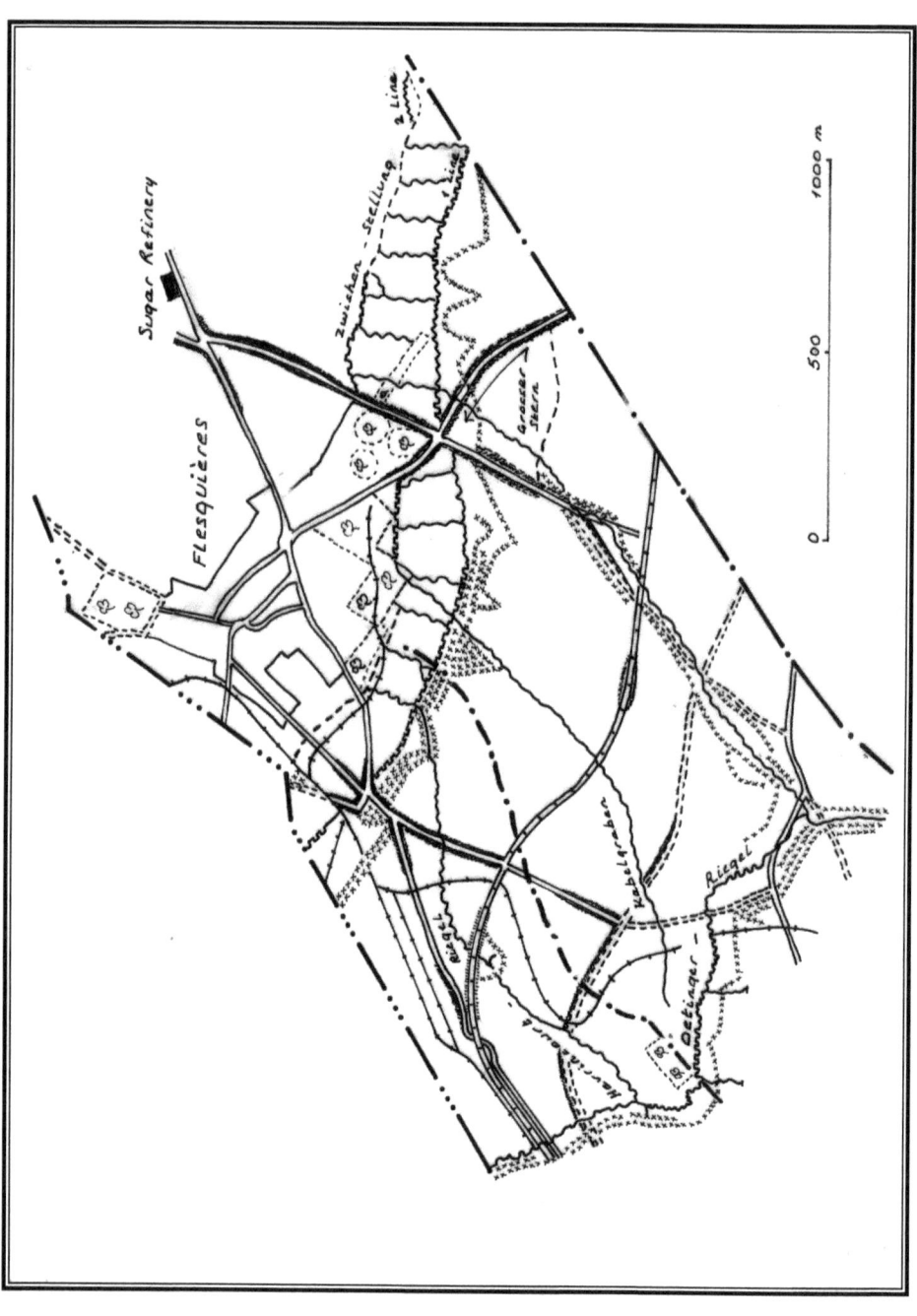

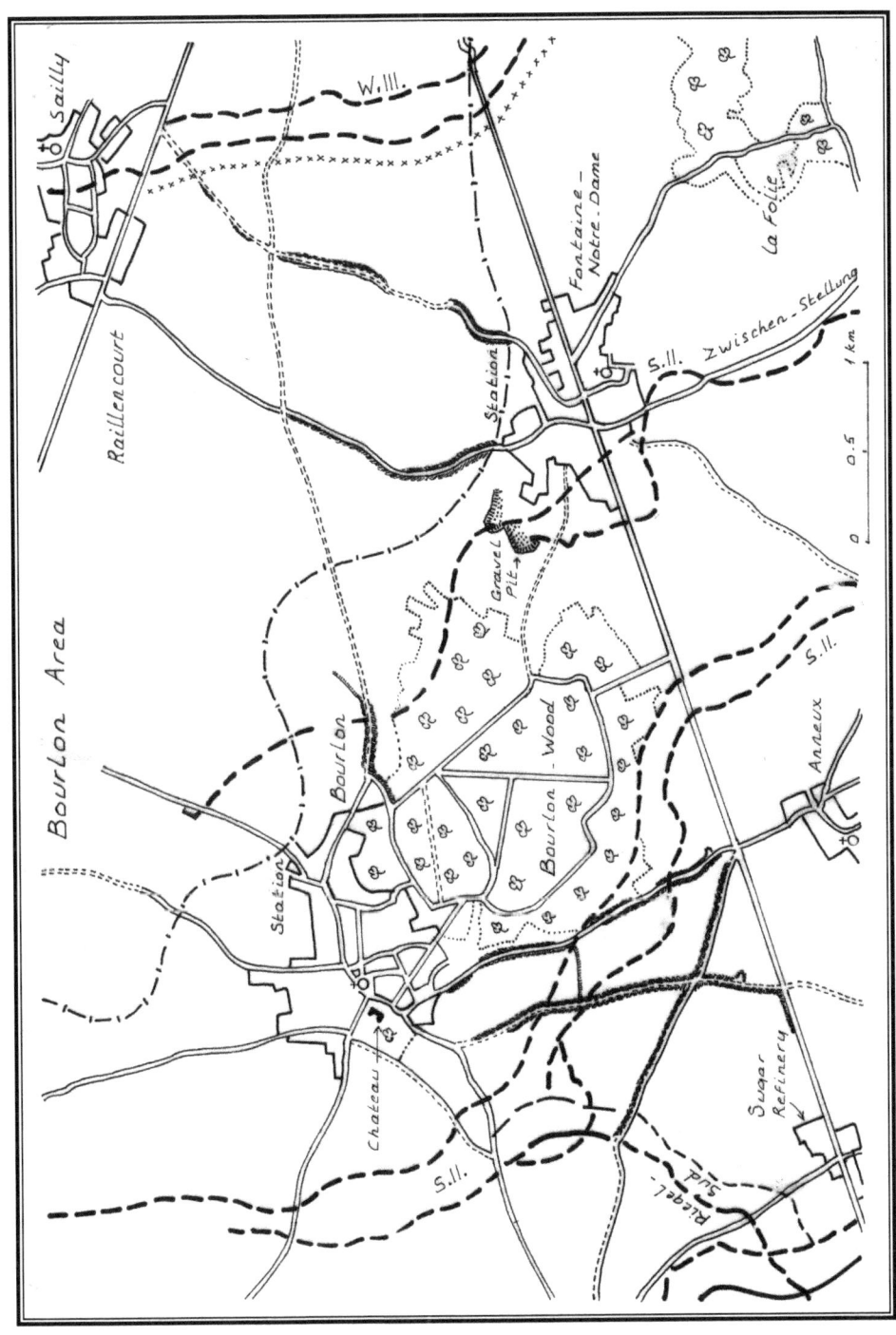

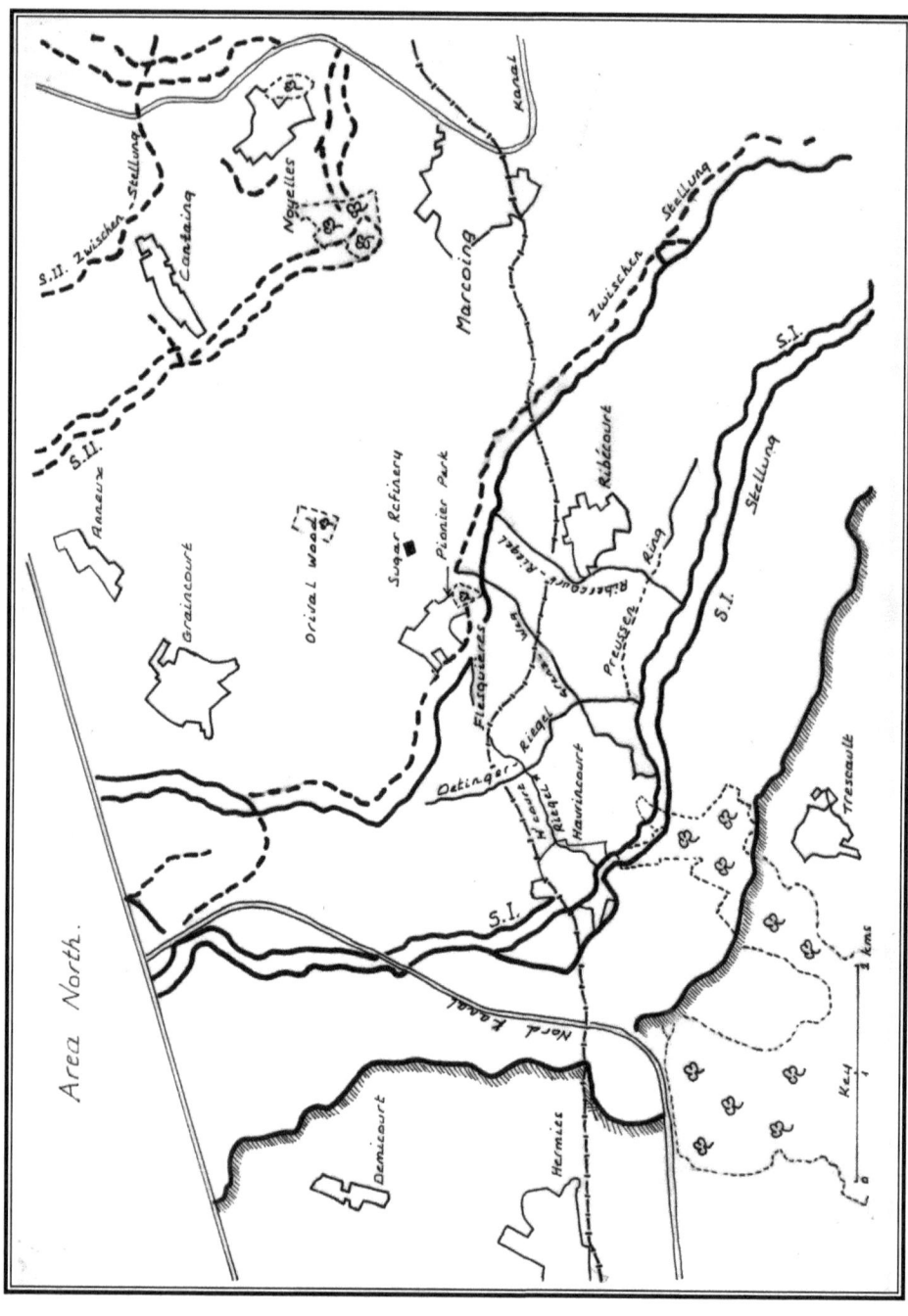

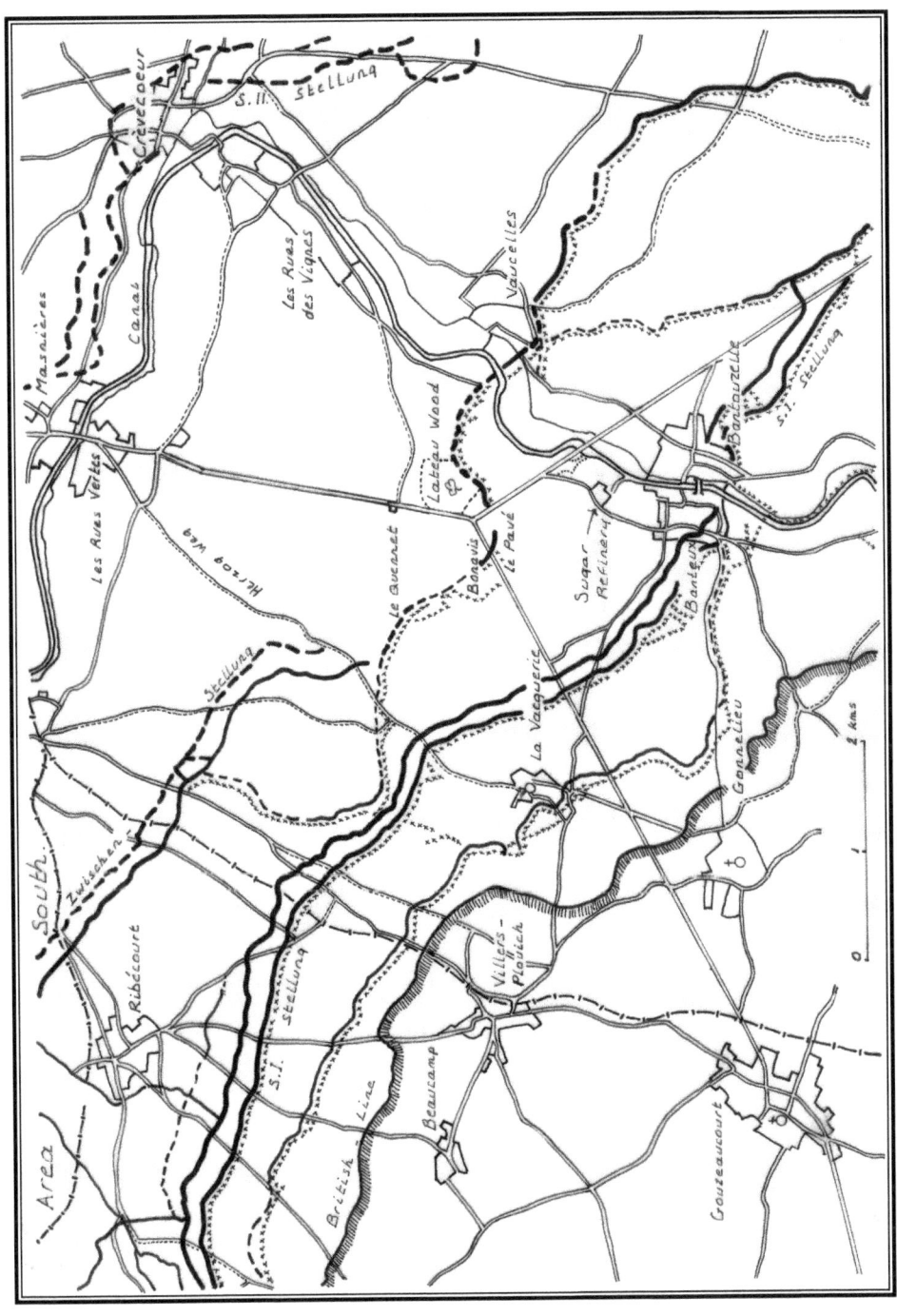

German – British
Comparison of Ranks

Generalfeldmarschall	Field Marshal
General der Infanterie General der Kavallerie	General of Infantry } General of Cavalry } General N.B. The holder of any of these last two ranks was at least a corps commander and might have been an army commander.
Generalleutnant	Lieutenant General. N.B. The holder of this rank could be the commander of a formation ranging in size from a brigade to a corps. From 1732 onwards Prussian officers of the rank of Generalleutnant or higher, who had sufficient seniority, were referred to as *'Exzellenz'* [Excellency].
Generalmajor	Major General
Oberst	Colonel
Oberstleutnant	Lieutenant Colonel
Major	Major
Hauptmann	Captain
Rittmeister	Captain (mounted unit such as cavalry, horse artillery or transport) It was also retained by officers of this senority serving with the German Flying Corps
Oberleutnant	Lieutenant
Leutnant	Second Lieutenant
Feldwebelleutnant	Sergeant Major Lieutenant
Offizierstellvertreter	Officer Deputy N.B. This was an appointment, rather than a substantive rank.
Feldwebel	Sergeant Major
Wachtmeister	Sergeant Major (mounted unit)

Vizefeldwebel	Staff Sergeant
Vizewachtmeister	Staff Sergeant (mounted unit)
Sergeant	Sergeant
Unteroffizier	Corporal
Korporal	Corporal (Bavarian units)
Gefreiter	Lance Corporal

Musketier
Grenadier
Garde-Füsilier
Füsilier
Schütze
Infanterist
Landsturmmann
Jäger
Wehrmann
Soldat
Ersatz-Reservist

} N.B. These ranks all equate to Private Soldier (infantry). The differences in nomenclature are due to tradition, the type of unit involved, or the class of conscript to which the individual belonged.

Kriegsfreiwilliger   Wartime Volunteer. This equates to Private Soldier.

Kanonier	Gunner	
Pionier	Sapper	N.B. These ranks
Fahrer	Driver	all equate to
Hornist	Trumpeter	Private Soldier.
Tambour	Drummer	

Medical Personnel

Oberstabsarzt	Major (or higher)
Stabsarzt	Captain
Oberarzt	Lieutenant
Assistenzarzt	Second Lieutenant

N.B. These individuals were also referred to by their appointments; for example, *Bataillonsarzt* or *Regimentsarzt* [Battalion or Regimental Medical Officer]. Such usage, which varied in the different contingents which made up the German army, is no indicator of rank.

| Sanitäter | Medical Assistant | N.B. These two |
| Krankenträger | Stretcherbearer | ranks both equate to Private Soldier. |

Frequently the prefix 'Sanitäts-' appears in front of a normal NCO rank, such as Gefreiter or Unteroffizier. This simply indicates that a man of that particular seniority was part of the medical services.

Bibliography

Unpublished Sources

Kriegsarchiv München

HGr Rupprecht Bd 125, Akt 206	*AOK 2 Kampfwertmeldung vom 17.11.1917*
1 R. Korps Bd 169	*Heeresgruppe Kronprinz Rupprecht Oberkommando* 1c No 4703 geh. *Der englische Angriff bei Cambrai am 20.1.1917. H.Qu. 4.12.1917.*
1R. Korps Bd 169	*1GRD Ia. Nr 6804 vom 26.11.1917: Erfahrung im Kampf gegen Tanks.*

Hauptstaatsarchiv Stuttgart

M 33/2 Bü 143	*54. Infantry Division Ia Nr. 2884 vom 16.11.1917; Lagemeldung des LIR 387 vom 20.11.1917 1030 Uhr & Fernspruch der Gr. Caudry an die 107. und 54.ID vom 20.11.1917, 10.50 Uhr*
M 33/2 Bü 256	*Gruppe Caudry Ia Nr.300 op.vom 11.11.1917*
M 33/2 Bü 373a.	*Gruppe Caudry Gen Kdo. XIII. (K.W.) A.K. Ia. 30.12.17 Die Tankschlacht bei Cambrai Anlagen 3 & 4 zum Bericht der Gr. Caudry:Die Tankschlacht bei Cambrai 232/Nov. Geheim! Armeebefehl Nr 15/Nov. vom 19/11/1917; Fernsprech Gr. Caudry an 107.ID vom 20.11.1817, 9.40 Uhr Vorm; Fernsprech Gr. Caudry an 107. und 54. I.D. vom 20.11.17 10.50 Vorm.*
M 33/2 Bü 374	*Gruppe Caudry Gen. Kdo. XIII Chef/Ia. 78 op geh. 28.11.17 5 Uhr 40 nachm. Gruppe Caudry Gen Kdo. XIII. (K.W.) A.K. Ia. Nr. 850 op. Erfahrung beim Angriff am 30.11.17 vom 9.12.17*
M 33/2 Bü 894	*Stärkemeldung Gruppe Caudry Abt. IIb. Nr. 20920 13.11.1917*

Bundesarchiv-Militärarchiv Freiburg im Breisgau

RH 61/50652	*Persöhnliches Kriegstagebuch des Generals der Infanterie a.D. von Kuhl*
RH 61/51507	*Die Deutsche Gegenangriff bei Cambrai 1917*
RH 61/51714	Solger: *Akten und Tagebuchauszüge (Heft/Akt 240) Schreiben der HGr Rupprecht an die OHL vom 29.10.1917 und Telegramm Ludendorffs (Ia Nr. 5337 geh. Op.) an die HGr Rupprecht vom 14.11.1917*
RH 61/51716	*Aktenauszüge aus OHL O Ia 'Operationen West 1.-30.XI.1917' HGr Rupprecht Ia Nr. 4517 geh. Vom 21.XI.1917 Besprechung S.K.H. des Kronprinzen von Bayern beim A.O.K. 2 vom 24.11.17*
	OHL Ia Nr. 5510 op.geh. vom 27.11.17
	OHL Ia Nr. 5617geh. op 7.12
	OHL Ia Nr 5655 geh. op. 9.12

Published Works (German: author known)

Anspach Hauptmann a.D. Siegfried and Flach Oblt. d.R. a.D. Dr Erhard *Das Kgl. Sächs. Reserve-Infanterie-Regiment Nr. 107* Dresden 1927

Arnold Paul *Regimentsgeschichte LIR 384* Hannover 1939

Bartenwerffer Oberst a.D. Erich v. & Herrmann Oberlt. d.R. a.D. Alfred *Das Reserve-Infanterie-Regiment Nr. 232 in Ost und West Teil II.* Celle 1927

Benary Oberstleutnant a.D. *Königlich Preußisches 1. Posensches Feldartillerie-Regiment Nr. 20* Berlin 1932

Brandes Ltn. d. Res. Heinz *Geschichte des Kgl. Preuß. Infanterie-Regiments v. Voigts-Rhetz (3. Hannov.) Nr. 79 im Weltkrieg 1914 – 1918* Hildesheim

Braun Major a.D. *Das Reserve-Infanterie-Regiment 104 im Weltkriege* Leipzig 1921

Bülowius Hauptmann a.D. Alfred & Hippler Hauptmann Bruno *Das Infanterie-Regiment v. Boyen (5. Ostpreußisches) Nr. 41 im Weltkriege 1914-1918* Berlin 1929

Christian Leutnant d.R. Karl *Das Heldenbuch vom Infanterie-Regiment 418* Frankfurt am Main 1935

Dahlmann Hauptmann a.D. Reinhold *Reserve-Infanterie-Regiment 27 im Weltkriege 1914/1918* Berlin 1934

Fasse Dr. Alex *Im Zeichen des 'Tankdrachens' (Doctoral Thesis)* Berlin 2007
www.edoc.hu-berlin.de/dissertationen/fasse-alexander-2007-06-21/PDF/fasse.pdf

Fischer Hauptmann d.R. *Das Reserve-Infanterie-Regiment Nr. 262 1914 – 1918* Zeulenroda 1936

Freydorf Oberstleutnant a.D. Rudolf von *Das 1. Badische Leib-Grenadier-Regiment Nr. 109 im Weltkrieg 1914-1918* Karlsruhe 1927

Führen Franz *Die Hohenzollernfüsiliere im Weltkrieg 1914 – 1918* Oldenburg 1930

Gerth Leutnant d.Res. Max *Geschichte des Infanterie-Regiments Nr. 395* Dessau 1933

Giese Leutnant d. Res.Franz *Geschichte des Res.-Inf.-Regts Nr. 227 im Weltkrieg 1914/1918* Halle 1931

Glogowski Oberlt. d.Res. a.D. *Das Kgl. Sächs. 6. Infanterie-Regiment Nr. 105 'König Wilhelm II von Württemberg'* Dresden 1929

Hansch Oberleutnant Johannes and Weidling Leutnant Dr. Fritz *Das Colbergsche Grenadier-Regiment Nr. 9 im Weltkriege 1914-1918* Oldenburg 1929

Hindenburg Generalfeldmarschall von *Aus meinem Leben* Leipzig 1934

Hüttmann Oberst Adolf & Krüger Oberleutnant a.D. Friedrich Wilhelm *Das Infanterie-Regiment von Lützow (1. Rhein.) Nr. 25 im Weltkriege 1914 – 1918* Berlin 1929

Kessler Major a.D. Wilhelm *Das Königl. Preuß. Res.-Feldartillerie-Regiment Nr. 9* Berlin 1938

Kuhl Gen d. Inf. a.D. Hermann v. *Der Weltkrieg 1914-1918 Band II* Berlin 1929

Lattorf Oberleutnant a.D. Claus-Just von *Kriegsgeschichte des Brandenburgischen Jäger-Bataillons Nr. 3 (Jäger-Sturm-Bataillon Nr. 3) 1914-1918* Berlin

Loebell Hauptmann v *Mit dem 3. Garde-Regiment z.F. im Weltkriege 1914/18* Berlin 1922

Ludendorff Erich *Meine Kriegserinnerungen 1914-1918* Berlin 1919

Mark Oberstleutnant a.D. Moritz *Das K.B.13. Infanterie-Regiment* München 1922

Moser General Otto von *Feldzugsaufzeichnungen als Brigade-Divisionskommandeur und als kommandierender General 1914 – 1918* Stuttgart 1923

Müller Major d.R Paul, Fabeck Oberst a.D. Hans von & Riesel Oberstleutn. a.D. Richard *Geschichte des Reserve-Infanterie-Regiments Nr. 99* Zeulenroda 1936

Müller-Loebnitz Oberstleutnant a.D. Wilhelm *Die Badener im Weltkrieg 1914/1918* Karlsruhe 1935

Müller-Loebnitz Oberstleutnant a.D. Wilhelm *Das Ehrenbuch der Westfalen* Stuttgart

Mülmann Oberst a.D. Paul von and Mohs Oberleutnant a.D. *Geschichte des Lehr-Infanterie-Regiments und seiner Stammformationen* Zeulenroda 1935

Naumann Hauptmann d.R. & Michaelis Leutnant d.R. *Das 3. Garde-Regiment zu Fuß im Weltkriege II.Teil* Oldenburg 1923

Peters Leutnant d.R. a.D. Erich *Das Reserve-Infanterie-Regiment Nr. 28 im Weltkrieg 1914-1918* Oldenburg 1927

Petri Oberstleutnant *2. Oberrheinisches Infanterie-Regiment 99* Oldenburg 1925

Piedmont Major a.D. Claus, Pieper Leutnant a.D. Hugo & Krall Oberstleutnant a.D. Paul *Geschichte des 5. Rheinischen Infanterie-Regiments Nr. 65 während des weltkrieges 1914-1918* Oldenburg 1927

Pries Hauptmann d.R. Arthur *Das R.I.R. 90 1914 – 1918* Oldenburg 1925

Puttkamer Oberstleutnant d. Res. a.D. Oscar-Jesco v *Das Königlich Preußische Reserve-Infanterie-Regiment Nr. 46 Im Weltkriege* Zeulenroda 1938

Rohkohl Pastor Lic. Theol. Walter *Reserve-Infanterie-Regiment 226 Teil II* Oldenburg 1926

Rosenberg-Lipinsky Hauptmann Hans-Oskar von *Das Königin Elisabeth Garde-Grenadier-Regiment Nr. 3 im Weltkriege 1914-1918* Zeulenroda 1935

Rupprecht Kronprinz von Bayern *In Treue Fest. Mein Kriegstagebuch, Zweiter Band* München 1929; *Dritter Band* München 1929

Schede Hauptmann *Das 2. Badische Grenadier-Regiment Kaiser Wihelm I. Nr. 110 im Weltkriege 1914-18* Heidelberg 1921

Schlörer & Schwinn *Kriegstagebuch der 1. Batterie 5. bay. Fußart.-Regiments* Bühl 1919

Schmidt Major a.D. Walter, Winkelmann Oberltn. a.D. Otto & Altermann Oberltn. a.D. Martin *Das Königlich 3. Posensche Infanterie-Regiment Nr. 58 im Weltkriege* Zeulenroda 1934

Schulenburg-Wolfsburg Generalmajor a.D. Graf v.d. *Geschichte des Garde-Füsilier-Regiments* Oldenburg 1926

Schwenke Oberstleutnant a.D. Alexander *Geschichte des Reserve-Infanterie-Regiments Nr. 19 im Weltkriege 1914-1918* Oldenburg 1926

Schwerin Rittmeister a.D. C. von & Schmidt Oberleutnant d.R. a.D. Dr. Karl *Reserve-Inf.-Regiment 261 in Ost und West* Berlin 1932

Simon Oberstudienrat Dr. Eduard *4. Magdeb. Infanterie-Regiment Nr 67*

Band II Oldenburg 1927

Soldan George *Das Infanterie-Regiment Nr. 184* Oldenburg 1920

Strutz Hauptmann a.D. Dr. Georg *Die Tankschlacht bei Cambrai 20. – 29. November 1917* Oldenburg 1929

Sydow Hauptmann a.D. Herbert v. *Das Infanterie-Regiment Hamburg (2. Hanseatisches) Nr.76 im Weltkriege 1914/18* Oldenburg 1922

Szymanski Leutnant d.R. a.D. Dr. Theodor *Das Reserve-Infanterie-Regiment Nr. 80 im Weltkriege 1914 – 1918* Wiesbaden 1935

Tschischwitz General der Infanterie a.D. *General von der Marwitz: Weltkriegsbriefe* Berlin 1940

Ulrich Oberleutnant d.R. a.D. Herbert *Res.-Inf.-Regiment 52 im Weltkriege* Oldenburg 1925

Viereck Oberleutnant a.D. Helmut *Das Heideregiment. Königlich Preußisches 2. Hannoversches Infanterie-Regiment Nr. 77 im Weltkriege 1914 – 1918* Celle 1934

Vogt Leutnant d. Res. Dr. Otto *3. Niederschlesisches Infanterie-Regiment Nr. 50 1914 – 1920* Berlin 1932

Voigt Oblt. d. Res. Hans *Geschichte des Füsilier-Regiments Generalfeldmarschall Prinz Albrecht von Preußen (Hann.) Nr. 73* Berlin 1938

Wißmann Oberst von *Das Reserve-Infanterie-Regt. Nr. 55 im Weltkrieg* Berlin

Zechlin Generalmajor a.D. Friedrich *Das Reserve-Infanterie-Regiment Nr. 60 im Weltkriege* Oldenburg 1926

Zunehmer Kgl. Preuß. Oberst a.D. *Infanterie-Regiment Graf Kirchbach (1. Niederschlesisches) Nr. 46 im Weltkrieg 1914/1918* Berlin 1935

Published Works (German: author unknown)

Der Weltkrieg 1914 bis 1918 Dreizehnter Band: Die Kriegführung im Sommer und Herbst 1917. Die Ereignisse außerhalb der Westfront bis November 1918 Berlin 1942

Die Bayern im Großen Kriege 1914-1918 München 1923

Verein ehemaliger Offiziere des Feldartillerie-Regiments Großherzog *Das Feldartillerie-Regiment Großherzog (1. Badisches) Nr. 14 im Weltkriege 1914 – 1918* Karlsruhe 1933

Mitteilungen des Reserve-Infanterie-Regiments 27 (Heft 24 1927)

Alte Kameraden der 54. Infanterie-Division *General Oskar Freiherr von Watter: Ein Gedenkbuch* Hamburg

Feldzugsteilnehmer ehem. Infanterie-Regts. von Manstein (Schleswiges)

Nr. 84 *Erinnerungsblätter der ehemaligen Mansteiner: 4. Folge Nr 6 (April 1923); Nr. 7(Mai 1923); Nr. 8 (Dezember 1923); Nr. 12 (April 1925)*

Mitkämpfer *Geschichte des 4. Hannoverschen Infanterie-Regiments Nr. 164* 1932

Das FAR Nr. 213 Zeulenroda 1930

Reserve Infanterie Regiment 261 Nachrichtenblatt Nr. 32 Berlin 1927

Published Works (English)

Cooper Bryan *The Ironclads of Cambrai* London 1967

Hammond Bryn *Cambrai 1917: The Myth of the First Great Tank Battle* London 2008

Horsfall Jack & Cave Nigel *Cambrai: The Right Hook* Barnsley 1999; *Cambrai: Bourlon Wood* Barnsley 2002; *Cambrai: Flesquières* Barnsley 2003

Miles Captain Wilfrid *Military Operations France and Belgium 1917: The Battle of Cambrai* London 1948

Turner Alexander *Cambrai 1917: The Birth of Armoured Warfare* 2007

Index